From Huntsville to Appomattox

From Huntsville to Appomattox

R. T. COLES'S HISTORY OF 4TH REGIMENT,
ALABAMA VOLUNTEER INFANTRY,
C.S.A., ARMY OF NORTHERN VIRGINIA

**Edited by
Jeffrey D. Stocker**

*Voices of the Civil War Series
Frank L. Byrne, Series Editor*

The University of Tennessee Press • Knoxville

The Voices of the Civil War series makes available a variety of primary source materials that illuminate issues on the battlefield, the homefront, and the western front, as well as other apsects of this historic era. The series contextualizes the personal accounts within the framework of the latest scholarship and expands established knowledge by offering new perspectives, new materials, and new voices.

Copyright © 1996 by The University of Tennessee Press / Knoxville.
All Rights Reserved. Manufactured in the United States of America.
First Edition.

The paper in this book meets the minimum requirements of the American National Standard for Permanence of Paper for Printed Library Materials. ∞ The binding materials have been chosen for strength and durability.

Library of Congress Cataloging-in-Publication Data

Coles, R. T. (Robert T.)
   From Huntsville to Appomattox : R. T. Coles's history of 4th Regiment, Alabama Volunteer Infantry, C.S.A., Army of Northern Virginia / R. T. Coles; edited by Jeffrey D. Stocker. — 1st ed.
      p.   cm. — (Voices of the Civil War series)
   Includes bibliographical references and index.
   ISBN 0-87049-924-6 (cloth : alk. paper)
   1. Confederate States of America. Army. Alabama Infantry Regiment, 4th.   2. Alabama—History—Civil War, 1861–1865—Regimental histories.   3. United States—History—Civil War, 1861–1865—Regimental histories.   I. Stocker, Jeffrey D., 1958–   II. Title. III. Series.
E551.5 4th.C65   1996
973.7'461—dc20   95-32487
                                                                CIP

Contents

Foreword	Frank L. Byrne	ix
Editor's Acknowledgments		xi
Editor's Note		xiii

HISTORY OF 4TH REGIMENT, ALABAMA VOLUNTEER INFANTRY, C.S.A., ARMY OF NORTHERN VIRGINIA

	Introduction	9
1.	Company Sketches	11
2.	The First Manassas Campaign—July 18 to July 23, 1861	18
3.	From Manassas to the Peninsula Campaign—July 23, 1861, to March 11, 1862	30
4.	Peninsula Campaign and Battle of Seven Pines—March 11 to June 12, 1862	37
5.	Seven Days Battle—June 12 to July 8, 1862	44
6.	The Second Battle of Manassas—July 8 to August 31, 1862	50
7.	Maryland Campaign—August 31 to September 18, 1862	60
8.	From Sharpsburg to Fredericksburg—September 18 to November 22, 1862	72
9.	Fredericksburg—November 22, 1862, to February 18, 1863	76
10.	The Siege of Suffolk—February 18 to May 5, 1863	89
11.	Incidents on the Rappahannock and Rapidan—May 5 to June 15, 1863	96
12.	Gettysburg Campaign—June 15 to July 14, 1863	100
13.	From Falling Waters to Fredericksburg—July 14 to September 10, 1863	130

14.	Chickamauga Campaign—September 10 to October 8, 1863	133
15.	Our Campaign in Lookout Valley—October 8 to November 4, 1863	139
16.	Knoxville Campaign—November 4 to December 23, 1863	148
17.	East Tennessee Campaign—December 23, 1863, to April 18, 1864	153
18.	Wilderness—April 18 to May 7, 1864	156
19.	Spotsylvania Ridge to the James River—May 8 to June 16, 1864	167
20.	Siege of Richmond and Petersburg—June 16, 1864, to April 2, 1865	179
21.	Petersburg to Appomattox—April 2 to 11, 1865	191
22.	Our Return Home	195

Appendix A. Letter of Captain Edward D. Tracy	199
Appendix B. Address by Capt. W. C. Ward	202
Appendix C. Chapters of Unwritten History by P. D. Bowles	214
Notes	223
Bibliography	305
Index	309

Illustrations

Figures

Adj. Robert T. Coles	3
Col. Egbert J. Jones	116
Col. Evander M. Law and Members of the 4th Alabama, 1861 or 1862	117
Gen. Evander M. Law, ca. October 1862	118
Col. Owen K. McLemore, in Prewar Regular Army Uniform	119
Col. Lawrence H. Scruggs, October 1862	120
Maj. Charles L. Scott, Postwar Photo	121
Capt. Nathaniel H. R. Dawson	122
Capt. Lewis E. Lindsay	123
Capt. Edward D. Tracy	124
Capt. Charles C. Sale	125
Capt. Robert P. Jones	126
Capt. William H. F. Lee	127
Capt. Reuben V. Kidd	128
Lt. John Breedlove After the War	129

Maps

Theater of Operations of 4th Alabama in Virginia, Maryland, and Southern Pennsylvania	4
Theater of Operations of 4th Alabama in Northwestern Georgia and Tennessee	5

Foreword

In its second year, the Voices of the Civil War Series again presents testimony from both sides of the struggle. This volume is the memoir of a southerner, written in the form of a history of his Confederate regiment. While some people in northern Alabama, where the 4th Alabama Volunteer Infantry Regiment mostly was raised, supported the Union, others like Robert T. Coles joined the movement to leave it. Later, in preparing to perpetuate the memory of his military unit, Coles refreshed his still-sound memory by consulting published records and surviving comrades. He produced a history both balanced and favorable to his unit.

To Coles's account, with its valuable recollections of army service, editor Jeffrey Stocker has juxtaposed alternative accounts by other witnesses. The result is a rare history of a remarkable regiment. Had comparable evidence been available for the Confederacy when postwar military historians began compiling lists of Union "fighting regiments," the 4th Alabama almost surely would have made the equivalent southern roster. Among the many major actions in which it participated were such great eastern battles as Antietam and Gettysburg. In the latter, the regiment gained immortality in the fight for Little Round Top involving Joshua L. Chamberlain's 20th Maine, as well as the 83d Pennsylvania and other units. Moreover, unlike many regiments, the 4th Alabama served in both the eastern and western theaters. A large segment of the book deals with fighting in and near East Tennessee, including the battles of Chickamauga and Knoxville. Yet the Alabamians returned to Virginia for the bloody campaign of 1864, to the fire-filled thickets of the Wilderness and the killing fields of Spotsylvania and Cold Harbor. Coles summarizes very well the siege of Petersburg and the final Confederate retreat.

All of this description is by an eyewitness who was present at almost every one of his unit's military actions, mostly at the central observation post of regimental adjutant. He writes in an engaging style, sometimes employing striking expressions. Thus he characterizes Antietam-Sharpsburg as "a perfect homespun Waterloo." He provides considerable human interest material, some rather unusual for a Victorian narrative. (One can think of no other that records an officer's reaction to having had an enema!) Stocker's carefully edited presentation of Coles's history and related documents casts new light on several aspects of the Civil War. While Coles's history stands on its own, readers might benefit by comparing his version of the fighting in the West with that of the Unionist William Marcus Woodcock, a companion volume in this series.

Frank L. Byrne
Kent State University

Editor's Acknowledgments

For as long as I can remember, I have been keenly interested in studying the Civil War. In fact, one of my earliest memories, from the time when I was a very small boy, is of being on the field at Gettysburg. For instilling this interest in history and encouraging my quest for knowledge, I would like to thank my parents, Donald and Louise Stocker.

A number of my associates in the Civil War Round Table of Eastern Pennsylvania merit special mention. Donald Stocker, Edwin Root, Rev. William Holberton, and Michael Snyder provided thoughtful input and suggestions concerning my endnotes. Jayne Holubowsky and Michael Snyder also aided me greatly in researching the muster rolls of the 4th Alabama in the National Archives, Washington, D.C.

I especially thank D. Scott Hartwig, supervisory park historian for Gettysburg National Military Park, for encouraging my efforts to see Robert Coles's "History of the 4th Alabama" published, so that now it can be read and studied by all. One of the premier Civil War historians in the country, Scott supplied many very valuable suggestions and ideas.

The National Park Service is to be commended for its many fine historians, who work hard making sure that visits to national military parks are both educational and enjoyable. In addition to Scott, the following are some highly knowledgeable historians who provided invaluable assistance as I gathered source material: Robert K. Krick, John Hennessy, and Donald Pfanz of the Fredericksburg National Military Park; Mike Andrus and Robert E. L. Krick of the Richmond National Military Park; and Michael Litterst of Manassas National Military Park. All unfailingly shared and helped me secure information, whether on the 4th Alabama or on the Union regiments whom the 4th encountered in battle.

Anyone engaging in research on the Civil War must consult the United

States Army Military History Institute in Carlisle, Pennsylvania. Richard Sommers and his talented staff put the rich resources of the institute at my disposal. Dr. Sommers, with his encyclopedic knowledge of the Civil War, provided many excellent leads and suggestions for securing rare photographs and information regarding the 4th Alabama. For this assistance I am most grateful.

I am deeply indebted, too, to Norwood Kerr of the Alabama Department of Archives and History for allowing me access to Coles's history and for giving me authority to publish this work. Norwood has been an invaluable source of support throughout this endeavor, providing manuscripts and articles on the 4th Alabama, supplying photographs, and granting access to the voluminous newspaper archives in his department.

David Guest of Hoover, Alabama, has been of immense assistance in researching the Alabama Newspaper Archives and in proofreading this work. He contributed greatly to bringing this book to fruition.

As a result of a fortuitous telephone conversation, Charles Rice of Huntsville, Alabama, provided copies of his extensive collection of 1861 and 1862 newspaper articles on the 4th Alabama. He also kindly provided biographical information on some officers of the 4th Alabama. Without his efforts, this work would not be as rich or comprehensive as I hope it is.

Nancy Adams of the Southern Lehigh Public Library was most helpful in securing, through Pennsylvania's Inter-Library Loan Service, microfilmed information on soldiers in the 4th Alabama.

Steven Wright of the Civil War Library Museum in Philadelphia was most cooperative in providing useful information and access to copies of the *Southern Historical Society Papers, Confederate Veteran,* and the *Official Records.*

Since my typing skills are almost nonexistent, I am thankful to Lisa Lawson Firth and Mary Ellen McWade for their skilled transcription work. I owe special thanks to my sister, Susan Stocker Phillips, who entered the entire manuscript in my computer and painstakingly made additions and revisions until the project was completed.

I also would like especially to thank Frank Byrne, editor of the University of Tennessee Press's Voices of the Civil War Series, and Dr. Edwin Bearss, chief historian of the National Park Service, for their assistance in editing my final manuscript and in bringing Robert T. Coles's work closer to publication.

Finally, I would like to thank my wife, Marliese Walter, without whose support, understanding, and patience this project could not have been accomplished.

Editor's Note

The next of our division to go into action was old General Benning's Georgians, then followed our brigade at a double quick into line. Here we found General Lee, who appeared to be very much perturbed over his misfortune, and the only time I ever saw him excited. Riding up to our brigade, he asked, "What troops?" "Law's Alabamians!" was the reply. "God bless the Alabamians," he said.

That stirring meeting between Lee and Law's Alabama brigade, as it went into action on May 6, 1864, at the Battle of the Wilderness, was described by Robert T. Coles, adjutant, 4th Regiment, Alabama Volunteer Infantry. It is but one of the hundreds of incidents, battles, engagements, and events vividly recounted by Coles in his history of that regiment.

In April 1861, the 4th Alabama was organized at Dalton, Georgia, when various unattached infantry companies from Alabama were formally mustered in under the banner of the 4th Regiment, Alabama Volunteer Infantry.

The regiment was ordered to Virginia on May 4, 1861. On May 7, upon arrival in Lynchburg, the men took the Oath of Allegiance to the Confederate States of America and were mustered in for a term of twelve months. Egbert Jones was elected colonel of the regiment, Evander Law lieutenant colonel, and Charles L. Scott major.

The 4th Alabama immediately was sent to the outskirts of Harpers Ferry, Virginia, where it made camp on Bolivar Heights. Training then was initiated to prepare the regiment for active service.[1]

Very few details of the life of Robert T. Coles are available, despite extensive research in old Alabama newspaper archives and in the Alabama Department of Archives and History. Robert T. Coles, the son of

Robert T. Coles, Sr., and Eliza Fearn Coles, was born on June 29, 1842, in Pittsylvania County, Virginia. By 1850, the Coles family had moved to Madison County in northern Alabama. Robert Coles, Sr., had died by this time, leaving his widow with seven children—three boys and four girls. Robert, Jr., was the second of the three sons.

The people of northern Alabama in 1861 were not solidly in favor of secession from the Union. A modern writer on the Unionist movement in northern Alabama during the Civil War states:

> The Civil War held little appeal for the mountain folk of northwest Alabama, the majority of whom had nothing in common with their more prosperous neighbors to the south and saw no need to fight and die in someone else's conflict. Most preferred to remain neutral, but when that option was denied, the hill folk either opposed the Confederate war effort at home or joined the Union army.[2]

At the Alabama Secession Convention of January 1861, held in Montgomery, the Ordinance of Secession passed by a vote of 61 to 39. During the course of the Civil War, 2,578 men from Alabama enlisted in the Union army.[3] In fact, Winston County, in northwestern Alabama, in 1862 even seceded from the state, in opposition to the Confederacy and the Confederate Conscription Act.

On April 26, 1861, just after the outbreak of the Civil War, Robert enlisted for a twelve-month term of service in the Huntsville Guards. This unit was to become Company F of the 4th Alabama Regiment. At the time of Coles's enlistment, he was a student at the LaGrange Military Academy. Possibly due to Coles's educational background, he was promoted to sergeant major of the regiment when it was mustered into Confederate service. When the 4th Alabama was reorganized in April 1862, he was appointed adjutant, the post which he held for the remainder of the war.

Adjutant Coles was present at practically all of the great battles fought in the eastern United States during the Civil War. He also fought with the 4th Alabama in the western campaigns in the fall and winter of 1863–64, when the regiment was transferred to that theater as part of Lt. Gen. James Longstreet's First Corps. Coles's service records indicate that he was wounded on June 27, 1862, in the Battle of Gaines' Mill; he also was absent due to sickness for one day in the Campaign of Second Manassas in late August 1862, and for several months during the siege of Petersburg in late 1864 and early 1865. He surrendered with the remnants of the 4th Alabama at Appomattox Court House on April 9, 1865. Coles, then, given his position as adjutant, his health, and his avoidance of injury, had a unique opportunity to observe the 4th Alabama throughout its entire term of service.

After his return home, Coles became a farmer in Madison County, Alabama. On April 10, 1873, he married the former Lucy V. Wortham in Huntsville, Alabama. He fathered four sons and a daughter.

On February 13, 1925, Robert T. Coles, who was using the honorary title of "Colonel," died in Huntsville, Alabama. The funeral service was held at the residence of his daughter, and was attended by his four sons, various friends, a contingent from the Daughters of the Confederacy, and the members of the Egbert J. Jones Camp of Confederate Veterans. A Confederate flag was draped over his casket, and another was placed next to his grave.[4]

One of Robert Coles's main interests after the Civil War was preserving the memory of the 4th Alabama and of his comrades who gave their lives to the Lost Cause. According to notes attached to Coles's history, he began writing the work formally in 1909 and completed it in 1910. In fact, in volume 17 of *Confederate Veteran* (1909), Coles placed an advertisement asking any of his old comrades who had any information on the regiment to send it to him so that he could accomplish his task more completely.

When I undertook this project, I decided at the outset not to write a history of the 4th Alabama using Coles's work as a base. Rather, I wanted to amplify his account by giving readers background information and pointing them to sources on the battles and campaigns discussed by Coles.

This book also provides biographical information on the various actors in this story—not only the officers but all the men in the 4th Alabama named by Coles. Since they were the ones who fought the battles, the modern reader should have some knowledge of their backgrounds.

Coles had a tendency to write long sentences with various thoughts and phrases connected by semicolons. Accordingly, some adjustments have been made in his prose style. Paragraphs are delineated. So as not to break the narrative's flow, I have avoided the annoying use of the word *sic*, as well as the use of brackets for inserted punctuation marks. These are the only changes that have been made in the manuscript.

Coles himself incorporated some information from other sources, such as quotations from the *Official Records* and other articles, books, and documents published after the Civil War. This information was copied directly by Coles into his original manuscript. Without exception, the sources of all such material are identified in the endnotes.

In addition, other sources have been cited which contain more information on the battles and campaigns that Coles discusses. Also included in the endnotes are accounts by other members of the 4th Alabama of their various campaigns, and by soldiers in the Union regiments confronting the men of the 4th Alabama in the various battles of the Civil War.

Finally, the appendices contain three unedited accounts, written by men of the 4th Alabama, of the fighting at the Battles of First Manassas, Gettysburg, and the Wilderness. These excellent narratives merited separate publication, rather than citation in small sections within the main work. The three battle descriptions are intended to stand alone. They are included to give the reader a different perspective on the edited work itself. They are so well written that editing them would have diminished their flavor and content.

It must be stressed again that this history of the 4th Alabama is the work of Robert Coles. The men in the 4th Alabama were fortunate indeed that the person who undertook the task of telling their story was their own Robert T. Coles. His work will preserve forever the memory of their gallant exploits.

History
of
4th Regiment
Alabama Volunteer Infantry, C. S. A.,
Army of Northern Virginia

—By—
R. T. Coles

An original member—
Sergeant Major of the Regiment
from its organization to March 6, 1862—
at which time was appointed
Adjutant in the Provisional Army
of the C. S. A. and assigned
to duty with the 4th Alabama Infantry,
serving in that capacity until
the surrender of the
Army of Northern Virginia
at Appomattox.

Adjutant Robert T. Coles.
Courtesy of the Alabama Department of Archives and History.

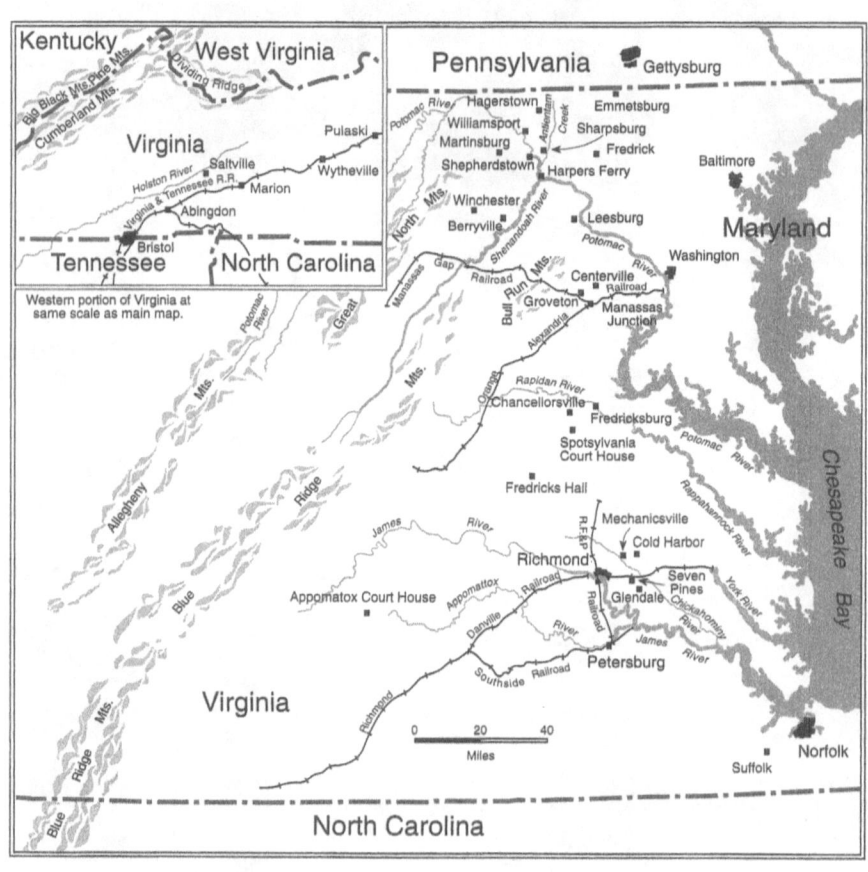

Theater of operations of 4th Alabama in Virginia, Maryland, and southern Pennsylvania. Courtesy of The University of Tennessee Cartography Laboratory.

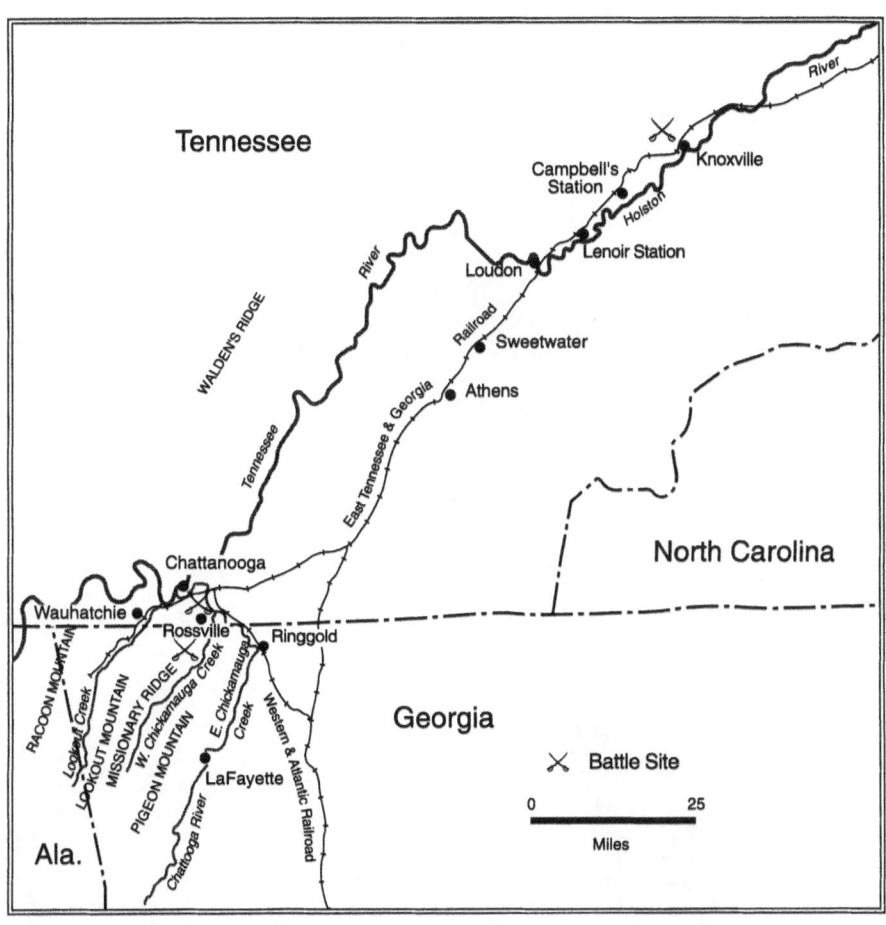

Theater of operations of 4th Alabama in northwestern Georgia and Tennessee. Courtesy of The University of Tennessee Cartography Laboratory.

*Dedicated
to
my wife*

Lucy Virginia Wortham Coles

Introduction

During the formation of the two companies during the latter part of April, 1861, in Huntsville, which afterwards became a part of the 4th Regiment of Alabama Volunteers, I was a cadet at Old LaGrange Military Academy in Franklin, now Colbert, County. With two other cadets, James C. Brandon[1] and Fielding Bradford,[2] I returned to my home in Huntsville and enlisted. Brandon and Bradford joined Captain Tracy's company and I Captain Jones' company.

On the organization of the regiment at Dalton, Georgia, about the 1st of May, I was appointed sergeant major of the regiment and served in that capacity until the 6th of March, 1862, when I was appointed adjutant of the regiment, and served as such until we stacked our arms at Appomattox. Having been present for duty in every battle, march and skirmish of the regiment, except the 29th of August, 1862, on the plains of Manassas, and a skirmish below Richmond in 1864, this experience, though blurred by time, has, with the assistance of a few of my dear comrades, afforded the means of following in the footsteps of the old regiment from its organization to Appomattox.

My great regret is that this sketch was not written by some member of this immortal old regiment who was more competent to undertake the work than myself, and before so many had passed away, who took an active part and added so much to make it one among the best regiments of the Army of Northern Virginia. After all efforts failed to induce others of the regiment to accomplish the task, fearing it would be too late, I undertook the work, to do the best I could under the circumstances.

On the return of the regiment from Appomattox in April 1865 to devastated homes, and throughout the entire Reconstruction period, thoughts, time and energies were directed in an entirely different channel from that in which they had so long been engaged. The war was a closed book, there being no leisure moments for writing history; still, after the smoke of battle had cleared away, the "Union League" subdued and carpetbagism banished, the time was right for some member of a literary turn to collect ample data to write quite a complete history of the regiment.

The kind and comradely words of encouragement and proffered help from comrades, some of whom have died since beginning this sketch, have been sufficient recompense for time and labor expended. To Dr. Thomas M. Owen, Director of Archives and History, Montgomery, and my esteemed friend and schoolmate, Dr. John A. Wyeth of New York City, I am grateful for information, assistance and advice. Of my comrades whom I wish especially to thank and acknowledge my indebtedness, are Captain P. T. Vaughan of Selma, Captain W. C. Ward of Birmingham, General P. D. Bowles of Evergreen and Major Joseph Hardie of Los Angeles, California.

I have confined myself, in all the operations in which we participated, to the regiment. Since where marked and conspicuous courage was so frequently displayed, it is impossible, at this late date, to give individual instances without encountering the danger of doing injustice to others.

1

Company Sketches

Company A

Governor's Guards—Captain Thomas J. Goldsby

In the latter part of 1860 this company from Selma offered its services to the Governor and was accepted and employed in taking possession of the forts along the coast of the State. It performed the duties required of it at Fort Morgan until April 1861, when it was relieved by regulars and returned home. During that time the Confederate Government made its first requisition on the State for troops. The Guards were among the first to offer their services, and were duly accepted on the 26th day of April, and sent to Montgomery.

From here the company was ordered, after being armed and equipped with what was known as the "Mississippi Rifle," to Dalton, Georgia to form a part of the 4th Regiment, Alabama Volunteer Infantry, to be organized there as twelve months troops. It contained 129 officers and men during its entire service. Captain Goldsby[1] was elected lieutenant-colonel on October 28, 1861, to fill the vacancy occasioned by the death of the lamented Colonel Egbert J. Jones.[2] He resigned at the expiration of his twelve months term at Yorktown in May 1862.

At the same time Lieutenant Jason M. West[3] was elected captain, and held that position until we surrendered at Appomattox, when one officer and 21 men were paroled. Captain West, in his report of this company, which was written in the trenches down on the Darby Town Road, below Richmond, in January 1865, says: "At the expiration of the term of enlistment of the company for twelve months, a re-organization and re-election of company officers placed J. M. West, Captain-elect of Company A, junior to the Captain-elect of "D," the Rifle Company, the left of the regiment, and therefore Company "A," without change of letter, was transferred from the right to the left of the regiment.

"In all else, the history of the regiment has been the history of the company. With officers and men ever at their post, cheerfully and faithfully performing every duty assigned them, there is no need to praise them above their sister companies, satisfied that 'Honor and shame from no condition rise, Act well your part, there all the honor lies.'

January 1865   J. M. WEST, Captain"

Company B

Tuskegee Zouaves—Captain E. M. Law

This company was organized in 1860. Its services were tendered to the Governor of the State in January 1861, and on the 7th was ordered to Pensacola, Florida, and placed in the 2nd (afterwards 3rd) Alabama Volunteer Infantry under Colonel Lomax.[4]

It was relieved from duty on the 14th of February and returned to its home in Macon County. Its services were then tendered to the Governor in April 1861 and were accepted. On the 2nd day of May it was connected with the 4th Alabama Volunteer Infantry, as Company B of that regiment during the entire war. All the other nine companies also retained their original letter until the close of hostilities.

Captain Law[5] having been elected, at the organization of the regiment in Dalton, Georgia, lieutenant-colonel, he was succeeded by T. B. Dryer,[6] who resigned April 21, 1862, and E. J. Glass[7] became captain, resigning May 16, 1863. He was succeeded by Bayless E. Brown,[8] who was killed at the Wilderness on May 6, 1864, and succeeded by John P. Breedlove,[9] who was permanently disabled for duty at Gettysburg July 2, 1863, but after the death of Captain Brown, retained the captaincy to the end of the war.

It contained during its service 124, aggregate. There were paroled at Appomattox 1 officer and 22 men.

Company C

The Magnolia Cadets—Captain N. H. R. Dawson

This company was enlisted in Dallas County and mustered into service

April 26, 1861. Joining the regiment at Dalton, it served as Company "C," being the center or Color Company.

Captain Dawson,[10] at the expiration of his twelve months service, resigned and was succeeded by Alfred Price,[11] who fell mortally wounded at the battle of Gaines' Mill on June 27, 1862. He was succeeded by M. D. Sterrett,[12] who having lost a leg in the Maryland Campaign of 1862, resigned and was succeeded by Frank C. Robbins,[13] who served until we laid down our arms at Appomattox. The company during its existence bore upon its rolls an aggregate of 136.

Captain F. C. Robbins was requested to give a sketch of his company, with the other companies of the regiment. It is dated, Darby Town Road, near Richmond, January 1865, and in which he says: "This company has always tried to do its duty cheerfully and bravely in all the difficulties and trying scenes through which it has been called to pass. The thousand individual acts of personal danger and suffering are all enshrined in the hearts of loved ones at home, and it is unnecessary to state them here."

There were present, and paroled, April 9, 1865, 2 officers and 22 men.

Company D

Canebrake Rifles—Captain Richard Clarke

This company was organized at Uniontown, Perry County, on the 25th of April 1861. It joined the 4th Alabama on May 2, 1861. This company, like "A" Company, was armed with the "Mississippi Rifle," a good arm, but not of suitable make for a bayonet. After the reorganization of the regiment at Yorktown, the company was transferred to the right of the regiment, the captain of "A" Company having become junior to that of "D."

On the 25th of April 1862 Captain Clarke[14] resigned and Thomas K. Coleman[15] succeeded him. On account of a controversy of long standing between Captain E. J. Glass and Captain Coleman as to which was entitled to the majorship, made vacant by the promotion of Colonel Law to brigadier general, the office of major remained vacant for some time. The matter was taken before the Court of General Longstreet's Corps and finally decided in Captain Coleman's favor, who, as major of the regiment, was killed at Chickamauga on the 20th of September 1863. He was succeeded to the captaincy by James Taylor Jones,[16] who served to the surrender.

The company contained during the four years of its enlistment 170 aggregate, and surrendered two officers and twenty-one men.

Company E

Conecuh Guards—Captain P. D. Bowles

This company was organized at Evergreen, and on its first formation went to Pensacola, Florida, on January 12, 1861. Its services not being required, it returned to its home in Conecuh County, and was re-organized on April 24, 1861. On the next day it proceeded to Dalton, Georgia, and with other companies formed the 4th Alabama as twelve month volunteers.

On August 27, 1862, in consequence of the vacancy created by the resignation of Major Charles L. Scott,[17] who was permanently disabled from wounds received at First Manassas battle, Captain Bowles,[18] being senior captain, was appointed to succeed him. Lieutenant Lee[19] succeeded to the captaincy and met his death at Gettysburg on July 2, 1863, and was succeeded by Archibald McInnis,[20] a gallant little Canadian, who was retired on account of wounds received below Richmond just before the close of the War. He was succeeded by J. W. Darby,[21] who served until the end and surrendered at Appomattox.

The company enlistment was 155. There were surrendered at Appomattox 3 officers and 34 men, being the largest company in the regiment to turn over their arms.

Company F

Huntsville Guards—Captain Egbert J. Jones

This company was organized and left Huntsville immediately after its formation for Dalton, Georgia, on the 29th day of April 1861, to join the other companies assembling there to form the 4th Alabama Regiment. At the organization at Dalton, Georgia, its captain being fifth in rank, it was designated as "F" Company.

Captain Egbert J. Jones, having been elected colonel of the regiment, was succeeded by First Lieutenant G. B. Mastin,[22] who was killed at the battle of Seven Pines on June 1, 1862. He was succeeded by W. W. Leftwich,[23] who was mortally wounded at Gettysburg on July 2, 1863, and was succeeded by James H. Brown,[24] who survived to the surrender. This company contained during its service 140 aggregate, and surrendered one officer and twelve men.

Company G

Marion Light Infantry—Captain Harry Mosely[25]

This company was organized the 16th of April, 1861, but did not leave Marion, Alabama, until April 24th, from which date the record is begun.

The history of the 4th Regiment, Alabama Volunteers, is but a compendium of the history of the various companies composing it, and as the stations, dates, marches, battles and so forth are therein fully set forth, I must be permitted to refer to it as embracing all I have to say with regard to the history of this company. It is not only idle, it is vanity in the extreme, to claim for any one company of such a regiment as this has been any preeminence among its fellows. Where all have done well, discrimination by an impartial observer might seem invidious; how much worse then would that discrimination appear if urged by any man or set of men as deeply interested as the members of this company must be in its fair fame. If the rising race shall ask of us our history, we care not to say that it stands traced in ink upon the tablets of the natural record by one primarily interested in casting around it a halo of self glorification, but we desire to say, and say truly, "our history is the common history of this great struggle for independence, engraven in characters of blood upon our Country's great heart."

The history of the regiment referred to above will be found appended to the "Record of the Field and Staff of the Fourth Alabama."

Orderly Sergeant M. M. Cooke[26] wrote a history of the regiment, which was published in the *Marion Commonwealth*, but, much to be regretted, no trace has been found of it except the first two chapters. These were used in the sketch.

Company H

Lauderdale Guards—Captain R. McFarland

The company was raised at Florence and mustered into service on April 28, 1861, and at the organization of the regiment, had enrolled 83, aggregate, and during its existence had a membership of 136. Captain McFarland[27] resigned after serving his twelve months, returned to Florence and raised a cavalry company, joining John H. Morgan's command. He was succeeded by Heslop Armistead,[28] who was killed at Gaines' Mill June 27, 1862; he was succeeded by William F. Karsner,[29] who served through to the surrender, when two officers and fifteen men were paroled.

No reports, which the commanders of companies were required to make out in January 1865, have been found of "F," "H," "I" and "K," the four North Alabama companies.

Company I

The North Alabamians—Captain E. D. Tracy

Was organized in Huntsville in April 1861. The company left there April 29, 1861, for Dalton, Georgia, and joined the 4th Alabama on the 2nd day of May 1861—on its muster rolls, one hundred and one aggregate and contained during its existence 139 officers and men.

On August 1, 1861, Captain Tracy[30] was appointed major of the 13th Alabama Volunteer Infantry, and was afterward promoted to the rank of brigadier-general. He was killed leading his brigade in the battle of Port Gibson, Mississippi, on May 1, 1863. Lieutenant C. C. Sale[31] succeeded to the captaincy and died of disease in the fall of 1861. L. H. Scruggs[32] succeeded him and was promoted to the rank of major on September 30, 1862. He was succeeded by Lieutenant Watkins Harris,[33] who, for the greater part of his incumbency, was absent on sick leave, and died before the close of the war. First Lieutenant Daniel H. Turner[34] commanded the company after we left Suffolk until the end.

No officers were present when we surrendered. The orderly sergeant, Stephen Murphy,[35] and ten men were all who were represented there.

Company K

Larkinsville Guards—Captain L. E. Lindsay

Was raised in Jackson County and composed principally of young farmers. It joined the regiment at Dalton with an enrollment of seventy-five officers and men and contained during its existence 129 aggregate. In the First Manassas battle Captain Lindsay[36] was killed; he was succeeded by James H. Young,[37] who resigned at Yorktown [in] May 1862. Young was succeeded by William H. Robinson,[38] who lost a leg at Gaines' Mill, resigned and was succeeded by James H. Sullivan,[39] who was killed at Sharpsburg, Maryland, September 17, 1862. Sullivan was succeeded by James H. Keith,[40] killed at Fredericksburg, December 13, 1862, who was succeeded by John D. Ogilvie,[41] who died of disease, February 24, 1864, and was succeeded by A. C. Murray,[42] who was killed at Petersburg, July

28, 1864. Finally, Murray was succeeded by R. P. Jones,[43] who was among the survivors when we surrendered.

The company, with only one officer (Lieutenant Newbill)[44] and nine men, surrendered at Appomattox, and all are now dead except Rufus Hollis[45] of Jackson County, who, as orderly sergeant, at the surrender, called the last roll of his company, and is the only living litter-bearer who helped to carry our beloved General Barnard E. Bee off the field at the First Manassas.

2

The First Manassas Campaign
July 18 to July 23, 1861

On the morning of July 18, 1861, intense excitement was created throughout camp, occasioned by an order from Headquarters to cook two days rations and to be ready to move at a moment's warning. It was the first of the many such orders which were afterwards issued when there was frequently much less to cook and nothing to move. The ladies of Winchester had shown every kindness to the regiment during their stay among them. The sick were taken into their homes and nursed with the greatest of care and tenderness. In after years the regiment always looked back upon their encampment among the good and noble women of Winchester as by far the most pleasant of any during the four years of its busy life in the Army of Northern Virginia.[1]

The regiment moved out from camp in light marching order on the evening of the 18th. Every one was in a jolly mood, in anticipation of meeting the enemy, until the town was reached and the head of the column turned in the opposite direction from the enemy. The street, as the regiment passed down it at a long swinging gait, was thronged with ladies, old men and children wringing their hands and crying out in distress: "Oh, you will certainly not leave us to the mercy of the Yankees." It was whispered among the men that the move resembled very much a retreat. Both the citizens and the troops became very much depressed as it appeared that General Johnston[2] purported evacuating Winchester and retreating from in front of General Patterson.[3] General Johnston perfectly understood his raw undisciplined troops and contrary to military rules, he kindly took us into his confidence, and as soon as the rear of the column had passed through Winchester, issued the following order:

(SPECIAL ORDER)
Headquarters, Army of the Shenandoah,
Winchester, Va., July 18, 1861
No. 1

The Commanding General directs the regiments to be informed immediately after they have left the town, on the march, that he had received the important news that General Beauregard and his brave army are being attacked by overwhelming forces. He has been ordered by the Government to his assistance and is now marching across the Blue Ridge upon the enemy. General Patterson and his command have gone out of the way to Harpers Ferry, and are now not in reach. Every moment is now precious, and the General hopes that his troops will step out and keep closed, for this march is a forced march to save the country.

(Signed) W. H. C. Whiting, Major and Inspr. General

This order revived the drooping spirits of the men as if by magic. It was greeted with cheer after cheer. They quickened their gait, and the march was continued until late in the night before we halted and went into bivouac.

After getting a few hours rest, the march was resumed before daylight, and we soon reached the Shenandoah, which was fordable. Had we been veterans, no time would have been lost in wading the stream, but at least five hours of valuable time was lost before the brigade reached the opposite bank.[4]

To have a column of infantry blocked, moving up a few feet at a time for hours, as all soldiers know, is the most trying and disagreeable position in which an already exhausted soldier can be placed. From the Shenandoah we hurriedly marched through Ashby's Gap across the Blue Ridge Mountains to Piedmont, a station on the Manassas Gap Railway, reaching there about an hour after dark. As this was our first long march and a forced one, the men were very much exhausted.

While awaiting cars to transport us to Manassas, the men procured a few hours sleep in the rain. Having consumed their two days rations issued before leaving Winchester, it was discretionary with the regiment whether we would proceed that night or wait until the next morning for rations. As the men were so intensely anxious to meet the enemy, they preferred going on at the earliest possible moment; the 4th Alabama, two companies of the 11th and the 2nd Mississippi (Generals Johnston and Bee[5] accompanying us) reached the Junction about noon on the 20th. The remainder of the Army of the Shenandoah, consisting of 6th North Carolina and 1st Tennessee of our brigade, Colonel Elzey's[6] brigade in charge of General E. Kirby Smith,[7] together with the remaining regiments of Colonel Bartow's[8] command, failing to secure transportation by rail from Piedmont in time, did not reach the battlefield until the evening of the 21st, although the President of the railway promised General Johnston to have them all there by the 20th. The artillery and cavalry marched through from Winchester to Manassas and reached there before the battle opened.

The 4th Alabama upon its arrival at the Junction was marched out in a northerly direction about two miles and bivouacked in a piece of woods. The men were all hungry and very much exhausted. Rations were issued and the soldiers spent until the following morning resting, eating and sleeping.

Early on the morning of the 21st artillery firing was heard away off in a northwesterly direction from our bivouac and soon after orders were received to march. Colonel Egbert Jones, mounted on his bay horse, "Old Battalion," after two or three ineffectual efforts to cross swords with General Patterson,[9] was at last to lead the regiment to its first baptism of fire.

General Bee was placed in command of the troops of the 2nd and 3rd brigades which had arrived from Winchester, consisting of 4th Alabama, two companies of the 11th, and the 2nd Mississippi, the 7th and 8th Georgia under Colonel Bartow, and Imboden's[10] battery. General Bee hurriedly led the column forward, the 4th Alabama leading. The firing of small arms was soon heard, and the smoke from bursting shells could be seen.

General Bee led us gradually to the left in direction of the heaviest firing, as General Johnston says of him in his report of this battle: "[General Bee] had with a soldier's eye selected the position near the Henry house, and formed his troops upon it."[11] Here we formed line of battle, and were ordered to load. We were now in position to support our attacking column in our front, which consisted of a part of a brigade commanded by General Evans[12] and was composed of six companies of the 4th South Carolina and five companies of Wheat's[13] Louisiana Tigers. General Johnston assumed command over both armies after his arrival on the 20th.

General Beauregard[14] had disposed his little army, known as the Army of the Potomac, from the stone bridge on Bull Run down that stream at the different fords for several miles, but had neglected to guard any point above the bridge. General Evans with his small force, before the battle opened, held the stone bridge, the extreme left of the Army of the Potomac, and the Army of the Shenandoah which had arrived, was intended to be the supporting column, but "the best laid plans o mice and men aft gang aglee."

Early on the morning of the 21st the Union General McDowell[15] dispatched a force, two divisions under Hunter[16] and Heintzelman,[17] by way of Sudley Springs Ford, two miles above the bridge, with the object of turning our left flank and reaching our rear.

A demonstration at the same time was being made against General Nathaniel G. Evans (an old Army officer and West Pointer dubbed by his schoolmates of that institution "Shanks") at the bridge. His suspicions were, however, aroused when he saw the dust arising above the trees on his left in direction of Sudley Ford. Leaving his skirmishers and two pieces of artillery to defend the bridge, with the rest of his command, he quickly marched about three quarters of a mile to his left and rear with the Louisiana Tigers on the right and the South Carolinians on the left in line of battle. The leading brigade of Hunter's Union division (Burnside's)[18] soon appeared and attacked. Evans with his small force drove Burnside back on the next Union brigade (Porter's)[19] and held his position for over an hour. With other Union troops of General Hunter's division, followed by General Heintzelman's men coming up, Evans was completely overpowered.

In the meantime the 4th Alabama had been marched from its original position on the Henry House Hill across an intervening valley, through which flows Young's Branch, and halted. From this position we were moved up the hill to a low fence surrounding a piece of growing corn. General Bee, who had been reconnoitering on our left, and finding Evans about to be repulsed, came riding down from that direction and upon reaching the centre of the regiment, with a wave of his hand, in a loud commanding tone called out: "Up Alabamians."

The men were rushed over the fence and advanced at a double quick to the crest of the hill;[20] before reaching there we met Colonel Wheat and his Tigers falling back.[21] Our position was on the right and somewhat in advance of General Evans' line. The right and part of the left centre of the 4th Alabama was in the cultivated field and the extreme left was in the pine woods. The part in the open did the most execution. The extreme left, being in such dense cover, did very little effective work. By the time we reached the crest of the hill, the turning column of the enemy, which had been attacking General Evans, had moved farther to our left, continuing their flanking movement. General Heintzelman's division now appearing in our front, the men firing at will, opened a terrific fire on his leading regiment.[22] Our battery (Imboden's) posted on the Henry House plateau lent its aid and did splendid execution.

For at least an hour we held our position, driving back regiment after regiment as they were led forward against us by General Heintzelman in person. The 4th Alabama was literally hanging in the air. General Bee ordered Colonel Bartow to take position on our right with the 7th and 8th Georgia, and he placed the rest of his command, the 2nd Mississippi and two companies of the 11th, in the timber on our left. This was by far the most critical period of the day's battle. Two strong divisions of the Union Army were attacking our front, and enveloping our flanks; Beauregard's Army was away off to the right guarding the fords. General Jackson,[23] who was also some distance on the right from us supporting Beauregard's forces, hearing the heavy firing in our direction, was hastening to our assistance. In the meantime Colonel Hampton[24] with his Legion of six South Carolina companies, who had arrived on the cars that morning from Richmond, advanced to the attack. His little force was held in check after we retired (and before Jackson reached us) together with the remnant of our scattered forces, which Generals Bee and Evans had hastily collected until Hampton, also hard pressed after two hours of hard fighting, was ordered by General Bee to fall back to the Henry House Hill.

No combination of men ever fought with more heroic courage and determination than the 4th Alabama while fighting on the crest of this hill, but they were not veterans. Enveloped on three sides, we were forced by overwhelming numbers to retire, and with one accord, without orders, the 4th Alabama melted away to the rear, leaving that grand old man, Colonel Jones, wounded unto death, surrounded only with the dead and wounded, supporting himself with his arm thrown across his saddle. Seeing the men falling back, he said feebly from loss of blood, "Men, don't run."[25]

The regiment fell back down the hill a short distance, and a rather fruitless effort was made by Lieutenant Colonel Law to reform it. It then moved across Young's Branch and over the fence, the enemy making no effort to pursue us.[26] A regiment (the 27th New York) was found standing on our left, after crossing the brook, in closed column by division and at support arms. Our signal, and the only one that was ever given in any battle, was given us by General Beauregard, when we arrived on the field, so as to identify our own men, viz., to raise either hand to the cap, palm outward, and the password, "Our Homes." After making repeated signals and crying out the password to no effect, the left company of the regiment fired a volley into the ranks of this unknown command, and instantly they deployed and poured a deadly volley into our already shattered ranks, which sent us retreating across the valley of Young's Branch beyond musket range where we rallied and collected together about two hundred very dejected soldiers of the regiment.[27] Captain Tracy of I Company, however, stepped out and delivered a patriotic address, ending it with Hallock's lines, "Strike for the green graves of your sires. Strike for your altars and fires, God and your native land."

By this time General Johnston and General Beauregard arrived from the right. As General Johnston rode up he asked, "Where are your field officers?" "Left on the battle field" was the answer. Some of the company officers then requested him to again place us in position. He stated that he would do so as soon as he learned the condition of affairs.[28]

Colonel Bartow rode up, wounded in the foot, and asked for reinforcements. "This regiment will support you," he [Johnston] said, pointing to the 4th Alabama. General Johnston then took charge of the regiment, riding on our left flank, and placed us near the Georgians. Colonel Bartow, a few minutes after, was killed. General Beauregard took personal charge of the troops engaged and "General Johnston rode back to Headquarters at the Lewis House to hurry forward such reinforcements as it was thought safe to withdraw from the fords."[29]

It was now about two o'clock. The enemy were preparing to advance with fresh troops over our line of retreat. At this particular stage of the battle, General Jackson says in his report: "Subsequently ascertaining that General Bee, who was on the left of our line, was hard pressed, I marched to his assistance, notifying him at the same time that I was coming to his support; but, before arriving within cannon range of the enemy, I met General Bee's forces falling back. I continued to advance with the understanding that he would form in my rear. His battery, under its dauntless commander, Captain Imboden, reversed and advanced with my brigade."[30]

General Bee, very much depressed at the unfortunate turn of affairs, then proceeded to collect his scattered forces. Riding up to the 4th Alabama, he inquired, "What regiment is this?" Captain Richard Clarke, or Captain Porter King,[31] quickly replied: "Why General, don't you know your own men—this is what is left of the 4th Alabama." After stating that this was the only part of his command he had been fortunate enough to find, he then said: "Come with me and go yonder where Jackson stands like a stonewall."[32]

As soon as the water detail which had been sent out returned and the men had satisfied their thirst, the regiment fell into line and followed General Bee to the support of General Jackson.[33] While getting into position with his battery, Lieutenant John Pelham[34] commanding Alburtis' battery, cut the regiment at the centre to pass through. When the two battalions joined, it was learned that our beloved and gallant leader, General Bee, had fallen severely wounded.[35] We then took position under command of Captain Thomas Goldsby as support to General Jackson, and remained in that position until four o'clock when the battle ended.

General Jackson had taken position on the Henry House plateau, exactly where General Bee had placed us in the morning before going into battle. His artillery consisted of four batteries,[36] all from the Army of the Shenandoah.

The Union troops advanced across the valley of Young's Branch, and up the slopes of the Henry House Hill. Then the battle again opened in earnest and continued with unabated fury for two hours, the enemy advancing gradually to our left and sending forward regiment after regiment of fresh troops until their assaulting column on the hill had increased to about eleven thousand men opposed to only six thousand Confederates. The struggle continued until four o'clock without either side gaining any advantage.

There then came into the engagement on our left flank General Kirby Smith with Elzey's brigade, who fortunately had stopped the train at Wellington before reaching Manassas, disembarked his men and marched across to the battle and joined in the contest against the enemy's flank. Soon after, General Early[37] of Beauregard's Army arrived with his brigade from the lower fords, and the battle was soon decided in our favor. By five o'clock there was not a Union soldier except the dead, wounded and prisoners on the south side of Bull Run. One of our batteries was run up quite close and opened on the fleeing enemy. While crossing Cub Run Creek on the north side of Bull Run, a wagon, in the confusion, was upset on the bridge; then the real panic began.

Late in the evening President Davis[38] rode past us in a gallop, going to the front. About sundown we were ordered to march back to the Junction. An ambulance passed us on the way, taking General Bee to the rear. He was sitting up and we entertained a hope that he would recover, but he died that night. No officer ever gained the affections of his men in such a short time as General Bee, and had he been spared to us he would, undoubtedly, have ranked among the first of our Generals.

The men dragged themselves wearily back, feeling that they had been disgraced for showing their backs to the despised Yankees, and sad over the loss of comrades. Lieutenant-Colonel Law and Major Scott were both wounded.[39] The former was unhorsed during our retreat, and as his little mare, badly frightened, passed me I caught the reins and held her until, with the blood streaming down his finger tips, I assisted him to remount. The loss of brigade commanders was particularly heavy in the Army of the Shenandoah, every one being either killed or wounded. The casualties in the 4th Alabama were greater than that of any other regiment engaged in the battle on either side of killed and wounded, which was 40 killed and 170 wounded. The Army of the Shenandoah, according to the official report of General Johnston, was 270 killed and 979 wounded. That of the Army of the Potomac, 108 killed, 510 wounded.[40]

The 4th Alabama having been very much depleted on account of sickness, principally measles, only carried into the fight five hundred and fifty-eight men, and several of these should have been left in the hospital. Some were just recovering from a severe illness and went into the battle positively against the orders of the Surgeon. This battle was fought on the beautiful Sabbath day.

When we awoke the next morning, we were very much surprised to hear nothing but exalted praise from everyone for the 4th Alabama. It was not, however, until General Heintzelman's official report was published and a statement from him, that we realized what we had actually accomplished.[41] Our Major, Charles L. Scott, who had gone to California in 1849 during the gold fever and had been elected to Congress for two terms from that State, and General Heintzelman at that time an officer stationed there, became warm friends. In General Heintzelman's official report he stated that an Alabama regiment had driven back four of his regiments in succession. Some doubted its being an Alabama regiment which opposed him. He then came out in a statement saying that he was not only positive that it was an Alabama regiment, but that he knew it was the 4th Alabama for he plainly recognized Major Scott through his field glasses.

Several members of the regiment, having become separated from it during the retreat from General Heintzelman's front, did not rejoin the regiment, and most of them who were not wounded fought independently during the rest of the day or joined other commands. Among this number was Private William Oakley[42] of H Company, who, late in the evening, after the enemy was routed, captured Colonel Corcoran[43] of the 69th New York of Sherman's[44] brigade. This brigade of Tyler's[45] division was the same which flanked us out of our position on our right when opposing General Heintzelman. Oakley brought Colonel Corcoran in and turned him over to the proper authorities, retaining his sword, which he sent to his home in Florence, Alabama. For this act of bravery by a mere lad in his teens, he was promoted to colorbearer of the regiment. He was a quiet, modest, unassuming country boy, as brave as the bravest, and no mistake was made when the Colors were placed in his hands. Nearly one year afterwards he and his Captain, Heslop Armistead, fell side by side in the charge at Gaines' Mill on the evening of the 27th of June 1862.

At this date (1909), of the litterbearers who bore General Bee when mortally wounded and unhorsed off the field, Rufus Hollis of K Company is the only survivor, and of the nine men and one officer of the company who surrendered at Appomattox, the last roll call on earth of that company having been called by him, all except himself have joined the ranks of those left on the field.[46]

One of the touching incidents, and there were many others, which occurred in this battle is involving George Anderson,[47] a youth of I Company. Left on the field dead when we retreated, some of the Union troops of the 71st New York Militia rifled his pockets and procured his diary, which afterwards fell into the hands of a Union war correspondent, was published, and went the rounds of the Union press. I will quote only one or two entries of this simple little narrative of a Southern soldier lad who loved his God, his home and his country:

"Sunday, May 18, 1861. What a cold day for the 19th of May. Everybody is acting as if it was Monday, all firing guns, cooking, playing cards, etc., had a dress parade, Colonel Jackson inspecting us. He is a large fat old fellow, looks very much like an old Virginia farmer. Returned to camp, prepared and ate a scanty dinner. Had Episcopal service and then a good old fashioned sermon from our Pastor Chadwick. Oh, how I love to listen to him; had another dress parade in the evening; rained all night." (He was mistaken as to the officer who inspected us. It was Major Deas,[48] afterwards a General, from Alabama, in the Army of Tennessee, whose report will be found in the official records: "The Alabama Regiment is well appointed, has brought its tents and camp equipage, and is well clothed. Arms in good order.")[49]

Anderson's last entry, in part, when we reach[ed] Manassas was: "Moved about two miles and camped in the woods, when some bread and meat soon reached us, and we walked right into it like a starved hound eats—now and then all day—slept a little and slept well at night; got up a little after sunrise on the 21st, broiled my meat and ate it with some old crackers full of bugs, expecting orders to march every minute. Will get them I think, for it is Sunday. We will fight I suppose before another week."

This was the end, and in a few hours after writing the last word Private George Anderson of I Company with many more of his gallant comrades was numbered among the dead.

There has always been no doubt in the mind of the writer that this battle made the 4th Alabama Infantry, as a brave and gallant regiment, a possibility. Its history as a first-class command dates from the close of that memorable event on the night of the 21st of July, 1861, when what remained of it collected at Manassas Junction and mourned in common over its dead and dying comrades.

From the organization of the regiment to this time there was discord in its ranks, originating it was said, with certain company officers desiring to depose Colonel Jones.

I will quote what Lieutenant Vaughan[50] of C Company, an able and efficient officer, one who stood true and steadfast to the last, recently said of this unfortunate affair, which in after years was deplored by every member of the regiment:

> One day while at Harpers Ferry papers were handed around in each company of the regiment for signature. I saw one of them recently (1909) —no doubt the only one in existence. It was a request of Colonel Jones that he resign his commission as colonel of the regiment. I cannot recall that I heard a charge of any kind against him. If there were such it did not reach me; I was a private. I remember only that we were told by some one, he had been a captain of a company in the Mexican War and had never gotten into a fight. This may have been idle talk, but it had its effect. An officer who had been in a war and had not gotten into a fight, when others were at it might be a very good soldier, but was not quite the man to lead the gallant 4th Alabama.
>
> At this time there was no distinction socially between officers and privates and so Colonel Jones was deeply mortified. He decided to lay the case before General Joseph E. Johnston and to him he went accompanied by his friend, Joseph Hardie,[51] Adjutant of the regiment. General Johnston being an old soldier told Colonel Jones to return the papers to the men and tell them to prefer charges against him. That settled it. There were no charges and so the matter ended. I am reminded by Mr. Randall Berry that Colonel Jones then told the men he would resign after the first battle. I have thought since, though undreamed of at the time, that some ambitious for promotion might have been at the bottom of that affair. It was a cruelly thoughtless act on the part of the men, for neither in the army nor at home was public sentiment in a sane condition, and any reflection upon a soldier by his comrades was a wound from which he hardly recovered. But at any rate it displayed in the regiment a martial spirit which was soon to be tested.
>
> In a few weeks, Colonel Jones led his men into battle and the above incident doubtless had something to do with his severe bearing on that occasion, and the slaughter of his men, for he held them against great odds until about one-third of them were shot down, nor could they retreat until he fell mortally wounded.[52] Then there was a revolution of sentiment, and messages of regret and sympathy were sent to him at Charlottesville where he died. Long after the war some who signed those papers could hardly speak of it without emotion.[53]

Major Scott and Captains King and Clarke also accompanied Colonel Jones to see General Johnston.

The terrible ordeal through which the regiment passed at Manassas brought a complete transformation as to the sentiment of the different companies. It resulted in binding them together as a perfect unit, which nothing could tear asunder. They had all suffered together for one common cause which they believed was right. They had all gone into battle elbow to elbow, "as iron, were baptised in fire and came out tempered steel," and before twelve months of arduous service had elapsed, became hardened veterans and the best of friends. From the 21st of July 1861 to April 9, 1865, the 4th Alabama continued to exhibit during these four eventful years the unsurpassed courage and fortitude which it first displayed upon the plains of Manassas.

The 8th Georgia, which came to our assistance on our right, did splendid execution and next to the 4th Alabama lost more men than any other regiment in either Beauregard's or Johnston's Army. The 7th Georgia, on the right of the 8th, also acted nobly but, not having the brunt of the battle, their loss was not so heavy; still it stood third in casualties, the 27th Virginia of the Stonewall Brigade being a close fourth.[54] After this battle the 8th and 7th Georgia were separated from us until after the battle of Fredericksburg, at which time they were placed in Hood's[55] division and remained with us to Appomattox, and there was and has always been a close comradeship between these two gallant regiments and the 4th Alabama.

It has often been stated by writers giving a description of this battle that General Johnston personally led a charge with the colors of the 4th Alabama Infantry in his hands. In the first place, he led no charge as stated, only having placed us in position, and, secondly, the colors of the 4th Alabama were never surrendered to friend or foe. From First Manassas to and including Appomattox the colors of the 4th Alabama never, in battle nor after we surrendered, left the hands of some member of that regiment for a moment and no regiment ever entertained more love or reverence for their flag than the 4th Alabama. It is a great consolation to the 4th to know that General Johnston lived long enough to correct this exaggerated statement. He says: "When we were near the ground where Bee was reforming and Jackson deploying his brigade, I saw a regiment in line with ordered arms and facing to the front, but two or three hundred yards in the rear of its proper place. On inquiry I learned that it had lost all of its field officers; so, riding on its flank, I easily marched it to its proper place. It was the 4th Alabama, an excellent regiment; and I mention this because the circumstance has been greatly exaggerated."[56]

General Johnston was the only full Confederate general I knew personally, having met him and his good wife after the war. He always spoke affectionately of the 4th Alabama and stated to me that it was his favorite Alabama regiment. This was quite natural, for we were the first Alabama regiment to be under his command, when first organizing at Harpers Ferry. The few troops there were thrown more in contact with him, he becoming more and more isolated as his army was being augmented. He knew all the commanders of companies and field officers personally and entertained a high regard for Colonel Jones.

General Heintzelman, in his official report, says that he first led up the 11th New York Zouaves against the 4th Alabama, which soon broke and ran. He then led forward the 1st Minnesota, which was repulsed. Next was led forward the 1st Michigan, "which was also repulsed and retired in considerable confusion." The 4th Alabama held its position until General Heintzelman led forward the 14th Brooklyn, which, he says, "went forward in gallant style, but soon after the firing commenced the regiment broke and ran," and he considered it useless to again rally it.[57] Finding our position untenable and without orders, as stated, the 4th Alabama, 2nd Mississippi and two companies of the 11th Mississippi of Bee's brigade, with Evans' command, and 7th and 8th Georgia under Bartow, all fell back toward the Lewis House, across the Valley of Young's Branch.

3

From Manassas to the Peninsula Campaign
July 23, 1861, to March 11, 1862

After the battle of Manassas, General Johnston, in command of both his troops and General Beauregard's, occupied his trenches at Centreville. The 4th Alabama was stationed at Bristow Depot on the railway southwest of the Junction. Our camp was well located near Broad Run, a tributary of the Occoquan, which flows by the station. Our wounded had been sent mostly to Culpeper Courthouse, Warrenton and adjacent points for better care, and almost daily we learned of the death of some one of the most severely wounded.

Many of us, after the excitement of the battle had subsided, began to feel the effects of the exertion occasioned by our severe experience encountered in our first battle, but we soon recovered and in a short time were ourselves again.[1] Major W. H. C. Whiting,[2] a West Pointer and a member of General Johnston's staff, was appointed brigadier-general to fill the place of the lamented Bee. While in camp here, General Whiting rode up to some 4th Alabama pickets playing cards in a ditch. "Suppose I had been the enemy," he said. They replied as they continued playing: "We would have surrendered." No doubt the idea was more strongly than ever impressed upon the mind of General Johnston, after his experience in battle with green volunteer troops, of the necessity for more rigid and thorough training of his raw levies. Wherever practicable, he appointed officers who were competent to bring his troops up to a high state of efficiency and in the shortest time possible.

As we had no field officers with the regiment and our senior Captains being only posted on company drill, General Johnston assigned Major Allston[3] of South Carolina to duty with us. He was a graduate of the U.S. Military Academy, and a lieutenant in the cavalry service before resigning from the U.S. Army. He was not at all suited for volunteer infantry service.

It appeared to be a difficult matter for some of the younger officers, West Pointers, who had cast their fortunes with the South, to discriminate between the material they had to deal with in the old army, men of low degree fighting solely for pay, and men of refinement and culture fighting for a principle. He visited the regiment every morning, hailing from no one of the regiment knew where, and after looking over the mails and examining the morning report, after being made out by the Adjutant, would mount and ride away, not to be seen until the next morning. He made an effort to drill the regiment, but having been only a cavalry officer since his graduation from West Point, had forgotten infantry tactics entirely, and made a complete failure.

Soon after Major Allston joined us, Major O. K. McLemore[4] of the 14th Alabama was also assigned to duty with our regiment. He had belonged to the 8th Regiment U.S. Infantry and graduated at West Point when John Pelham entered that institution. He was a splendid drill master, in fact the best the regiment ever had, and was a fine disciplinarian.

Not yet being initiated into all the innumerable intricacies of military life, having been under the supervision of volunteer citizen officers, the harsh, distant and stern manner displayed by our West Point instructors was to many very humiliating and at times mortifying. There had been, up to this time, between the officers and men of the regiment very little distinction socially. Consequently the sudden change from slack training to strict military rules, which had been drilled into our new instructors from the time they entered West Point as a "Plebe" until it had become a second habit, was accepted with very poor grace by a 4th Alabamian. The morning Major Allston took command, Mr. Kennedy[5] of "A" Company, who as the mail carrier for the regiment and dubbed by the boys "the Pony Express," came dashing up as usual to the Adjutant's tent and cried out, "Here is your mail, come out and get it." Major Allston was perfectly astounded, and in a very preemptory manner ordered him to dismount and bring the mail in.

This is one instance of several which wounded the proud spirits of those who were reprimanded for some little breach of discipline, the men claiming that they came out to fight, and when called upon to do so were at all times ready and willing. Colonel W. C. Oates,[6] whose regiment, the 15th Alabama, was one among the best, was associated with us from January 1863 to Appomattox, understood thoroughly the material of which the 4th Alabama was composed, and says in his book: "The regiment [4th Alabama] was composed of the very best material. It was the only regiment I ever saw that would fight about as well without officers as with them. The discipline was not of a high order, nor did it seem to be necessary."[7]

When still encamped at Bristow Station, General Johnston, in the reorganization of his army, placed our brigade, the 3rd, as it was still called, and the Texans,[8] Hampton's Legion, and the 18th Georgia as a division under Major General Gus Smith,[9] also a West Pointer and formerly an engineer in the U.S. Army. The Texans were associated with the 4th Alabama from this time until we parted, to return to our homes, at Appomattox, fighting side by side in every engagement without a single exception. Colonel John B. Hood of the 4th Texas was appointed brigadier-general of our brigade.

An effort at this time was being made by the Confederates to close the navigation of the Potomac River below Washington near Dumfries in Prince William County, and seal up that city as a port. For this purpose a number of large siege guns were placed in position on the bank of the river and were known as the "Cockpit Batteries." Our division was sent from Bristow Station to Dumfries as support for the batteries. General McClellan[10] at this time was in command of the Union Army opposing us, and Yankee public opinion scored him severely for permitting the Rebels to accomplish their object unmolested. Here we remained until the spring campaign of 1862 opened.

Majors Allston and McLemore were both with us here, sometimes one and then the other. One cold frosty morning, H Company, commanded by Captain McFarland, was detailed to relieve the company on duty at the batteries. We left camp some time before daylight; as Major Allston had never been there, he ordered me to accompany him. I concluded to walk, and as we hiked along in the cool bracing air kept very comfortable, while Major Allston sat his horse shivering like a leaf. After marching some distance, he asked me if I did not wish to ride; of course I declined. He then asked Captain McFarland, who also declined. Finally, becoming so uncomfortably cold he could stand it no longer, he dismounted and handing the reins to the Captain, said: "Captain, I order you to ride, sir." Captain McFarland was a fat Scotchman, a lawyer of Florence before becoming a soldier, and a splendid, companionable man. The exercise of walking had heated up his robust and corpulent body. After mounting, it was only a few minutes until he was suffering agonies, but he was under orders and like a good soldier obeyed.

Colonel Jones, after undergoing great suffering from his wound, died on the 1st of September 1861 at Charlottesville, Virginia.[11] Lieutenant-Colonel Law and Major Scott were still absent on account of their wounds, and not until some time in October did Colonel Law recover sufficiently to report for duty.[12] Law became colonel and on the 28th of October, 1861, Captain Goldsby was elected lieutenant-colonel. The West Pointers were relieved and returned to their respective commands. To show their aversion to Major Allston, the regiment made a great demonstration over the return of Colonel Law, Lieutenant Lily Spraggins[13] taking an active part because he was reprimanded by the Major for accepting an invitation to dine with his men and partake of some of the viands received from home.

It was while here and about this time that the members of the regiment, to show their esteem, love and admiration for General Whiting, contributed among themselves one thousand dollars to purchase a horse and present it to him. The regiment was called out and formed into line the day of presentation. The guns and accoutrements, all new and the best the Union army could afford, the spoils of Manassas, with the bayonets glistening in the autumn sunlight, and the uniforms which had not yet become entirely too much faded, presented a fine appearance. Samuel H. Moore[14] of I Company, who had been appointed messenger boy by Colonel Jones, rode forth the war horse. Colonel Law made the presentation address, and the horse, a magnificent animal, was accepted by General Whiting, who named it in honor of the 4th Alabama.

As cold weather was fast approaching and it was expected that we would spend the winter here, preparations had to be made to make us more comfortable. Colonel Goldsby took a great deal of interest in superintending the location of our new quarters, which were located in a more elevated position. Colonel Goldsby looked after clearing off the grounds, laying off the streets, and the erection of cabins; among the latter he had a commodious and comfortable cabin with chimney built for the Adjutant's office. When complete, we had quite a respectable little town, with rather a variegated assortment of buildings, mostly tents with chimneys intermixed with cabins. Several displayed their mechanical ingenuity by inventing miniature wind mills and weather vanes. Others displayed remarkable talent in fashioning with their pocket knives, from the root of the laurel, many little trinkets which were sent to Alabama as souvenirs.

Major Scott returned and reported for duty before the spring campaign opened, but still suffering with his wound, resigned and returned to his home after remaining with us a short while.[15] Captain Bowles, a senior captain, was next in promotion, but was not appointed major until the 27th of August, 1862.

Major Scott was not a military man, a typical old Southern gentleman he was, as true as steel to his friends, the soul of honor and one of the most dignified old gentlemen imaginable. Barlow Bradley,[16] a private of I Company, professed to be too much of a gentleman to perform any of the duties incumbent upon the members of the different messes, and in consequence, was not permitted to mess with any of his company, and was, therefore, compelled to impose upon his friends for his meals. He was a frequent uninvited guest at the Field and Staff table. Major Scott was a great smoker and carried his tobacco in his pant's pocket. On one occasion when Bradley was a guest, after eating a hearty meal at headquarters, he approached the major holding a short stemmed pipe in one hand and tapping the bowl of it with the forefinger of the other and said: "Major, will you be kind and condescending enough to present me with a sufficiency of fumigating material to replenish my fumigator?" The Major ran his hand down into his capacious pocket and brought forth a handful of tobacco, and handing it to Bradley, remarked: "Is that what you wish, sir?" Bradley finally concluded to perform his part of the drudgery and was initiated into one of the messes of I Company. He was one of the four reported captured on Raccoon Mountain near Chattanooga in October 1863, and was never exchanged.

Once a week we sent our wagons down to Fredericksburg for supplies and as Christmas approached, boxes from the loved ones at home for some of the companies were brought up. D Company was the fortunate one a short time before Xmas, and they must have indulged too freely, for when we assembled for dress parade on the evening after the receipt of the boxes, Dr. W. O. Hudson,[17] who was at that time the orderly sergeant of the Company, in making his report to the Adjutant, said sufficiently loud for all the regiment to hear him: "All present or accounted for except Uncle Dick and thirty-seven." Captain Richard Clarke of D Company was called by all of us "Uncle Dick" and never did any military duty. He said he only came out to take care of the boys. We could very easily account for his absence from dress parade, but not so with such an excess of absentees until an investigation was made. Dr. Clarke not only looked after the health of his own company, but he was untiring in looking after the welfare of other members of the regiment. He was a grand old man and several of us would have suffered had it not been for his watchful care and attention immediately after the battle of Manassas.[18]

There was a box brought up from Fredericksburg, a large heavy one, directed to the 4th Alabama, but evidently intended for some other Alabama regiment. It was held in the Adjutant's cabin until after Xmas. This office was a nightly resort for the boys after the older ones had retired. As the luxuries from home had become exhausted, several of the boys were anxious to investigate the contents of this box, and every night the first question asked on entering was: "Have you found the owner of Briggs' box?" When answered in the negative an appeal was made to open it. After giving up all hopes of finding the rightful "Briggs" it was pulled out from under a bunk and opened. Everything that a soldier's heart could wish was stored away under its cover and what a feast we had. Lieutenant Newt McGraw,[19] of C Company, is remembered as one of the party, and how he enjoyed the brandy cherries of which there was a half-dozen large bottles. As long as it lasted, "Briggs" was regularly patronized by the fortunate ones who had introduced themselves to him. A common theme around the campfires when rations were scarce among those who helped to exhaust "Briggs," was an enumeration of its contents and how they enjoyed it, until "Briggs" became a by-word. As every military aphorism is attributed to Napoleon, of course it was he who said: "An army is only a collection of stomachs."

During the first year of the war it seemed that the 4th Alabama had to contend with every conceivable disease which flesh was heir to. The regiment had scarcely recovered from measles before it was afflicted with that detestable affliction, Yellow Jaundice. Our hospital was down at Old Man Merchant's hotel, which was provided with cots and nice clean bedding; our hospital steward, Dr. Duryee[20] of I Company, was an efficient officer. We also had a bakery attached which made splendid bread. There was one large ward and several small ones. Dr. Bradley[21] of C Company and Dr. Kirksey[22] of A, both privates, were detailed to assist Dr. Slaughter.[23]

In one of the small wards four of us were placed; among the number was Lieutenant Karsner of H Company, a boon companion and a brave and gallant officer, that is, when he was well. When ill he was a perfect nuisance to those around him—irritable, quarrelsome and melancholy. He declared the jaundice would kill him and knew he would never see his dear mother again. All our efforts to cheer him were perfectly exhausted without the least effect in quieting him. When his malady became somewhat complicated, though not at all serious, the nurse, whom we termed our baby, came in smiling and stated that the surgeon had ordered him to perform an operation on Lieutenant Karsner. When the nurse displayed the instrument which he was to use, Karsner, having a very vague idea of its use, declared he could not survive such treatment. We begged and pleaded with him, stating that his only chance of recovery was to comply with the instructions of the surgeon. Finally he submitted. After the departure of the nurse, he became very quiet for half an hour or more and peace and quiet at last reigned in our ward, much to our relief. One of the boys became alarmed at the unusual quiet of our patient and remarked: "Do you suppose that operation has really killed him?" He at the same time tip-toed gently over to Karsner's cot, to find him wide awake. He was asked in a very sympathetic tone: "Lieutenant, how do you feel now?" "Oh," he said, "God bless enemas, when I recover I shall certainly take one every morning." Whether he ever adhered to his own prescription or not, he was never seriously sick again and never missed a battle in which the regiment participated, was a jolly good fellow and a brave, efficient and capable officer.

Our camp at Bristow Station was named in honor of Colonel Jones; this one was named in honor of Colonel Law. During January 1862, as every preparation was being made by the contending forces for a prolonged war, nearly all of the regiment re-enlisted for three years.[24] As there was a probability of no active operations being resumed until spring on account of cold weather and bad roads, and the regiment having been very much depleted in consequence of death, wounds and transfers as officers of newly formed regiments, several of those who re-enlisted, both officers and men, were ordered home on sixty days leave of absence for the purpose of securing recruits.[25] By March all had returned, and with the recruits obtained, together with the return of several who had recovered from their wounds, the regiment was very much augmented. Most of the Union troops who fought us at Manassas were ninety day levies and their time was then fast expiring.[26] One of its regiments and a battery claimed their discharge on the opening of this battle and, as remarked by General McDowell, "moved to the rear to the sound of the enemy's cannon."[27] In this respect, as to the hasty mobilization and organization of its raw troops, the Confederate Government exhibited a better military system than the Washington Government did.

4

Peninsula Campaign and Battle of Seven Pines
March 11 to June 12, 1862

On the 9th of March 1862 General Joseph E. Johnston withdrew his forces from his works at Centreville, and at the same time called in his detachments from the Potomac batteries. The 4th Alabama joined the main army south of the Rappahannock. Ewell's[1] division was ordered to reinforce General Thomas J. Jackson, who had been previously sent back to the Valley. About the middle of April the remaining part of the army, under the immediate command of General Johnston, moved in the direction of Richmond. From this time until the end, our hardships and trials increased and multiplied until the Confederate soldier had a greater burden to bear than it was possible for human endurance to undergo.

Although gradually becoming weaker in number as the War progressed, the heroic and determined spirits who stood bravely to their colors, continued throughout the conflict imbued with a determined effort to win out or die in the attempt. After the novelty and enthusiasm began to wear off and we were being initiated into the realities of a desperate and prolonged undertaking, there was found many laggards and cowards who used every subterfuge to avoid the hardships of camp life and its attendant dangers. A prolonged war is an ideal position to bring out a man's good or bad qualities; there they will crop out and rise plainly to the surface so distinctly that, "He who runs may read."

General George B. McClellan had been placed in charge of the Union army opposed to us as already stated. At the time of his assignment, no one could have been selected who would have been more acceptable to the Union press, the people and the army. He had been graduated second in the class of 1846, the class in which Stonewall Jackson was graduated seventeenth and George E. Pickett[2] fifty-ninth. About the 8th of March there was a tacit understanding between the Washington authorities and

General McClellan that he move his army on Richmond by water to Urbanna on the lower Rappahannock, only two-and-a-half days overland march from our Capital. General Johnston, no doubt, through some means secured information of this move on the next day, for by the 11th of March, only three days after this contemplated move, he had concentrated his army south of the Rappahannock and about the same distance from Richmond as General McClellan would have been at Urbanna. With the right of his army at Fredericksburg and his left at Culpeper, General Johnston was censured by the authorities in Richmond for his hasty abandonment of his works at Centreville. His critics, Southern writers principally, have also condemned this movement alleging he left there so precipitately, much property was destroyed.[3] General Johnston's purpose was to checkmate General McClellan's contemplated move as promptly as possible, and he did so most effectively. General McClellan then determined to make an effort to capture Richmond by transferring his army by water to Fort Monroe, which was in possession of the Union forces. Norfolk was held by the Confederates under General Magruder[4] with eight thousand troops, and about twenty-five miles up the Peninsula at Yorktown were about as many more under the Confederate General Huger.[5] The Peninsula lies between the York and James Rivers and is a low, level and marshy region.

As soon as General Johnston discovered that McClellan purported making Fort Monroe his first base, he marched us down the Peninsula from Richmond over the worst roads we had encountered up to that time. The 4th Alabama went into camp at Yorktown, having reached there the last of April. While encamped here some radical changes were made in the regiment. Our twelve months enlistment having expired, the regiment was reorganized. Most of the men remained, but very few of the officers stood for reelection. It was with sadness and regret we saw the departure of many officers whose comradeship for the past twelve months had become endeared to many of us. But after several months of strenuous military experience the men were in fit condition to elect company and field officers of ability, trial and practice, and fortunately there was, of which advantage was taken, good available material left to select from as leaders. In several instances selections were made from noncoms and privates. The following officers formed the new organization. All officers after this election were appointed. Captains Glass of B, Bowles of E, Mastin of F, and Scruggs of I were the only Captains reelected. Lieutenant Jason M. West of A, Sergeant Alfred C. Price of C, 1st Lieutenant T. K. Coleman (who had been virtually the Captain) of D, Lieutenant W. M. Robbins[6] of G, Private Heslop Armistead of H, Private W. H.

Robinson of K were elected captains of their respective companies. Colonel E. M. Law was reelected colonel, Major O. K. McLemore of the 14th Alabama elected lieutenant-colonel, and Major Charles L. Scott reelected major.

General Magruder held the trenches and we were bivouacked a short distance in their rear, among the old breastworks of General Washington, which were still plainly visible. We had no cooking utensils; however, as it was springtime, the boys procured and peeled hickory bark and placed their dough on it before the fire, Indian style, and cooked their bread. We procured a good many oysters.

There was a sudden and most terrific firing opened on our front along Huger's line of works about taps one night. Judging from the roll of musketry it appeared that the whole of General McClellan's army was storming our works, creating the greatest excitement and confusion in the regiment, men running over each other in the dark searching for misplaced arms and accoutrements. The long roll was being sounded in every regiment. Many of the 4th Alabama ran out as the line was being formed, with accoutrements in one hand and clothes in the other. By the time the line was formed the firing ceased as suddenly as it had commenced. Soon after, a staff officer of the brigade rode up and informed us that we could return to our bivouac, that the firing had been caused from a false alarm on the part of Huger's men, and the enemy had not fired a gun. This was our first experience with a stampede and was a wholesome lesson to us: to always have everything in its place and be prepared for any emergency. After General McClellan had placed his army in front of Magruder's forces, General Johnston, on reaching Yorktown, found this Confederate General strongly entrenched behind his formidable works, extending on his left from near Yorktown a distance of thirteen miles across the entire Peninsula to Lee's Mills on our right.

Finding our position too strong to be taken by direct assault, General McClellan ordered a number of large siege guns and heavy mortars to be mounted along our front. By the 5th of May everything was to be in readiness to annihilate the Confederate army. At this time the Union army had been increased to 105,000. General Johnston carried down with him 35,000, and with the troops found there under General Magruder, his army barely amounted to 50,000 effectives. It was confidently expected that the Confederates could not sustain for more than a few hours the terrible fire of the Union siege guns and mortars. General Johnston wisely concluded not to await his destruction. On the night of the 3rd of May he withdrew his army and commenced his retreat up the Peninsula to Richmond.

Before reaching historic Williamsburg, which is only twelve miles from Yorktown, the 4th Alabama received orders to move rapidly to the front, together with the other regiments of the 3rd Brigade and the Texans, Hampton's Legion and 18th Georgia, get ahead of the whole army and proceed to West Point on the York River (the head of navigation where the Mattaponi and Pamunkey rivers unite), and there intercept General Franklin's[7] Union Corps, which at that time was embarking on transports at Yorktown for the purpose of moving against our army and wagon trains. The mud was so deep that the regiment made slow progress. Entirely without rations, we floundered on without a stop until late in the night; the men dropped down to sleep perfectly exhausted and worn out from the fatiguing march. Until dark we plainly heard the battle in progress back at Williamsburg, between our rear guard and the advance of McClellan's army.[8]

Before reaching Eltham's Landing, opposite West Point, we learned that General Franklin had passed us and was landing and throwing out his forces in our front at this point. The 5th Texans, under Colonel Archer,[9] being in front, immediately threw out a strong line to meet them. In the early dawn, General Whiting, our brigade commander, passed us going to the front with his hands clasped and his face turned heavenward, when some of the boys remarked that he was praying. General Hood with his gallant brigade succeeded without much opposition in driving the enemy back under cover of his gunboats, and his (General Whiting's) prayer was answered. The 4th Alabama had very little work to do aside from slight skirmishing.[10]

That night while the army was passing on its way to Richmond, we procured some rations from the supply trains. Orderly Sergeant Hartley[11] of I Company and Private John Cussons[12] of A were sent out in our front on the night of the 6th as scouts that dark night. Cussons returned the next morning and reported the brave and gallant Hartley killed. He reported that while scouting, the first intimation they had of the presence of the enemy was the click of the gun locks of the Union pickets only two or three paces from them; both sides fired at the same time and Hartley fell instantly killed.

In the "History of the 27th N.Y. Volunteers" is a photograph of an open roll book pierced by a bullet. On one of the open pages is the roster of company and non-com officers, with a note below, as follows:

"Roll Book of Co. D 27th New York Regiment"

"The scar shows where a bullet passed through the roll book and entered the heart of Lieutenant (formerly Orderly Sergeant) John L. Bailey, who carried the rollbook in his breast pocket. Lieutenant Bailey was shot by a Confederate picket named W. Hartley of the 4th Alabama the night of May 6, 1862, at West Point on the York River.

"Hartley was shot and instantly killed by Corporal H. M. Crocker, whose name, the eighth in the list of corporals, was obliterated by the tear and bloodstains."

William Hartley was a native of Connecticut, a civil engineer who came South but a short time before Alabama seceded. It was only a short time after our organization at Dalton, Georgia, that his company discovered his real worth and elected him orderly sergeant and reelected him at Yorktown. He was among the best in the regiment, a disciplinarian, and through his efforts the morals of his company, which were not the best, were very much improved. Not only his company, but the entire regiment deplored his death.

I am here reminded of a little incident which occurred back in our infancy and green squad days, on Bolivar Heights, at Harpers Ferry in May 1861, when General Joseph E. Johnston was organizing his little army. Hartley while we were here reprimanded a hotheaded youth, the youngest in his company, A. B. Shelby,[13] for some breach of discipline. Shelby became furiously angry and gave Hartley to understand that he would not be dictated to by a damned Connecticut Yankee, at the same time landing a terrible blow with his fist in Hartley's breast. The latter did not resent it, nor did he hasten to his Captain to report the offense committed, but serenely folded his arms and gave Shelby a most significant look—who, with bowed head, walked away. As he has said to me long after the close of the war (he is still living), in speaking of the incident, he received the severest chastisement ever inflicted on anyone, and he can never speak of Hartley without the deepest emotion. He was stung to the quick and never forgot the rebuke Hartley gave him.

This was the only casualty in the regiment. Why Franklin did not make a greater effort to drive our two little brigades from his front with his full Corps and gunboats and get possession of the road on which General Johnston was retreating before the arrival of Confederate reinforcements, always remained a mystery with us. We held our position until the army and trains passed. We then followed on unmolested and went into camp around Richmond and for three weeks enjoyed a good, quiet rest.

Then came the Battle of Seven Pines as we termed it; Fair Oaks the Union.[14] On the evening of the 30th of May, the regiment was marched out beyond Richmond and bivouacked among some oaks. Against one of them the Marion Light Infantry boys (G Company) stacked their guns. During the night a most terrific electrical storm occurred; lightning struck the tree under which G Company was lying, demolished the guns, killing Porter Graham,[15] seriously disabling sixteen and slightly thirty of the company. There was scarcely a corporal's guard left for duty of those refined, cultured young men. Early the next morning with only time to drop a tear to the dead and maimed, we were hurried off to the battlefield.

When our regiment, after seven or eight miles of marching, reached Seven Pines the enemy had been driven out of their encampment before our arrival, which was left with their fly tents all standing.[16] This camp was situated in a low place and before each tent was a hole dug about three feet deep in which the water came nearly to the surface and was used presumably for drinking and culinary purposes. We were maneuvered about in different positions until late in the evening without becoming engaged, and finally were placed across the Richmond & York River Railway, our colors resting on the track. On our left was the piece of woods in which was the abandoned camp; in our front was an open field in which was a Union battery in full view.[17]

As soon as we took our position, the battery opened on us and soon got the range. We were being peppered most unmercifully—no other regiment so far as we could see was near us. While lying here, General Johnston rode slowly, alone, and quietly up within a few paces of our line, and sat there for some time looking intently to the front. As there was no Union infantry in our front to keep us occupied, we were compelled to lie there and submit to the shelling, and cast an occasional glance back at General Johnston with the hope that he would retire; before doing so, a piece of shell struck him on the shoulder and he was unhorsed. He had scarcely fallen before the litter bearers of the 4th Alabama ran to him and bore him from the field.[18] This was the last time he was ever seen by the regiment.

The position of the regiment being so exposed, it was moved by the left flank under cover of the woods to the abandoned Union camp, and in doing so, a shell exploded just before reaching the head of F Company and rear of D, killing Captain Gus Mastin and his orderly, Sergeant E. M. Croxton,[19] and killing and wounding several others of both companies. We took position to left and rear of the abandoned camp, when the Union infantry advanced on us about dark.[20] After a lively fight of several minutes, the enemy retired and left us in possession of their camp, where we slept that night supplied with an excess of water and few rations. Before the enemy retired, Mr. Davis rode up close behind the firing line, but it was too dark for us to know his presence until the firing had ceased, and he then came among us and complimented the regiment for its bold and determined stand.

Major General Gus Smith, who commanded the division to which the 4th Alabama was attached, being next in seniority to General Johnston, took command of the army and the battle was fully expected to be resumed the next morning. General Smith, however, omitted to bring on a general attack. About 2 P.M. on the 1st of June, General Lee[21] arrived at General Smith's headquarters and, in compliance with an order from President Davis, assumed command of the Confederate army. That night he withdrew the army to its original position in the entrenchments around Richmond. Our casualties in this battle were 8 killed and only 19 wounded, none missing. General Gus Smith, on account of ill health, was relieved of command of our division and never afterwards held any position in the Army of Northern Virginia. General Whiting succeeded to the command of the division, and Colonel Law, being senior colonel of the brigade, was placed in charge of it. The regiment again secured a rest of two weeks. The Confederate army in the meantime had been reinforced by about 15,000 troops from points south of Richmond.[22]

5

Seven Days Battle
June 12 to July 8, 1862

A rumor was circulated and went the rounds among the boys of the 4th Alabama as they were lounging around camp at Richmond a few days after the battle of Seven Pines, to the effect that General Lee purported sending us to the Shenandoah Valley to reinforce General Jackson. The latter had just completed his brilliant campaign against the forces of Banks,[1] Fremont,[2] and Shields,[3] and was then resting his little army near Staunton at Brown's Gap.[4] This camp rumor, in which the regiment placed very little credence, was thought to be too good even to be realized. About the 12th of June the report was confirmed and made public that our brigade and the Texans, and Lawton's[5] brigade sent from the South,[6] were the fortunate troops selected to be sent to General Jackson.

The 4th Alabama was perfectly elated at the idea of once more getting back into the Valley. The report was circulated throughout the army, an unusual occurrence, and no doubt was immediately conveyed to Washington through the Union Secret Service.

The Union General McDowell's[7] Corps of 40,000 men was then at Fredericksburg under orders to reinforce General McClellan before Richmond. This order was immediately countermanded and McDowell was hurried back to Washington to defend it against the invincible Jackson and his "Foot Cavalry." At this time General McClellan had crossed his vast army to the south side of the Chickahominy, except Porter's[8] Corps, and was confronting General Lee only seven or eight miles below Richmond.

We were entrained at Richmond and transported after lying over two days at Charlottesville, to Staunton, and from there joined General Jackson on the 17th of June. General Lawton with his six Georgia regiments was placed in General Ewell's division. Our division under General Whiting embraced the Texas brigade, commanded by Brigadier General John B. Hood, and ours under command of Colonel Law, with the two batteries of Captains Reilly[9] and Balthis.[10]

General Jackson had given his little hard marched and much fought army a needed rest of five days before our arrival. As soon as we reported, General Jackson put his army in motion, with the distinct understanding that we were marching under secret orders. Leaving nearly all of his cavalry to conceal the movements of his army, now increased to about 25,000 men and thirty-four cannon, he abruptly turned the column in direction of Richmond at a rapid gait. This was continued until we reached Frederickshall Station on the 22nd (Sunday).

The next morning General Whiting sent an order to us to be prepared for inspection by 9 o'clock A.M. As the boys were busily engaged in cleaning their guns and accoutrements, another order was received from General Jackson stating that in lieu of inspection there will be held divine service in the afternoon. Dr. Dabney,[11] Chief of Staff, delivered a splendid sermon, and it appeared that the whole of Jackson's army attended the service. The rest of the day was occupied in cooking rations and resting.

Early the next morning we took up the line of march, continuing in the direction of Richmond. Exactly eight days after forming a junction with General Jackson's forces (we had marched about one hundred and fifty miles and rested during that time one day) we found ourselves at the end of this time, June 25th, bivouacked around Ashland, twelve miles from Richmond. We were now in rear of McClellan's army, nearly at the point from whence we had started, with all of our fond anticipations of meeting our good friends of the Valley blasted.

On the morning of the 26th we left Ashland for Cold Harbor, our division in the lead and the Texans in front of our brigade. There being nothing so far to impede our progress, we marched rapidly on down the Ashland road, crossing the Central Railroad about 10 o'clock. Upon reaching Totopotomoy Creek, which could only be crossed on a bridge, our Texas riflemen were thrown forward to drive back the Union pickets at that point. After succeeding in doing so, the bridge was found to be partially destroyed to impede our progress and the enemy was also on the opposite side of the creek busily engaged in felling trees obstructing the road, and endeavoring to delay us as much as possible.

General Whiting rode forward and soon had the bridge in condition for us to cross over. After old Captain Reilly had given the woods in our front a good shelling, we moved cautiously and slowly, removing the obstructions in our front, marching on down the north side of the creek to Hundley's Corner, where we went into bivouac for the night. As we marched that evening, heavy and continued discharges of artillery were heard in direction of Mechanicsville, announcing the engagement of General A. P. Hill[12] with the extreme right of the enemy. General Lee had sent A. P. Hill's division to our side of the Chickahominy to cooperate with us early that morning, but hearing nothing from General Jackson and becoming impatient, he made the attack alone and was repulsed.[13]

Early on the morning of the 27th with Ewell's division in the lead, we left Hundley's Corner for Cold Harbor, inclining as we advanced, to the left. General A. P. Hill having joined us, General Jackson placed him on one road and we took another. The former, meeting with no obstructions, reached Cold Harbor some time before we did. As on the day before, we met with obstructions of felled timber, which together with the enemy's sharpshooters, very much retarded our progress.

At one time as the 4th Alabama was lying on each side of the road while our scouts and pickets were reconnoitering and clearing the road in our front, a splendidly equipped ambulance drawn by a fine pair of bays came driving slowly through the regiment in the direction we were marching. When the driver reached the centre of the regiment, he observed our colors and excitedly inquired: "Who be you?" In an instant the men near the centre jumped up and rushed for the ambulance, falling over each other and almost smothering the poor frightened driver in their efforts to secure something eatable. Orderly Sergeant Parker[14] of D Company, who was sitting by me, was among the first to get in, and in a few moments emerged from the scrambling crowd with his cap full of nice, ripe, red currants which he placed on the ground at my side with an invitation to join him, and no two soldiers ever enjoyed a more refreshing repast. The ambulance was soon relieved of its contents by the fortunate ones who succeeded in getting into the vehicle. The driver stated that he belonged to General Porter's Union Corps and had been out in the country foraging for the headquarters mess, and had not received any intimation of our presence.

In a few minutes afterwards we received orders to move forward. The road now being clear and nothing to impede us, we moved briskly forward in the direction of the firing, which now became very heavy. We soon passed the abandoned camp of General Porter with everything intact, tents, officers' tables and other camp furniture standing as if it was their intention to return after a temporary absence. General Porter had fallen back to Gaines' Farm about half a mile from Cold Harbor and fortified himself. General A. P. Hill had preceded us about two hours and General Jackson, finding he was hard pressed, hurried on to his relief.

Before reaching the firing line, Capt. W. M. Robbins of G Company, as was generally the custom with him before going into battle, all the regiment kneeling, delivered a prayer. As we lay for a few moments, after emerging through a dense undergrowth and swamp, General Jackson ordered us forward to the relief of A. P. Hill, who had been hotly engaged for over two hours along his whole line.[15]

Our brigade occupied the extreme right. In our front was an open field a quarter of a mile in extent which we had to cross to reach the enemy's position. The position taken by the enemy was naturally strong, and was further strengthened by hastily thrown up artificial cover. His forces in our front were posted in an open wood on an abrupt bluff running nearly parallel with the Chickahominy. At the foot of this bluff was a deep ravine and beyond was the first line of infantry posted. Farther up the bluff was a second line of infantry firing over the heads of the first. On the top was the artillery supported by a third line of infantry.[16] It was, in fact, a perfect Gibraltar and had we been aware of the strength of the almost impregnable position before making an effort to storm it, the bravest of the brave would have blanched at the undertaking.[17]

As we advanced across that stormswept field, the artillery and small arms were perfectly deafening.[18] The smoke had settled down heavily, and one standing erect could scarcely see ten feet in his front. General Field's[19] Virginia brigade of Hill's division was found lying down in the field in front of the enemy's line, while the shrapnel and bullets poured into them as thick as hail. They would neither advance nor fall back; they were perfectly exhausted and out of ammunition.

Lieutenant Colonel McLemore took position in front of the 4th Alabama as we marched up in rear of the Virginians and walking backwards, he called out as coolly as on drill, "Guide centre; keep the step—one, two, three, four; one, two, three, four," and continued calling out the step until we passed over the Virginians, and then he gave the order to charge. With a bound and a yell every man sprang forward and made a rush for the works. Those who were not shot down never halted until they crossed the ravine and jumped into the first line of works. Then on up the steep ascent over the second line to the crest of the hill, exposed to a deadly fire they pressed on until they had driven the enemy from their stronghold.[20] The position was carried from right to left of General Jackson's line, and as he says: "The shouts of triumph which rose from our brave men as they, unaided by artillery, had stormed this citadel of their strength, were promptly carried from line to line."[21]

Jim Harrison[22] of D Company in his eagerness to reach the crest of the hill, fell into a trench filled with the enemy. After shooting down one of them, the others, twenty-two men and an officer, surrendered to him. Securing the officer's sword and pistol, he marched them to the rear and returned before the battle ended.[23] The Federals, routed at every point, and aided by the darkness of the night, escaped across the Chickahominy.

A large number of prisoners and fourteen pieces of artillery fell into our hands.[24] Captain Heslop Armistead, a most estimable and popular officer, was killed, and Captain A. O. Price of C Company mortally wounded. Lieutenant Colonel McLemore was among the wounded. Our casualties were 2 officers and 21 men killed and 7 officers and 100 men wounded and 2 missing.[25] After the wounding of Lieutenant Colonel McLemore, which occurred before the regiment crossed the ravine in the charge, Captain L. H. Scruggs took command. Among the prisoners captured was Colonel McLemore's old company of the 8th U.S. Infantry, of which he was a lieutenant before the commencement of hostilities.

The 28th was spent in caring for our dead and wounded and repairing the bridge across the Chickahominy, which the enemy had destroyed in their retreat. The regiment crossed the Chickahominy on the morning of the 29th and followed the retreating enemy to Malvern Hill. There McClellan made a stand, and it being a strong position, he could not be dislodged.[26] The 4th Alabama was subjected to severe and constant shelling from the large guns of the enemy while supporting our batteries.

The next morning it was found that the enemy had retreated some time during the night, leaving their dead and some artillery and small arms on the field. General McClellan retreated to Harrison's Landing on the James River under cover of his highly esteemed gunboats. It is said of him that he was so elated when stepping aboard of one after reaching there, he remarked: "A gunboat should be in every family."

General Jackson moved all of the force under his command, except D. H. Hill's[27] division which was badly cut up at Malvern Hill, down near Harrison's Landing, reaching there on the 3rd of July. The 4th Alabama remained there until the 8th, when General Lee ordered all of his army back to Richmond. As far as the 4th Alabama was concerned, our temporary connection with General Jackson was, on our return to Richmond, severed and we never again served under him, except in the battle of Sharpsburg.

Our casualties at Malvern Hill were 2 men killed, Jordan[28] and Patton,[29] two of the tallest men in the regiment, and 2 officers and 11 men wounded. Captain J. T. Jones of D Company, one of the officers wounded, had a ten dollar gold piece in his pocket. A ball struck it and buried it partly in the flesh. Gangrene set up around the wound and it came very near costing him his life. After the war, he was a member of Congress from the Mobile District and died a few years ago—a Judge of the First Judicial Circuit.

The writer, having been one of the wounded at Gaines' Mill, found on his return for duty the last of July the regiment still in camp at Richmond. General Lee reorganized his army and formed it into two Wings or Corps. Major General Longstreet[30] was placed over the First and Major General Jackson the Second. The 4th Alabama was assigned to the First. Colonel Law still retained command of the old 3rd brigade and was afterwards made Brigadier General of it. General Hood's brigade of Texans, together with the Hampton Legion and 18th Georgia, were still with us. General Whiting having been transferred to North Carolina, General Hood succeeded to the command of the division.

6

The Second Battle of Manassas
July 8 to August 31, 1862

Soon after McClellan's defeat and retreat to Harrison's Landing on the James River, more extensive and determined preparations than ever before were made by the authorities at Washington to capture Richmond and "crush the Rebellion." The Army of Northern Virginia, with its depleted ranks and inadequate facilities for coping with an adversary so far superior not only in numbers but in every appointment required to conduct hostilities, knew there was before it a Herculean task. At the time the Seven Days Battles around Richmond were being fought, the Valley of Virginia had almost been entirely denuded of Confederate troops, through the withdrawal of General Jackson from there. Mr. Lincoln organized the "Army of Virginia," composed of Banks', Fremont's and McDowell's forces, and General John Pope[1] was called from the West and placed in command.[2] This Union force, meeting with no opposition, advanced as far south as Culpeper Court House during the early days of July.

On the 13th of July, only about two weeks after we defeated McClellan, General Lee sent General Jackson with two divisions up to Gordonsville, to keep watch on the movements of General Pope. There Jackson remained until the 7th of August, at which time he was reinforced by General A. P. Hill's "Light Division" of six brigades. He then advanced with his entire force across the Rapidan, and at Cedar Mountain, about 8 miles south of Culpeper Court House, met and defeated a part of Pope's army, commanded by General Banks.[3]

On the night of the 11th, after burying his dead and caring for his wounded, and permitting the enemy to do the same, General Jackson had numerous campfires built in order to deceive General Pope, who was advancing with a large force against him, and retreated back to Gordonsville. On the 14th of August General McClellan began moving his army from

Harrison's Landing around to Aquia Creek and Alexandria to the support of Pope's army and the defense of Washington.[4]

In the meantime the 4th Alabama was moved with the remaining part of General Lee's army from Richmond to join Jackson at Gordonsville. The 4th Alabama was among the first troops to leave Richmond. We had up to this time remained around the city for over three months. It is true we fought two battles, but much of the time was spent in camp, and before leaving, the men became restless and were anxious to be out and going.

The only respite we had enjoyed during this time was the few days of outing, when we were sent to the Valley to join Jackson. In camp for any length of time soldiers became quarrelsome over the most trivial matters, homesick, and subject to disease. Each member of a mess, which consisted, generally, of from three to five men, took his turn at cooking. The utensils, when in camp, comprised usually for each mess, a camp kettle, frying pan and "spider" or skillet. In the latter, biscuits were baked when fortunate enough to secure flour. The centre biscuit was always the largest, and there would frequently arise an animated and heated controversy, when on short rations, as to who was entitled to the "middler," and this discussion would finally end in a "scrap," the best man securing the lion's share. The Adjutant of the regiment being, as it were, the guardian of the musicians, Freid,[5] Fogarty[6] and Hickey,[7] on account of the frequent disputes and disagreements as to who of the three was entitled to the prize, in order to keep the peace in his little family, kept a record tacked in a conspicuous place on his desk showing to whose lot the precious biscuit should fall. On the march and all during an active campaign, however scant the rations, nothing but brotherly love existed and everything worked along harmoniously. Without any incident worthy of mention we joined General Jackson, who had advanced his Corps from Gordonsville to the Rapidan River and was there awaiting us.

By the 20th of August all of General Longstreet's Corps having arrived from Richmond, General Lee now in charge of both Corps, crossed the Rapidan and advanced rapidly in the direction of Culpeper Court House in the vicinity where General Pope had his own army concentrated, and was being strengthened daily by reinforcements from General McClellan's army, hurrying to his assistance from Aquia Creek and Alexandria. General Pope declined to await our coming and hastily retreated across the Rappahannock. The good people of Culpeper and vicinity hailed our coming with enthusiasm, and related many incidents of cruelty and depredations inflicted on them by the camp-followers of Pope's army.

With Stonewall in the lead, and our two little brigades composing Hood's division, which formed the vanguard of the First Corps, we kept close on the heels of Stonewall, marching as it were by the left in front. On the 22nd of August we moved on up the south bank of the Rappahannock, constantly under heavy fire of the enemy's batteries on the opposite side of the river. Trimble's[8] brigade of Jackson's Corps, which was guarding the wagon train directly in our front, became engaged with a force of the enemy which had crossed the river for the purpose of capturing the train at Freeman's Ford. Trimble called on General Hood for assistance. Our brigade was hurried to the left and the other took position on the right of Trimble. The river, from the incessant rains, had become very much swollen. As soon as we got into position our three brigades, enveloping the force opposing us, made a charge and drove the enemy pell mell into the swollen stream, killing, drowning, and capturing several with small loss to us.[9]

In consequence of the frequent rains and exposure, many of the 4th Alabama fell prey to fever, myself among the number, and were left behind in the care of the goodhearted citizens of Culpeper and Fauquier Counties.

On the next day the 4th Alabama relieved a regiment of the Second Corps up at Waterloo Bridge, and General Jackson then disappeared, moving on up the south bank until he passed beyond General Pope's right flank. On the morning of the 25th he crossed the Rappahannock and proceeded on the longest and most hazardous flanking movement he had ever undertaken, while we were left on the Rappahannock to amuse General Pope.[10]

It has seldom fallen to the lot of an army to be placed in such a precarious position as when General Lee sent half of his army on this perilous task over a long and circuitous route to turn the right flank of General Pope. Of course we of the line were ignorant of General Lee's plans, and the two Corps were divided by many miles before we were aware of it. Still when we discovered that our Corps alone was confronting a force of splendid fighting material, superior in numbers and daily augmented, no fears were entertained of the ultimate result. Shoeless, on short rations and exposed to alternate rains and oppressive heat, we had perfect faith in our peerless and aggressive leader, who still remained with the First Corps.

Captain (afterwards Major of the regiment) W. M. Robbins expressed his fears that General Lee had too much confidence in his men, then modifying his remark, said, "No doubt we have a grand army, which has been sifted and sifted until nothing but the very quintessence is left." Lieutenant Colonel Henderson of the British Army, says of this campaign: "Lee violated both of the maxims of Napoleon, never to divide an army into two columns unable to communicate, or to attempt a junction in the presence of a concentrated enemy, but Lee knew his men. He violated the last section of his maxim because he knew Pope, and the first because he knew Jackson. It is rare indeed that such strategy succeeds. Napoleon, although he several times attempted it, never carried out the operation referred to, except at Ulm, with complete success."[11]

On the 26th of August the 4th Alabama crossed the Rappahannock and continued on the flank of the now retreating army of General Pope, our route being the same circuitous one which had been previously taken by the Second Corps. That night we went into bivouac at the village of Orleans, a slow march, having been very much retarded by the enemy harassing our flank. On the 27th we were again delayed by the foe, going into bivouac at dusk near White Plains. Here the roads fork, the right hand leading to Thoroughfare Gap in the Bull Run Mountains.

Early on the morning of the 28th, after taking up our march for Thoroughfare Gap only six or seven miles distant, the column was suddenly and unexpectedly halted. Unexpected because General Lee's order to march was invariably, unless delayed by the presence of the enemy, to march fifty minutes and rest ten in every hour. Everything being quiet in front, to us the delay could not be fathomed. On that day the 4th Alabama brought up the rear of the division.

When the line of march was finally resumed, the 4th Alabama soon reached the forks of the road referred to, where the head of the regiment had halted during the stop. In the forks, as the regiment rapidly passed, we saw dangling by the neck in mid-air, suspended by a bridle rein to the limb of an oak tree, a well-dressed but bootless young soldier in the full garb of Confederate uniform. Information soon passed down the lines to us that a Union spy had occasioned the delay and had paid the penalty with his life for his rashness. The 6th North Carolina, leading our brigade that day, some members of it witnessed the execution of the spy, one of whom was credited with having deprived the spy of his boots as soon as life was extinct. Colonel Law and Lieutenants Cussons and Tom Christian[12] of Law's Staff, all 4th Alabamians, were present during the execution, at the head of the division. Lieutenant Cussons has written a full and interesting account of the particulars leading up to the execution, which will be found in the appendix.[13]

It was late on the evening of the 28th of August when our two brigades reached Thoroughfare Gap. The troops in our rear were brought forward, and as soon as gotten into position the advance was made. This was a formidable position to carry by direct assault, being a deep and narrow defile with precipitous sides, with barely space sufficient for the railroad and county road to pass through. On account of the importance of this position to the enemy, we expected to meet with determined opposition against a large force. General D. R. Jones'[14] division, having been sent into the Gap, met the enemy in force.

The 4th Alabama had an arduous and difficult task to perform in scaling the almost perpendicular heights to the left of the Gap, in order to flank the enemy out of his strong position.[15] Three divisions were engaged in this movement, Jones, ours and Wilcox.[16] The latter was sent three miles to the left to Hopewell Gap. We succeeded in gaining the east side of the mountain about dark and bivouacked for the night on very scant rations.

The next morning (29th) the regiment awoke to find the enemy had retreated during the night. The way was now open to form a junction with "Old Jack," a march of about nine miles. "The excitement of battle," said General Longstreet after leaving the Gap early that morning, "seemed to give new life and strength to our jaded men."[17]

Our riflemen rapidly drove in direction of Gainesville the fast retreating enemy. General Hood was compelled on more than one occasion to halt the riflemen for the main column to take our accustomed rest. After a rapid march we emerged at Gainesville into the Warrenton Turnpike and turned abruptly to the left in the direction of the Stone Bridge on Bull Run. Although Jackson had attacked and fought Pope on the evening before when we were making strenuous efforts to drive the enemy from the Gap, and Jackson heard the welcome sound of our efforts to reach him, through the "clatter" of our arms, not a sound did we hear of the desperate fighting by Jackson's men which extended far into the night.[18] Nor were we aware that he had become engaged in a general battle until we reached Gainesville.

At a quickened pace we proceeded down the pike and formed line of battle about midway between Gainesville and the Stone House, the latter situated at the crossing of the pike and the Sudley Ford Road. We formed on the left of the pike and at right angles to it. The Texans, 18th Georgia, and Hampton's Legion connected with us on the right of the pike and our left joined on to Jackson's line. Being the first troops of the right wing to reach our hard pressed and almost exhausted comrades of the left wing, as soon as we got into position, our arrival was sounded down Jackson's line, its entire length, with prolonged cheers.

With our riflemen reinforced we drove those of the enemy until a position was reached in close proximity to his main force of infantry and artillery. We halted at this point until our artillery arrived on the field, which took position to our left and rear and opened on the enemy. We remained in position here under a heavy artillery fire, and continued skirmishing until four o'clock P.M., at which time the general battle opened in earnest in General Jackson's front. Here a sad accident occurred. The 6th North Carolina was thrown immediately in our rear, and through the accidental discharge of a rifle in the hands of one of its men, Jasper Stinson[19] of E Company was instantly killed.

The right brigade of Jackson's line in our immediate left emerged from the woods led by General Bradley T. Johnson,[20] encountered the enemy and drove him back some distance, capturing a 3-inch rifle. Colonel Law then moved the 4th Alabama forward on a line with the Virginians.

About 6 o'clock a large body of the enemy's artillery and infantry appeared in our front, advancing up the turnpike.[21] His artillery had scarcely unlimbered when the intrepid Hood ordered Colonel Law to charge. The enemy's artillery opened on our line with telling effect before coming in range of their infantry as we rapidly advanced.[22]

When the 4th Alabama reached the cover of the hill on which the enemy was strongly posted, his artillery could only be depressed to affect us but little. As the regiment half-bent ran up under the belching guns, several members of the 4th Alabama were powder-burned in hands and faces. Brave little Captain McInnis, as he ran up the hill in a stooping position beneath the blazing cannon, the back of his coat became ignited, burning a hole as large as one's hands before it could be extinguished. All the enemy's guns limbered up except one howitzer and escaped with the retreating infantry. The piece that remained fought valiantly and continued to fire until some of the 4th Alabama ran up and wrested the sponge-staff from a brave gunner as he was driving his last charge home. Colonel Law detached a part of the brigade to meet a force about to flank our part of the line on the right of the pike, but the 4th Alabama pressed forward and drove the enemy until black darkness put an end to the pursuit.

We then halted and formed our line across the pike a half mile in advance of our first position. Here we remained until after 1 o'clock A.M. when General Hood ordered the regiment to return to our original position in rear of the hamlet of Groveton, where General Lee was reforming his lines. While driving the foe several prisoners were captured. Among the number was a captain of artillery, George A. Gerrish and Captain J. A. Judson, assistant adjutant-general to General J. P. Hatch.[23] While reconnoitering, Lieutenant John Cussons was captured and sent north to prison. We found on our arrival on the field that morning, when the two Confederate wings united, that Stonewall's command extended from in rear of Groveton to Sudley Church. Most of the country here is open, and the ground in many instances identical with the First Manassas battle.

When General Jackson disappeared from us on the Rappahannock five days before on this perilous movement, he proceeded rapidly via Thoroughfare Gap and Gainesville. He then pushed on with his usual celerity to Bristow Station, reaching there on the evening of the 26th, just two days after leaving us, having marched nearly sixty miles. Here he found and destroyed, after supplying his men, a large amount of stores, ammunition and sutler's goods, besides burning railroad bridges and rolling stock in abundance, which soon placed the Union soldiers on half rations. From Bristow he dispatched infantry and cavalry six or seven miles up the railroad to Manassas Junction, captured the garrison and destroyed everything at that point. He was now divided by thirty-five miles and Pope's army from General Lee and the right wing.

In the meantime, General Pope abandoned his line on the Rappahannock and hurriedly retreated in direction of Manassas Junction. On his (Pope's) near approach General Jackson took up his position where we found him at noon on the 29th. His casualties of the previous evening (28th) were comparatively small.[24] Being well protected by the cuts and embankments of an unfinished railway he held his position against the onslaught of the enemy who fought heroically and with a determined effort to crush him before our arrival. The fatal mistake General Pope made in his attempt to defeat our left wing before the arrival of our right was in not sending, and he had ample time and means to do so, a sufficient force to hold Thoroughfare and Hopewell Gaps and prevent the junction of the two Confederate wings. But the battle of the 29th was only the forerunner of what was to come on the morrow.

All that night the remainder of the right wing was arriving and taking position in line of battle assigned them on our right. There was very little sleep for the regiment. With looking after our wounded, the incessant rumbling of the artillery moving into position, and the continual tramp of the infantry there was very little chance for rest. By daylight Saturday morning August 30th all of our Corps which had reached the field were in position on Jackson's right and at right angles to his line, extending from the rear of Groveton across the pike reaching out in direction of Bull Run below the Stone Bridge.

Colonel Law, who had been only slightly wounded on the 29th, was sufficiently recovered to relieve Colonel Stone[25] of the 2nd Mississippi, who had commanded the brigade during his absence. When as stated we abandoned our position at 1 o'clock A.M. and moved back to Groveton our pickets were also withdrawn and the 12-pound howitzer which we had captured was left on the field, both wheels having been cut down. At daylight, General Pope, finding the howitzer had been left on the field and none of our pickets where he expected them to be, conceived the idea that we were retreating and immediately ordered his whole line "in pursuit" of the fleeing "rebels." Major General Irwin McDowell of the 3rd Union Corps, who met his Waterloo on the same field thirteen months before, was by special order of General Pope assigned to pursue the enemy and press him vigorously during the whole day.[26]

As the 4th Alabamians were endeavoring to snatch a few hours sleep they were awakened at dawn by the familiar sounds of our pickets carrying on a brisk duel with the enemy. Heavy skirmishing and artillery firing was continued until about four o'clock P.M, when a most vigorous attack by the enemy's infantry commanded by the Union General Morell[27] was made on our left wing and in close proximity to the 4th Alabama.[28] It was only a few minutes before our entire left wing was engaged in a fierce and sanguinary struggle with the enemy. The right wing being at a right angle to the left and our brigade connecting with it, the regiment had a full view of the grand and beautiful panorama spread out before it. All of the reserve artillery in charge of Colonel Stephen D. Lee[29] was parked in a piece of timber about two hundred yards in rear of the regiment. The enemy advanced a column of infantry out of the woods across the open field almost to the woods, near the edge of which were lying Jackson's men in the railroad cut. At close musket range Jackson opened with a galling fire, and after a prolonged and desperate effort in a hand-to-hand encounter the enemy recoiled and retreated across the field to the cover of the woods from whence he came.

Then Union column after Union column advanced only to be hurled back like their predecessors. As viewed from our position this was an ideal battle, and the only one of any magnitude in which the 4th Alabama was merely a spectator. The successive, sustained, and heroic charges of the enemy had caused our men to exhaust their ammunition. So impetuous were the assaults that General Jackson called for reinforcements from the right wing; not, however, until his men had exhausted their last cartridge, and some were holding their positions by driving the enemy back with stones picked up in the railroad cut.[30] To give an idea of the obstinate fighting which was being engaged in near us, Colonel Bradley T. Johnson, whose brigade connected with ours, on our left said, "I saw a Federal flag hold its position for half an hour within 10 yards of a flag of one of the regiments in the cut, and go down six or eight times, and after the fight 100 dead were lying 20 yards from the cut, some of them within 2 feet of it."[31]

When General Longstreet was requested to send troops to General Jackson's relief the former had just reached our part of the line, and after taking in the situation, determined to enfilade the enemy about to overwhelm Jackson with his artillery. When the artillery firing began, General Lee's order to support Jackson was repeated to General Longstreet. It was evident to General Longstreet, that the attack against General Jackson could not be continued for ten minutes under the fire of the eighteen pieces under Colonel S. D. Lee, which were then belching forth confusion and destruction on the charging columns of the foe. Therefore, he considered it unnecessary to aid General Jackson with his infantry at that time and it would have taken four hours to have done so.

Having relieved the left wing with artillery, General Longstreet, anticipating General Lee's wish, threw the right wing forward against the forces in our front. As if by intuition, at the same instant, both wings rushed forward in one of the grandest charges on record.[32] The troops sprang to their work and moved forward with all the steadiness and firmness of war worn veterans.

The attack was led by our two brigades. The ground here is rolling, a succession of hills, one after another running at right angles to the Warrenton pike. As each elevation was reached by the 4th Alabama the gallant artillerist S. D. Lee was promptly by our side, unlimbered and ready to open on the fast fleeing enemy. The regiment, very much exhausted, was halted at the hamlet of Groveton several minutes with orders to support a battery. Here we were subjected to a severe artillery fire. We then moved on down to the famous Dogan House, where the enemy's infantry was met in force.[33]

After driving away this line as it advanced against us on the right of the house, an effort was made by the regiment to capture the battery stationed at this point, but it limbered up and escaped.[34] From this time until dark we drove the enemy without encountering any, or very little, opposition, having achieved a glorious victory, but at a cost of some of the best blood in the regiment. Our casualties in the encounters of both days were twenty killed and forty-three wounded. We bivouacked that night not far from Sudley Ford on Bull Run.

The regiment on its march from Gordonsville and before reaching the Rappahannock were sadly in need of shoes. Lieutenant Colonel McLemore ordered me to call on General Hood and get some relief if possible. I found him during the march at the head of our little division. He ordered me to go back to Louisa Courthouse, where a detail from the division, a member of C Company being one of the number, were making shoes. At the same time, he gave me an order on the Quartermaster for a wagon, with orders to bring back all the shoes made. Arriving at the shoe factory, I found only a scant supply on hand and waited a day longer, hurrying up the men to furnish as many as possible. Overtaking the regiment with a hot burning fever I reported to my esteemed friend, Dr. Hudson, our surgeon, who was in the rear of the division with his hands full of patients similarly affected. "You shan't go any further," he remarked, "and as soon as I can do so, I will place you in a comfortable position."

Before crossing the river he placed me with Mr. Ashby, uncle of our lamented General Ashby.[35] The same evening Dr. Hudson sent back Lieutenant Colonel Scruggs, who had also fallen prey to the fever. The only occupants of the household being the kind, quiet and gentle old Virginia gentleman and his daughter, Miss Mary, who proved to be a perfect angel of mercy. Dr. Hudson sent me, by Colonel Scruggs, a bottle of Fowler's Solution, but the rest and kind attention we received from our refined host was much more efficacious in breaking our fever than the Doctor's pills, powders and solutions.

Colonel Scruggs, the day after we reached Mr. Ashby's, was lying on a rug in front of the fireplace with an upturned chair and pillow as a support for his head. Happening to turn over with his face toward the chimney, I saw him intently gazing up at something in which he appeared to be very much interested. He sat up and beckoned for me to come and take a peep. I crawled out of bed, and looking up the chimney beheld numerous luscious old Virginia hams which had escaped the vigilant eyes of Yankee marauders.

Our fevers broken and our horses fresh, we bade farewell to Miss Mary and the Colonel (as we called Mr. Ashby) and hastened to join the regiment, reaching it the night of the 29th, after its first day's battle. Every member of the regiment whom I met that night gave me his individual experience as well as that of the regiment, so I was better posted than had I been present.

I distinctly remember how disappointed I was on our return from this campaign when, on reaching within a mile of two of Mr. Ashby's, our regiment, at the forks of a road, turned off abruptly to the right. One of Mr. Ashby's servants who had been patiently waiting for Colonel Scruggs and myself, ran up to us and stated that Miss Mary had sent him up to invite us down to dinner. I remained with the servant while Colonel Scruggs hurried to the front of the column to get permission to attend the feast which I knew was then awaiting the two hungry soldiers. But Alas! commissioned officers were positively forbidden to leave the ranks. That night while eating our barely sufficient meal I knew Colonel Scruggs' mind reverted to the contents of the chimney and other good eatables down at Mr. Ashby's when he remarked, "doggone a soldier's luck," and I fully agreed with him.

7

Maryland Campaign
August 31 to September 18, 1862

On the 31st, which was Sunday, we rested and attended to duties which were always incumbent on troops immediately after a battle. The dead were buried; lists of casualties and reports made out and forwarded to Headquarters. Better and by far more wholesome rations were issued than we had been accustomed to since leaving Richmond. In this respect Stonewall's men fared much better than the right wing, for while they were reveling in Rhine wine and other captured luxuries during their "Rebel Raid,"[1] we were on scant rations of very inferior quality. As was invariably the result immediately after a battle, the rain poured down in torrents and added very much to our discomfort, the weather becoming quite chilly.

Late that evening the regiment went into bivouac for the night. Lieutenant Tom Samuel[2] of A Company was captured on the 30th by Sigel's Dutch[3] but in the confusion of their hasty retreat Tom escaped and rejoined the regiment. He had many amusing incidents to relate of his experience during his brief captivity in the hands of the badly whipped, but brave and jolly Dutchmen.

Early the next morning the 4th Alabama crossed the Ford, our division of two little brigades in the lead of the right wing. General Pope, with his "Headquarters in the Saddle," at the head of the Union army, was hurriedly retreating in the direction of Washington. General Jackson with the left wing preceded us at noon on the day before, crossing at the above Ford with orders to overtake the rear of Pope's army and take him in flank, and arrest his retreat before reaching the fortifications of Washington, while our division was to strike him in the rear. Near Chantilly, in Fairfax County, General Jackson came up with the enemy's rear. On the same day we crossed Bull Run, a half day's march ahead of our division.

The rain continued and we had a most miserable time. Between Chantilly and Centreville we bivouacked, every man in sad plight, cold and wet to the skin. We worried through the night and resumed our march early the next morning. As we had heard the report of cannon in our front the evening before (at which time Dump Sterling[4] called out to the boys as he floundered in the mud and rain to hurry up for old Jack had done treed), the supposition was that we would overtake General Jackson's forces engaging the enemy and join in the battle with them. On arriving at Chantilly we found that a part of the left wing had intercepted the rear guard of the enemy in the drenching rain of the previous evening, and after a spirited contest, had failed to arrest him and he was then scurrying on in the direction of Washington,[5] the enemy having lost gallant old General Kearny.[6]

Here General Lee gave up the chase and turned the head of his column in the direction of Leesburg, near which place, on the 6th of September, the 4th Alabama crossed the Potomac at White's Ford into Maryland and continued north to Frederick City, Maryland. From there, on the 10th, we marched across to Hagerstown, Maryland, crossing the mountain at Boonsboro Gap.

We were sadly disappointed in the reception accorded our army when we reached the shores of Maryland. There was very little of it for us Confederates. The sentiments of the people were about equally divided, and before invading her soil a rumor had gone abroad, circulated by Union sympathizers, that, as soon as General Lee should reach there he purported making a conscription of all able-bodied men. Nearly all such, of both Union and Confederate sentiments, had absconded before our arrival. The 4th Alabama did get one recruit, J. I. Hager,[7] now of Little Rock, Arkansas, a finely developed, robust youth, who proved to be an excellent soldier. He ran the gauntlet from Boonsboro Gap to Appomattox without any broken bones, but in his planing mill at Little Rock (where I saw him in 1910) he has lost a thumb and one leg. A few others enlisted in other regiments, so there was no flocking to our standards by any means. The "Maryland Line," a battalion in the Army of Northern Virginia, from Baltimore principally, made such excellent soldiers that the 4th Alabama hoped to secure several recruits to increase its depleted ranks, of the same material as the Baltimore boys' contingent, but were doomed to disappointment.

In fact our Maryland Campaign was a very disagreeable and unsatisfactory venture. We of the line had full consciousness of having accomplished all that could be done, but the equipment and numbers were wanting to have made a successful issue of the campaign.

Of course, General Pope was deposed and General McClellan reinstated.[8] He consolidated Pope's army with his original Army of the Potomac and at this time was slowly marching from Washington in direction of Frederick, Maryland, one hundred thousand strong, to either capture or drive our little army south of the Potomac. Back in Virginia at Martinsburg and Harpers Ferry were Union garrisons which General Lee feared, if left there, would interrupt his communications. He therefore, before we reached Hagerstown, sent General Jackson with over half of the army to capture or dispossess them.

The 4th Alabama went into camp near Hagerstown to await developments. There was a great contrast, we found, after reaching Hagerstown, where the people had not felt the ravages of cruel and merciless war, compared with the barren waste we left in northern Virginia. We had been so long inured to short rations and misery, not only among ourselves, but also to the devastated fields, and want of the necessaries of life among the citizens, it was hard to realize that during all this turmoil between the two sections these people had been living in the enjoyment of ease and plenty with access to the outside world. While resting here we were anxiously, eagerly looking for the return of General Jackson from Harpers Ferry, as we confidently believed, with victory inscribed on his banners, to unite with us in ample time to meet the slow plodding McClellan.

Early on the morning of the 14th of September the 4th Alabama received hurried orders to prepare rations, fall in and march back to Boonsboro Gap. There ever have been, and always will be, as long as wars are waged, blunders, omissions and miscarriages in all battles and campaigns. General D. H. Hill's division, which was the rearguard of our army, remained at Frederick City until the near approach of the Union vanguard, and from there General Lee ordered him, with his five brigades, in our direction, to hold Boonsboro Gap. This sudden and unexpected retrograde movement on the part of the 4th Alabama was the direct cause of the fatal loss of a copy of Confidential Special Order No. 191, issued by General Lee to each of his division commanders at Frederick City during our stop there on September 9th. It was said to have been picked up, wrapped around three cigars, by a Union soldier in the camp at Frederick City, but recently vacated by General D. H. Hill, and handed to General McClellan on the night of the 13th.[9] General McClellan, who had been advancing cautiously and timidly, with 97,000 men, against our force of only 45,000, was only eight or nine miles a day, in the direction of Frederick City, from Washington. As soon as he was apprised of the genuineness of his find, he immediately gave orders for a rapid and vigorous forward movement.

Many theories have been advanced by as many writers as to how this famous instrument could have suffered loss in which was minutely detailed General Lee's plans for the movements he required of each of his division commanders. The copy which fell into the hands of General McClellan was direct from General Lee's headquarters, addressed to General D. H. Hill and found in his vacated camp, but, strange to say, Colonel Archer Anderson, Adjutant General of D. H. Hill's division, afterwards produced a copy of the order in General Stonewall Jackson's handwriting and addressed to General Hill. The former, it is said, considered General Hill under his command. Both General Hill and Colonel Anderson declared it impossible for the copy exhibited in full in General McClellan's official report to have been received by General Hill. The part as to how it was lost as far as I know still remains a mystery. As the 4th Alabama regarded it, it was a most serious and irretrievable misfortune, by far the most deplorable in the chapter of accidents which ever befell the Army of Northern Virginia.

The reader must bear in mind that now General Lee with his entire force was on the west side of the mountain, his army scattered from Harpers Ferry to Hagerstown, with only a small part of it in front of General McClellan, who, holding that fatal order in his hand, was rapidly advancing on the east side to get possession of the Gap, and make quick work of our scattered forces before General Lee was able to unite his army. Situated as we were, for the safety of the Confederate army, it was absolutely necessary for General D. H. Hill to hold the Gap with his small force until our arrival.[10]

After a march of fourteen miles, which taxed to the utmost the energies of every man in the regiment, we arrived none too soon, between three and four o'clock P.M. We found General Hill had been making a gallant and stubborn fight all day against immense odds. There were too many opposed to him, and he was fast losing ground. The 4th Alabama was first ordered to attack the enemy on the left of the road. Soon afterwards we were ordered to the right through an orchard, the trees growing among huge boulders luxuriantly, many loaded with tempting fruit and not a minute to spare to eat a single apple. There we met Drayton's[11] brigade falling back in confusion, stating that they had been flanked. We moved still further to the right, and secured a position to meet the advancing enemy. General Hood, in his official report, says: "I at once ordered the Texas Brigade, Colonel W. T. Wofford[12] commanding, and the Third Brigade, Colonel E. M. Law commanding, to move forward with bayonets fixed, which they did with their usual gallantry, driving the enemy and regaining all of our lost ground."[13]

It was now dark and the 4th Alabama, for better protection, was transferred to a sunken road running obliquely across the Gap, the enemy still keeping up an incessant firing, inflicting but little damage, as the road afforded good protection. On the embankment next to the enemy was a fence; on the opposite side was a dense laurel thicket. The bullets of the enemy striking the laurel leaves caused a loud report, and created the impression that the enemy were firing explosive bullets. During the heaviest part of this night engagement, Colonel McLemore climbed upon the fence in our front to reconnoitre. He soon fell back into the road, shot through the shoulder.

There being no possible way to replenish our ammunition, and as it was fast disappearing, the men were ordered to only keep up a desultory firing, while Captain Scruggs, who took command after the wounding of Colonel McLemore, went down on our right to the 2nd Mississippi, the nearest regiment, to prevail upon Colonel Stone to divide ammunition with us. Captain Scruggs also found that of the 2nd very much reduced, and failed to secure any. While talking to Colonel Stone a Union soldier who had been sent with several canteens for water became lost in the darkness and walked up to them, and was captured. Scruggs brought back two of the filled canteens, and water never tasted sweeter than it did that night, or at least my share of it.

During Scruggs' absence the enemy also checked up in firing, no doubt for the same reason that we stopped, for their men could be plainly heard drawing out the tins to replenish their boxes.[14] We then remained unmolested until after midnight, having great difficulty in keeping the men awake. When the order did come for us to retire about midnight, most of the men were fast asleep, in spite of the efforts of the officers to keep them awake.

As the men were awakened, they were ordered to go quietly one at a time down to the main road, which led to Sharpsburg and there reform. We placed Colonel McLemore on a litter and carried him with us. When all the army had passed on its way to Sharpsburg, we formed the rear guard of the Corps, marching the rest of the night, until noon on the 15th. We reached the Antietam River near the town of Sharpsburg, where all the regiment took a much needed bath, and, in the meantime, hung their clothes on a limb to dry, after giving them a partial washing.

That evening the regiment was ordered to take position about a mile from Sharpsburg on the Sharpsburg and Hagerstown Pike near the Dunker Church, and remained in this position under the fire of the enemy's shells until nearly sunset on the evening of the 16th. General McClellan having crossed a force to our side of the river[15] (Antietam) our division was ordered forward to meet it. Colonel Stephen D. Lee had placed a section of one of his batteries on the crest of a hill in our front under Lieutenant Elliott, a South Carolina battery,[16] and the 11th Mississippi and the 4th Alabama of the old 3rd Brigade were ordered to its support.

Colonel Law ordered a heavy line of skirmishers to cover our front. As we marched up to the battery through a pasture, there was a perfect tornado of bursting shells from the long range guns of the enemy playing on us from the opposite side of the river. This, added to the clatter of our small arms and Elliott's two pieces, which were being superbly served by that gallant artilleryman, kept up such a din that the commands of the officers could with difficulty be heard. A flock of quail, just before we reached the battery, so completely paralyzed with fear, were creeping about in the grass unable to fly as the men advanced over them, when the writer stopped, picked up a brace and placed them in his pocket. As he had no means of cooking them, he presented them to the assistant surgeon of the 11th Mississippi, who could prepare and enjoy eating them, back at the Field Hospital. The artillery continued firing until some time after dark, and each flash of Elliott's howitzers made the most beautiful picture imaginable. Could it have been possible to transfer it to canvas exactly as viewed by us that dark night, no battle scene could have been more exquisitely beautiful, and each one of the immortal old 4th Alabama would then have had a place in the picture by the flashing of the guns.

About nine o'clock P.M. the 4th Alabama was moved from this position and placed farther to the right in a freshly plowed field enclosed with a high Virginia rail fence. We were some distance in front of our main line, in an isolated position, on outpost duty. In our front and on the opposite side of the fence was, as well as could be seen in the darkness, a pasture field with small scattering growths. The men made themselves as comfortable as possible by lying down in the corners of the "worm" fence, where the ground was not plowed, with their guns resting through the fence. The constant rumbling of artillery and caisson wheels of both armies was kept up all night, getting into position, preparing for the bloody ordeal which was to open at daylight. The men were completely worn out from hunger and want of sleep, and it was almost impossible to keep them awake. To add to our discomfort, it had become very cloudy and dark, with a cold misty rain falling.

Everything in our immediate front was perfectly quiet until about 10 o'clock P.M., when the tramp of a body of Union infantry was heard advancing directly on our position. The column continued to advance until almost at the fence. Then the order was given by Captain Scruggs to fire, and every gun fired at the same instant. For several minutes there was a commotion of retreating footsteps and groans of the wounded and dying. A wounded Union officer cried out: "I am an officer of distinction, an officer of rank, for God's sake come over and send my dying words to my family." Captain William M. Robbins, getting assurance from him that he would be protected, made a slip gap in the fence so that he and the litter bearers could crawl through, and the wounded officer was brought to our side and taken to the field hospital for treatment. The men were all curious to discover the name and rank of that "distinguished" officer, and were very much disappointed when Captain Robbins informed them that he was only a lieutenant of the 5th Pennsylvania Reserves with a picket force of about thirty men. He died that night, so we were informed. As the records of that regiment only show one officer killed and ten men killed and wounded in this engagement, therefore the officer reported as killed, Lieutenant Hardman P. Petrikin, is presumed to be the one in charge of the picket line and killed by the 4th Alabama.

Everything again becoming quiet in our front, the officers resumed their efforts to keep the men awake. Our position having been discovered by the enemy, we were fearful of a second advance. The most earnest and pathetic appeals were made to the writer to endeavor to get permission to go back and get Colonel Walker,[17] commanding Trimble's brigade, to relieve us, he being bivouacked a short distance to our rear and left. I at first refused on the grounds that Walker's brigade had just arrived that evening from the capture of Harpers Ferry,[18] being a part of Jackson's forces, and were as much exhausted as we were. Finally, the company officers, becoming so discouraged in their attempts to keep the men awake and the urgent appeals of the men for food and rest, that I was ordered to make an effort to secure relief wherever it could be found.

It was with great reluctance that I undertook the execution of this order, to request to be relieved by men who had undergone hardships of equal severity. Colonel Walker's men were found asleep, wrapped up snugly in their blankets. Attracted by a dim light while stepping over and among the men, Colonel Walker was discovered sitting with the cape of his overcoat pulled up over his head and the skirts of his coat partially concealing a few live coals between his feet. After explaining the object of my mission, much to my relief, he willingly consented to send one of his Georgia regiments to our relief. When those old heroes, after much difficulty, were aroused from their deep slumber, they arose, shook their blankets, rolled and tied them up, adjusted their accoutrements and fell into line, to my surprise laughing and joking.

While conducting the relief to our outpost, I learned from the officers with whom I conversed on the way that all of Jackson's forces had reached the field, except A. P. Hill's and McLaws'[19] divisions. The former was left at Harpers Ferry to receive the surrender of the garrison. After being relieved we returned to the Dunker Church, secured a few rations and procured a little rest before dawn of the 17th.

There was only one man at this stage of the war, a member of the regiment, who was regarded as a downright coward. Several attempts had been made to pull him into a battle, but all efforts of his officers so far had failed—as for personal courage he had plenty and some to spare. He could whip any three of the best soldiers in the regiment when around the camp fire, but became perfectly demoralized at the first sound of a bullet or shell. He stuck to his colors in camp and on march, did all the drudgery cheerfully and willingly, and never appeared to have any disposition to leave, as was the result with other skulkers who had long since departed. When we returned to Dunker Church he made his appearance, having been absent on a skulking expedition since the evening before when we went forward under shot and shell to the support of the battery. Lieutenant James Stewart,[20] commanding the company in which he claimed a membership, remarked that night that if he could not force him into the coming fight he intended to kill him.

At 3 o'clock A.M. the battle was opened by General McClellan attacking the two brigades under General Lawton in our front, which had relieved our division the night before. For an hour and a half the battle raged furiously. Shells and minnie balls fell thick and fast in and around our bivouac near the church. General Lawton hurried a messenger back to General Hood that he was wounded, his men hard pressed, and to come to his assistance or he would be compelled to fall back. Quickly getting the division into line General Hood ordered both brigades forward, with the 4th Alabama advancing obliquely across the open field in front of the church and parallel with the Smoketown Road, to a piece of woods, now designated on the military maps as East Woods. As the regiment passed through the field under a perfect hail storm of shot and shell, and before reaching the woods, the 4th Alabama preserved as perfect an alignment, though marching rapidly, as if on drill.

Immediately after leaving the Church Joe Frame[21] fell out of line. Lieutenant Jim Stewart, who was keeping a close eye on him, with his pistol in one hand, caught Joe by the collar with the other and tried to force him forward, but Joe, falling down on his hands and knees, held his position against the struggles of his Lieutenant. Finding that the regiment was rapidly leaving him behind, Stewart gave Joe a vigorous kick and turned to overtake the fast disappearing regiment, while Joe made Gilpin speed back in the direction of Dunker Church.

The 4th Alabama occupied the right of the brigade,[22] in fact it was the right regiment of the left wing of the Confederate army. Colonel Law says in his official report: "The 5th Texas Regiment (which had been sent over to my right) and the 4th Alabama pushed into the wood in which the skirmishing had taken place the evening previous, and drove the enemy through and beyond it"[23] out into the open.

As we entered the wood, Captain Scruggs was wounded, though not seriously, and Captain William M. Robbins took charge of the regiment. Here we had much the advantage over the force contending against the 4th Alabama; good cover afforded by the timber, and being veterans, we were quick to take advantage of it. The nervous condition of the regiment from want of food and rest caused them to fight desperately, even savagely. Major John M. Gould, then Adjutant of the 10th Maine, the force which opposed the 4th Alabama at this particular juncture, states in his regimental history of the opposition he encountered from the 4th Alabama: "It was an awful morning; our comrades went down one after another with a most disheartening frequency, pierced with bullets from men who were half concealed, or who dodged quickly back to a safe cover the moment they fired. On all other fields from the beginning to the end of our long service, we never had to face their equals; they were all good marksmen and the constant call of their officers to aim low appeared to us entirely unnecessary."[24]

The other regiments of our brigade, as well as the Texans, South Carolinians, and 18th Georgia, being in the open on our left suffered terribly; the 1st Texas losing a larger percentage of men engaged than any other regiment during the war in the Army of Northern Virginia.[25] At the stage of the battle when the 4th Alabama was driving the enemy through East Woods, a battalion of skirmishers which had been previously engaged applied to Captain Robbins, commanding the regiment, for permission to join onto us, as they desired to continue in the battle. Captain Robbins placed them on the right of the regiment. They advanced with us and stood nobly to the front doing good execution, shoulder to shoulder with the 4th Alabama. I think this detachment was composed of one company each from Colquitt's[26] brigade of D. H. Hill's division on our right, commanded by Captain William Arnold.[27] They had been on the firing line for some time fighting before we were ordered in and they became separated from their brigade. They were about two companies strong and all Georgians, except one small company from the 13th Alabama.

We were fighting at right angles to the general line of battle, our division fronting about north, and the right of us about east; the 4th

Alabama being next to the left of D. H. Hill's division, Ripley's[28] brigade, and it being at right angles to the 4th Alabama and holding their part of the line. This permitted the enemy to pour a heavy fire upon the flank and rear of our regiment.[29] We had now been engaged, as afterwards learned, almost three hours, fighting desperately without any intermission. Most of the men had exhausted their ammunition, and all had exhausted themselves in their efforts to drive the enemy from his position.

Before accomplishing this, however, the Union General Greene,[30] with two fresh brigades, made a terrible and overwhelming attack on our front, which, together with the fire on our right flank and rear, caused us to fall back. General Hood then withdrew the rest of the division, which had also exhausted their ammunition, along the entire line. Having no support to take our places in front, and the enemy so heavily reinforced, we feared he would closely follow us up. But he failed to do so, which gave us ample time to re-form and replenish our ammunition boxes.

General Hood kept his staff and couriers busy going over the field directing the scattered men of the division to assemble in rear of Dunker Church. Just as we reached the Church, Lieutenant King[31] of F Company, a man born and reared on the Tennessee River in Morgan County, who dropped his plow to enlist in the 4th Alabama, and who was promoted from the ranks for sheer merit by the aristocrats of his company, had the whole top of his head blown off by a shell.

As jovial Captain Karsner, Lieutenant Dan Turner and I were slowly wending our way in that direction, a shell of the enemy from over on the right of the line burst near us, and a fragment struck Karsner's too prominent nose. The shock was so great it knocked him for a severe fall, at full length upon his back. We ran to him, thinking he was killed. On examination, as he still remained where he fell, though bleeding profusely, we found the wound very slight. With the blood running down in his eyes and mouth, he presented, lying there, a most ludicrous sight, so much so that it was impossible to avert a smile on our part. He imagined that the missile had gone entirely through his head, so great was the shock; and when he observed that we entertained so little feeling for a "dying" comrade, he promptly arose and, still quite dazed, abused us soundly for our lack of sympathy. After being convinced that it was nothing serious he soon regained his usual merry mood.

Just then General Hood was seen approaching from the rear. After showing the division where to re-form, Lieutenant Turner remarked, "Captain, wipe that blood from your face before General Hood reaches us." "No," he said, "I will see if I can make *him* sympathize with me." He then, with his hands, smeared the clotted blood thickly over his face. General Hood exclaimed as he rode up, "My God! Captain, I am sorry to see you so seriously wounded." "Yes, General," he said, "I came very near getting my face shot off." General Hood was as sympathetic as a woman.

We had no idea of the time consumed in this battle. General Hood said we went into action a few minutes after 6 A.M. and retired at 9 A.M.[32] About an hour after retiring, McLaws' division arrived on the field from Harpers Ferry, moved to the front and soon became engaged, while we were held in reserve near the Church in his rear. This desperately fought battle, a perfect homespun Waterloo, continued until darkness put a stop to the bloody work, neither side having gained any advantage.

It was the severest clash of arms in which the 4th Alabama ever participated and the gamest fight against the greatest odds in which the Army of Northern Virginia ever engaged. Fighting under cover of East Wood, the casualties in the 4th Alabama were much less than those of any of the other eight regiments, even less than Hampton's Legion, which had only six companies, of the division. Our casualties were eight killed and thirty-six wounded. Those of our comrades on our left, in the open, amounted to eight hundred and ninety-six, an average of one hundred and twelve killed and wounded in the other eight regiments. The 1st Texas suffered the greatest loss, over eighty per cent, and also lost their colors, which have since, after many years, been returned to them.

It was reported in the Union camp after the battle that our brigade was completely annihilated and the colors of the 4th Alabama captured. This, as to the capture of the 4th Alabama flag, was a gross error. Our flag was never captured, and was not even surrendered at Appomattox. In regard to this matter, Major Gould, Adjutant of the 10th Maine in this engagement, wrote me: "The 111th fellows (referring to the 111th Pennsylvania, a part of General Greene's forces which made the final 'onslaught' on the 4th Alabama) wrote to me, and also stuck up a wooden sign board in East Woods in 1894 telling where they went and what they did. They claim that they captured the flag of the 4th Alabama, but Robbins (of the 4th Alabama) swears by all the gods that the flag was carried to Appomattox and there *torn up* and not surrendered at all. I wrote to the 111th fellows about it, and they *modified* by saying it was only a *piece* of the flag, the *staff* and *inside* of the flag 'got away' but Major Robbins would not accept the amendment." Major Gould carried on quite an extensive correspondence with Major Robbins and me relative to this battle when writing the history of his regiment, and met our Major Robbins at Sharpsburg, when the latter, at the time and until his death, was one of the commissioners of the Gettysburg battlefield.

Lieutenant-Colonel McLemore we conveyed to Shepherdstown and from there to Winchester, where he died, after intense suffering, from his wounds, on the 30th of September 1862.

For three consecutive days before and during the battle of Sharpsburg, we had only a half ration of beef for one day and green corn, and if there is any exercise which will give a soldier a ravenous appetite it is marching and fighting.

Late on the evening of the battle the 4th Alabama was moved to the right nearer Sharpsburg and procured a good rest that night and all the next day. Some time during the night of the 18th we folded our blankets, marched to the Potomac and crossed to the Virginia side. The 4th Alabama entered the battle with one hundred and fifty-four and recrossed the river with not exceeding one hundred rifles. The battles, marches, sickness from improper food and other hardships of the previous four months had made a heavy drain on our ranks. Seven Pines, the Seven Days battles around Richmond, Second Manassas, Boonsboro Gap, Sharpsburg and numerous skirmishes each claimed its share of victims, fifty-seven buried in the field and two hundred and twenty-three wounded.

8

From Sharpsburg to Fredericksburg
September 18 to November 22, 1862

After recrossing the Potomac near Shepherdstown on the night of the 18th of September, the 4th Alabama turned west and went into camp near Martinsburg, Virginia, on the Oppequon Creek. The next day, to make his alleged victory a complete success, General McClellan sent a large body of infantry and cavalry in pursuit of General Lee. A part of Jackson's Corps and our cavalry were left at the river to protect our rear. Late that evening a part of Porter's Union Corps rushed across the river and succeeded in capturing four of our cannon. The following morning, the 20th, elated with their success of the evening before, two more divisions crossed the river to make a reconnaissance in force. General A. P. Hill, of Jackson's Corps, with his Light Division of six brigades, met and drove the enemy back across the Potomac.[1] General McClellan, after this, was satisfied with his laurels won, and remained on his side of the river.

The 4th Alabama went into camp with the rest of the army in the fertile valley of the Oppequon Creek to recuperate from its hard campaign, while General Lee kept watch upon the movements of the Federal army. Here we remained quietly in camp resting and writing letters home. The North Alabama boys of the regiment, "orphans," as we were called, seldom had the pleasure of hearing from home during the war. The enemy, having taken possession of that part of the South early in the action, held it under their control most of the time. Upon reaching this camp, we of North Alabama were the happiest set of mortals that ever existed when informed that northern Alabama had been relieved of the Yankees, and that section was "fancy free" for a time at least, during Bragg's[2] invasion of Kentucky. The "orphans," however, when cut off from their homes, fared about as well as the Southern Alabama boys, for there were many angels of mercy, relatives of our comrades, who, when supplying the wants of their loved ones, remembered the "orphans" and sent donations, as far as their limited means in those trying times permitted.

I take the liberty of quoting from a letter dated September 24, 1862, written from near Martinsburg, Virginia, by me to my mother, as follows:

> How happy I am to learn you are once more free. Oh! How glad was I to receive those more than welcome letters which I have so long looked for. I could not contain myself, gave several rebel yells, and—very unbecoming in a veteran—wept. We are camped between Martinsburg and Oppequon Creek not far from the Baltimore and Ohio Railroad, and about twenty miles from Winchester, where we had such a jolly time summer before last. I was actually so dirty when I reached here that I did not feel like I was a white boy. Have endured many hardships, been hungry a great many times, had not changed my clothes for several weeks, as our baggage wagon was not with us after we left Richmond. Crossing a small creek in Maryland, General Hood was sitting on his horse on the bank of it, to make us hurry across and blocking the column in our rear, one of the boys asked him when our wagons would be up, that we were all as lousy and dirty as the dickens; General Hood said, 'Step out, step out, and cross over, so am I.' All the boys in hearing presented him with a lusty cheer—misery loves company, you know. The rest of the boys whose parents are not in the Yankee lines have been very kind to us. There is a company in the regiment from Tuskegee. Their good people sent us a large box of clothing before we left Richmond. Our former Adjutant, Joe Hardie, of whom I have so often written, whom I superseded, left us at Yorktown last May; has written me several kind letters. His mother, through him, sends a message to me to call on her for anything I need in the way of blankets, clothes and so forth. I also received before leaving for Maryland, a kind letter from his wife, who spent some time with us, when Lieutenant Hardie was our Adjutant, so if the Yankees return, don't bother about me for my friends will take care of me. I shall never wish to place my foot on Maryland soil again. We saw very little of States rights sentiment. All the male population ran away, having heard that General Lee would conscript them. All the citizens were very much surprised at the good behavior of our troops. General Lee impressed upon us in his orders that we must respect private property, and that we were not making war on women and children. It is strange, but not a member of the old 3rd Brigade was satisfied while we were in Maryland. All wished to return to 'Old Virginia' and no one wanted to fight out of the Confederacy.

The regiment moved down from near Martinsburg and went into camp between Bunker Hill and Winchester on October 1st and remained here for several days. Our position remained unchanged until the latter part of the month, when we were marched down near Winchester. On October 29th our Corps all left for Culpeper Court House, leaving Jackson's Corps in the Valley to watch McClellan, who had crossed the Potomac on the 26th of October. On November 1st we crossed the Shenandoah and the men fairly yelled when they struck the cold water. We crossed the Blue Ridge at Chester Gap and arrived in position at Culpeper Court House on November 6th. Our cavalry had numerous engagements with the enemy on our march from Martinsburg to Culpeper and guarding the gaps in the Blue Ridge. Our division was compelled to go to their relief at Manassas Gap, but the 4th Alabama was not called into action.

After our return to Virginia our regiment was very much increased by the return of the sick and those on detached duty. General Lee augmented his two Corps until their number was almost twice that of his shattered command on their return from Maryland. The positions of the Confederate and Union armies on November 6th bore about the same relation to each other as in August when our Corps on the Rappahannock was divided by Pope's army and thirty-five miles from Jackson. General McClellan had advanced across the Blue Ridge and was concentrating his vast army of eight Corps in the vicinity of Warrenton, when our Corps reached Culpeper Court House only twenty miles distant. Jackson with the Second Corps was still up in the Valley in Clark County, in the vicinity of Berryville and Millwood, about forty-five miles on a straight line from us, and with no direct road by which the two Confederate Corps could unite.

It is now a matter of history that the time had come for McClellan to strike in between Culpeper Court House and Washington and separate the two wings of the Confederate army and beat them in detail or else force them to concentrate as far back as Gordonsville. He proposed making the effort at once, but the Washington authorities intervened, and prevented the carrying out or undertaking of his project. The very next day (November 7), after we reached Culpeper Court House, Mr. Lincoln relieved General McClellan of the command of the Union army and appointed his personal friend Burnside in his stead.[3] General Lee still retained General Jackson in the Valley, while he held our Corps at Culpeper awaiting the developments of General Burnside.

General Lee having discovered that General Burnside had adopted via Fredericksburg as his "On to Richmond" route, instead of attacking our Corps in our position, immediately placed us under marching orders.

Our regiment left Culpeper Court House on the 18th of November, McLaws' division preceding us. By the 22nd of November all of our Corps had assembled at Fredericksburg on the south side of the Rappahannock, ready to oppose the enemy's crossing. In this, his first move, General Burnside had been so far arrested in his attempt to reach Richmond.[4]

9

Fredericksburg
November 22, 1862, to February 18, 1863

On our arrival at Fredericksburg the 4th Alabama was placed in camp near Hamilton's Crossing, below the town. Soon after reaching here our old brigade commander, General W. H. C. Whiting, who had been assigned to the Department of North Carolina, made a special request of the War Department to have the 4th Alabama transferred to his command. The request was not complied with. He was afterwards killed defending Fort Fisher.

The men were allowed a good many liberties during the day and were only required to answer roll call and attend dress parade. We had no picketing to do, as McLaws' men, who were the first to arrive, were found picketing the bank of the river and silently watching the Union pickets on the opposite bank. The day after our reaching there, orders were issued by the officer of the day prohibiting any communication with the enemy's pickets, but the order was daily violated during the absence of the officers, not only by the pickets, but by the soldiers generally whenever an opportunity offered, until some of them became quite chummy. Thanksgiving occurred a few days after our arrival among the Union troops, and it was whispered in camp that Lieutenant W. T. Turner[1] and one or two other men of the regiment had accepted an invitation to go over and partake of turkey and cranberry sauce. They actually went, so it was reported, were most cordially welcomed and bountifully entertained by their hosts, and not a word mentioned of the war by either Union or Confederate.

General Lee ordered General Jackson to join us from over the Blue Ridge, and by the last of November all of the Army of Northern Virginia was concentrated at and near Fredericksburg along the bank of the Rappahannock. The two hostile armies now occupied the opposite banks of the Rappahannock; the Union army 122,000 strong, the Confederate 78,500. Jackson's Corps[2] occupied the right of the line, Longstreet the left, and the 4th Alabama was placed on the right of Longstreet's Corps, thus causing us to be about the center of the line. Two shots in quick succession from the heavy artillery were to be the signal to notify us when General Burnside would make an effort to cross the river.

We were very comfortably quartered, being supplied with tents and fire wood convenient. Our rations were such an improvement over what we had been accustomed to on our recent arduous campaign that the men were quite contented. Down in our front on the banks of the Rappahannock was an elegant mansion, the Bernard House, known as Mansfield, perhaps a mile and a half below Fredericksburg. General Hood kept a regiment of the division there on picket duty along the bank of the river. Only on one or two occasions did it fall to our lot to be detailed for that purpose. Had it been left to our choice, we would have remained there. The house was vacant, including the outhouses, which extended back to the banks of the river; there was sufficient room to quarter a large regiment. General Lee kept a signal station in the tower on top of the main building. On the walls were several fine paintings and there was a splendid library. It was afterwards learned from the Texans who were on picket at the Bernard House immediately after Burnside was defeated, that the Union troops destroyed and carried away everything in the house; they gutted it completely.

As time wore on, and before we were sent down, the Confederate boys progressed in their intimacy with the Union pickets on the opposite bank until negotiations were opened for a commercial treaty between the two parties, strictly on a free-trade basis. The North side wanted our tobacco, we their coffee. The craft which plied between the two ports, and which conveyed many a pound of freight, consisted of a board about twelve inches wide and three feet long with a mast. When leaving a Northern port the sail consisted of a late Northern paper, and when returning with a cargo from the Southern port a late Richmond paper was the motive power.

On the 11th of December about 4 o'clock A.M. the signal guns fired. Then the long roll sounded. Everyone knew his duty and it was done orderly and quietly, but with dispatch. The regiment marched out and took its position in line. Heavy firing was heard down at the town. We learned that Barksdale's[3] Mississippi brigade, of McLaws' division, which was on picket there, was trying to prevent Burnside's men from crossing. With his men concealed along the river front he did such execution [that] the enemy was unable to put down his pontoons; nine distinct and desperate attempts were made to complete the bridge. This continued until about ten o'clock, when General Hunt[4] of the Union army began his bombardment of the ill-fated town, with his heavy artillery on Stafford Heights.[5] Swinton, the historian, who was an eyewitness, says: "There opened up from the massive concentration of artillery a terrific bombardment, that was kept up for above an hour. Each gun fired fifty rounds, and I know not how many hundreds of tons of iron were thrown into the town."[6]

We could see from our elevated position the town on fire. How dreadful to think of the suffering brought upon the helpless and innocent women and children who we learned were huddled in cellars and the depot, fleeing in every direction for safety. Three Union regiments[7] were finally placed in boats and effected a crossing, capturing about one hundred of the Mississippians; Barksdale returned to our position. Three pontoons were placed at Fredericksburg and two below. Our pickets retired from the lower ones, and the enemy was permitted to cross over.

While Burnside was crossing, General Lee was quickly moving us from our camps and bringing up his detachment from the lower fords. The 4th was moved up further to the left and took its position in line on the right of Longstreet's Corps near Deep Run, as at first proposed.

The regiment had been so long at Fredericksburg unoccupied that it had wandered over the town and surroundings until the topography of the country was familiar to many of the men. As the art of war was our only occupation, it was natural that the more intelligent and ambitious of both officers and men should study our positions when a chance offered from a military viewpoint. Dick Jones,[8] of D Company, was a close student and became quite proficient in the art of war; though only a private, he would have made a colonel of a regiment of whom any body of men would have been proud to follow, and there were others, efficient and capable, serving in the ranks, but who were fully entitled to promotion. I only mention this instance to show of what material the 4th Alabama was composed.

After our troops retired from Fredericksburg the enemy soon completed their pontoons and began entering the town. The shelling from both sides continued at intervals along some portions of the line until night.

The 4th Alabama had a dreary day's experience. Burnside was slower than we expected in crossing his men, and nothing wears out a soldier more than to be waiting, waiting, expecting momentarily to be called into action, and in the meantime be under a heavy artillery fire. It is by far more trying than to be actually engaged in battle. Such was our experience on the first day in line of battle, and most miserable it was.

During the night of the 11th and morning of the 12th, Franklin's Grand Division[9] of two Corps had crossed over on the two lower bridges in Jackson's front with one hundred and sixteen guns. Sumner[10] with his Grand Division of two Corps had crossed on the three bridges at Fredericksburg with one hundred and four cannon in front of Longstreet's line. On Stafford Heights were one hundred and forty-seven heavy guns in position ready to sweep the plain in our front between our position and the river. In addition, Hooker's[11] Grand Division of two Corps were left on the north side and ready to cross over.

To meet this grand army General Lee had arranged, commencing on the left above the town, Anderson's[12] division, his left resting on the river; then came McLaws' division with Howell Cobb's[13] Georgia Brigade in the sunken road behind the stone wall in front of Marye's Hill and directly in rear of the town, by far the strongest position on our line. Next came Pickett's division, then our little division of only two brigades. This constituted Longstreet's Corps.

General A. P. Hill of Jackson's Corps joined on to us and extended back to Hamilton's Crossing towards the river below. General Jackson's was the shorter, and also the weaker line, or more difficult to hold of the two, on account of the nature of the ground. General Hill had his six brigades in two lines, with three brigades in each. In rear of his rear line was a third composed of Taliaferro's[14] and Early's divisions. Off to their rear and right, still closer to the river, was D. H. Hill's division. General Jackson also had with him Stuart's[15] cavalry and John Pelham's Horse Artillery. General Lee had three hundred and six cannon, Burnside three hundred and sixty-seven, not including the artillery of Hooker's Grand Division.

Our line extended back along the ridges to the centre, forming an irregular obtuse angle. The position of our regiment was about a mile from the river and about the farthest of any other with an unobstructed view from our elevated position almost to the river. On the morning of the 12th we were moved a little to the left of our line, as we had no breastworks, and placed behind an embankment which afforded very good protection. The artillery both from the enemy's batteries in our front and from Stafford Heights opened early on us. Very few of ours had up to this time opened, as it was not necessary, and nearly all of them along the entire line were masked and awaiting an attack before disclosing their position.

Volunteers were called for to go on picket to drive back a line of skirmishers over the rise in our front; a sufficient number promptly responded and went forward. We saw some of our Generals as they passed along our front. "Old Stonewall" was dressed out in the new uniform General Stuart is said to have presented him; Generals Lee and Stuart also passed.

The 12th had proven a repetition of the 11th, a day of shelling and misery. About dark we were marched back in direction of our winter quarters, presumably to secure rations. As we passed along the road which wound around the base of the ridge thousands of camp fires on the slopes where soldiers had gone into bivouac lighted our way and the boys became quite cheerful. John Young[16] of I Company called out to us and wished to know why that hillside resembled a drug store. Many and various were the guesses, but none were correct. Some were very amusing and the boys became really merry. He finally informed us "because it was full of camp hire" (the old way of writing camphor).

Colonel Bowles, who was in command of the regiment, was absent, but present on the 13th. The office of Major was vacant on account of a controversy between Captain Glass of B Company and Captain Coleman of D as to seniority. The matter at this time was pending in our military courts and was finally decided in Captain Coleman's favor, his appointment being dated back to October 3, 1862.[17] Captain Glass resigned May 16, 1863, and Captain Robbins became senior captain.

The next morning (Saturday the 13th) we returned to our former position of the evening before, somewhat refreshed, and found brisk skirmishing and artillery firing going on along the line. This was the commencement of the third day. Burnside was making his preparations to attack us, and nothing done except to harass us with shelling and skirmishing. We hoped he was ready to cross swords with General Lee today and let the matter be done with.

The firing soon became heavy on Jackson's front, who was engaged with the forces of General Franklin. The latter had been reinforced by two divisions of Hooker's Grand Division, which increased his force to 50,000 men. Jackson's force amounted to only 30,000. The battle raged on this end of the line until two o'clock without any decisive results. General Jackson was acting on the defensive and had often said that the enemy might not be driven from a position by his men, but it could never take one from them; therefore, we on the centre felt secure as to our right. We expected a desperate effort would be made on that part of the line, as it was very plain that had the Union forces succeeded in defeating General Jackson the Union army would then have been between us and Richmond, but we felt secure, and did not fear any such result.[18]

That morning until about 11 o'clock A.M. a dense fog obscured everything in our front, when it lifted and revealed to our artillerymen the dense masses of troops in and around the town. From their position on the heights on Longstreet's part of the line, they opened a vigorous shelling and the battle began in earnest with our men in the sunken road behind the stone wall. French's[19] division attacked first in column of brigades. Cobb's[20] Georgians waited until the front brigade had approached to within about two hundred yards when they opened fire. The front brigade reached within sixty yards and halted. The other two went no farther and all were forced to retire. Our gallant Kershaw[21] with his South Carolinians hurried to the support of the Georgians. The line now behind the wall was four ranks deep. General Hancock[22] next made an effort with his division to drive the Confederates out. He got within thirty or forty yards, but no farther and he had to retire. Pickett's division was also attacked on our left, but he too held his ground and drove the Union troops opposed to him back.

At the very time that Hancock was driven back in front of Cobb's and Kershaw's brigades, having lost one-half of his men, General Jackson drove the enemy back from his front. General Burnside, still determined to take Marye's Hill, ordered Franklin to again attack General Jackson with his whole force so as to draw attention from the stone wall. For this purpose General Hooker was ordered to make the attempt with two of his divisions. Hooker brought his remaining divisions from the other side of the river and was about to renew the attack when he met French and Hancock, who advised him of the hopelessness of the assault.

Hooker returned to Burnside and begged to be relieved from leading his men to their death. By this time General Lee had four brigades, eight ranks, behind the wall, and old Colonel Walton[23] still with his battalion of the Washington Artillery on top of the hill. Burnside ordered Hooker back saying "that height must be carried this evening." Hooker returned and prepared for the assault by concentrating several batteries hoping to trench the wall, but General Lee had had the wall reinforced with earth and it withstood the bombardment. General Lee had also sent Pickett's division and one of our brigades (the Texans and 3rd Arkansas) up as support from the centre, but they were not needed.

It was now about 4 o'clock P.M. Hooker gave the signal for the assault and Humphrey's[24] division sprang forward to the charge; crushed, it fell back. General Sturgis[25] had again attacked on Hooker's left and he also had failed. Twilight came on and Hooker ordered his men to fall back. "Finding," he said, "that I had lost as many men as my orders required me to lose, I suspended the attack."[26]

The battle of Fredericksburg was virtually ended. General Franklin failed to attack General Jackson, as ordered by General Burnside, because, as he says, it was too late to do so after the order was received.[27]

All during the day the regiment was subjected to more or less shelling. In the afternoon, as the enemy was seen massing on our right, we were placed nearer A. P. Hill as support on Jackson's left.

Late that evening we were ordered to move quickly down the road. At a double quick by the flank we moved for some distance. We halted under a terrible shelling, and formed line of battle. We had scarcely performed this movement before an order came for us to move as quickly as possible to the front. We had moved but a few paces when we came into view of a large regiment of Confederate troops which had never before been under fire, and were demoralized by the terrible shelling they underwent. They were going to the rear as fast as their legs could carry them.[28]

On the crest of a slight elevation in our front was a battery; the gunners were working their pieces as fast as they could load and fire. Shells were tearing up the earth around us, and missiles from the small arms were flying thick over our heads. It appeared that we were soon to have a real fight at last. There came dashing down the gentle slope from the battery, meeting us, a young mounted artillery officer waving his cap in a frantic manner, who, upon approaching within speaking distance, suddenly reined in his horse and exclaimed in a very excited and positive manner: "Don't come up here unless you will promise to support me," and began a tirade against the regiment which had deserted him. This young officer was Major Latimer[29] of Jackson's Corps. Without checking our speed someone in the 4th Alabama replied: "Go back, Captain, to your battery, this is the old 4th Alabama." "Thank God, I am safe," he said, then turned his horse and went flying back to his battery.

We ran up in the rear of the hill, getting under cover as quickly as possible, and dropped down completely out of breath, at the same time throwing out D Company in front as skirmishers. Over the hill in front of the battery at a double quick, and deploying as they ran, D Company soon disappeared and became hotly engaged with the enemy's skirmishers. We fully expected a column of the enemy's infantry soon to appear against our front, our pickets driven in, and a desperate fight defending the battery the result. We were in great suspense. Captain Cussons and Virginius Smith,[30] both of Colonel Law's Staff, passed us and rode out on the picket line. In a few minutes Cussons came dashing back bareheaded, his long black hair waving in the breeze, and stated that the gallant little courier "Jimmie" Smith was killed.[31] Billy Ware[32] of D Company was also killed on the skirmish line.

Darkness soon coming on, the firing almost ceased and the day's work, which was a bloody one on the right and left, was ended. While lying behind the battery after dark, as an occasional bullet from the enemy's skirmishers fell over the hill among us, William Caldwell,[33] who was lying asleep on his back, was struck by one, which had sufficient force to penetrate his heart. Turning over quickly on his stomach with the blood gushing from his mouth, he died almost instantly.

It was afterwards discovered that the demonstration in our front by the enemy was only a feint to hold the Confederate centre from reinforcing the left at Marye's Hill contending against General Hooker's forces. When everything became quiet the regiment was moved back a short distance in a piece of woods and there slept until the next morning. Then E Company relieved D as skirmishers.

Skirmishing and artillery firing was resumed. The regiment was moved into the open near the edge of the wood to the rear and right of the battery. The enemy were firing solid shot from their batteries on the opposite side of the river on Stafford Heights. As Captains Keith, Karsner and I were conversing, while standing on the edge of the wood in the rear of the regiment (Keith, with his hands in his pockets, facing the front, and Karsner and myself with our backs to the enemy), a ricochet ball came bouncing in our direction, the men giving the alarm to us to look out. Before we could move, the ball passed between Karsner and me and struck poor Keith squarely in the breast. Both he and the massive solid shot fell to the ground together. His breast was crushed into a jelly and he died before the litter bearers reached the field hospital.

Gilchrist R. Bouleware[34] came in from the skirmish line wounded. He is still living (1909) in Conecuh County. That morning a shrapnel shell burst in the regiment near Ben Love[35] and we thought he was knocked to pieces, but he only suffered the loss of one finger. He now lives in Texas. There appeared in the *Confederate Veteran* a picture of Ben, his wife and twelve children.

During the afternoon there was a lull in the battle. Up to this time we had not resorted to artificial cover on our part of the line. General Lee, still anticipating another general attack from General Burnside, ordered that we entrench ourselves and the night of the 14th was spent in bringing logs from a nearby marsh and digging dirt.

On the 15th no demonstration was made against us until late in the evening, when we received a slight shelling. H Company, Lieutenant Newsome[36] in command, this day was on the skirmish line in full view of the regiment. As there was nothing doing all during the morning, Newsome and the Lieutenant in charge of the Union skirmishers in his front met halfway and held a friendly conversation. Old Stonewall was seen coming down the line and Newsome hastened back to his position. After Jackson had passed, the Union officer inquired the name of the officer. "Stonewall—had you known who it was no doubt you would have shot him," said Newsome. "Oh! no," said the Lieutenant, "I am in favor of keeping him; we may, after whipping you, need him."

On the 16th, as usual after a battle, we awoke to find it raining. We were glad to see Lieutenant Colonel Scruggs back with us from a leave of absence. Cheering was heard on our right and left and soon reached the centre. The report was that the enemy had retreated across the river during the night and that all of Burnside's army was back on Stafford Heights. Lieutenant Newsome and the writer, among others of the regiment, went out on the battlefield. Newsome and I hastened over to the left to see Marye's Hill. Our loss behind the reinforced wall was slight, but it was awful among the Union troops out in front of it. The ground was literally covered with their dead.

On our return, being hungry, we inspected the haversacks of the dead, and found on a handsome Union boy a full haversack of provisions and love letters. We were eating sweet chocolate and destroying the letters when we met General Hood. He told us to return to the regiment and tell Colonel Bowles to take us back to our camp. Reuben Nix,[37] who was among those who had gone out on a tour of observation, and one who could pick up more than any other member of the regiment on such occasions, came in just before we started back to camp with three prisoners, three horses and two dogs.

We returned to camp, and after making out our report of casualties found there were five killed and seventeen wounded. For six long weary days we had done nothing but skirmish and were subjected from day to day to almost incessant shelling. As a regiment we had not fired a shot.

In this battle the Union loss alone of killed and wounded at the base of Marye's Hill in front of the reinforced wall was sixty-three hundred, and their loss in front of General Jackson and the centre was only thirty-nine hundred and eight. Our loss along the whole line was fifty-two hundred and nine. That in the centre was very slight.[38]

Fortunately for the illy clad Confederates in this engagement, the weather was unusually mild for the middle of December. On the night of the 14th there was an aurora borealis which lit up the earth equivalent to a bright moon light. The morning of the 15th Steptoe Chapman[39] (son of ex-Governor Chapman of Alabama), who was on General Longstreet's staff and formerly a member of the 4th Alabama, came by to see us. Among other things that he told us was of the consultation of the Generals held by General Lee on the night of the 13th after we had repulsed General Burnside. Each one was called upon to give his opinion as to the best course to pursue. General Jackson was lying on his blanket fast asleep during the greater part of the conference. Generals Longstreet, A. P. and D. H. Hill and Jackson were present. Chapman said that when General Jackson was awakened to give his opinion, before rising from his blanket he said, "Drive them in the river. Drive them in the river." His idea was to strip the men of all their clothing so that they could be better identified in the dark.[40]

History has recorded a good many interesting incidents connected with this battle, of the mistakes, lost opportunities, and miscarriages. It is stated that a courier was intercepted and captured by one of our scouts on the north side of the river on the night of the 13th, bearing dispatches from General Burnside to the commanders of two of his Grand Divisions to renew the attack against us early on the morning of the 14th. The capture of this dispatch caused General Lee to call the conference above mentioned, and he finally decided to act on the defensive. Burnside, not knowing his dispatch had been delivered to General Lee, instead of to his commanders, fully expected a renewal of the attack. There being none, he renewed the order late on the 14th. His Generals protested so strenuously, believing they would meet with a second repulse, that Burnside countermanded the order. Had General Jackson's idea of acting on the aggressive been adopted by General Lee, it doubtless would have been successful, but at a great sacrifice of killed and wounded in our ranks. General Jackson, knowing the heavy loss and disheartening effect created in the Union army from the disastrous repulse on the 13th, no doubt believed it was the opportune time to act, one of his maxims being that "a defensive campaign can only be successful by taking the aggressive at the proper time."

General Lee was so confident that General Burnside would renew the attack that he dismissed his Generals after the conference with orders to act on the offensive as soon as General Burnside was repulsed. After finding that General Burnside delayed attacking, General Lee then determined to advance against him. The heavy ordnance ordered from Richmond to counteract the effect against our right of the Stafford Heights' batteries was so difficult to get into position that General Lee deferred that attack until the next day. On the morning of the 16th we awoke to find that the enemy had recrossed the river and were back in their positions on Stafford Heights.

Soon after we returned to our camps, the weather became bitterly cold. To those who could reach their homes, General Lee granted "furloughs of indulgence," as the winter campaign was over.

The drum corps of the 4th—and there was no better in the Army of Northern Virginia—was composed of three boys, George Fogarty, John Freid and James Hickey. All three deserted from the U.S. Army before the Civil War, were employed as musicians before the commencement of hostilities at the University of Alabama, from there joined the Tuskegee Company and were appointed musicians of the regiment after its organization. They remained with the regiment until we surrendered at Appomattox, and were bright and intelligent and fond of reading. When Colonel Albert Sidney Johnston[41] with twenty-five hundred regulars was sent to Utah in 1857 to bring old Brigham Young to terms, they accompanied him as musicians and shared all the hardships with that command when blockaded by the snow in the winter of 1857–58 in the Rocky Mountains. When the muster rolls were being made out here on the first of January 1863, Hickey came to the Adjutant's office tent and requested that his name be changed to Morgan Scullen, his proper name, stating that when in New Orleans after he deserted he met an honorably discharged soldier of the U.S. Army, Hickey by name, and secured from him his discharge papers and from that time took the name of Hickey. His request was complied with and he was afterwards known in the regiment as Morgan Scullen, and so reported on the muster rolls.

About the time all the papers were completed and sealed up, ready to be forwarded to Richmond, Captain Karsner came blustering into the office tent on a friendly call. He drew a camp stool up to the fire and began stroking his long black beard and complaining of the severe cold splitting the ends of the hairs. Scruggs threw down his book and picked up the bottle of mucilage from the table, which had been used in sealing the papers, and expatiated on the purity and excellency of the hair oil it contained. To convince him of its genuineness, Scruggs stuck his forefinger over the mouth of the bottle, shook it vigorously and doubling down that finger rubbed his own beard with the middle one. Karsner then poured out a copious amount in the palm of his hand and anointed his beard thoroughly. Sitting before the hot fire, it became in a few minutes as stiff as a horn. Without a word he arose and went back to his company. The next evening he returned in as jolly a mood as ever and said that Gabe (his servant) had to heat three camp kettles of water before he could get his beard back to its normal condition.

In January we had two or three snowstorms and there occurred one or two severe, bloodless snowball battles. Upon our arrival back in our camps, under the law requiring the army to be brigaded by the States, much to the regret of the old 3rd Brigade (4th Alabama, 2nd and 11th Mississippi and 6th North Carolina), which had stood together in so many hard fought battles from 1st Manassas to and including Fredericksburg (the 2nd and 11th Mississippi was taken out of the brigade before the Fredericksburg battle) was here dissolved and wiped out of existence. The 4th remained in its camp and the other regiments were sent to join other brigades. The 15th, 44th, 47th and 48th Alabama regiments were brigaded with us, and we remained together until the surrender at Appomattox. Colonel Law having been made a brigadier general, we were known as Law's Alabama Brigade, Hood's division, Longstreet's Corps. These four Alabama regiments, which with the 4th formed the new organization, remained as such without any change until the end at Appomattox. There was also no permanent change otherwise, only in brigade and division commanders.

All four regiments were transferred from Stonewall Jackson's Corps, and no better troops were enlisted from Alabama. The 15th Alabama had from April 1862 seen much service under Stonewall Jackson in the campaigns in the Valley and under General Lee up to this time. The 44th had participated in all the battles from Second Manassas. The 47th and 48th fought from Slaughter Mountain or Cedar Run;[42] therefore, all were veterans and equal to the best and did their work nobly and well until their colors were furled on the 9th of April 1865.

I have stated that the Texans were closely associated with the 4th Alabama beginning in the fall of 1861 and ending at Appomattox. Although permanent transfers of every other regiment of our two brigades were made to other parts of the Army of Northern Virginia, the 4th Alabama and the three Texas regiments were never separated from the same division. There being only three Texas regiments in the Army of Northern Virginia (not a sufficient number to complete a brigade),[43] the Hampton Legion and the 18th Georgia were taken out and the only Arkansas regiment in the Army of Northern Virginia, the 3rd, was substituted. No further change in this brigade was ever made. In reality the name given it by historians, "the Texas Brigade," is a misnomer, and historians are known to have even gone farther and fallen into the error of terming our whole division the "Texans." The three Texas regiments were composed of good fighting material and made a fine record. The same can be said of all the other regiments who fought in the same brigade and division. All are entitled to equal honors. As time progressed, there will soon be none of us left to contradict the many errors committed. I have come to the conclusion that history is nothing more than a "Blue Book" of lies anyhow.

From this time to the 9th of April, 1865, Brigadier General Benning's[44] and Brigadier General George T. Anderson's[45] Georgia brigades were placed in our division, increasing it to four brigades—and a noble set of fellows they were, too. The gallant old 7th and 8th Georgia, who poured out their lifeblood by the side of the 4th Alabama on the plains of Manassas in 1861, were members of Anderson's brigade and were a welcome acquisition to our division.

We remained in camp at Fredericksburg all of January 1863. On the 18th of February the regiment was ordered to Richmond and placed in camp on the south side of the city.

10

The Siege of Suffolk
February 18 to May 5, 1863

The forces which the 4th Alabama accompanied from Fredericksburg to Richmond consisted of our division (Hood's) and Pickett's. General Burnside had been relieved of the command of the Union army and "Fighting Joe" Hooker was selected by the Washington authorities to fill his place.[1] We left General Lee strongly entrenched from Banks Ford to Skinkers Neck, a line twenty miles long, on the hills on the south side of the Rappahannock, in our original position, confronted by Hooker occupying the north side on Stafford Heights. After detaching Hood's and Pickett's divisions, General Lee was left with only two divisions (Anderson's and McLaws') of our Corps, and all of Jackson's Corps, barely sixty thousand men and one hundred and seventy cannon. Hooker's army by spring had been augmented to 130,000 men in infantry and artillery with 404 cannon. We were perfectly ignorant of General Lee's object in sending us down to Richmond, which was menaced by Union forces from both Fort Monroe and Suffolk.

During February we remained in camp. Some of the men obtained furloughs, and several had the smallpox, among the latter our Assistant Surgeon, Dr. Duncan[2] of Savannah, Georgia, a most estimable gentlemen. Sergeant Walke[3] of D Company received a leave of absence to visit his home, and it was rumored in camp after his return to the regiment that he contracted smallpox on reaching home and all except himself, of his family, died.

Orders were received about the 1st of March to go to Ashland, sixteen miles north of Richmond, for what reason we never knew. The weather was very cold and many of the men were barefooted; several had almost no shoes at all. We reached there late in the evening and went into bivouac in a piece of woods and soon had immense fires built, and slept in our blankets by the fires and kept quite comfortable until the next morning. The yelling of those who first crawled out from under their blankets at dawn aroused the rest of us, and as we threw the cover from over our heads where we were comfortably lying, five or six inches of snow poured down in our faces. Then there was more yelling. Our fires had become extinguished, and we thought we would freeze before getting them again lighted. We had hardly gotten comfortable before we were ordered to march back to Richmond.

There was more suffering on those sixteen miles than on any other of the same length during our experience as soldiers. The barefooted and illy shod, like Washington's soldiers of the Revolution and Napoleon's on his retreat from Moscow, left a trail of bloody footprints behind them. Tired, hungry, and disgusted with plodding through slush and mud all day, as we wearily dragged ourselves through Richmond, several girls and young men, the latter clothed in immaculate gray and brass buttons and holding "bomb proof" positions[4] in the different departments, were standing on the pavement watching us pass through. Dump Sterling called a dudish-looking young man to him, protected from the gibes of the soldiers amidst a bevy of girls. When he approached, Dump said, "Ain't you a bird." "Yes, I am," he replied, "is that all you called me out here for?" "No," said Dump in a whisper, "I want to tell you that if you will just march with us out of the city I'll catch you a worm."

Sometime during the month of March we were sent down near Petersburg and remained there until April, when, on the 6th, we took up our march to Suffolk. Besides our two divisions, there was a detached brigade under General Roger Pryor[5] sent with us, all under command of General Longstreet.

Our regiment reached the Blackwater River one evening on the march and bivouacked at the ford. The Superintendent of a large plantation had a number of negroes there seining the river for mullet. We tried to purchase some for the regiment, as they had caught a large quantity. The man in charge stated that he needed them for the negroes, but that we could pay them something to make a haul for us. Colonel Scruggs gave them ten dollars, and they soon caught enough to supply the regiment. As fresh fish was quite a treat to us, the men remained up late in the night cooking and eating fish.

The next morning we resumed our march, and by the 12th of April were within four miles of Suffolk. We formed line of battle and the Texans indulged in a little skirmishing. While the regiment advanced slowly in direction of Suffolk, we threw forward four companies as skirmishers.

Amid picket firing and occasional shots from the raw Union artillerists we advanced and by the 15th had the town invested. We threw up a good substantial line of works in a piece of pines.

Our cooking camp was established back out of range of the Union batteries, and our rations [were] brought up to us. On our left was the Nansemond River, where we kept one or more companies constantly on picket duty. A five-gun battery occupied the left of the regiment. We had orders not to fire on the enemy unless we were attacked, but the enemy exhausted a large amount of ammunition doing very little execution. Their batteries annoyed us a good deal every night until after taps. A youth by the name of Weaver came out from North Alabama to see his brother. While asleep the first night he came (April 25th) a fragment of shell struck him and he was instantly killed.

In rear of the breastworks was the Field and Staff tent; but frequently all the regiment, except the picket, after the firing ceased, would go over in front of the works and sleep on the pine logs. Colonel Scruggs had gotten a few bundles of fodder from an old citizen nearby, to send back to the cooking camp to his horse. He made a bed of it, and went to sleep over in front of the works. A stray horse from the battery on the left wandered over and began to pull it out. The Colonel awoke and drove him off, but he insisted on returning. Finally the Colonel got up, tied a bundle of fodder to the poor old horse's tail and stuck a lighted match to it. The men were all lying thick on the ground asleep and the horse went at full speed right over them back to the battery. The men began to yell and the lighted fodder shining above the tree tops caused the Union batteries to open and we received a terrible shelling. Everyone ran into the breastworks and indulged in a hearty laugh, after finding there were no casualties.

Old man John McCalley, who lived in Spotsylvania County, had a son in the 4th Alabama and he frequently visited the regiment. His son's friends and mess mates were always delighted to see him, for he always brought something good in the way of eatables. The old man visited the regiment while at Suffolk. He left his horse at the cooking camp and walked over, carrying his well-filled saddle pockets on his shoulder. When he reached the regiment he found that his son (Bolivar)[6] was with his company down on the Nansemond on picket duty. Colonel Scruggs invited him to stay with him until his son was relieved. At supper the Colonel expressed fears that the old man would be disturbed by the shelling. "Oh no," he said, "if I ever get to sleep it will not disturb me in the least." He was given a bunk in the tent, with his saddle pockets and boots placed in easy reach. The old man was soon snoring away, when the battery opened on us as usual. After about the third shot a fragment of shell struck the ridge pole. This was too much for the old gentleman. Seizing his boots in one hand and his saddle pockets in the other, he disappeared, and sent word the next morning by the servant who brought our breakfast from the cooking camp for Bolivar to come back there, if he wished to see him.

We came to the conclusion after reaching Suffolk that General Lee sent us down there to collect supplies for the Army, and everything pointed that way.[7] We had the enemy cut off from trespassing on the country and General Longstreet kept all the wagons constantly occupied gathering up bacon (for which this section of the country is noted) and other supplies. Our pickets had quite a trying and disagreeable experience exposed constantly to both infantry and artillery fire, while the regiment proper was only subjected to artillery fire.

Lying in or near our breastworks became quite monotonous during the day. The crack of an occasional rifle out on the picket line was unnoticed as the men lolled idly about. The Field and Staff whiled away many hours playing "Mumblepeg." At that time there was attached to the regiment, as Assistant Surgeon, Dr. DeGraffenreid,[8] who had formerly been in that capacity in the old Army. The Doctor being endowed with a very prominent nose, every effort was made by Dr. Taliaferro,[9] Lieutenant Colonel Scruggs and myself to defeat him, in which we were generally successful, driving the peg down, apparently blindfolded, as deep into the ground as possible. We amused ourselves in seeing the Doctor making strenuous efforts to extricate the peg, which it was impossible for him to do until he scooped out sufficient space in the ground to accommodate his nose.

One morning I accompanied Lieutenant Colonel Scruggs down on the Nansemond to inspect the ground near the river where one or more companies from the 4th Alabama was daily detailed for duty. It was a low, level country back from the river. Remote from where our pickets were stationed were several large siege guns, apparently unprotected. It appeared to Colonel Scruggs and myself that all the enemy had to do was to land from their boats, drive back the small picket line and come out and claim them as their own. The only animate life we saw on that part of the field was a number of donkeys grazing on the open fields.

Lieutenant Dan Turner, now living in Madison County, Alabama, was in charge of his company at this time and detailed for duty on the Nansemond. That night being very dark, the enemy made an effort to land a superior force in his front. Knowing it would be useless for a small company to contend against such odds, he resorted to a ruse by calling out in a loud voice, which the Federals distinctly heard, saying, "Go back and hurry forward those other two regiments." The enemy then hurriedly returned to their gun boats—the ruse was effective in a satisfactory manner to Company I.

While sitting in the office tent the next morning making out my report, after Company I was relieved by sending down another company from the regiment, Lieutenant Turner came in and related his experience of the night before. I jokingly remarked to him, "Oh, that was only an hallucination of yours, Dan, you only saw in the dark that flock of donkeys and imagined they were a brigade of Yankees." Only to while away the time I began, after the departure of the Lieutenant, a sketch depicting Dan with his sword aloft urging on his little company against the imaginary foe. I had about completed it, donkeys and all, when Cussons came over from Brigade Headquarters with some instructions from General Law to Colonel Bowles. I related to him Lieutenant Turner's experience and the joke which prompted the sketch; he laughed and said, "Give it to me." "I will do no such thing," I said, "Turner is one of the best friends I have in the regiment and should you make it public in the brigade it might create a wrong impression." I then left him to deliver the orders to Colonel Bowles, but when I returned, Cussons and my rough sketch had both departed. I was very much angered and troubled over the matter, fearing I had carried my joke too far, and as soon as I made out my morning report, hurried with it over to Headquarters, determined to get my sketch and destroy it. But when I reached there, Cussons had taken his pencil and made such great improvement on my poor efforts as an artist that I never would have recognized it. He finally returned it to me, very much to my relief.

On the 28th of April an incident "after the manner of gentlemen" occurred at General Law's Headquarters, a full account of which is given by Colonel Oates of the 15th Alabama in his book—who was an eyewitness to the whole proceeding.[10] The double duel was brought about by Captain Terrell,[11] Assistant Adjutant General on General Law's staff, and Captain Cussons, Law's aide, who reported to Law that Colonel Connelly's[12] regiment, the 55th North Carolina, had acted disgracefully down on the Nansemond, having retreated and permitted the enemy to capture some of our heavy siege guns, thereby raising the blockade of the river.[13] Colonel Connelly and Captain Terrell were to fight with double barrel shotguns loaded with balls, at forty paces; Major Belo[14] of the 55th North Carolina and Cussons to fight with Mississippi rifles at the same distance. The Major and Cussons missed at the first fire; the guns were re-loaded, and at the second fire Major Belo was slightly wounded in the neck. A parley was then held and the matter amicably adjusted between all parties interested without any further bloodshed.[15]

For several days it rained almost incessantly, and filled our trenches with water, which made it quite disagreeable when we were compelled to repair to them for protection against the shells, which the enemy did not appear to stint themselves in throwing to us.

On the 30th of April, General Longstreet received an order from General Lee to return to Fredericksburg. He (Longstreet) replied that he could not do so, as all of his wagon train was absent collecting supplies. The order was repeated and General Longstreet dispatched to General Lee to know if he must hurry forward and abandon his wagon train, but to this he received no reply. It was not until the night of the 3rd of May that General Longstreet abandoned his position to go to the relief of his Chief.

All that day our skirmishers, four companies of the regiment down on the Nansemond, were busily engaged with the enemy and the regiment, the six remaining companies, were subjected to a perfect bombardment from the Union batteries over in Suffolk. Late that evening our skirmishers were called in and reached the breastworks in the midst of the shelling and were compelled to run the gauntlet in reaching the works, which they heroically did by jumping into them waist deep in water.

That night we bade farewell to Suffolk, although the enemy used every effort to hold us there to prevent our re-enforcing General Lee. All night we marched in a westerly direction and by noon the next day arrived at Franklin on the Blackwater River. From there, after resting and cooking rations, we resumed our march about sundown up the right bank of the Blackwater to Ivor Station, on the Norfolk & Western Railroad, and from there took the cars for Petersburg, which we reached about dark.

A short stop was made there, and as a soldier never lost a chance to eat when there was anything eatable in sight, nearly every member of the regiment made a rush for the dining room of a hotel near the depot. About the time we became seated we were ordered back to the train. The officers hurried the men back to the cars, but not until each one appropriated what he could carry off, leaving the table perfectly bare.

We were there long enough to learn from the citizens that General Lee, with his small force, had won the battle of Chancellorsville, but that General Jackson was seriously wounded.[16] As General Lee said at the time of this sad misfortune, "Jackson has lost his left arm, and I have lost my right." We were hurried on through Richmond by rail to Fredericksburg, but before reaching there were disembarked, on the 5th of May, at what is now White's Station on the Fredericksburg and Potomac and Piedmont Railway. There we remained for several days, and were then moved down near Raccoon Ford on the Rapidan.

Had General Longstreet been in position to move to General Lee's assistance on the 30th of April we could have reached him in ample time to have joined in the battle of Chancellorsville.

There is no record of the casualties of the regiment during the siege of Suffolk. The writer cannot recall anyone who was killed there, but there were some wounded among the skirmishers. Taking into consideration the vast amount of ammunition so lavishly expended against us, it would appear that we certainly should have been entirely exterminated. Our small losses were attributable to the raw and inexperienced soldiers who were opposing us.[17]

Incidents on the Rappahannock and Rapidan
May 5 to June 15, 1863

Our comrades who had participated in the hard fought Battle of Chancellorsville accomplished such wonders against immense odds that the 4th Alabama would have much preferred to have had the pleasure of inscribing, with them, upon its banner, "Chancellorsville," in lieu of "Siege of Suffolk."[1] The Army of Northern Virginia, or at least that part of it which met the enemy in the Battle of Chancellorsville, for half of Longstreet's Corps was absent, deserves more credit for overcoming the great preponderance of numbers opposed to it than in any battle that the army ever engaged in. With General Lee's strategy, and the divisions of Generals McLaws and Richard Anderson of the First Corps and General Jackson of the Second executing the orders given them by their Chief, the apparently impossible feat was accomplished, but at such a sacrifice. The moment Stonewall Jackson fell mortally wounded, the Army of Northern Virginia sustained a far greater loss than in any other battle during its existence. This was the last battle in which General Lee attempted to divide and re-unite his army in the presence of the enemy.

Had one half of the brave men who hurled the Union forces back across the Rappahannock, crestfallen and defeated, been sacrificed in the attempt, a greater gloom could not have been cast upon the 4th Alabama when I read the following order at dress parade on the Rapidan, on the evening of the 11th of May, 1863.

> Headquarters Army of Northern Va.
> May 11, 1863
>
> General Order No. 61.
> With deep grief, the commanding general announces to the army the death of Lieut. Gen. T. J. Jackson, who expired on the 10th instant,

at 3:15 P.M. The daring, skill, and energy of this great and good soldier, by the decree of an all wise Providence, are now lost to us. But while we mourn his death, we feel that his spirit still lives, and will inspire the whole army with his indomitable courage and unshaken confidence in God as our hope and strength. Let his name be a watchword to his corps, who have followed him to victory on so many fields. Let officers and soldiers emulate his invincible determination to do everything in the defense of our beloved country.

R. E. LEE, General[2]

The position assigned the 4th Alabama on the Rapidan at Raccoon Ford above Fredericksburg was the same which Lafayette crossed on his march to Yorktown in June 1781.

After the death of General Jackson, General Lee re-organized his Army, forming an additional Corps. General Longstreet still retained command of the First, Ewell was given the Second and A. P. Hill the Third. General Richard Anderson's division was taken out of our Corps (Longstreet's) and given to General Hill.[3] Our division (Hood's), however, was increased from our two brigades to four. The two placed with us were both Georgians. One was commanded by General George Anderson, a West Pointer, whom we dubbed "Old Tige," and the other by that grand old Roman, General Benning, whom the boys will insist on calling "Old Rock." Our old friends of the 7th and 8th Georgia of Bartow's old brigade were a part of General Anderson's command and we were glad to welcome them near us again. Both brigades were composed of as fine a body of soldiers as Georgia furnished the Confederacy.

We remained near Raccoon Ford until the 3rd of June, when orders were received to cross the Rapidan and march to Culpeper Court House. By the 8th, General Lee had the troops of the First and Second Corps concentrated there. General A. P. Hill was left at Fredericksburg to watch the movements of the Union army, which was still in its position, to which it had been twice driven by the prowess of the Southern soldiery, looking down at us from Stafford Heights.

The 4th Alabama was among the first regiments to reach Culpeper. All the cavalry was concentrated under its matchless leader, General Jeb Stuart near Brandy Station between us and the Rappahannock River. On the 8th of June General Lee ordered a review of the whole of General Stuart's Corps. The 4th Alabama was present and witnessed the grandest and most spectacular display of the largest body of cavalry they had ever seen massed on one field. General Stuart was in all his glory. Mr. Davis, his Cabinet, and a large number of ladies from Richmond and the surrounding country were among the spectators.

That evening General Stuart entertained his visitors with a sham battle. To several members of the 4th Alabama there was only one thing to mar the occasion— the absence of the dashing Alabama artillerist of Stuart's Horse Artillery, John Pelham, who was killed leading a cavalry charge only a few miles from where we then were, on the 17th of March, 1863.[4] That night the little village of Culpeper was filled to overflowing with beautiful women and brave men, where a dance inaugurated by the cavalry continued until long after we infantry had retired to our respective blankets.

Along in the "wee small hours" of the 9th of June when "mutual eyes" were loath to part, the cavalry pickets came rushing into the village from above at Beverly Ford reporting the Union cavalry crossing the Rappahannock and marching in direction of Brandy Station. Soon after, other couriers came dashing in stating that both cavalry and infantry were crossing below at Kelly's Ford.

To counteract the Union infantry, which was advancing with the cavalry against us, our division was at dawn aroused from its slumbers and ordered to the support of the cavalry. The cavalry soon became engaged and when night closed on the scene, the grandest cavalry engagement of the Civil War had been fought and won by the Confederates and the enemy driven back across the river with a loss of 907 and three pieces of artillery, though not until General Hooker had discovered through this reconnaissance in force that General Lee had so far stolen a march on him and had the greater part of his army concentrated thus far on his contemplated invasion of Pennsylvania.[5]

On the day following the cavalry fight, General Lee sent forward the Second Corps under General Ewell, via Berryville, Winchester and Martinsburg. Each one of these places were successively carried by our troops, with a large number of prisoners, supplies and equipment falling into our hands. The Valley of Virginia was now, with small loss to us, cleared of the enemy, and all accomplished in five days after General Ewell departed from us at Culpeper.

General A. P. Hill was ordered on the 13th to join our Corps at Culpeper, the enemy having abandoned Stafford Heights. The three Confederate Corps were now strung out over many miles, which caused Mr. Lincoln, upon being informed of our scattered condition by General Hooker, to reply to that officer: "If the head of Lee's Army is at Martinsburg and the tail of it on the Plank Road between Fredericksburg and Chancellorsville, the animal must be very slim somewhere. Could you not break him?"[6] General Hooker failed to make the effort.

At 11:30 P.M. on the night of the 14th of June, General Hood was ordered to have his division in readiness to go forward the following morning. By one o'clock A.M. the courier had delivered the order to the 4th Alabama. Campfires were soon lighted and each mess busily engaged in preparing two days rations for the haversacks.

12

Gettysburg Campaign
June 15 to July 14, 1863

Early on the morning of the 15th of June, in the best of spirits, the 4th Alabama, in common with the other gallant regiments of the First Corps, took up its long march northward from its encampment at Culpeper Court House. Lieutenant General Ewell of the Second Corps was far afield, and many miles intervened between us. Lieutenant General Hill of the Third Corps remained at Fredericksburg until he saw the last of the Union Army disappear over the hills of historic old Stafford, and then hurried on to join us. General Lee, who remained in the centre with our Corps near General Longstreet, had now resolved to shorten the distance between the "tail" of his Third Corps and the "head" of his Second. General Hooker, after his reconnaissance with his cavalry on the 9th, rapidly moved his army from Stafford Heights up the north bank of the Rappahannock in order to throw it between General Lee and Washington.

Our first day's march was a record one. When we went into camp that night in the vicinity of Little Washington, in Rappahannock County, near a beautiful spring, the men were almost completely exhausted. The day was extremely warm, and we had covered at least thirty miles.[1]

On the 16th and 17th General Lee led us along the eastern slope of the Blue Ridge in order to conceal our movements from the enemy. On the 18th we crossed the mountain from Upperville and forded the Shenandoah at Berry's Ford in the afternoon. The rain poured down in torrents all that evening and we bivouacked on the west bank of the river a short distance from Snicker's Ferry.

On the morning of the 19th as the regiment had just commenced cooking rations, hurried orders were received to fall in, cross the river, and ascend the mountain for the purpose of holding Snicker's Gap. A detail was left to complete the cooking, and off we marched at a rapid gait.

Without disrobing, the men plunged into the rising stream to the east side and ascended the mountain, forming in line of battle on right and left of the Gap. Here we remained in a dense fog and heavy mist until the next evening, awaiting the approach of the foe. Failing to make his appearance, we were ordered to return to Snicker's Ferry and recross to the west bank of the Shenandoah.

On account of the heavy rains, the river was very much swollen and quite deep for wading. A detachment of cavalry was placed a short distance below the ford to catch any soldier who should lose his footing and be swept down the stream, but no such accident occurred. Again the regiment, without stopping to disrobe, plunged into the rapidly rising stream, after adjusting the cartridge boxes on the bayonets to keep them dry. Several of the boys in the rear hastily handed me their valuables from their pockets to carry over for them. Just before I reached the west bank my little mare deliberately dropped down, her head only appearing above the surface of the water. I scrambled out completely drenched, much to the amusement of those near me. As it was late in the afternoon when we crossed over, we went into bivouac a short distance from the Ferry.

After a good deal of marching and countermarching along the west bank of the Shenandoah, the evening of the 22nd of June found the regiment encamped a mile beyond Millwood, only ten miles on a straight line from our bivouac of the night of the 20th. In this quiet, beautiful valley we rested all of the 23rd on the estate of a wealthy gentleman. There was a magnificent spring on the place, and a large deer park, which contained a herd of English fallow deer.

Early on the morning of the 24th we resumed our march and by 7 o'clock A.M. had reached the fortified town of Berryville. General Rodes[2] (the best General officer furnished the Confederacy by Alabama) of Ewell's Corps, on the 13th of June, with his division, captured this place, although well fortified and garrisoned.[3]

That night, after a long march, the old regiment rested its weary limbs two miles beyond Midway. General Lee was now hurrying us forward in order to shorten the gap between Lieutenant General Ewell's Corps and his two rear Corps. Lieutenant General Hill had overtaken us on the Shenandoah and passed into the Valley above us. It was impossible for General Lee from this time until the Battle of Gettysburg was half fought to obtain accurate information of the movements of the enemy, on account of General Stuart taking nearly all the cavalry off on a raid.[4]

At daylight on the 25th the regiment moved out in the direction of Martinsburg, reaching that place about noon. On the 14th of June General Rodes with his division, after taking Berryville on the 13th, captured the garrison at Martinsburg. He took 700 prisoners, 5 pieces of artillery and a considerable quantity of stores.[5]

That night saw the 4th Alabama go into bivouac near the Potomac, not far from Falling Waters. The next morning about 8 o'clock we were wading across the Potomac into Maryland at Williamsport. Hill's Corps crossed at the same time below us at Shepherdstown. We marched out a short distance from the town and halted. General Hood secured several barrels of whiskey and had surgeons issue a certain quantity to each member of the division.

We crossed the line into Pennsylvania and camped in the neighborhood of Greencastle, Pennsylvania. We had breakfasted in Virginia, dined and wined in Maryland and taken supper in Pennsylvania. It was reported by some that we had marched in four states that day, the fourth being in a state of intoxication.

General Lee scarcely gave us time to cross the Potomac before he gave us to understand that the destruction of personal property, the burning of rails, even for cooking or any other purpose, was positively forbidden.[6] I saw one evening after we had gone into bivouac a soldier run a chicken under General Hood's chair and catch it and the General appeared perfectly unconscious of the act, so intent was he on examining a map, while sitting in the yard of a Pennsylvania citizen. This was the only piece of apparent wantonness I saw perpetrated during our campaign in Pennsylvania, and doubtless in this instance the owner had obtained full value for his property.[7]

For miles and miles the Army of Northern Virginia marched along roads flanked on both sides by fields of luxuriantly waving corn and wheat, and all remained untouched. On the 27th of June the regiment passed through Greencastle, and reached Chambersburg that evening. Marching two miles beyond the town, we went into camp.

On Sunday the 28th we rested. The Army of Northern Virginia was, on this day, in the following positions: Longstreet and Hill at and near Chambersburg; Ewell, with two divisions of his Corps, at Carlisle, a day's march from Harrisburg; Early with the third division of Ewell's Corps was advancing east from South Mountain to York.

This same Sunday night information was brought, not by General Stuart, who was then on his "too fascinating" raid, entirely lost to General Lee, but by General Longstreet's famous scout Harrison,[8] who delivered to General Lee the first complete account of the operations of the Union army since disappearing from our front on the Shenandoah. This scout, or more properly, spy, reported that General Hooker had thrown the Union army across the Potomac into Maryland and was advancing northward, and that the head of his column was then at South Mountain, thus menacing our communications with the Potomac, through Hagerstown and Williamsport. This forced General Lee to concentrate his army as speedily as possible east of the mountain. We also learned through Harrison that General Meade[9] had succeeded General Hooker in command of the Union army.

On the 29th the 4th Alabama enjoyed another day of rest, and materially reduced the supply of apple butter and light bread of our Pennsylvania Dutch hosts. Hill's Corps moved out in the direction of York by way of Cashtown to cooperate with General Ewell. The greater part of our Corps was ordered to move in the same direction via Greenwood.

The 4th Alabama, with the other regiments of the brigade and a battery, was detached from the Corps on the morning of the 30th and sent by way of Fayetteville to New Guilford on outpost duty, where we arrived on the morning of the 1st of July. Here we again reveled in apple butter and light bread until two o'clock on the morning of the 2nd.

In the meantime, the other commands of the Confederate army were either in the vicinity of Gettysburg, ten miles to the east of Cashtown, or on the march for that point, except Pickett's three brigades left at Chambersburg in charge of the wagon train, and our brigade at New Guilford. Some time during the night we were awakened by the unwelcome voice of a courier asking to be directed to the Colonel commanding. General Longstreet had sent for us to join him at Gettysburg without delay.

By two o'clock A.M. we were on the march; the 4th Alabama was in the rear of the brigade. Twenty-eight good miles intervened between New Guilford and the position we were to occupy in line of battle.[10] By 3 o'clock P.M. the hospitals were reached, and until we arrived at our division which accompanied the extreme right of the army, the litter bearers of the Second and Third Corps, with the dead and dying of both friend and foe, were continually passing to the rear.[11]

We found the Texans and 3rd Arkansas occupying the right of the division. We marched beyond them and took position on their right. This threw our brigade on the extreme right of the Confederate army, which extended for six miles in the shape of a fish hook, the right representing the shank. The 48th Alabama was the right regiment of the brigade, the 4th Alabama the left, touching elbows with the 5th Texas.[12] Old Captain Reilly, whose battery always accompanied our brigade in battle, was there on our right. His brave gunners from the Old North State welcomed our arrival with suppressed cheers; beside one of his pieces was lying a three-inch burst rifle. Without giving us time to fill our empty canteens after our long and unbroken march under a broiling sun, General Longstreet gave the order to advance against the enemy's stronghold.

In our front was a field of growing wheat, and beyond across the Emmitsburg Road was the mountain, 1000 or 1200 yards from us.[13] When the order was given to charge, the whole division made a mad rush down through the wheat, firing and yelling like demons, the enemy in the meantime sweeping the field as we advanced with numerous pieces of artillery stationed on the side and crest of the mountain.[14] The 4th Alabama at the point of the bayonet routed the enemy from behind a stone wall upon reaching the foot of the mountain.[15] Here we halted to reform our lines.[16]

Colonel Scruggs fell from sheer exhaustion and was carried to the rear by the litter bearers, one of whom, while doing so, was killed, James H. Cooke[17] of G Company. Three of the five regimental commanders fell from exhaustion in the brigade before the close of the battle that evening. Major Thomas Coleman, who succeeded Colonel Scruggs in command of the regiment, after halting at the foot of the mountain, ordered me to return to the shell-swept field and urge on to the front those who had become too much exhausted to keep up with the regiment in its rapid, sudden and headlong advance. Several of the men were met trying in their broken down condition to reach the regiment; some were found, and whom I knew to be good and fearless veterans, unable to go further.[18]

One soldier, whom I was certain was Charles Halsey,[19] was found lying in the tangled wheat, face downward. He was one of the best fighters in the regiment, and could always be found on the firing line. I touched him lightly with the point of my sword and ordered him to get up and join the regiment, at the same time calling him by name, but he refused to look up or move. As I had no time to lose, I hurried through with my work and reached the regiment just as the advance up the mountain began. We swept on up the rocky mountain side, some of the men assisting each other over the boulders, while others passed between them. While about halfway up, still driving the enemy, right in front of me was Charley Halsey. I said, "How in the world did you get here?" "Get here," he said, "I've been here all the time." It was simply a case of mistaken identity.

We advanced up the mountainside (known as Little Round Top) when we encountered a strong force of the enemy in a fortified position.[20] We made three attempts to carry it, but it was impossible to take it by direct assault and our ammunition had become almost exhausted.[21]

Major Coleman caused us to fall back a short distance to reform what remained of us, and while doing so, a staff officer of General Longstreet, apparently drunk, came dashing up the mountain side and booted, gloved and spurred, and rode among us. Reining up his horse he inquired in a loud voice: "Who is in command of this regiment?" Someone too breathless to speak pointed in direction of Major Coleman, who was beyond us busily engaged in getting the line into shape. This officer, mistaking me for Coleman, spurred his horse to my side, and placing his whole weight down upon my shoulder ordered, "Get your men into line, sir, and charge that position." I politely informed him that Major Coleman was the proper one to receive his order and directed him to that officer, but he abruptly turned his horse down the mountain and disappeared, having by his uncalled-for action caused a good deal of excitement and a few harsh epithets thrown after him from some members of the regiment.

At this stage of the battle I take up in part Colonel Scruggs' official report, written August 8, 1863: "Owing to the exhausted condition of the men and the roughness of the mountain side, we found it impossible to carry this position. We retired in good order, though not until we had expended our ammunition. Having received a fresh supply of cartridges about dark, we remained in the enemy's front, some 200 yards distant during the night. Early the next morning, we threw up a line of breastworks composed of rock, and assumed the defensive."[22] I learn (1909) from members of the regiment who have recently visited that historic battlefield, that this breastwork of rock is still there in the same condition as we left it.

It is now (1909) forty-six years since this battle was fought, and there has been more written about it than on any other battle of the Civil War. Of the errors and omissions committed, all of the principal officers of the Army of the Potomac and the Army of Northern Virginia who participated have had their say from their own view point. It is not, however, for those who bore the brunt of that awfully bloody struggle over ground "inaccessible to man" to read its true history. That will come some time after the last one shall have passed away. There is still much more to be added.

Since 1880, when the first of the series of War Records were published, the historian has gained much valuable information. The rolls of the two armies are now being published and will, when completed, in addition to that already written of this battle, furnish the future student of military history, in my opinion, a more interesting chapter to work out than any other engagement in which the 4th Alabama participated.

All the survivors of this battle now know it was General Lee's wish the battle should open anew on the morning of the 2nd with the troops then on the field, commencing the attack on the extreme right, and to be taken up successively to the left, Ewell on the extreme left to attack when he heard Longstreet's guns. All of the three Corps were either up or in striking distance of the field, except Pickett's division of 3 brigades of our Corps, and our brigade.

Most of the morning was consumed by General Longstreet in moving his seven brigades (McLaws' four and Hood's three) around to the right. He lost at least two hours in his effort to find a route that would conceal him from the enemy's signalers on Little Round Top. Then he says in his official report, "Fearing that my force was too weak to venture to make an attack, I delayed until General Law's brigade joined the division."[23] This delay no doubt caused us to lose both the Round Tops, either of which was the key to the position.

Finally when we did reach the field and double-quick into line on the right, our formation was as follows: the 48th Alabama, Colonel James L. Sheffield,[24] on the right; on his left was the 44th Alabama, Colonel Wm. F. Perry.[25] In the centre was the 15th Alabama, Colonel W. C. Oates. On his left was the 47th Alabama, Lieutenant Colonel M. Bulger.[26] The 4th Alabama, Lieutenant Colonel L. H. Scruggs, occupied the left. The other brigades of the division occupied the following positions: the three Texas regiments and 3rd Arkansas, commanded by General Robertson,[27] on our left, and next to them was General George T. Anderson (Tige) with his Georgians. Old General Benning with the other Georgia brigade was placed in the rear of our brigade as support.[28] Our division, now complete with its four brigades, was ready for General Longstreet to make his long deferred attack.

Looking outward from our position across the Emmitsburg Road, Big Round Top loomed up, our right regiment, the 48th Alabama about opposite its centre. North of it was Little Round Top. Still farther northward, forming a part of Little Round Top, was Devil's Den, a treeless, uncanny gorge covered with immense boulders.[29]

Still further toward Gettysburg was the famous Peach Orchard. McLaws was in position on our left along Seminary Ridge fronting Devil's Den and the Peach Orchard, Kershaw and Barksdale on the front line, and Semmes[30] and Wofford in reserve. Our division extended beyond the enemy's left flank. There were so far no Union troops occupying the Round Tops. The 3rd Union Corps under General Sickles[31] occupied in strong force, in front of General McLaws, the Peach Orchard and the spur which formed the south side of Devil's Den.[32]

Long before we arrived from New Guilford General Hood had discovered through his scouts that there were no Union troops on either of the Round Tops and this is corroborated by General Warren,[33] at that time Chief Engineer of the Army of the Potomac, during an inspection of Little Round Top about the time our attack began.

When it finally did begin, as already only partially described, for then we only saw that which was immediately in our front, General Longstreet left-obliqued us in direction of Little Round Top. Dear old General Benning with his invincible Georgians, whom we relied on for support, became completely lost from our brigade and, falling in with Robertson's brigade, became commingled with the 1st Texas and 3rd Arkansas off to our left in Devil's Den, where they were having a strenuous time with Sickles' men.

About this time General Hood received a severe wound and was borne from the field. General Law, a senior brigadier of the division, took command. Both the Georgia brigades and the left of Robertson's (1st Texas and 3rd Arkansas) were making a perfect inferno of Devil's Den against the gallant men of Sickles and the reinforcements swarming to his support. General Law hurried Colonel Perry with the 44th Alabama to the support of our hard-pressed left. Shortly afterwards he withdrew the 48th Alabama, Colonel Sheffield, and sent them in the same direction. After an hour or more of the most desperate fighting, our mixed-up brigades succeeded in taking Devil's Den, capturing three ten-pound Parrot guns,[34] a few standards, and prisoners, but in spite of all he could do, General Law could advance no farther. He then took a position on the Spur, and acted on the defensive. This ended the fight for the division on the left that evening.

In the meantime the two remaining regiments of the brigade on the right of the 4th Alabama were not idle. Colonel Oates states in his history of the 15th Alabama that General Law rode up to him as we were advancing across the Wheatfield and informed him that he was then on the extreme right of our line, and for him to hug the base of Big Round Top and go up the valley between the two mountains, until he found the left of the Union line, to turn it and do all the damage he could, and that Lieutenant Colonel Bulger of the 47th Alabama would be instructed to keep closed on his regiment. If separated from the brigade Bulger would act under his orders.[35]

After going a short distance he encountered a body of United States sharpshooters, but recently arrived there. With his two regiments he drove them up and over Big Round Top, and met a part of the force the 4th Alabama was fighting as he ascended Little Round Top, and there, like the 4th, was brought to a stand-still. Finding he was about to be flanked by reinforcements of the enemy swarming up the mountain, he sent his sergeant major with a request, as he states in his book, to the 4th Alabama, the next in line on his left, to come quickly to his relief.[36] The sergeant major returned to him within a short time and reported that none of our troops were in sight, the enemy was between him and the 4th Alabama, and was swarming in the woods south of Little Round Top. His two regiments became in a few minutes completely surrounded and were compelled to fight their way out, several of both (the 15th and 47th) having been captured and losing heavily in killed and wounded.

This ended the fighting for that evening on the right of the 4th Alabama. The 4th and 5th Texas were the only regiments which advanced up Little Round Top with the 4th Alabama, and they too became separated from us. No regiment in either army made a more determined effort nor exhibited a bolder front, unsupported and exposed on both flanks, than the 4th Alabama in its three different efforts to dislodge the enemy. Colonel Oates says: "All the regiments of the brigade did their full duty at Gettysburg, but the 15th struck the hardest knot."[37] I don't know, perhaps it did, but I do know the eleven companies of the 15th carried into the battle about double the ten companies of the 4th. The official reports of both the regimental commanders and that of Surgeon LaFayette Guild, Medical Director of the Army of Northern Virginia, gives of those killed exactly the same in each regiment—seventeen.[38]

The total of the casualties of the killed and wounded in the 15th in this battle amounted to 20 1/2 percent killed, and in the 4th to 26 percent. It was almost invariably the result in every battle in which we engaged, the percent killed in proportion to the wounded was greater than any other regiment in the brigade. (The 15th reported seventeen more wounded than the 4th.)

Colonel Oates calls attention to this in his book, in referring to the 4th Alabama, and attributes it to the daring and reckless individual exposure of its members.[39] Should the killed and wounded be an index by which a correct judgment can be formed of the bravery and endurance of soldiers, I cannot see that the three brigades of Pickett's had much, if any, in heroism the advantage of the regiments of Hood's division. The brigades of Benning, Anderson, Robertson and Law charged across that open field of wheat, up the boulder covered slopes of Little Round Top, and through Devil's Den, capturing artillery and many prisoners, and driving the enemy to a standstill on the formidable heights of Little Round Top, amid the almost unsurmountable difficulties which we were compelled to undergo.[40]

The three brigades, Garnett's,[41] Armistead's[42] and Kemper's,[43] comprising Pickett's division, had an average of 74 2/3 killed and 380 wounded in each brigade during their charge on the 3rd, while Hood's four brigades had an average of 84 3/4 killed and 370 wounded in their encounter on the evening of the 2nd against the Round Tops. Those brave men of Hood's division have never received the meed of praise to which they were justly entitled. Pickett's, Trimble's, and Pettigrew's[44] divisions are entitled to all the praise that can be accorded them.

Our casualties were seventeen killed, forty-nine wounded and twenty-one missing. Some of the mortally wounded breathed their last almost before reaching the field hospital. I am reminded of one instance which was so indelibly impressed upon my mind that I remember distinctly. During our third and last ineffectual effort to dislodge the enemy from his stronghold, there emerged from our scattered ranks a youth whom I well knew in our boyhood days, Rufus Franks.[45] He walked erectly and rapidly to the rear, still grasping his rifle, with no apparent evidence whatever of being the least wounded. A man hard hit invariably will drop his gun. As he brushed past me he remarked in a trembling voice, his face deathly pale, "Adjutant, a handful of men can't drive those Yankees from that place. Can't you get Major Coleman to call the boys off before all are killed?" I knew he was a good soldier, yet his actions forced me to imagine, "There goes a soldier whose heart is gone." I called in a rather pleading tone to him to come back. Without looking back or stopping, and still with his gun at a trail, he replied, "I am wounded." Thinking he was only slightly wounded, I dismissed the incident, and in the confusion of battle would henceforth have been forgotten, had I not learned, as we lay in our rude breastwork of rock the next morning that he was shot in the bowels and died soon after he was taken to the hospital. Lieutenant Henry Roper[46] (as I write, the Circuit Court Clerk of Madison County), while we were climbing up the mountain side, was shot through the lungs and incapacitated for duty ever afterwards. He informed me that he and Franks were taken from the base of Little Round Top in an ambulance to the field hospital. Although Franks knew he was mortally wounded, it was perfectly pathetic to hear him repeatedly apologizing to Roper between violent spasms of vomiting in the ambulance for his unavoidable demeanor.[47]

All during the night of the second, the 4th had several scouts out among the boulders in our front, some of whom were captured. Lieutenant Tom Christian, formerly of D Company, then on General Law's staff, was captured with twenty-two men of the brigade while posting them. Several of our best men were captured, and the 4th Alabama had a greater number to report missing (21) by far than in any other battle. One of the 4th Alabama scouts advanced sufficiently close to overhear loud talking between the two Union cavalry Generals, Kilpatrick[48] and Farnsworth.[49] The former was in command of a division occupying the front of our right flank, which was defended by a thin line of our infantry skirmishers, the line extending back nearly at right angles to our line of battle. It appears from what our scout caught of the heated conversation that Kilpatrick had ordered Farnsworth, a brave and ambitious young brigade officer, but recently promoted, to charge over our picket line and turn our right flank. Farnsworth earnestly protested against such a fool's errand, whereupon Kilpatrick angrily remarked, "Then, by God, if you are afraid to go, I will lead the charge myself." Farnsworth then without further protest determined to make the effort. This was immediately reported to General Law, and preparations made during the 3rd to meet it.[50]

John Young of I Company, who before entering the army was an editor, while scouting, had his rifle lying on a large rock with his right hand resting on the barrel. As he stood partially concealed behind the boulder, a Union sharpshooter fired and knocked off his middle finger. He came down to the regiment and holding up his hand, manipulating his thumb and forefinger, remarked: "Well, boys, there is one consolation about this loss; I can, when this cruel war is over, set type as well as ever."

We remained behind our rock breastwork until about 1 o'clock P.M. on the 3rd. Comparative quiet prevailed along our entire battle line.

Then there opened on our left a most terrific and deafening cannonading. A good many shells of inferior make from our batteries, bursting prematurely over our position on the side of the mountain, compelled many to take refuge from them on the side of the boulders next to the enemy. This continued for almost an hour before it began to slacken.[51] Then General Pickett made his historic charge, which has so often been described. In it, besides his three fresh brigades, participated six others from Hill's Corps.[52] Alabama was represented with the 13th Regiment and 5th Battalion of Archer's brigade, Archer having been taken prisoner on the 1st. The gallant Colonel Fry[53] of the 13th Alabama commanded the brigade, composed of the 13th Alabama and 5th Alabama Battalion and three Tennessee regiments.[54] This resulted in a more complete failure than the charge of our division the previous evening.

There was again a lull in the battle until late that afternoon. Rapid firing of both small arms and artillery then opened on our right, opposite our thinly protected flank. A few minutes elapsed. Then a courier came dashing up to the regiment at full speed with orders to double quick to the right. Without awaiting orders from Lieutenant Colonel Scruggs, who had early that morning returned from the hospital partially recovered from his exhaustion of the evening before, everyone, without the semblance of order, with rear in front and only keeping with each other, companies all commingled, the most fleet-footed leading, ran through the woods in the direction of the firing. We at the time were perfectly ignorant of the cause of the sudden and unexpected call, and were not aware of the extent or nature of the disaster which had befallen our unprotected right flank, nor whether it was cavalry or infantry we were to meet.

Just as we were about to emerge from the timber into the open field we saw a squadron of Union cavalry bearing down upon us at a gallop. It came in smashing style from the direction of Captain Reilly's battery, which occupied the same position on the extreme right flank we found it in when we arrived from New Guilford the evening before. The men, on account of the long hot and rapid march of the previous day and the strenuous time we encountered after reaching the battlefield, were unusually nervous, and our limbs were stiffened and sore from over exertion. As soon as our foe was found to be cavalry, the excitement was materially allayed, for nothing afforded the regiment more delight than to have a scrap with them whenever a chance presented itself.

One little fellow of C Company, a new recruit, was particularly rattled, with pallid cheeks and trembling limbs. He advanced with the rest of us, determined to stand by his colors, let the consequences be what they may—an illustration of many cases which occurred under similar circumstances of "triumph of mind over matter." When Lieutenant Vaughn of his company called out in a loud voice, "Cavalry, boys, cavalry; this is no fight, only a frolic; give it to 'em," the little fellow exclaimed, "Well, I will be dog-goned if we ain't got the best Lieutenant in this whole army." Cool and with steady aim he commenced firing. Doubtless his gallant Lieutenant felt flattered and grateful for the compliment. Only a few fitly spoken words at the proper time on the firing line has often revived the spirits of many.[55]

In the confusion Sam Whitworth[56] of F Company, not seeing me in his front, threw his rifle around to his right as the Vermonters[57] came down in gallant style from that direction, and struck me on the left side of my head with the barrel of his piece and fired. I was only shocked for an instant but brave old Sam never tired afterwards with apologies for his carelessness, when discussing Gettysburg around our campfire.

When Sam fired, the Union troopers leading the charge were not ten paces from us, and our whole line scattered along the edge of the timber was pouring a deadly fire into their ranks. A young trooper's beautiful sorrel mare fell shot in the breast only a few paces from our line. The trooper came down with her, standing erect on his feet, astride of her. Instead of surrendering he quickly threw up his carbine and discharged it directly in our faces, but fortunately no harm was done. Then, throwing down his gun, he jumped from over his horse and ran. A puff of dust flew out of the blouse which never covered a braver heart, as the bullet penetrated between the shoulders, and he fell, meeting the same fate as his horse.

Clearing our front we rapidly advanced eastward across the open field.[58] In the meantime several other regiments had reached that part of the field from the left of the division under orders from General Law, and were scattered in every direction, apparently from our position, all intermingled with the Union cavalry. In the direction of Captain Reilly's battery could be seen a small force of Union cavalry, which appeared to a few of us to be surrendering, as we imagined we could discover them displaying a flag of truce. However, before reaching that part of the field the firing continued, and those of the enemy not killed and captured after the firing ceased, escaped back into the Union lines.

We advanced on up near the battery and there learned that the officer in charge of the flanking movement, Brigadier General Farnsworth, had been killed and that he wore a long light-colored havelock which we had mistaken for a white flag, and that at the time he was trying to rally his scattered and badly defeated troopers, and make an effort to regain his lines.

I heard that evening two or three versions of how General Farnsworth met his untimely death, and have been told others since. None of the 4th Alabama that I can remember were sufficiently close to witness it. Lieutenant Adrian of the 44th Alabama, at the time General Farnsworth with his few followers appeared to some of the 4th Alabama to be surrendering, had advanced sufficiently close for General Farnsworth to draw his pistol and order him to surrender. Adrian replied with a volley from his carbine and the rifles of those nearby, unhorsing Farnsworth and two or three of his troopers. The latter, with his pistol still in his hand showed no disposition to surrender. Adrian walked up to him and remarked, "Now *you* can surrender, sir." Preferring death to captivity, with an oath that he would not surrender, he turned his pistol on his own body and fired, expiring almost instantly. Lieutenant Adrian was one of the best known and most popular of the company officers in the brigade, and was afterwards promoted to a captaincy for his gallantry. This is his version of the affair as he related it to us, and I believe it to be the correct one.

A squad of us stepped over to old Captain Reilly's battery. Some of the gunners laughingly informed us that they had a hot time defending their guns but they had knocked two cavalrymen from their mounts with a rammer and captured them. Reub Nix, who is mentioned as having made a good haul after the battle of Fredericksburg, climbed over a fence as we sauntered over the field, to examine the pockets of some dead cavalrymen. He returned in a few minutes with a roll of green-backs. The 1st Texas was, before the cavalry charge, on picket behind a low stone fence, protecting our right flank, not far from where we then were. The 4th Alabama was ordered down to relieve them. They stated that the Union cavalry leaped over the fence and were on them before they had time to fire, and as the troopers never halted to capture them, they jumped on the opposite side and continued firing until the cavalry got out of range of their rifles. We held this advanced position until some time after dark. We were then ordered to the rear, and [to] connect to the remainder of the brigade on the right.

It has been demonstrated that heavy cannonading causes rain. In this terrible battle through which we had just passed, and in which more cannons were used than any two other armies ever experienced, we knew it was sure to come. The night of the 3rd rain came in torrents and continued for several days. All of the 4th we remained quietly in our position. A victory on this day for General Meade would have been such a nice present to send Mr. Lincoln.

Our aggressive Commander-in-Chief had fought his little army against superior numbers in a strong position until there was little left to him in numbers and ammunition. All that day we acted on the defensive, inviting attack. As General Meade would not attack him in the open field, General Lee began his retrograde movements in direction of the Potomac early on the morning of the 5th.

All our seriously wounded were left at Gettysburg. When the regiment took its departure, several were permitted to go by the hospital and bid them farewell. Among those left is remembered Captain W. W. Leftwich, who was mortally wounded,[59] and Lieutenants Breedlove and Roper, and W. C. Ward,[60] who, although thought to be mortally wounded, recovered. At this time the Union authorities would not permit the exchange of officers. A member of Breedlove's company (B) removed his cap, which by the gold braid indicated Breedlove's rank, and placed his own over the face of his wounded officer. Lieutenant Colonel Scruggs tore the braid from his hat and took Roper's better one, knowing that should Roper recover, it would be a long time before he should need one.

General A. P. Hill's Corps moved out first, ours next. The rear of the Third Corps did not get away until nearly noon of the 5th.[61] Ours being the centre Corps, General Lee placed the prisoners, about 4,000 of them, under our charge. He paroled 2,000 before we left.

We proceeded across the mountain by way of Fairfield to Hagerstown through a terrible rainstorm, reaching there on the 6th. We never left a battlefield more leisurely, after defeating the enemy on other fields, than we retreated from this.

We took up position a few miles from Hagerstown, threw up a good and safe line of works, and from then until the night of the 13th of July awaited an attack, ready and anxious to meet our old adversary. For the last few days after the enemy had sat down in our front and fortified, there was more or less skirmishing along some part of our line, which extended in a semi-circle, with both flanks resting near the Potomac. In our rear was our pontoon bridge at Falling Waters, and the ford at Williamsport.

General Meade afterwards reported to a committee of Congress that his army when in our front from the 6th to 13th of July had been increased to about one hundred thousand men.⁶² The field returns of the Army of Northern Virginia made out on the 10th of July as we lay in position awaiting the attack show only 40,485 effectives for duty. The remnant of Pickett's division and the artillery of A. P. Hill's Corps were not included. General Lee, having every reason to believe that General Meade would attack, issued the following patriotic address:

> Headquarters Army of Northern Va.
> July 11th, 1863
>
> GENERAL ORDERS NO. 76
> After long and trying marches, endured with the fortitude that has ever characterized the soldiers of the Army of Northern Virginia, you have penetrated the country of our enemies, and recalled to the defense of their own soil those who were engaged in the invasion of ours.
>
> You have fought a fierce and sanguinary battle, which, if not attended with the success that has hitherto crowned your efforts, was marked by the same heroic spirit that has commanded the respect of your enemies, the gratitude of your country, and the admiration of mankind.
>
> Once more you are called upon to meet the army from which you have won on so many fields a name that will never die.
>
> Once more the eyes of your countrymen are turned upon you, and again do wives and sisters, fathers, mothers, and helpless children lean for defense on your strong arms and brave hearts.
>
> Let every soldier remember that on his courage and fidelity depends all that makes life worth having, the freedom of his country, the honor of his people, and the security of his home. Let each heart grow strong in the remembrance of our glorious past, and in the thought of the inestimable blessings for which we contend, and, invoking the assistance of that Divine Power which has so signally blessed our former efforts, let us go forth in confidence to secure the peace and safety of our country.
>
> Soldiers! Your old enemy is before you! Win from him honors worthy of your righteous cause—worthy of your comrades dead on so many illustrious fields.
>
> R. E. LEE, General⁶³

On the night of the 13th of July orders were issued to recross the Potomac, Ewell's Corps by the ford at Williamsport and Longstreet and Hill on the bridge at Falling Waters. In the forenoon on the 14th the 4th Alabama reached the bridge, after floundering through mud and rain for at least ten hours. When the front of the regiment reached the Virginia shore, General Lee, who was sitting on old Traveler on the bank of the river, ordered Lieutenant Colonel Scruggs to file us to the left out of line, with instructions to remain there until all of the army had crossed over, and then to take out and load the pontoons on the wagons.

He stated that a squadron of cavalry was bringing up the rear, and as soon as it should get over to proceed to taking it out. Good rifle pits had been provided for our protection, and Lieutenant Colonel Carter's[64] battalion of artillery (Reeves' battery[65] of Alabamians was a part of this battalion, of which the Honorable John Purifoy, now a state official of Alabama, was a member) left with us.

The officer in charge of the troopers, when he crossed over, informed us that there were no others left behind. But he was mistaken, for just as we untied the cable on the Maryland side, and the bridge began to swing around, a Confederate trooper came dashing at full speed and barely had time to leap from his horse and jump on the bridge. His horse, apparently as anxious to get back into old Virginia as his rider, plunged into the rapid stream and swam over to the Virginia side.[66]

We fully expected a hot time with the enemy before getting the boats, flooring and so forth out and loaded on the wagons, but we were not molested. A small force of the enemy did appear in the distance, but a few well directed shots from the artillery caused them to retire, and thus ended the Pennsylvania Campaign.

The following sad letter was written by John W. Mosely,[67] of Company "G," 4th Alabama Volunteer Infantry. Although excused from duty on account of illness, he joined his company and fought until he fell on the slopes of Little Round Top.

> Battle Field—Gettysburg.
>
> My Dear Mother:
>
> I am here a prisoner of war and mortally wounded. I can live but a few hours more at farthest. I was shot within forty yards of the enemy's lines. They have been exceedingly kind to me.
>
> I have no doubt of the final result, and hope I may live long enough to hear the shouts of victory before I die. I am very weak. Do not mourn my loss. I had hopes to have been spared, but a righteous God has ordered it otherwise and I feel prepared to trust my case in his hands. Farewell to you all.
>
> Your affectionate son,
> John

Colonel Egbert J. Jones.
Courtesy of the Alabama Department of Archives and History.

Colonel Evander M. Law, taken either late 1861 or early 1862, with other unidentified members of the 4th Alabama. Courtesy of the Cook Collection, Valentine Museum, Richmond, Virginia.

*General Evander M. Law, taken possibly in October 1862.
Courtesy of the Albert Shaw Collection, Virginia Historical Society, Richmond, Virginia.*

*Colonel Owen K. McLemore, in his pre-war Regular Army uniform.
Courtesy of the Alabama Department of Archives and History.*

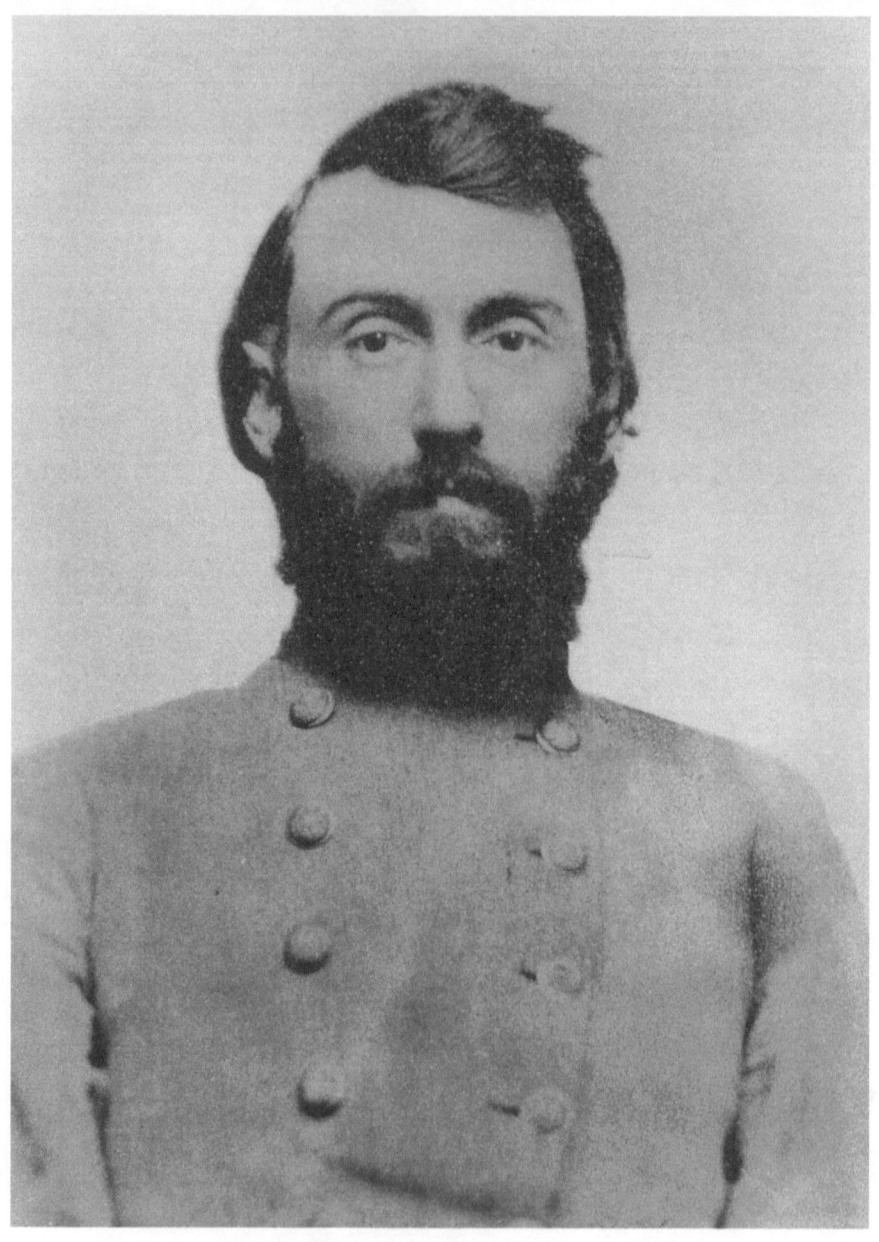

*Colonel Lawrence H. Scruggs, taken in October 1862.
Courtesy of the Alabama Department of Archives and History.*

*Major Charles L. Scott, in a post-war photo.
Courtesy of the Alabama Department of Archives and History.*

Captain Nathaniel H. R. Dawson.
Courtesy of the Alabama Department of Archives and History.

Captain Lewis E. Lindsay.
Courtesy of Robert A. Quinn and the Alabama Department of Archives and History.

Captain Edward D. Tracy.
Courtesy of the Special Collections Library, Duke University.

Captain Charles C. Sale.
Courtesy of the Alabama Department of Archives and History.

Captain Robert P. Jones.
Courtesy of the Alabama Department of Archives and History.

Captain William H. F. Lee.
Courtesy of the Alabama Department of Archives and History.

Captain Reuben V. Kidd.
Courtesy of the Alabama Department of Archives and History.

*Lieutenant John Breedlove, in a post-war photo.
Courtesy of the Alabama Department of Archives and History.*

13

From Falling Waters to Fredericksburg
July 14 to September 10, 1863

After leaving Falling Waters on the evening of the 14th, we marched via Martinsburg and Darkesville to Bunker Hill, reaching there on the 16th. Here we remained and rested until the 20th. The incessant rains had so swollen the Shenandoah that General Lee apprehended trouble in getting his army across that stream and safely through the Blue Ridge Gaps before the enemy reached there from down at Harpers Ferry.

On the 20th the 4th Alabama was hurried on to Millwood, our object being to cross and get possession of Ashby's Gap. Here we found the river past fording, the enemy in possession of the Gap and their pickets down on the river banks ready to oppose our crossing. We then marched on up the river to Front Royal. Although we found the river here much swollen and very swift, we succeeded in wading across at Berry's Ford.

At daylight on the 23rd of July we took the road from Front Royal to Linden, intending to cross at Manassas Gap. Here, too, this Gap was found in possession of the enemy with a large force of cavalry and artillery. We immediately formed line of battle and threw out a strong line of skirmishers and made such a demonstration that the enemy fell back further into the Gap late that evening. General Law, in command of the division, moved all of it that night to Chester Gap, except General Benning's brigade of Georgians and the 4th Alabama. He gave orders for us to hold our position until midnight, when we would be relieved by General A. P. Hill's Corps, which was in our rear.

It was 9 o'clock A.M. the next day before any of General Hill's troops came to our relief. We then started to overtake our division. When we reached Chester Gap it was found to be perfectly blockaded with the wagon train of General Hill's Corps and our division gone. The whole day was occupied in our efforts to pass the train, and by night, we were bivouacked only two miles beyond Flint Hill, on the east side of the mountain, and two days march in rear of our division. The 4th Alabama loved and admired General Benning and his noble Georgians; therefore, we felt "perfectly at home" and contented to be thrown with our esteemed friends the Georgians.

On the morning of the 25th we left our bivouac about daylight and halted for a short time at Gaines' Cross Roads to await the arrival of the 15th Alabama of our brigade, which had been left at a mountain road until the arrival of General Hill's vanguard to relieve it. As soon as Colonel Oates joined us, we resumed our march, General Hill's Corps still in our rear. The enemy's artillery and cavalry, which was continually hanging on our flanks, hoping to find an opportunity to pounce down on our wagon train, annoyed us a great deal.

Before reaching the ford across Hazel Run, General Hill sent forward a staff officer requesting General Benning to endeavor to get in the rear of the enemy's cavalry and either drive it off or capture it. The 4th Alabama was assigned this movement, piloted by a very willing and enthusiastic old citizen, who guided the regiment over a circuitous and lengthy route, over very rough ground, in order to reach the rear of a body of cavalry. The old citizen led us up to within fifty yards of the column and directly on its flank. Before being aware of our presence, we fired a volley and without scarcely returning the fire, the column disappeared and their artillery limbered up and beat a hasty retreat. We had been successfully led by the old fellow in between the main force and the picket line.

Lieutenant William T. Turner, a private of the regiment whose name I do not remember, and myself ran up to a road leading through a woods pasture with the hope of intercepting the pickets, presuming they would on hearing the firing in their rear return in haste to join their comrades. We had scarcely reached the pasture gate before we saw the pickets approaching at a gallop. All could have easily escaped from only infantry, but we succeeded in capturing one of them, who galloped directly up to the gate. Lieutenant Turner and the private with us claimed the contents of the trooper's saddle pockets. The horse and saddle fell to my share.

Lieutenant Turner appropriated a toothbrush among his share of the spoils. When asked what use he proposed to make of it, he remarked that he valued it more than any other trophy we had captured which fell to his lot, as he intended to give it a thorough boiling and use it for the purpose intended.

We were not molested any more during our march. We had been delayed here for nearly a half a day, had marched four or five miles over a very rough country and fought quite an exciting little skirmish, after which we returned to the road and crossed Hazel Run, reaching Culpeper the next day. We found our brigade in camp here, where we remained, enjoying a much needed rest, until the first of August.

From Culpeper Court House, or near there, we marched to Fredericksburg, and went into regular camp, reaching there about the 6th. We had now returned to nearly the same position we had vacated about two months before, completing a most arduous campaign, having marched about four hundred miles and fought in one of the most sanguinary engagements of the Civil War.[1] After quietly resting here until the second week in September, General Lee ordered General Longstreet to report to General Bragg near Chattanooga with our division and that of General McLaws.[2]

14

Chickamauga Campaign
September 10 to October 8, 1863

All necessary arrangements having been completed for our transfer by rail to join the Army of Tennessee, by the 11th the 4th and 48th Alabama were embarked on one section, and proceeded on their cramped, uncomfortable, and tiresome journey to Georgia. General Bragg was falling back in front of Rosecrans'[1] army from Chattanooga, and was then in the vicinity of Ringgold, Georgia. General Hood had recovered sufficiently from his wound received at Gettysburg to take charge of our division before we left Virginia.

In addition to our four brigades, Jenkins'[2] brigade of South Carolinians, then in South Carolina recruiting their strength, was ordered to report in Georgia to General Hood. These five brigades and General McLaws' four composed the nine brigades sent from Virginia under the command of General Longstreet, and not the whole of the Corps, as has been currently reported. Only five of these reached their destination in time to take part in the Chickamauga battle of the 19th and 20th of September.[3]

The people along our route were generous and kind. Several stops were made to permit the men to partake of lunches prepared for our benefit. All of our horses and ambulances were ordered to reach us over the highways. Our artillery did not reach us until some time after the battle. For want of transportation from Atlanta, we remained there for twenty-four hours and reached Ringgold, where we disembarked on the night of the 17th. Everything, except the guns and cartridge boxes, was left behind. Our surgeons, surgical instruments, and litters were in the rear. We were in no condition whatever to go into battle.

We saw several commands of General Bragg's army during the day preceding the battle. They were all poorly equipped, using rough road wagons for conveying the wounded, and were deficient in artillery. General Lee had, before we left Virginia, caused to be issued to us clothes and shoes. Frequently, Bragg's men proposed to exchange a "Bragg" jacket for a "Lee" jacket, and would make a good many comments about General Lee requiring his Brigade and Field Officers to walk. General Benning carried an axe on his shoulder as he marched at the head of his Georgians. A member of our regiment asked him why he did not carry a blanket. He replied that an axe kept him warmer than two blankets. The nights were becoming cool, but there had been an extended drought and the marching, counter-marching and maneuvering of the troops made wading through the dust very disagreeable.

On the 17th, 18th and 19th, General Rosecrans of the Union army and General Bragg maneuvered for positions, and there was constant skirmishing on some parts of the line, and sometimes there would be quite a brisk engagement and desultory fighting. On the evening of the 19th, the 4th Alabama was standing in line of battle in the rear while quite a battle was progressing in our front. We opened our line for a battery to pass going to the front. Lieutenant Newsome recognized a schoolmate as its captain and remarked to him that should the enemy capture his battery to let us know and we would recover it for him, which we did the next day.

Colonel Sheffield of the 48th, senior colonel, was in charge of the brigade, General Law of the division and General Hood of the Corps. General Longstreet had the honor of commanding the left wing and General Polk[4] the right. General Hood came by to see us as we stood in line, and informed us that, as we were not prepared, we would not be ordered to go into battle that evening. Generals Polk and Forrest[5] also came by, the first and only time we ever saw them.

Colonel Sheffield in some manner secured transportation for, and was permitted to bring, his horse, a magnificent iron grey with long flowing mane and tail, presented to him by his regiment of mountain boys of North Alabama. He was placed in a car attached to our train. Somewhere en route the door of his old car flew open and he jumped out while the train was going at full speed. The train was stopped and he was caught and placed back in his car, uninjured from his rash leap.

While we stood there congratulating ourselves on the good fortune of not having to go into battle, the firing in our immediate front became closer and heavier. Colonel Sheffield, waving his hat, came dashing along our front on his gallant grey, and cried out in that tremulous and quavering manner of voice peculiar to him: "Forward, 4th Alabamians, forward! You have a name that will never, never die," and forward we went.

Advancing blindly and rapidly through a dense undergrowth, we ran unexpectedly right into a column of infantry, which poured a deadly fire into our ranks.[6] Colonel Scruggs was here shot down. The ball had entered close to his sword belt buckle and had come out through his sword belt on the opposite side. We pronounced him mortally wounded, and so informed him, but on closer examination found that the ball had struck the edge of the buckle and passed halfway around his body between the flesh and his undergarment, very much bruising him, but scarcely breaking the skin.

For a moment the regiment was stunned and dazed from the suddenness of the fire. Then, before the enemy had time to reload, with an unearthly yell, we again went forward, the enemy retreating out into and beyond the Chattanooga Road into the woods on the opposite side. Here we were exposed to both their artillery and infantry, and were apparently too much in advance of our right and left flanks. Nothing is more demoralizing to a body of American soldiers, veterans or not, than finding they are, or are about to be, flanked. Lieutenant Newsome, a gallant officer, whose valuable services were prolonged until during our last struggle around Richmond, when he fell mortally wounded, pointed to the left in an opening on the Chattanooga Road, and called my attention to a body of the enemy driving back a column of Bragg's troops. Without thinking what effect it might produce, he called out to his Captain, W. T. Kershaw,[7] who was some distance from us, "Captain, we are about to be flanked." He replied, "Go to h——l, Buck Newsome, don't you see those are our own men?"

Major Coleman, perceiving the danger we were in, moved us back a short distance and threw the two left companies out as skirmishers. As usual in going into battle, the Texans and 3rd Arkansas were on our left and were ordered to keep closed on our brigade. But after getting into the road, a heavy force of the enemy appearing on their left flank, General Law directed them to change front. This caused our left flank to be unprotected. Fortunately, only a small force had penetrated between us and the Texans, which were easily driven back by our two companies thrown out as skirmishers, reinforced by two companies each from the 15th, 47th and 48th Alabama. In the rapid rush through the timber we entirely lost the 44th. We remained in our position until dark and were then moved farther around to the left, where we secured rations and remained all night.

This battle on our part of the line was a most bungling affair.[8] We were in an exposed position, without a solitary piece of artillery, confronted by a strong force of both infantry and batteries.

Our losses being consolidated in the two days battle, there is no record of this evening's battle, but we carried with us, when we retired, on a tarpaulin cloth, having no litters, as grand a soldier as ever went into battle. The loss of Captain Reuben Kidd[9] was deeply deplored by the whole regiment. He was a splendid specimen of manhood and his clear ringing voice could be distinctly heard from left to right of the regiment, amid the din of battle.

Here, for the first and only time, we drew a ration of rice flour. The men made it into biscuits, and the "shortening" being quite short, they managed to eat some of them while warm and freshly baked, but when they became cold, they were as hard and equally as durable as marble or bronze. It is a fact that some of these same biscuits were taken back to Virginia eight months afterwards.

The next morning was Sunday, September 20, 1863. The right wing under General Polk was to begin the attack at daylight and, if possible, push back General Rosecrans' left wing, until the Lafayette and Chattanooga Road was uncovered, and cut off Rosecrans from Chattanooga. Then we were to move forward and crush him. General Polk was late getting into action,[10] and after engaging the enemy made no progress in the accomplishment of his object. General Longstreet waited on him until about 11 o'clock, and then with a "soldier's eye," saw it was time to act, and threw forward his first line. The 4th Alabama was in the second.[11]

After the first line had been engaged for some time, we received orders to go forward. Advancing over a good deal of ground through which the enemy had been driven, we proceeded through the timbers, over the dead, dying, and wounded. One peculiar thing we noticed and had never seen before were a good many ramrods buried partly in the trees, that the Yankees, in their haste to fire, had not, in loading, withdrawn from their guns.

The 4th Alabama advanced to the foot of quite a steep hill, and halted on the edge of the timber. The slope of the hill was bare and on its crest, in full view of us, were two batteries supported by infantry, a very difficult position to assault and capture.[12] For some time we kept up a rapid fire, the men protecting themselves in the best manner possible, under cover of the hill and the timber. Old man Quimby[13] of E Company was exceptionally tall and lank. He stood erect and alone out in the open, taking deliberate aim at the gunners. When told he was exposing himself too much and to get under cover, he replied, "No, a man born to be hung will never be shot," believing "what is written is written." He came out of the battle unharmed, but a regiment that would adhere strictly to his belief would soon find a bullet that was moulded for each member of it.

On both the right and left of the 4th Alabama, our division was forcing the enemy back, relieving the pressure in our front. We charged up the hill, under the fire of both artillery and the infantry supports, and succeeded in securing six pieces of artillery before they could be withdrawn, our regiment running them down the hill by hand.[14] The rest of the guns and all of the caissons had disappeared. We discovered, in a sink-hole near where the battery had been stationed, several of the gunners, who were taken prisoners and sent to the rear. Nearly every man had fired his last cartridge. One of Bragg's batteries remained with us until we reached the hill, which excited our admiration for the manner in which the gunners so bravely and energetically handled their pieces and kept in line with the regiment.

It was now about 2 o'clock. At this stage of the battle, General Longstreet says, "Hood's column broke the enemy's line near the Brotherton House, and made it wheel to the right. In making this movement Major General Hood fell severely, and it was feared, mortally wounded by a Minie ball breaking his thigh.[15] He had broken the enemy's line, however, and his own troops and those to his right and left continued to press the enemy with such spirit and force that he could not resist us. Brigadier General Law succeeded to the command of Hood's division, and Brigadier General Kershaw to the command of the two brigades [his own and Humphrey's[16]] of General McLaws' division."[17]

General Grant, in his memoirs, leaves the impression that the whole of Longstreet's Corps participated in this battle,[18] when there were only the above five little skeleton brigades, about equal to five full regiments.

The regiment this day, as it had the day before, suffered a severe loss in one among its best officers. Major Thomas Coleman fell early in the engagement, shot through the leg; he bled to death before he could be carried from the field.

Other troops which General Longstreet had held in reserve took up our movement and we retired to rest, replenish our ammunition and get rations, for we had not eaten anything since the night before. Our casualties during that day and the evening of the 19th were, killed fourteen, wounded fifty-four.

By night the enemy were in full retreat to Chattanooga and the Confederate army had gained a complete victory. Jenkins' South Carolina Brigade, having arrived after the battle, was placed in our division. General Jenkins, being senior to General Law, took command of the division. This caused a rivalry between these two officers as to who should secure the position vacated by General Hood and, unfortunately, continued until our return to Virginia in the Spring of 1864.

We found among the Army of Tennessee a former 4th Alabama private, Colonel Bush Jones,[19] commanding the 58th Alabama, and Colonel, afterwards Brigadier General, George D. Johnston,[20] a former Lieutenant of Company G, 4th Alabama, commanding the 25th Alabama.

We learned that General Bragg the next morning after this battle called on General Longstreet for suggestions. "Move instantly against Rosecrans' rear to destroy him," was the reply.[21] No doubt General Bragg adopted this view, for that evening, the 22nd, the right wing received marching orders and ours, the next morning at daylight, for a contemplated movement.

We marched about ten miles, reaching Red House Ford on the Chickamauga about noon. Remaining there for a short time, we were ordered to retrace our steps to our former position in front of Chattanooga. We then plainly saw that our victory was a fruitless one, and proved what General Longstreet so much feared when he bade General Lee farewell on our departure from Virginia. General Lee had followed General Longstreet to his horse to see him off. As the latter placed his foot in the stirrup General Lee said: "General, you must beat those people."

General Longstreet replied: "General, if you will give your orders that the enemy, when beaten, shall be destroyed, I will promise to give you victory, if I live, but I would not give the life of a single soldier of mine for a barren victory."[22] From this time until we severed our connection with the Army of Tennessee in November there was apparently no concert of action between these two officers.

15

Our Campaign in Lookout Valley
October 8 to November 4, 1863

After the Battle of Chickamauga General Bragg, satisfied with the laurels secured in his first and only complete victory, won for him by General Longstreet, contented himself with fortifying his lines in front of Chattanooga and sitting down, and permitted the enemy to do the same. All of our two divisions, Hood's and McLaws', had now arrived from Virginia and were placed on the extreme left of the army next to, and on, Lookout Mountain. We fortified and remained in our position until the 8th of October,[1] when the 4th Alabama, alone, was ordered across the mountain into Lookout Valley. The object being to act as sharpshooters, the men were ensconced along the overhanging bluffs of the Tennessee River on Raccoon Mountain, the river there being about three hundred yards wide, to shoot down the mules of the wagon trains of the enemy which were compelled to pass, after crossing over from Chattanooga, along the narrow road between the bluff and river, on the opposite side. We held the railway on the south side from Lookout Valley to nearly opposite Bridgeport, thus forcing the Union Army to secure their supplies by wagon train from Bridgeport and Stephenson, their nearest bases.

The day after reaching the valley we were reinforced by the 15th Alabama, Colonel Oates in command. He brought over with him a section of Barret's battery,[2] which he had great difficulty in getting up and over the mountain into the valley. Colonel Oates deployed his men and picketed from Brown's Ferry, which is nine miles by the river below Chattanooga, down to our line. His position was principally along the river bank, ours up among the bluffs. The line occupied by the two regiments extended about five miles. It was understood that the other regiments of the brigade, the "fortycans," as we called them, would be sent over to support us.

We secured sufficient supplies for our needs in the valley and were progressing very well in our isolated retreat, shooting mules to our heart's content, and enjoying the sport immensely, until we had reduced the Union army to half rations by forcing it to secure supplies by a more difficult and circuitous mountain road. On the 25th of October we were very much surprised to learn that the rest of the brigade, the 44th, 47th, and 48th Alabama, which had been ordered over to support us, had been ordered back across the mountain to the main army. We were perfectly aware that we were inflicting great damage on the enemy, and that we would not be permitted to remain there much longer without an effort on the part of the enemy to dispossess us.

We had brought our Whitworth rifles from Virginia with us. These were placed down the river on our extreme left to shoot down the front teams, which after being done, the road was entirely blocked. We then proceeded in a leisurely manner to use our English rifles. The road was too narrow between the bluff and river for the teams to turn around or escape in any manner, and they were compelled to stand until all were shot down. I saw one of the Whitworth rifles, an English gun, with a globe sight, carrying a large ball, a few of which had run the blockade in the hands of one of our sharpshooters, kill two mules at one shot, the heavy missile passing through their necks.[3]

On the 16th, a few days after we arrived here, General Grant[4] was placed over the Mississippi Department by the Union War Office, in which was included the department of the Union army opposing us here. At the same time General Rosecrans was relieved and General Thomas[5] placed in command of the Union forces at Chattanooga. General Thomas, after taking command, gave such a gloomy account of the situation that General Grant deemed it necessary to repair to this point in person and remedy, if possible, the condition of affairs. He gives the condition as he found it after his arrival there on the 24th of October: "A retreat would have been almost certain annihilation, for the enemy, occupying positions within gunshot of and overlooking our fortifications, would unquestionably have pursued our retreating forces. Already more than ten thousand mules and horses had perished in supplying half rations to the troops by the long and tedious routes from Stephenson and Bridgeport to Chattanooga over Walden's Ridge. They could not have been supplied another week. The enemy was evidently fully apprised of our condition in Chattanooga and of the necessity of our establishing a new and shorter line by which to obtain supplies, or we could not maintain our position."[6]

General Grant, with his unlimited resources, was not long in taking advantage of the weak and frivolous attempts made by General Bragg, and the half-hearted manner of General Longstreet of conducting affairs on the left which were entrusted to his care. It was plainly apparent to all in the regiment that General Longstreet, who had distinguished himself by the able manner in which he handled the left wing of Bragg's army in the Battle of Chickamauga, that his interest, after this battle, began to wane, as it did before the Battle of Gettysburg. If he was ever over on our side of the mountain while we were on duty there, no one of the regiment saw him. We were left alone and to our own resources. Of the General Officers, General Law was the only one who studied, kept in touch with, and understood thoroughly the perilous position in which we were placed, and he was perfectly ignored by those higher in authority.

Colonel Oates, in his book, gives a graphic account of the exciting part played by the gallant old 15th during our stay in the valley. Among other things, he says that on the 24th of October he notified General Jenkins, our division commander, of his apprehension of an attack on his part of the line. On the evening of the 27th he received a message from General Duke,[7] commanding the remnant of Morgan's[8] cavalry, and operating at that time on the south side of the Tennessee between our position (Raccoon Mountain) and Bridgeport. A heavy force of the enemy, consisting of infantry and artillery, was attempting to cross the river below Raccoon Mountain, near Bridgeport, and that he was powerless to prevent them, and that when they did so, and advance in our direction and turn Raccoon Mountain, we would be cut off and captured.

These forces alluded to by General Duke were the re-enforcements sent from Virginia to augment the Union army in Chattanooga (the same troops we had fought in Virginia),[9] which had reached Bridgeport by rail and were crossing over to the south side with the intention of marching up through Lookout Valley by way of Brown's Ferry to Chattanooga. Colonel Oates says he immediately sent a message to General Longstreet apprising him of this fact (for which he received a receipt), stating that he feared an attack that night or early the next morning. No response, he says, ever came.[10]

The bend in the Tennessee River below Chattanooga begins at that city and curves around in the shape of a horseshoe, Chattanooga being at the heel of the shoe at its upper end, and Brown's Ferry exactly opposite at the lower heel. It is only a short distance, about two miles, across the heel from Chattanooga to the Ferry, but nine miles around by the river. The scenery in the vicinity of Raccoon Mountain is grand and wild. The bluffs on both sides of the river, which almost approach the water's edge, loom up hundreds of feet perpendicularly, while the river winds its turbulent and tortuous way through them. The writer, having had occasion to visit this locality at different times since the Civil War, the topography of the country and many of the incidents which occurred here in the fall of 1863 are still kept green in his memory.

At Brown's Ferry is a series of ridges running parallel with the river, the road from that point running through a gap in the ridge up Lookout Valley and crossing the railway at Wauhatchie. Extending back from the river up the valley for three or four miles and dividing the valley near about its center for some distance is a succession of hills about two hundred feet high, with precipitous and very thickly timbered slopes, what we termed "hog backs," one after another, with very narrow crests, in many places not over two to six feet across. The position of the 4th Alabama was different from that of the 15th Alabama. Being up among the bluffs on Raccoon Mountain, no direct attack could be made upon us from the river. The only way to get us out was by a flank movement of the enemy.

Our duties, which are summed up in a few words by Colonel Oates, were: "Law sent the 4th Alabama to do this perilous and all-important work down to the point of Raccoon to act as sharpshooters and prevent the use of the river and the wagon road on the other side of the river; and the 15th Alabama to picket the river from the right of the 4th up to Brown's Ferry..."[11] These were the only instructions received by the 4th Alabama.

The transportation of the 4th Alabama consisted of one poor old pack mule, which we kept busy packing supplies up the mountain. We surrounded ourselves with a strong picket line day and night. Sampey[12] of E Company fired his gun one night and called the Corporal of the Guard and created thereby, among the few of us not on duty, no little consternation and uneasiness. When the corporal reached the post he was informed by Sampey that, hearing someone approaching, and not obeying his challenge, he fired, and was positive he had killed a Yankee, for he heard him struggling in the dry leaves. He and the corporal then made an examination, and found that Sampey had shot a large coon squarely through the head.

One cool frosty morning, October 27, 1863, just before daylight, when the fog was hanging low and heavy along the Tennessee River, picket firing was heard up above us among Colonel Oates' men. As the firing continued for some time, we became very apprehensive that the enemy was forcing a crossing in Colonel Oates' front at Brown's Ferry. The firing had scarcely ceased when our pickets from the extreme right came running in and stated that the 15th Alabama pickets, after making a gallant resistance against a large force, had been driven out, and that Colonel Oates was brought out badly wounded.[13]

At that time most of the men of the 4th Alabama were off duty; "D" and "I" were the only companies on picket. We hastily called in the nearest men and sent messages to the others to get out the best they could. Our cooking utensils were quickly strapped on our mule and we were soon ready to evacuate Raccoon Mountain. From some cause the mule, in the confusion, not placing our utensils on his back to exactly suit his fancy, got away from the man leading him and went braying and kicking down the mountain trail, the boys laughing and yelling and picking up scattered utensils.

We flanked around, crossed the road from Brown's Ferry to Wauhatchie and safely got over the "hog back" ridges next to Lookout Mountain. On our left, as we retreated, the enemy was seen on the ridges with axes busy felling trees and making breastworks. After getting in the valley we surrounded our mule and succeeded in capturing him, after he had kicked off everything except one skillet handle. Out of breath, we fell back slowly across the bridge which spans Lookout Creek and retired under the crest of Lookout Mountain, where we found Oates' reserves and the section of Barret's battery, the latter firing an occasional shot at the enemy fortifying on the ridges. General Law came over and brought back our other three regiments and our friends, the Texans and the 3rd Arkansas, that evening. That night D Company came in; of Company I four failed to get out and were captured. This was our only loss. The 15th Alabama pickets also got out and came in that night.

Colonel Timothy R. Stanley of the 18th Ohio Volunteers, who had in Chattanooga the task of superintending of boats, crews and so forth for the expedition which was for the purpose of dislodging the 15th and 4th Alabama, says in his official report: "I directed boats' crews to consist of one corporal and four men, and each of two boats to be under command of a sergeant, each detail to be under command of a commissioned officer. I afterwards added a large flat, in which I carried 60 men. The pontoons each carried 25 men besides the boats' crews, making in the whole fleet fifty two boats and 1600 men."[14] This expedition left Chattanooga at three o'clock on the morning of the 27th of October and floated with the current down to Brown's Ferry, where it surprised the pickets of the 15th Alabama, disembarked, attacked, and drove the 15th Alabama away. This Union force was only a part of General Hazen's[15] brigade. The rest of his command, together with General Turchin's[16] brigade, was sent across the narrow neck of land from Chattanooga to Brown's Ferry. General Hazen is remembered as the first husband of Admiral Dewey's wife.

Boats were near at hand to bring them over as soon as a lodgment was secured by the expedition, which came down by water. General Law reconnoitered their position and found nothing could be done, as the enemy was now perfectly secure in his position, and had about completed a pontoon bridge across the river at Brown's Ferry. The river was virtually opened from Bridgeport to Chattanooga, and the Union army was safe.

The enemy was perfectly elated because of their easy dislodgment of the 15th and 4th Alabama and were greatly surprised to meet with such little opposition, for they fully expected a large force to meet them, and to be compelled to fight and to fight hard for the coveted prize. General Hooker, in his official report, says: "From its [Lookout Valley's] proximity to the enemy's line of investment around Chattanooga, and his facilities for detaching heavily from his masses, it was apprehended that the enemy would make unusual efforts to prevent the transfer of its possession, as a failure on our part to establish new communications involved a fact of no less magnitude than the necessity for the early evacuation of Chattanooga, with the abandonment of much of our artillery and trains."[17]

[As] for the irreparable loss of Lookout Valley to the Confederate forces, General Bragg attributed it to General Longstreet and he in turn to General Bragg. This disaffection and want of cooperation, it matters not upon whom the burden of blame should fall, whether upon one or both, was deplorable, when concert of action by those highest in authority was so essential to the success of our arms.

On the 28th of October, the way now being open to the enemy over the short route from Bridgeport to Chattanooga, General Hooker, in command of our old antagonists of Virginia, the 11th and 12th Corps, having crossed at Bridgeport to the south side, was marching in direction of Lookout Valley, on his way to Chattanooga. That same evening General Longstreet met by appointment General Bragg on Lookout Mountain, for the purpose of examining the new position of the enemy at Brown's Ferry. While there one of General Longstreet's signal party guided him and the commander-in-chief about a mile distant to a projection on the mountain, where they looked down into Lookout Valley and saw a column of Hooker's command file past and unite with Generals Hazen and Turchin's forces at Brown's Ferry. They afterwards saw what they presumed to be the rear guard, estimated by them not to exceed fifteen hundred men, halt and go into bivouac about three miles from, and in the rear of, the main force. They conceived the idea of capturing this force, with our division and McLaws', by a night attack.

This rear guard had no sooner halted than General Longstreet sent orders to General Jenkins, commanding our division, to concentrate all of his command in Lookout Valley that night. Our brigade and the Texans and 3rd Arkansas were already on the west side of the mountain, in charge of General Law. The rest of the division, Jenkins' brigade, commanded by Colonel Bratton[18] and General Benning's Georgians, were on the east side of the mountain with the main army, and could not reach us until after dark, at which time they would be concealed from the enemy's batteries while crossing the mountain. General Longstreet says he estimated our four brigades at five thousand men. Our other Virginia division (McLaws') failed to put in an appearance as promised. General Bragg failed to send it, and General Longstreet omitted to countermand the order to attack, after finding that it would not join in the proposed engagement.

The 4th Alabama received orders that evening to be ready to cross the bridge over Lookout Creek and take our position. The night of the 28th was a beautiful moonlit night, and as soon as our other two brigades from east of the mountain reached us, we moved out. I suppose it was about midnight before getting fully under way.

After crossing the bridge we were ordered to take possession of the ridge, or "hog back" before mentioned, which ran parallel with the road from Brown's Ferry to Wauhatchie. Before reaching the ridge we threw out our pickets and were soon notified that it was unoccupied by the enemy. We then quietly climbed to the top and threw together a few chunks and logs for our protection. We secured here a prisoner who was very drunk, and the only information we could obtain from him was that he belonged to Howard's Corps.[19] As the other regiments arrived they formed on our right and left, the 4th Alabama in the center. The Texans and 3rd Arkansas were then brought up and placed on our left. Colonel Law commanded both brigades. Colonel Sheffield of the 48th was in charge of our brigade.

Our position along the ridge overlooking the road was within about thirty yards of the road on our left and about one hundred and fifty or two hundred yards from it on the right. There was quite an interval, perhaps three quarters of a mile, intervening between our right and the river. To protect us at this point, Colonel Sheffield placed a company of the 15th Alabama as videttes, and each regiment threw out in its front a picket line. We were supposed to be about midway between the force at Brown's Ferry and the supposed rear guard up at Wauhatchie.

Our instructions were to hold this force near Brown's Ferry from reinforcing the rear guard at Wauhatchie while General Jenkins with his brigade, under Colonel Bratton, and General Benning's Georgians in reserve, was to either capture or disperse it. As the South Carolinians had never been on the west side of the mountain, Colonel Bratton requested Colonel Scruggs to furnish him a guide. Two or three of the best scouts in the regiment were furnished him.

We remained in our position for an hour or two patiently awaiting

Colonel Bratton's attack on the rear guard. When he did open it, everything in the Union camp became busy. Our videttes reported a heavy force moving toward Wauhatchie from Brown's Ferry to the support of the rear guard. Our orders were not to fire until the head of the column had reached our left. A volley was then fired by the whole brigade, which created a great deal of confusion in the enemy's ranks and sent them back towards the river. In a short time they rallied and made a desperate effort to charge up the ridge, and were again driven off.

Other Union forces arrived on our left and the right of the Texans and 3rd Arkansas. These were also repulsed. There was an interval of several minutes and then another effort was made to push us back, but we were secure in our well-protected position and, as in the other attempts, the enemy failed. Colonel Sheffield, thinking his right not sufficiently secure, sent two more companies in that direction to be deployed, one from the 15th Alabama and the other from the 44th Alabama. Still finding that his right was not sufficiently protected, he informed General Law, who sent the 4th Texas, which promptly took position on our extreme right and had scarcely reached there before a determined attack was made on the front of the 15th, 44th and 4th. The 15th and 4th succeeded in clearing their front, but the enemy rushed through the interval made by taking out the company from the 44th and broke its line. In an instant the 4th Alabama, seeing the perilous position in which we were placed, made a right wheel at charge bayonets, [and] with a yell and rush through the thick undergrowth, losing nearly all of our headgear, re-established the line.

The old 44th, all of whom were good soldiers, rallied and were soon back in line again, but several had received slight bayonet wounds. This was the last attempt by the enemy to drive us from our position. As it was impossible for our two brigades on the right to prevent, as instructed, the enemy from rushing re-enforcements from Brown's Ferry by our front to the relief of their rear guard at Wauhatchie, General Law, fearing the South Carolina brigade would be surrounded and captured, dispatched to Colonel Bratton notifying him of the fact, and suggested a withdrawal of his brigade, which he did in good order, carrying out several of his wounded.

General Law in the meantime sent the 1st Texas back to Lookout Creek bridge to hold it in the event the enemy should follow us. Our two brigades then withdrew from the ridges and retired in an orderly manner across the bridge, the enemy making no effort to pursue.

We had emerged from a veritable hornet's nest of vastly superior numbers, and had it not been for our promptness in retiring before the enemy recovered from the surprise of the suddenness of our attack, every one of us would have been surrounded and killed or captured. This night attack on our part is referred to by General Alexander,[20] Chief of Artillery of our Corps, as one of the most foolhardy adventures of the war. General Law states in his official report that when General Jenkins came over to join us on the night of the 28th of October, he (Law) ventured to remark to him that four small brigades were insufficient for the accomplishment of the end in view, and that nothing but failure would be the result.

"I was satisfied," he said, "from close observation, that a large force had been thrown across the river at Brown's Ferry from Chattanooga, that one corps had passed my position moving to that point from Bridgeport and that another of the same strength was following."[21]

General Jenkins replied "that he had positive orders to proceed on the expedition," and, of course, could do nothing but obey.[22] This minor affair has, at the hands of Union soldiers, received its full quota of exaggeration. They give glowing accounts of heroism displayed, the immense number of killed, wounded and captured Rebels and the complete rout of Longstreet's entire Corps.[23]

General Hooker, in his bombastic official report of this battle of Wauhatchie, as he terms it, says: "Of the loss of the enemy, it cannot fall short of 1500. Geary[24] buried 153 Rebel carcasses on his front alone . . . The force opposed to us consisted of two of Longstreet's divisions."[25] General Grant, who was not present, relied on the reports received from those who participated in the engagement, and writes as history incidents for which there is no foundation in fact.[26]

The casualties of the 4th Alabama were one man killed—Anderson[27] of E Company—and not a man wounded or captured. Our loss in the four brigades amounted to thirty-four killed, three hundred and fifteen wounded and sixty-nine missing. Almost the entire loss fell on the South Carolinians. The enemy's loss, according to its official report, was four hundred and twenty, about equally divided between the two Corps engaged.

Whatever the errors committed and indifference displayed by our officers who inaugurated this movement, the men of the line performed with zeal and promptness all that was possible for them to accomplish. The 4th Alabama, in the Lookout Valley Expedition, accomplished more and inflicted greater damage to the enemy, with less loss to itself, than in any other campaign in which it participated during its four years service.

The regiment, the next night, crossed to the east side of the mountain, and sat down with General Bragg's army in front of Chattanooga.

16

Knoxville Campaign
November 4 to December 23, 1863

On November 5, 1863, the regiment bade adieu to Bragg's army and marched to Tyner's Station on the East Tennessee & Virginia Railway. From here we were ordered to Tunnel Hill to take the cars for Sweetwater, Tennessee. After much delay we finally reached that place, and found that the rest of our division had gone on to Loudon. We then overtook the division, crossing on a pontoon below the town.

Brigadier-General Jenkins, commanding the division, had thrown out a strong line of skirmishers in his front from Bratton's brigade. All that was required of the 4th Alabama was to follow in the rear until we reached Lenoir's Station, where the enemy was found in force. Up to this time there had been constant skirmishing by our vanguard from the time we crossed the river at Loudon. It was now the 15th of November, and it was cold and raining. On very short rations, the regiment remained in line of battle all night.

On the next morning we discovered that our guide had placed us on the wrong road and the enemy had escaped during the night leaving a large number of cut down wagons loaded with commissary, ordnance and sutlers' stores. It was a race from here to Knoxville in our efforts to intercept and bring the enemy to bay. General McLaws' division was sent on one road and ours on another, both converging at Campbell's Station about twelve miles from Lenoir's. From some alleged mismanagement, which General Longstreet attributed to General McLaws' misconduct, we failed to accomplish anything after passing Campbell's Station. The enemy again escaped and continued on to his entrenchments at Knoxville.[1]

Late that evening the regiment made a rapid march on the flank of the enemy, over stony ridges, through thick undergrowth of briars and scrub oak, without time to secure rations, with the hope of cutting off the rear of Burnside's[2] army in its rapid retreat to Knoxville. We were sorely disappointed when finally, almost exhausted and ravenously hungry, we looked over the ridge down into the road to see the extreme rear guard of the enemy hastily disappearing. The men did their work cheerfully and zealously, but it appeared that our General Officers were at cross purposes, which, of course, caused all of our toils and hardships to result in failing to accomplish our object.[3]

Before going into bivouac another effort was made to intercept and cut off a portion of the enemy's rear, but darkness coming on, we abandoned the movement and went into bivouac. The only field officer I remember being present that night was Major W. M. Robbins, and I was the only staff officer.

Our march was so hurried we had no time to secure rations, except a few Irish potatoes, and it fell to my lot to divide them out equally to the officers and men. After a careful count, with the assistance of Lieutenant William Turner of D Company, it was found that each one was entitled to two potatoes. Lieutenant Turner suggested that he and I draw straws for who should have the four. It nearly broke my heart when Turner proved to be the winner, but, fortunately, one of the men, who had obtained from a citizen a small piece of fat bacon, generously gave me a slice. In some way Major Robbins had secured about a handful of peas. We boiled his peas and my meat in an oyster can, and these, with the Major's two potatoes, which he kindly divided with me, was the menu of the Field and Staff of the 4th Alabama that night.

Early the next morning we followed on, driving the enemy towards Knoxville, arriving in front of that place on the 17th of November, 1863. For the first and only time during the war, we were issued two days back rations, which consisted of flour, bacon, mutton, sugar and coffee. We captured a large lot of sugar and coffee. The men were so hungry they ate too much and nearly all were made sick. Our surgeons attributed our illness to what they termed "sick flour."

As soon as the regiment had completely gorged itself on back rations, it was ordered to the north side of the town in line with the other regiments of the division, and completely invested the place on the north side. As soon as we got into position, it was the general belief of every man in the regiment that General Longstreet would make an effort to bring General Burnside to terms then and there, but no further advance was made. A determined and bold effort on our part, as was afterwards learned from Federal officers, would have caused the garrison to capitulate. General McLaws says: "I believe that if Knoxville had been assaulted on the evening of our arrival there, that we could have forced an evacuation that night."[4]

A day or two after reaching Knoxville, the 4th Alabama was ordered to occupy an entrenchment during the night under the guns and in close proximity to Fort Loudon,[5] the strongest and most important position occupied by the enemy. Just before daylight on the following morning, the enemy in the Fort, taking advantage of the heavy fog, advanced a column of infantry directly on our front. Our pickets, being only a short distance in our front, ran in and aroused us in time to prepare for the enemy's reception. The column advanced within a few paces before exposing the line to view in the dense fog, and doubtless was ignorant of the fact of our presence. We fired a deadly volley at close range, which was so unexpected that it caused a retreat to the cover of the Fort, leaving a number of dead and wounded. The latter were brought in by our litter bearers and conveyed to the rear. Among the number was one seriously wounded, who was afterwards reported by the bearers as being a brother of a member of one of the "fortycan" regiments of our brigade.

In order to make his work more thorough, General Longstreet, on the 21st of November, dispatched our brigade and the Texans and 3rd Arkansas, crossing on flat boats, to the south side of the river below the town, our object being to get possession of some commanding ridges on that side and held by the enemy. Here the 4th Alabama remained for several days. After quite a brisk fusillade, in which all the regiment was engaged, we secured possession of the desired heights. Colonel Porter Alexander in command of Longstreet's artillery, brought over seven or eight heavy pieces and posted them on the heights.[6]

While our regiment was having a comparatively easy time over on the south side of the Holston, General Longstreet was making preparations to assault Fort Loudon opposite to us on the north side. The heavy guns which Colonel Alexander had posted on the south side were to cooperate with McLaws' division and the other three brigades of our division in making the assault. Our brigade, the Texans, and the 3rd Arkansas were to make a diversion on our side in order to prevent reinforcements of the enemy going to the aid of Fort Loudon.[7]

On the 26th and 27th of November rumors reached us, circulated principally through our telegraph operators, that there had been a battle at Chattanooga and that General Bragg had been defeated. This, although not official, was a sad blow to us. After all our sufferings and hardships, when we had the enemy right in our grasp, through Bragg's defeat, all was lost.[8]

The assault on Fort Loudon was arranged for the 28th, but on account of the rain and stormy weather, it was postponed to the morning of the 29th. Early that morning the regiment was ordered out to attack and hold the enemy. C and F Companies, about sixty-five men, were thrown forward and soon became engaged. Our heavy guns on the south side joined in the firing with our lighter artillery and the infantry on the north side, in the attack on the Fort.

Companies C and F of our regiment were doing most of the fighting in our front. They drove back the strong skirmish line opposed to them and held their ground for some time after the enemy were re-enforced by a heavy column. No order was given to the other eight companies of the regiment to go to the relief of our gallant comrades. We stood under cover of the ridge with the bullets of the enemy passing over and doing but little damage to the eight companies in reserve, but fast thinning out the ranks of brave and gallant old C and F. The firing of both artillery and infantry having slackened on both sides of the river, General Law sent for us to retire.

Most of the casualties which were incurred in the siege of Knoxville occurred in this encounter, in C and F, and most nobly they stood their ground until the enemy's position was turned. "This diversion," says General Longstreet, "on the south side I have learned since had the effect to prevent the reserve intended for the enemy's fort reinforcing there."[9]

General Longstreet instituted court martial proceedings against General McLaws for his failure to capture the fort, and states that there were only one hundred and fifty of the enemy in it at the time of our attack. Although the 4th Alabama was only indirectly engaged in the capture of this stronghold, it is no more than justice to our noble comrades to state that the opposition met by those who made the attempt was much more than stated by General Longstreet. The 79th New York, a full regiment, five companies of the 29th Massachusetts and two of the 20th Michigan were the infantry, besides the gunners, inside of the Fort, and a strong support was within reach.[10]

Some time during the day a dispatch was received from President Davis confirming the report of the defeat of General Bragg and ordering us to report to General Bragg. General Longstreet held a consultation with his two division commanders and Colonel Alexander, and the result was that under the circumstances it was impossible, on account of the nature of the country, to reach him. It was determined, much to our delight, to move in the opposite direction, nearer Virginia.

On the 1st of December a courier bearing dispatches from General Grant to General Burnside was captured. From this we learned that General Grant had dispatched three columns from different directions to his relief, so it behooved us to abandon the siege and get away as soon as possible.[11] On the 3rd we moved out in front of the division; our brigade, the Texans and the 3rd Arkansas were in charge of the wagon train.

It was predicted when we left Knoxville that our two brigades would have the hardest duty to perform, as we had a long train to guard, over miserable roads, but we were agreeably disappointed. McLaws' division and our other brigades, before the campaign ended, had nearly all the fighting to do, and we marched almost unmolested until the 9th of December, when we rejoined our division up near Rogersville, Tennessee.

Here we remained until the 14th, when the regiment was ordered to march back to Bean's Station and meet the enemy's forces, which General Grant had sent from Chattanooga to drive us out of East Tennessee. The battle was fought and ended before we reached there, by part of McLaws' and Bushrod Johnson's[12] commands and our cavalry, and resulted in a complete surprise to the enemy and a victory for the Confederates.[13]

On the 15th of December, with the worst of roads and still in charge of the wagon train, we did not reach our division until late in the evening, completely worn out and censured by General Longstreet for our tardiness. The enemy retreated during the night. Early the next morning General Longstreet made elaborate plans to capture the greater part of the Union forces with our two divisions and his cavalry, but he says: "As I rode to the front General Law preferred a complaint of hardships, etc. General McLaws was not yet fed, and there seemed so strong a desire for rest rather than to destroy the enemy, that I was obliged to abandon the pursuit."[14]

A part at least of McLaws' division was moved out in position and the 4th Alabama was stationed on the south side of a gap in Clinch Mountain to act in concert with our cavalry, which was to come down on the north side of the gap and engage the enemy stationed in our front. We waited patiently until noon, but learning nothing of our cavalry or the enemy, the men became restless while lying in an old field overgrown with underbrush and briars. Although we had orders to remain perfectly quiet, one by one they sauntered to the rear, under one pretext or another, until a rabbit in front of someone jumped out of a briar thicket. With a yell several gave chase, and in a few minutes most of the regiment was engaged in the sport. It was afterwards found that the enemy had retreated from the gap during the night.

For a week longer we remained on the north side of the Holston River between Rogersville and Blain's Cross Roads. Having exhausted all the supplies on that side within our reach, we crossed the Holston on the 23rd of December and went into winter quarters near Morristown, ending one of the severest and most trying campaigns of the Civil War. Our casualties in this campaign were five killed and twenty-four wounded.

17

East Tennessee Campaign
December 23, 1863, to April 18, 1864

As soon as we reached Morristown we proceeded to erect shelters and make ourselves as comfortable as possible under the circumstances. Our forage wagons were kept busy going over the country between the Holston and French Broad Rivers, collecting supplies. We were being constantly annoyed by the Union cavalry, and the population being mostly Unionists, we were compelled to send with our wagons a force to protect them. There was always found more than enough volunteers to accompany the wagons when ordered on a foraging expedition. The detail would generally return with a supply of provisions to last them for some time.

As it was too late when we reached camp (December 23rd) to order a Christmas dinner, the field and staff of the regiment ordered a turkey from Lynchburg, Virginia, for New Year. When it reached us it proved to be a goose, as a turkey was not to be found. The cost was seventy-five dollars and the freight. The mess cook, being a very ignorant negro, failed to dress the goose properly, which entirely destroyed the appetite of the men when the carver, who was appropriately the Surgeon, proceeded to divide out each one pro rata share of the costly bird. The negro had omitted to remove the crop and it was cooked and placed on the mess table in this manner.

Although January was bitterly cold, we were frequently called out to assist our cavalry in driving off the enemy's cavalry. On one occasion the 4th Alabama was sent down to the bend of Chuckey River and remained several days on outpost duty. We were bivouacked without any protection in a sugar maple grove near the river. Then came a severe snow storm of several inches depth, and the men had a great deal of fun, and some meat, catching rabbits. The sap began to run from the maple trees, which were already bored. We caught and boiled enough of the sap to fill our canteens with nice syrup by straining it through our handkerchiefs, of which a few were found in the regiment.

When ordered to return to camp I was sent to bring in the pickets. Sergeant Tom Mathis[1] of K Company was stationed at a barn about half a mile down the river, with a detail of about twelve men. They had stolen a hog and were butchering it when I rode up. As the regiment had left and there was danger of our being captured, and no time to hunt up the owner, the meat was divided out, each man filling his haversack. We overtook the regiment just as it was going into bivouac for the night. The next morning the headquarters mess had pork steak for breakfast, and Colonel Bowles, who now lives at Evergreen, Alabama, doesn't know to this day that he ever ate stolen meat.

The latter part of the month, January 24th, we were ordered to Dandridge, Tennessee, to meet the enemy, which was concentrating there to inaugurate a move against us. The regiment found our cavalry, when we reached there, dismounted and having quite a hot time with the enemy. The 4th Alabama became engaged and after a brisk little fight drove the enemy from the field, though not until one of our best officers, Lieutenant B. O. Peterson,[2] was killed and two or three men slightly wounded. "Bat," as we called Lieutenant Peterson, was a capable officer and one of the most popular in the regiment. He was detailed during the Gettysburg Campaign on Law's staff, and for a time was Acting Assistant Adjutant General of the division.

We returned to our camp and remained there until, with the 44th Alabama, we were sent down to Panther Springs. During inclement weather most of the regiment and Colonel Jones[3] of the 44th Alabama occupied a church on the hill beyond the little hamlet. All of our sick and barefooted were left up at Morristown. There was a family of good Southern people, an exception in that section, living in a large Colonial house on the hill in our front, and in rear of our pickets. They were very kind and hospitable, the two sprightly girls of the family giving us free access to their extensive library.

One day while here Newsome and I were sitting by a fire built against a log, reading, when the pickets commenced a rapid fire over the hill. All of the men, without orders or officers, [as] most of the latter had gone down to Morristown, seized their guns and cartridge boxes and ran in the direction of the firing. We dropped our borrowed books on the burning log and followed. As we passed the mansion the girls were on top of the fence, frantically waving their sunbonnets and pointing in the direction of the Federal Cavalry, perfectly oblivious to the dangerous bullets striking the house and pillars and regardless of appeals to run back out of danger. Each company, knowing its position so well, hastily took its place in line and after a few shots drove the enemy off. When we returned, those borrowed books, which we left in our haste lying on the burning log, were almost ruined from the effects of the fire. We were very much troubled over the matter and were in a dilemma as to the excuse we should make for our gross carelessness. We finally decided to draw straws for who should be the unfortunate one to return them, or at least what was left of them. The burden fell on Newsome, and he brought back an invitation for both of us to come up and take dinner.

A day or two afterwards we were relieved by the cavalry and returned to our camp at Morristown. General Longstreet, in March, moved us over about Bull's Gap, where supplies and provender were more plentiful. It appeared that General Longstreet had in East Tennessee a good deal of trouble with his general officers. The failure of General Law to hold his position in Lookout Valley on the night of the 28th of October, when we certainly would have met with nothing but disaster had we remained longer, had excited General Longstreet's enmity against that officer and unfavorable comments were made on every move, as is plainly shown in all of General Longstreet's reports after Chickamauga, against General Law.[4]

Generals McLaws and Robertson also came under the bane of his displeasure, the former on account of not making a successful assault at Fort Loudon, and the latter for criticisms made with regard to General Longstreet's manner of conducting affairs in the Knoxville and East Tennessee Campaigns. As fast as he placed them under arrest or relieved them from duty, they were returned to their respective commands by the authorities at Richmond. These two officers finally refused to serve under him.

General Law, as ordered, returned to duty with us after being released, when the rest of our division was ordered to report back to General Lee in Virginia. General Longstreet, knowing it was our heart's desire to also go back, transferred us to Buckner's[5] division, to remain in East Tennessee. We made an effort to get back regardless of General Longstreet's wishes, and on the 18th of April, 1864, the following order was received: "Major General S. B. Buckner, Bristol, Tenn. Send Law's Brigade to Charlottesville to report to General Field. General Law will be relieved from arrest and put in command of it. The charges against him will not be further entertained. S. COOPER, Adjutant and Inspector General."[6]

This was glorious news. We bade farewell, without any regrets at parting, to old East Tennessee, and went on our way triumphantly rejoicing,[7] back to old battle-torn Virginia and "Mars' Robert."[8]

This was the coldest winter the regiment experienced, and we suffered more hardships than during any other winter campaign of the four years of incessant marching and fighting.[9] Our casualties, however, were small, one officer killed and five men wounded.

18

Wilderness
April 18 to May 7, 1864

By slow stages on our dilapidated cars, the 4th Alabama, in company with the other regiments of the brigade, joined the rest of our division between Charlottesville and Gordonsville, though nearer the latter place. We had scarcely become reestablished with our Corps before General Longstreet again placed General Law under arrest. Colonel Perry of the 44th Alabama was placed in charge of the brigade.[1] General Hood, having been with us from the organization of the division in the fall of 1861 to the Chickamauga Battle, where he was wounded, severed his connection forever with the division. He had, through his leadership, made of the four brigades constituting his command, one among the best in the Army of Northern Virginia and through our long service under him we had become his devoted followers. The same relation existed, only still closer, in regard to our brigade commander, General E. M. Law.[2] Not having the leaders with whom we had associated so long and had learned to love, admire and respect, was much to be regretted.

Still our return to Virginia to again enlist under the banner of our beloved Chief more than counterbalanced other considerations and we congratulated ourselves on our good fortune with the hope that General Law would again soon be restored to the brigade. Immediately after the Battle of Chickamauga General Lee wrote to General Longstreet: "My whole heart and soul have been with you and your brave Corps in your late battle . . . Finish the work before you, my dear General, and return to me. I want you badly and you cannot get back too soon."[3]

All during our eight months' absence no general battle had been fought by the Army of Northern Virginia, but it had been by no means idle. We in the meantime had scored one more victory to our credit.

When our two divisions left for the Army of Tennessee in September,

Pickett's division of our Corps was also detached and sent to Petersburg and from there to North Carolina. This left General Lee with barely 46,000 men on the defensive, south of the Rapidan. General Meade, still in command of the Union forces, confronted him on the opposite bank.

On October 9th, just one month after we left for the Army of Tennessee, General Lee determined to act on the offensive by crossing the Rapidan, moving via Madison Court House and turning the right flank of General Meade. We learn from General Lee's official report that he felt justified in making this move as the 11th and 12th Corps of the Union Army under General Hooker were sent south to Chattanooga, thus weakening General Meade's forces. As has been stated, we met these old antagonists of ours in Lookout Valley on the Tennessee River, below Chattanooga on October 29, 1863.

During the night of the 10th, General Meade retreated across the Rappahannock and evaded all attempts to bring him to bay. General Meade finally crossed Bull Run and reached the fortifications at Centreville. General Lee then gave up the chase and withdrew his army to its former position south of the Rapidan, giving as his reason for withdrawing the following: "Nothing prevented my continuing in his front but the destitute condition of the men, thousands of whom are barefooted, a greater number partially shod, and nearly all without overcoats, blankets or warm clothing. I think the sublimest sight of the war was the cheerfulness and alacrity exhibited by this army in the pursuit of the enemy under all trials and privations to which it was exposed."[4]

Our two divisions were undergoing the same sufferings and wants in East Tennessee as here depicted by General Lee during, by far, the severest winter experienced in our four years service.

General Meade returned from Centreville in the footsteps of General Lee and took up his original position on the north side of the Rapidan in the vicinity of Culpeper and Warrenton.[5] The two opposing armies were occupying these positions on our arrival from East Tennessee about the middle of April, 1864. We left General Grant at Chattanooga when we departed from there in November 1863 for Knoxville, but found him here wearing the laurels of Vicksburg and Chattanooga, directing General Meade to fight General Lee between the Rapidan and Richmond.[6]

The rivalry which had existed in our division between Brigadier Generals Jenkins and Law as to who should command the division since the wounding of General Hood at Chickamauga was here ended by the powers at Richmond appointing General Charles Field to the command. General Field had previously been in command of a brigade of Virginia troops in A. P. Hill's Corps, and was an officer of commanding appearance, large, handsome and an officer of the old Army. He it was who rode at the head of the Cadet Corps at West Point when the late King Edward of England came over, as a boy, and during his visit took in the Point.[7]

Soon after reaching the Army of Northern Virginia, General Lee rode over to welcome our return and review our two divisions; Miss Mildred, his daughter, accompanied by several other ladies, was present.[8]

On the 2nd of May General Lee, from his signal station on Clark's Mountain, saw sufficient evidence of busy preparations in General Meade's camp across the Rapidan for a general advance, to justify him in getting ready to resist the vast horde which was about to inaugurate its overland march to Richmond. On the 3rd of May orders were issued to the regiment to cook two days' rations and make all other preparations to move at a moment's warning. At 9 A.M. on the 4th, the signal flag on Clark's Mountain was waving the news to General Lee's Headquarters that Grant's tents were folded and his army was in motion around the Confederate right flank. At once the order was given to advance.

General Meade was then throwing his army across the Rapidan below our army at Ely's and Germanna Fords, under the direction of Lieutenant General Grant, now Commander-in-Chief of all the United States forces in the field. At the beginning of this campaign General Lee's total strength was 61,953 men and the number of field guns 224, and that of the enemy was 120,000 enlisted men and 318 field guns, a difference of 59,000 men and 94 field guns in favor of Grant's forces.

This disparity in numbers on our part was to be overcome as far as possible through the generalship of our peerless leader, opposed to the brute force of his antagonist. General Grant states in his "Memoirs" that his train would have reached from the Rapidan to Richmond, the distance between these two points being sixty-five miles.[9] One of his officers asserted that the best clothed and best fed army that ever took the field was Grant's invading host.

To intercept and bring to a halt this mighty invading host which was crossing the Rapidan and filing into the dense thickets and marches of the Wilderness was Lieutenant General Ewell with the Second Corps, about 17,000 strong, followed by Lieutenant General A. P. Hill of the Third with 22,000 effectives. Longstreet back at Cobham Station near Gordonsville with Brigadier General Kershaw in charge of McLaws' old division and ours under Major General Field, both numbered 10,000 muskets; 4,800 officers and men constituted the artillery, and 8,300 troopers followed the black plume of Jeb Stuart. Sixty-two thousand ragged, shoeless and half-fed veterans was the sum total which the intrepid and dauntless Lee had the audacity to throw across the pathway of the enemy.

General Ewell was distant from the field of battle 18 miles, General Hill 28, and our two divisions 42. Both Generals Ewell and Hill moved out promptly at 9 A.M., as instructed by General Lee, and by rapid marching both Corps, except R. H. Anderson's division of Hill's Corps, which was left on the Rapidan, were in position by eight o'clock P.M. Twenty-nine thousand invincibles were ready to dispute the progress of Grant at the dawn of day on the 5th.

The 4th Alabama moved out at 4 o'clock P.M. on the 4th, marched twelve miles by dark, rested and fed and resumed the march, which extended without intermission through the night and all of the 5th until sundown, having marched 36 miles. The regiment went into bivouac that evening on the Catharpin Road near Richard's Shop, away off to the right and rear. General Lee, fully anticipating our arrival, gave orders to General Ewell on the morning of the 5th to bring him (the enemy) to battle now as soon as possible. Grant's army extended all the way from the Rapidan to the battleground of Chancellorsville. The left wing (Ewell) was across the Orange Turnpike and the centre (Hill) was astride the Orange Plank Road. Both these roads converged near Chancellorsville. The Catharpin Road, on which we were encamped the night of the 5th, was nearly parallel with and six miles south of the Plank Road.

The battle of the 5th raged furiously all day by Ewell and Hill of the left and right respectively, while the right under "Old Bull," as the boys were wont to dub General Longstreet, was far afield. How our comrades stood that day's incessant hammering and held their ground opposed to such overwhelming numbers as were arrayed against them was almost inconceivable. Wellington at Waterloo never looked with more anxiety for the coming of Blucher, nor General Lee for Stuart at Gettysburg, than he did on this day for the arrival of his First Corps. It has been said that several times during the day he remarked, "What can delay General Longstreet; why don't Longstreet come?" At eight o'clock that night General Lee dispatched Colonel Venable, his Adjutant-General, to General Longstreet to hasten to the front.[10]

At two o'clock the next morning the 4th Alabama, having plodded along after General Longstreet until our haversacks were empty, was aroused and marched under the direction of a guide for the nearest point on the Plank Road. The road on which we were marching forked a short distance before reaching the Plank Road. Kershaw's division took the right-hand fork and ours the left. Kershaw was leading by about one hundred yards when we overtook him on the Plank Road. Dick Anderson's division, which had been left on the Rapidan, was coming up just in our rear. This was the only time I ever saw two divisions marching into a battle side by side.

For some time before reaching the Plank Road we knew from the continued roll of musketry that the battle was on in earnest. Directly in our front as we were hastening forward, the sun, blood red, from the effect of the smoke of battle, was just appearing above the Wilderness, which caused the prediction, "There will be a hot time in the Wilderness today, for there is blood in the sun." Litter bearers were continually passing with the severely maimed and a stream of wounded able to leave the battle line filled both sides of the Plank Road. I never before or after witnessed such excitement and confusion. It was perfectly appalling. Staff officers were urging their mounts at topmost speed back and forth; orders were repeatedly received for us to quicken our steps. The number of wounded and stragglers increased as we drew nearer the firing line, all stating that we were holding our own, unwilling to acknowledge that disaster had befallen them. The 4th Alabama, which brought up the rear of our two divisions, chafed most unmercifully their retreating comrades.

All this turmoil was caused by the enemy attacking A. P. Hill before our arrival.[11] The blow fell on Heth's[12] and Wilcox's[13] divisions. Their men made a most stubborn resistance until Wadsworth's[14] Union division struck their left flank and Hancock Corps their right, doubling them up and forcing them from the field. General Lee's line was broken.

Generals Heth and Wilcox on the night of the 5th, after their hard day's battle, had occupied the right of Hill's Corps. Having no reserves, they had been fought almost to a finish. Tired and worn out, they had been promised by General Lee, who was momentarily looking for our two divisions to join him, that they would be relieved at dawn on the 6th. Without making any preparations to protect themselves in the event of an attack before the arrival of the promised relief, every man dropped to the ground and was soon fast asleep and did not awake until the skirmish line was driven in, closely followed by the enemy.[15]

"Old Bull" was not a minute too soon. "Tige" Anderson's Georgians were leading the division and the first brigade to become engaged.[16] Next came the three Texas regiments and the 3rd Arkansas, commanded by General Gregg.[17] The next of our division to go into action was old General Benning's Georgians, then followed our brigade at a double quick into line. Here we found General Lee, who appeared to be very much perturbed over his misfortune, and the only time I ever saw him excited.[18] Riding up to our brigade, he asked, "What troops?" "Law's Alabamians," was the reply. "God bless the Alabamians," he said.[19]

After the 4th Alabama passed General Lee something over two hundred yards, we came, after passing through a tangled depression, to the crest of a hill of slight elevation, where we were halted and ordered to form our entire brigade for an advance. By the time this was done, General Field, our new division commander, came down the line in person and called to Colonel Bowles to throw forward a good skirmish line, and at the command, "Advance!," to keep the right of the 4th Alabama on the Plank Road, stating at the same time that the 4th Alabama was the directing battalion of the brigade. Our skirmishers, about fifty yards in advance of the regiment, were halted at the edge of a dense thicket.

A few minutes elapsed, then the whole line was ordered to advance. The 4th Alabama went forward at a double quick. As the skirmishers were fired on after advancing only a short distance, they awaited our coming up. By the time we reached them, the firing of the enemy had become quite brisk, and was apparently only a short distance from us. A charge was then ordered through the tangled undergrowth. We had gone not exceeding one hundred yards when we reached a hastily thrown up breastworks vacated by the enemy. Here we halted again, throwing out our picket line well in our front, who kept up a desultory firing for several minutes.

The 47th Alabama was the next regiment on our left, and its Colonel being absent, it was placed under the supervision of Colonel Bowles. "Tige" Anderson's brigade of Georgians, which went into battle on the south side of the Plank Road, judging from their gunfire, were well up and apparently abreast of the 4th Alabama, and so far there was no danger of our getting too far in advance of them, or any others on that side of the road. A column of the enemy advanced on our front, driving in our pickets as we were lying down behind our temporary works. A volley or two was fired into it, checking its advance. On our extreme right, overlooking the Plank Road, the men of the regiment immediately on that part of the line were able to partially get a glimpse of the foe, so as to fire with some degree of accuracy, but on our left we were firing into an impenetrable thicket.

A second column, and in greater force than before, advanced against the 4th Alabama. Colonel Bowles then ordered a charge over our low works. We went tearing through the Wilderness perfectly ignorant of the numbers in our front. After going a short distance, we routed the foe from behind their second line of protection, which proved to be quite substantial and safe works, the enemy in the meantime falling back slowly and doggedly firing as they retired.[20] Behind this second line we felt quite secure and we all congratulated ourselves on our capture.

I was ordered to go to the left to look after the 47th Alabama and to see if our left was properly protected. On reaching there, I was surprised to find none of the other regiments of the brigade were in sight except the 47th Alabama. The other three were gone, and as I hurried back to the right I imagined we would be surrounded and captured before I could reach Colonel Bowles. I, with the other members of the regiment, had a perfect horror of being captured, and Grant had just issued his edict that there would be no more exchanging.[21]

When I got back to the regiment I was very much fatigued and excited, and hastily suggested that we withdraw to our first line of works. I found every man busily occupied in loading and firing, perfectly ignorant of our critical condition. I had scarcely expressed my fears of the situation in which we were placed when the bullets began to come thick and fast from the enemy on the opposite side of the road. We had evidently passed beyond our troops on the south side of the road, or they were being driven back and we were receiving a heavy fire on our right flank, which, of itself, forced the right to beat a hasty retreat to its first line of works with the exultant foe closely following.

On they came, through the tangled undergrowth, to within thirty yards of our frail works. Our only alternative was to check them with a countercharge, and for the second time, the regiment, as one man, leaped over our slight protection, which had served only as a rallying point, and with a discordant yell we again rushed through the brush and repeated our first effort in driving the enemy from their second line. In the meantime our comrades south of the road had made sufficient progress to now be abreast of us, and were of material aid in relieving the pressure by firing across the road into reinforcements of the foe advancing in heavy force directly in front of our apparently doomed little lone regiment.

This was the most critical moment of that awful, bloody, strenuous day's battle as far as the 4th Alabama took part, but thanks to the enemy for their breastworks, which we had for the second time wrested from them. On they came—a gallant and brave body of men they were too— only to be hurled back at each successive charge. Our ammunition was becoming dangerously low and it appeared that either one side or the other would soon have to give way, and we very much feared it would fall to our lot to be the first to quit the field. Fortunately for the 4th Alabama, the other regiments of the brigade returned to their proper positions on our left (after chasing Kitching's[22] Heavy Artillery armed as infantry back to the Lacey House, where was Grant's Headquarters)[23] and, throwing an enfilading fire into the foe in front of the 4th Alabama, caused them to scatter like partridges back to the Brock Road.[24] A conspicuous Federal officer, just before we broke their line and sent them back in disorder, leaped his horse over some obstructions in the Plank Road and was unhorsed. Some of the 4th Alabama who went down into the road returned and stated that a wounded general officer was lying in the road, who it was afterwards stated to be General Wadsworth.[25]

During this last and desperate encounter with as gallant a foe as the 4th Alabama ever met on any field, I was near Major Robbins, second in command of the regiment, who was waving his sword and exhorting the men to aim low and keep protected. Suddenly he faced about, his sword flying from his grasp several feet from him, at the same time falling heavily to the ground. I called Colonel Bowles' attention, and pointed to our dear, pious old Major, whom I was certain was dead. Several of us hurried to him and on turning him over found that he had only received a scalp wound and was not dangerously wounded. My old friend Quimby, also apparently dead, we found lying on his face. I was reminded of his remark to me at Chickamauga that a bullet and not a rope was foreordained to be his fate, I thought, as we looked down at his motionless form. But he too, like Major Robbins, was only stunned by a spent or glancing ball, and in two weeks was back for duty.

After repulsing the enemy, we made no effort to advance, but were relieved by one of General Anderson's brigades of Hill's Corps and ordered some distance by the left flank where we found the other regiments of our brigade taking position on the right and connecting with Brigadier General Perry's[26] brigade of Florida troops. It was now about 9 o'clock A.M. and perfect quiet prevailed along the entire battle line, and we patiently awaited further developments, for we knew the battle was yet not over.

General Lee, taking advantage of the lull in the battle, determined to strike the flank and rear of Grant's left under Hancock with four improvised brigades under General Mahone.[27] On our part of the line, we were ordered to hold ourselves in readiness to conform our movements to those of the troops first making the assault on Hancock's Corps. General Longstreet, in command of the right wing, placed Colonel Sorrel,[28] his Adjutant General, in charge of this important move, instructing him to "form a good line and then move, your right pushed forward, and turning as much as possible to the left, hit hard when you start, but don't start until you have everything ready; I shall be waiting for your gunfire and be on hand with fresh troops for further advance."[29] By 11 o'clock A.M. Colonel Sorrel was ready for the attack, having successfully reached the extreme left of Hancock's Corps. The assault was then made with a sudden and irresistible charge by Mahone.

Each successive Confederate brigade to the left joined in with their comrades of the right. We listened with intense interest as the heavy roll of musketry rapidly extended in our direction, assuring us that in a few minutes we would be called upon to take part in the contest. The roll of musketry gradually died away and again there was a stillness. It was impossible to divine the cause. Mr. Swinton, then a correspondent with the Union Army, thus describes this critical moment: "It seemed indeed that irretrievable disaster was upon us, but in the very torrent and tempest of the attack of the Confederates it suddenly ceased, that in the very fury and tempest of the Confederate onset, the advance was of a sudden stayed by a cause at the moment unknown. This afterwards proved to have been the fall of the head of the attack."[30]

General Mahone with his four brigades had completely routed and was driving and doubling up Hancock's Corps as if it were a wet blanket, in a northern direction, while General Longstreet struck the enemy as he led Jenkins' South Carolina brigade down the Plank Road in an easterly direction, thus throwing his two columns at right angles to each other. General Mahone halted his troops just before reaching the Plank Road. Generals Longstreet and Jenkins with their staffs appearing in his front were mistaken for the enemy and fired into, killing General Jenkins and seriously wounding General Longstreet.[31]

This was the cause of the sudden and sad ending of General Lee's well-laid plans, which up to this time had been so successfully executed. It was a singular coincidence that both of our leaders of an important movement, on almost the exact spot, in different battles of a year's interval, and under similar circumstances, should have been stricken down when victory was on the eve of crowning our efforts.[32] When Longstreet fell, "down the Plank Road," says General Francis Walker of the Union army, "from Hancock's centre a stream of broken men was pouring to the rear, giving the onlooker the impression that everything had gone to pieces."[33] General Lee had no one, when the battle joined, to take the place of his second in command. Our division commander, Major General Field, was the only General of his rank near at hand to take charge immediately after General Longstreet had been stricken down.

General Lee hastened to that part of the field to rectify matters, and it was three or four o'clock in the afternoon before he was ready to resume operations. By this time the enemy had recovered from his panic and was ready to meet us.

As we still remained unoccupied in our position, Colonel Perry became apprehensive of an attack from our left and on his own responsibility, as he afterwards stated, he sent forward the 15th and 48th Alabama from the left of the brigade, both under command of Colonel Oates, to "feel" of the enemy.[34] Colonel Oates states in his history of the 15th

Alabama that he informed Colonel Perry when the movement was suggested to him that he would meet with very strong opposition on his left flank before advancing any distance and gave good reasons for his belief, but Colonel Perry differing with him, he moved forward with the two regiments.[35] In the "feeling" process, should the movement prove favorable, Colonel Perry's plan was to advance the 44th, 47th and 4th Alabama respectively from left to right, in echelon at forty paces distant, by battalions, in support of Colonel Oates.

We at the time knew nothing of Colonel Perry's little coup de main, which he was inaugurating on our extreme left, and were quietly lying on the ground, the majority of us rubbing and nursing our spent ball and glancing shot bruises, when Colonel Perry rode from the right of the line. He stopped in front of me as I was lying down with my back resting against a tree, a short distance in rear of our lines. With a very self-satisfied manner, he drew himself up and remarked to me, "Well, Bob, I propose this evening to make a spoon or spoil a horn." I had been a soldier too long to inquire of him his strategical plans, so only wished him success, in I knew not what. He then passed on the left of the brigade and ordered forward the 15th and 48th, and just as Colonel Oates predicted, he was hit hard before going one hundred yards, and caught it heavily on his left flank. The 15th and 48th fought stubbornly and for some time stood their ground, but were hard pressed by a largely superior force.[36]

The gallant Major Carey[37] of the 44th went to Colonel Oates' assistance. His help availed but little, and he too was unable to stem the desperate onset made against them. Colonel Perry made an effort, with the 47th Alabama, just to our left, to check the enemy but they too were swept away and joined the other three regiments in a hasty run for the rear.

The 4th Alabama was perfectly amazed as we stood in line under heavy fire from the oncoming enemy, and saw to our left our four regiments going at full speed to the rear with the enemy right at their heels, yelling like devils and cursing the Rebels, Yankee officers and noncoms leading and urging on the privates. It required only a moment to convince the regiment that this was no place for them, and all of us on the right of the regiment moved directly up the line as fast as it was possible for our legs to carry us, expecting to get in rear of the three Florida regiments,[38] but when we reached the point where they should have been they too were gone. We learned afterwards that General Perry of the Florida Brigade (who survived the war and was afterwards Governor of Florida) had been inveigled into this spoon movement, as we afterwards termed it, by Colonel Perry, and had advanced his brigade at the same time the

48th and 15th were sent forward, and in consequence they too became badly smashed.

Heth's division of the Third Corps, which had been in our rear since their disaster of the early morning, came promptly to our help, pushed the enemy back and re-established our line. We circled around and joined our other comrades in the Widow Tapp field, very much exhausted from our hasty run and day's work. Each man as he came up dropped down in the old field, and, as soon as we could take in the situation through which we had so suddenly passed, laughed most heartily, giving Colonel Perry full credit for his miscarried little coup de main.[39] I can only recall one of the regiment who was wounded, Tom Melton[40] of C Company, shot severely in the foot, and who was brought out by his comrades.

This terrible and bloody struggle, which continued for two days, was brought to an end late in the evening by an attack of General John B. Gordon on the extreme left of our line. This continued in his favor until darkness caused him to halt, though not until he had driven the enemy some distance and captured two Brigadier Generals and six hundred prisoners.[41]

General R. H. Anderson being the senior Major General in the Army of Northern Virginia, General Lee placed him in charge of our Corps.[42] The 4th Alabama remained in its position that night and all the following day unmolested by the foe, who was strongly fortified a short distance in our front.

Our casualties in this entire day's work were fifteen killed and fifty-nine incapacitated for duty. Several of the men were struck with spent and glancing balls, on account of the undergrowth and timber, who were not entered on the list of wounded. During our engagement of the early morning, of the casualties which occurred, I can recall Captain Bayless Brown of B Company killed; Lieutenant Coonsey[43] of E Company, Lieutenants William Newsom of H, Stearnes[44] of E and Jones of K, and Captain James Brown of F were wounded. Lieutenant Henry Figures,[45] a gallant soldier and esteemed friend, a youth of decided military talent, was killed during our evening encounter. He was appointed Adjutant of the 48th Alabama, having been orderly sergeant in Company F, 4th Alabama, and an original member of the regiment.

As General Grant, in his attempt to again evade General Lee in his movement on Richmond, moved out on the night of the 7th, by way of Spottsylvania Court House, at 11 o'clock P.M., the same night the 4th Alabama was marching over a newly cut and rough road on a nearly parallel line with his forces. His dead and some of his wounded were left to the mercy of the decayed burning timber and forest leaves.

19

Spotsylvania Ridge to the James River
May 8 to June 16, 1864

Between the Po and Ny Rivers is what is known as Spotsylvania Ridge, on which is located Spotsylvania Court House, the point to which we were rapidly marching in order to reach there in time to throw a line across Grant's pathway.[1] Kershaw's South Carolinians[2] were in the lead, and the 4th Alabama followed close in their rear without a halt, except a few minutes' stop in the early morn to eat a hasty meal from the haversacks. We reached the Court House in the middle of the forenoon, after a march of nearly twelve hours. We met General Stuart's cavalry falling back, closely followed by the enemy's cavalry and infantry. In the race we had only won by a neck, as it were. General Law, having been restored to the command of the brigade by the War Office at Richmond, again assumed command of the brigade.

The enemy, no doubt anticipating encountering only cavalry falling back in their front, advanced boldly, meeting unexpectedly the South Carolinians, who had by then obtained possession of the Court House cross roads. A quick, sharp and bloody encounter on their part, in which bayonets were freely used, resulted in driving back the enemy in their front.[3] In the meantime our brigade was advanced in line of battle on the left of the South Carolinians and after quite a spirited engagement we were left in possession of the field. Our stubborn resistance with a display of infantry convinced the foe that General Lee, by his promptness and skill, had outstripped Grant in reaching the goal.

General Lee was now in position to array his line across the Ridge. As the rest of the army arrived it was moved to the right, and by dark our Corps and the Second (Ewell's) were in position. When the Third Corps (Hill's) had reached the field and gotten into position on the right of the Second, our line extended across Spotsylvania Ridge nine or ten miles.

Both wings were thrown back until they were almost at right angles to each other, our Corps (First) forming the left and the other two the right. In the angle was formed the famous salient, but the men persisted in terming it "the Mule Shoe," during the battle, and afterwards always referred to it as the "Bloody Angle."

On the morning of the 9th, the old 4th Alabama could be found well-protected behind its breastworks of logs and dirt, on the right of the brigade. Our division occupied the left of the army. The Texans and 3rd Arkansas occupied the left, and its left rested on the Po River. The enemy were similarly fortified only about two hundred yards in our front.

All the 9th we were engaged in skirmishing, and were subjected to a galling, enfilading shelling from heavy artillery on our left flank. General Lee soon put a stop to this by sending Heth's division of A. P. Hill's Corps across the Po below the Court House on up the west bank, the river flowing due south at this point. General Heth met and drove back the enemy and we were not molested from that direction any more.[4] Now, with our flank secure, we were ready to meet the enemy without any fear of being shot in the back.

About 10 o'clock on the 10th General Grant threw a heavy force against our division, in an attempt, by direct assault, to turn our left. From right to left of our entire division there was a perfect flame of fire, but of short duration. The 4th Alabama felt so secure behind its works, that it cheered to the echo and begged the Yankees to come on, but they recoiled and disappeared from our front.[5]

A detail was sent over the works to collect the guns and ammunition from the dead in our front. We also ordered up a fresh supply of ammunition. The wooden boxes with rope handles were brought up from the ammunition wagons, two men to a box, each box containing eight hundred cartridges. The boxes were distributed at regular intervals behind the regiment, opened; the thick paper wrapping was taken out, spread upon the ground and the cartridges placed on it. The officers assisted in loading.

About three o'clock another attempt was made against our works, which resulted in making us still strong in guns and somewhat replenishing our ammunition. We now had four or five guns to a man. We had often thrown together frail obstructions, but this was the first time we had ever fought behind real, artificial cover.[6] Behind it the men felt safer than in the open; consequently their aim was more deadly.

As our army was a continuous unbroken line, the men could pass a message from one to another back and forth. About sunset "Lookout on the left, massing in your front," was passed down to the left from the right wing. We had been previously assaulted by only Hancock's Corps. This time both Hancock and Warren were massing their two Corps for a grand charge against our thin line of gray. In two lines, Hancock in front, they hurled themselves against our works.[7] As fast as a gun was fired it was thrown back to the rear to be reloaded. Often the officers would only take time in their haste to bite cartridges, insert in the muzzle, and with a quick sharp blow of the butt of the piece on the ground send the cartridge home. In our front we broke both lines and sent them scurrying back to their entrenchments, leaving many dead and wounded behind them.[8]

The Texans and 3rd Arkansas always imagined, up to this time, that a bayonet was a useless weapon and not worth the trouble of carrying. They succeeded in driving Hancock's men back but Warren's came on with such vim and pluck that they went headlong right over among the Texans and Arkansas boys, and for a while there was quite a strenuous time with clubbed muskets on the part of the Texans and bayonets by Warren's men. The Texans came off victors, but made a requisition for bayonets the next day, and were never without them afterwards.[9] General Grant had thoroughly tested the strength and determination of General Lee along the whole line, had met with signal defeat, and thousands of his bravest had fallen before our unerring rifles.

The prolonged and terrible musketry and artillery fire brought down the rain, making our cramped and confined positions still more uncomfortable. Certain demonstrations on the part of the foe caused General Lee to infer that Grant was withdrawing from his front; he therefore ordered all the artillery difficult of access to be withdrawn and held in readiness for the march. As coming under this order all from the Salient were taken out except two pieces.[10]

The next morning (12th) at daylight Grant threw forward against this point twenty-two brigades of his best troops,[11] defended only with wet muskets and the two pieces of artillery; of the former many failed to fire. The Confederates were overpowered and the enemy obtained temporary possession of the works.

General John B. Gordon,[12] who led the forlorn hope in retaking the lost "Mule Shoe," gives in his book, "Reminiscenses of the Civil War," a most thrilling and eloquent account of General Lee with all its details of wonderful pathos, at this critical moment, of how the soldiers "gathered around him turned his horse in the opposite direction, some clutching his bridle, some his stirrups, while others pressed close to 'Old Traveler's' hips, ready to shove him by main force to the rear."[13]

While this bloody drama, which is likely to remain without a parallel, was being enacted only a short distance on our right, General Grant was throwing column after column against our whole line. In front of the 4th

Alabama we gave them such a warm reception with our numerous collection of rifles that they were soon driven back.[14] When night put a stop to the terrible butchering, General Grant had nothing but disaster to show for it.

Since leaving Gordonsville we had been under a terrible strain from loss of sleep, constant marching, fighting in the open, and resisting assaults. Fear of a night attack kept the whole line constantly on alert. Someone down on our left, perhaps a Texan, dreaming of having a hand-to-hand encounter with a Warren man, broke the stillness of the night by a shot from his rifle. Instantly a terrible roll of musketry opened and quickly extended from the left to and beyond the 4th Alabama. For a few minutes the fusillade continued, before the half-awakened and startled men could be convinced that it was only a panic occasioned by their strained and nervous condition.

From the 13th to the 15th we remained in our same position, with Grant's troops still fortified a short distance in our front, annoyed only by his sharpshooters.

Most of the officers and men in the 4th Alabama were good shots. There were found some, to our sorrow, who were equally as expert in hitting the bull's eye among the foe. One of the latter, on the 12th, was very annoying and difficult to locate. Finally he was discovered some distance off behind a tree. Colonel Scruggs took position with a rifle, on the right of the regiment, while some of the boys on the left with a few shots turned the Yankee to the Colonel's side, as they were accustomed to "turning a squirrel" down in Alabama. He fired, and that night one of the men crawled out and brought in the dead man's cap with a bullet hole through it. He proved to be a member of a Michigan regiment.

With those clumsy army guns the soldiers frequently shot squirrels from the topmost branches of the loftiest trees, but that was not their manner of securing them. When one was found, a squad of the boys surrounded the tree and with a few unearthly Rebel yells poor bunny, in his fright, would be certain to leap to the ground and become the prey of some hungry rebel.

Colonel Bowles, wishing to make a reconnaissance on our immediate right, requested me to accompany him. It being a warm day, he carried his cap in his hand. While crossing a country road which ran at right angles to our line, through a pine thicket, a sharpshooter fired and knocked the Colonel's cap out of his hand. The Yankee, no doubt out of pure mischief, continued firing, cutting the scrub pines on our side of the road to prevent our securing the cap. We finally obtained a pole and fished it out of the road.

In the interval of six days from the 13th to the 18th General Grant gradually moved his forces southward. The 4th Alabama in the meantime was transferred from our position, keeping step on a parallel line with the enemy until we reached Crutchfield's farm about the 15th. Our casualties were four killed and eleven wounded from the 8th to 15th inclusive.

On the morning of the 18th of May General Grant made his last struggle against the "Bloody Angle," which, although at a great loss in killed, wounded and prisoners, to us, was still tenaciously held by Ewell's Corps. Before scarcely getting within rifle range, General Lee was this time prepared, not with only a section of artillery and drenched rifles as on the 12th, but twenty heavy pieces hurling spherical case and canister, which did the work with but little participation of our infantry.[15]

At Crutchfield Farm we occupied the right of the army, and more digging had to be done. We constructed, as we were becoming as expert as the Yankees, quite a strong line of works—and were proud of our efforts and skill—just east of the dwelling and barn. Our position was a good one, it being on the crest of a hill looking east with an unobstructed view in our front. Here we remained for several days, hoping General Grant would repeat Spotsylvania, but he entirely ignored us, except to "make believe" with only a heavy line of skirmishers and a few shells. Our works, which we took so much trouble to construct for his reception, were for naught, as it was impossible to carry them with us.

We left here on the 21st for the North Anna River, which we crossed on the 22nd with the foe pressing our rear rather severely, so much so that the 4th Alabama was sent back to its support and remained near the bridge until the last of our Corps had crossed over. We were then ordered down the river and placed across the Richmond, Fredericksburg and Potomac Railway fronting the railroad bridge. Here we, of course, constructed more works. On two or three occasions we had thrown together for our protection, before this campaign, slight obstructions, but they were rude and inefficient makeshifts. Now we had become so reduced in numbers and so vastly outnumbered by the forces of our antagonist that it behooved us to protect ourselves as much as possible, and thereby lengthen out General Grant's attrition, as far as was in our power.

It was during the desperate assaults against our lines on Spotsylvania Ridge that General Grant, on the 11th, sent his famous "All Summer" dispatch to Washington calling for re-enforcements, with the hope that they would be sent as fast as possible and in as great numbers. Further he says: "I am satisfied the enemy are very shaky and are only kept up to the mark by the greatest exertion on the part of their officers, and by keeping them intrenched in every position they take."[16]

As to our officers' efforts to keep the men up to the "mark," they were equally as enthusiastic, determined and cheerful in the work before them as the officers, and had it not been for the numerous and formidable lines of entrenchments the Army of Northern Virginia had to contend against on the 6th in the Wilderness, the result of that battle would probably have been a victory for Southern arms. Had Heth and Wilcox on the night of the 5th used the same precaution in the Wilderness that Hancock's men availed themselves of in their front, having erected strong works, instead of dropping down to sleep without any protection whatever, the disaster to these two Confederate divisions could possibly have been averted. The Northern soldier was more inclined to construct artificial cover than his Southern brother. It was a variety of labor we disliked to perform, however urgent it was.

The 4th Alabama charged more entrenchments than it ever constructed from the First Manassas to Spotsylvania Ridge, and never failed to carry the works in a single instance. Our entrenchments here were constructed of green timber and earth; the tree tops, left from the timber utilized in the erection of the work, were trimmed up and pointed as they remained out in our front, which answered very well for an abatis. Two or three demonstrations in force were made in our front, driving in our pickets, but after feeling the strength of our line, the enemy retreated before reaching the abatis.

General Lee had his army drawn up in form like a wedge, the point resting against the river, the extreme left extending back to Little River and the right stretching back to Hanover Junction. Neither wing of the foe could reinforce the other without marching over a circuitous route, and at the same time crossing the river twice.

On the 27th General Grant withdrew his forces, having received a complete checkmate, and proceeded on down the north bank of the Pamunkey with the intention of making another effort to throw his army in front of General Lee. The enemy had eight miles the advantage, but our cavalry under General Fitz Lee[17]—General Stuart having been killed on the 12th[18]—held Grant's forces in check until the arrival of the infantry in his front.

The 4th Alabama covered twenty-five miles in as many hours by way of Ashland to the right of our army, which brought us down near Mechanicsville. The 4th then became engaged in intermittent entrenching, maneuvering and skirmishing, continually moving to the right, until we reached the vicinity of our former battleground, that of Gaines' Mill. Here we found excellent works which had been erected by troops which had preceded us. Some time during the day on the 2nd of June, rapid firing was heard some distance down the line on our right. With orders to repair to that point, the 4th at double-quick soon reached our troops engaged out in an opening, but without our help the enemy was soon repulsed and driven back to the timber. We lost one man here after returning to the breastworks, E. F. Powell[19] of E Company, shot in the head.

A sharpshooter of unerring aim, and doubtless the same who killed Powell, finding no heads to practice on, tried his skill on our flag staff, shooting it down as fast as we could replace it, until some of the men discovered him in a tree out some distance in our front. For some time our riflemen engaged his attention without effect. Then, substituting a Whitworth rifle for an Enfield, he was brought down with the first shot.

For perhaps an hour perfect quiet prevailed, and we were left to hold the works while our troops that we relieved marched on farther to the right on our "sliding" movement. A column of the enemy's skirmishers then was seen emerging from the timber on the opposite side of the opening. We threw over a company of pickets to meet them. These pickets of the enemy were soon followed by a column of infantry, which necessitated, on our part, a stronger force to meet it. Two companies from each of the other regiments were thrown forward, under Lieutenant Colonel Scruggs of the 4th and Major Carey of the 44th. After quite a spirited little fight the enemy were driven back into the timber.

Scruggs and Carey had scarcely gotten back to our line before the usual order was issued for a still farther movement to the right. Two more miles brought us to Cold Harbor, which we reached before sunset. The finished works continued on down to and beyond this point to the Chickahominy, and we entertained a hope that we would at least get one good night's rest, but our hopes were in vain. As soon as it became dark we were put to work entrenching. A salient, with the apex of an acute angle to the front, was allotted our brigade, but the position appeared to General Law so untenable that he ordered the salient to be leveled.[20] Having in person staked off a line across its base, we went to work by the light of the stars, and not having sufficient tools, bayonets for loosening the soil and hands in lieu of shovels were brought into requisition.

This was rather severe work, after our fatiguing toil of several days without rest, but the boys went to work good humoredly and with vigor on the new line. Lieutenant Vaughan of C Company, who was setting a good example to the men by the vigorous manner in which he handled the shovel, was accosted by Orderly Sergeant Steve Murphy of I Company, who stopped in his work long enough to compliment the Lieutenant on his graceful and deft manipulations. Steve, in his effeminate voice, remarked, "My goodness, Lieutenant, you can certainly beat any of us at it." "Yes," said Vaughan, "and if you realized what is going to happen in the morning you would be at it yourself."

By daylight our work was completed. The parapet was five feet high, with a ditch four feet deep in front and a wide shallow ditch on the inside, and a banquette for the men to stand on when firing. Major Carey of the 44th had charge of the skirmish line, as Lieutenant Vaughan had predicted, before sunrise on the morning of the 3rd a few shots were fired by our pickets, and our videttes on the parapet called out, "Look out, they are coming."

Before our pickets reached the parapet a heavy line of blue was seen emerging from the timber on our right opposite Anderson's Georgians. Five lines deep, and at trail arms, they rushed forward, evidently intending to surprise and take the salient, but finding the works leveled, followed in the wake of our fast retreating pickets. On they came until within musket range of General Anderson's front, when a murderous fire was opened by his entire brigade. Then our brigade and the artillery joined in with a right flank fire, causing the front column to hesitate, thus throwing the rear lines forward in a confused mass. It only required a few more volleys from our two brigades and two pieces of artillery to cause the enemy to retreat to the cover of the woods.

This, the first attempt to capture our works on our part of the line, was merely the forerunner of a general advance against our entire line of entrenchments, in which the Army of Northern Virginia repulsed the enemy at every point, except on the extreme right of the line near the Chickahominy, where a small part was broken, in Hill's Corps, but was soon retaken by Finegan's[21] Florida Brigade, with heavy loss to the enemy.

Only a few minutes elapsed, when a second and more determined assault was made on our immediate front. This time the enemy charged with uncapped guns, with orders not to fire until reaching the top of our parapet. Not a shot was fired by their infantry, but their artillery was freely used to hold us under cover. Our artillery, giving double shotted canister at not exceeding one hundred yards, did most effective work, while our infantry poured repeated and destructive volleys into the apparently solid mass of blue. We were fighting a brave and determined foe, but their ranks were so severely shattered they were compelled to again retreat.[22]

About half an hour after the ending of this second assault, a Federal regiment, entirely alone and unsupported, very suddenly emerged from a ravine on the right front of the position occupied by the 4th Alabama. Their colors flying, the Colonel in command waving his sword and urging his men forward, they advanced directly on the 4th Alabama. Their heroic courage and dash excited the admiration of every member of the old 4th. It appeared to be downright murder to kill men in the performance of an act so courageous. The 4th Alabama had, after the second assault against us, replenished their ammunition and extra loaded guns were in readiness to be thrown to our men standing on the banquette.

When this Federal regiment reached within sixty or seventy yards of our entrenchment, two or three volleys were fired point blank by the 4th, together with a flank fire on our right and left. When the smoke from our rifles cleared away, not a man was standing, except one, and he was shot down as he ran away.[23] We learned from the prisoners, several of whom were not wounded but fell with the dead and wounded, that three hundred reported for duty that morning before going into battle. I find from the official reports that the 25th Massachusetts belonged to Brigadier General George J. Stannard's[24] brigade, Martindale's[25] division of W. F. Smith's[26] Corps. The brigade was composed of the 23rd, 25th and 27th Massachusetts, and 55th Pennsylvania. Of the three hundred there were two hundred and twenty killed, wounded and prisoners. The prisoners stated that all of the above regiments were brought under cover of the ravine for the assault, but the 25th Massachusetts was the only one to obey orders.[27]

This was the last attempt on our front, but the enemy's sharpshooters continued to keep our heads below the parapet. We saw a little Yankee raise his head up out of the grass out a short distance in front and called to him to come in. He jumped up and made a rapid run for our works, followed by several shots from his friends. On learning from our little prisoner that there were several more out in our front not wounded, Colonel Perry (who was again in command of the brigade, General Law having been wounded) was requested to send a detail over and bring them in. Several volunteered to go over, and they brought back several officers and privates.

Our list of casualties was small: Lieutenant Tom Samuel and Sergeant Harris,[28] also Lieutenant Newbill and Sergeant Zahm,[29] both of whom were struck by the same ball. Another member of the regiment was wounded on picket but I can't recall his name. Total wounded five. General Law, after recovering from his wound, was transferred to the cavalry.

As soon as it was dark we brought in some of the enemy's wounded. Among them was a young man mortally wounded, who was placed near where Dr. Duncan and I had spread our blanket to take a much-needed rest. His repeated cries for "Wa-ter, wa-ter" were so pitiful I arose and gave him the contents of my canteen, but still he cried for water. I saw there was no sleep for me, however exhausted I may be, as long as he continued his plaintive cries. I awoke the Surgeon and requested him to give the poor fellow some relief. He administered a dose of morphine, and as I dozed off that single word, "water," incessantly repeated, grew fainter and fainter and finally ceased. The next morning when I awoke the man was lying on his back, a heavy dew covering his face and hair as he laid there cold in death.

It was then that one of the videttes, who had been on duty during the night, laughingly told me of a Federal captain of artillery, having rode up to our works while I was sound asleep, and inquired, "What regiment is this?" Upon being told it was the 4th Alabama he quickly turned his horse and started back to the enemy's lines. He and his horse both having been shot down, he was brought in shot in the leg, limping and cursing, "If the damned fools wanted my battery planted in the Confederate lines, they could do it themselves." He was out looking for a position to place his battery and probably was lost in the darkness. How he managed to escape our pickets, I never could understand.

When we first reached Cold Harbor we were put to a great deal of inconvenience and trouble to obtain our rations, which were brought to us from the cooking camp some distance in the rear. Nor could we get water and ammunition without going a long way up our line of works in order to get to the rear. Behind us was a spring of good water several feet below our position, and only a few yards in the rear, but it was impossible for anyone to go directly to the rear without being shot by a sharpshooter. After dark on the 3rd I staked off a zig-zag trench in the rear of the centre of the regiment, and by digging from both ends it was soon completed and ready for use the next morning.

I had frequently noticed a pretty pointer dog wandering around a dwelling just over our works and to the right of the regiment, which had been left there when his owner had departed for a safer retreat. While sitting on the bank of dirt thrown out of the zig-zag trench, eating my cold corn bread, this dog came over the parapet, hungry no doubt, and approached me. As I was in the act of handing him a morsel of my bread, a sharpshooter sent a ball which struck the side of his head just behind his ear and glanced off. He went off howling most piteously, and I know the poor animal imagined I was the aggressor, when in reality he had saved me from a severe wound, and perhaps a mortal one.

On the 4th several feeble attempts were made on the right of our division, which were easily repulsed. We learned that General Grant sent orders to his Corps commanders to renew the attack at 9 A.M. on the 3rd; Generals Smith and Hancock refused to obey the order. General McMahon, Chief of Staff of the 6th Corps, says that the order was repeated two or three times, to attack, and he further stated: "To move that army farther, except by regular approaches, was a simple and absolute impossibility, known to be such by every officer and man of the three corps engaged. The order was obeyed by simply renewing the fire from the men as they lay in position."[30] In other words, merely by sharpshooting, as the enemy was entrenched only a short distance from our line.

On the 5th, two days after the heavy assault, not a dead or wounded soldier of the Union army was buried or taken off the field, except a few near our works, which we risked our lives to bring over the parapet and care for. The 4th Alabama had witnessed many a field of carnage and blood, and imagined before reaching Cold Harbor that nothing could surpass the horrors and brutalities of cruel war which we had for three and a half years been encountering, but this, the Battle of Cold Harbor, was the most horrible of any we had ever experienced. Under the rays of the hot June sun, the bodies of the fast-decomposing dead sent over into our trenches a most sickening and nauseating stench, while the helpless and fly infested wounded were left to die a most horrible death. General F. A. Walker, a Union officer, and author of the life of General Hancock, gives the reason for General Grant's failure to care for his dead and wounded, when he stated: "It was due to an unnecessary scruple on the part of the Union Commander-in-Chief. Grant delayed sending a flag of truce to General Lee for this purpose because it would amount to an admission that he had been beaten on the 3rd of June. It now seems incredible that he should for a moment have supposed that any other view could be taken of that action."[31]

A flag of truce, on the 5th, appeared in our front, which was met by one of our staff officers, who returned bearing a unique proposal from General Grant to General Lee, the purport of which was, that, hereafter, when no battle is raging, either party be authorized to send to any point between the pickets or skirmish lines unarmed men bearing litters to pick up their dead or wounded without being fired upon by the other party. This proposition was not acceded to by General Lee. He suggested that General Grant should follow the regular method of asking a truce. A short time elapsed when General Grant sent another message requesting a truce of six hours only, to bury his dead, which was granted. General Lee had forced Grant to divulge the true condition of affairs in his front, but by this time all the wounded were numbered among the dead. General Grant then attempted to lay the blame for the delay on General Lee.[32]

We sat on top of our breastworks and watched the numerous details as they busily worked at the gruesome task out in our front, but when the six hours allotted General Grant expired, the dead still remained thick upon the ground. General Lee having acceded to an extension of the truce, the task, much to our relief, was ended. We then placed ourselves below the top of the breastworks and resumed our occupation of sharpshooting. This continued until the 10th of June, when Grant withdrew from our front sometime during the night, and moved by his left to Bermuda Hundred on the James River, there to unite his shattered army with that of General Butler.[33] On the 11th the 4th Alabama left the trenches and moved on in the direction of the James River.

On the 16th we crossed to the south side of the James River, as General Grant was concentrating his army at Petersburg.[34] In counting up the list of casualties of the regiment in this campaign, we found that twenty had been left dead and buried on the field of honor; of the seventy-three wounded, many, slightly so, returned for duty before reaching the James.

When the 4th Alabama left the North Anna River on the home stretch on the 29th of May, Pickett's division, composed entirely of Virginians, joined us, having come up from the coast of North Carolina. This was the first time we had met since our departure for the Army of Tennessee in September '63. Our old Corps of three divisions was now complete. General Longstreet still being absent by reason of his wound, Major General Richard Anderson continued to hold temporary command over it.

Generals Breckenridge's[35] and Hoke's[36] divisions also came up to us about the same time. These were all the re-enforcements, not exceeding nine thousand muskets, which the Richmond Government gave General Lee to replace our depleted ranks during this entire campaign. In the meanwhile, General Grant had been furnished by Mr. Lincoln fifty-five thousand muskets, principally bounty jumpers, who were poor substitutes to take the position in our front once occupied by the flower of his army.

20

Siege of Richmond and Petersburg
June 16, 1864, to April 2, 1865

The 4th Alabama ended its part of the campaign from the Rapidan to the James when it crossed to the south side of the latter stream on the 16th of June, after forty-one days of almost incessant fighting, skirmishing and being subjected to artillery fire, with nine desperate combats to its credit, in which it repulsed the enemy in every assault made upon its front. In the combats engaged in by the Army of Northern Virginia from the 5th to the 19th of May, Colonel Venable, General Lee's Assistant Adjutant General, is authority for the statement that General Lee's ordnance officers reported they had gathered up more than 120,000 lbs. of lead, which was recast in bullets and did work again before the 1864 campaign ended.[1]

On the 13th, when the 4th Alabama moved out of the trenches and crossed the Chickahominy, the three days it lingered before crossing the James proved to have been a useless expenditure of time. General Lee, anticipating an attack on Richmond, was slow in dispatching troops to Petersburg to the assistance of the small garrison of Confederates assembled there, although General Beauregard,[2] in command, had sent repeated requests for him to do so. It was not until the 15th that General Lee became fully apprised that the enemy was concentrating in front of Petersburg.[3]

General Grant shielded his movement to the south side all during the 13th, 14th and 15th, crossing below Bermuda Hundred. General Alexander, who commanded the artillery of our Corps, gives a description of the bridge over which the greater part of Grant's forces crossed. "This," he says, "was the greatest bridge the world has seen since the days of Xerxes. At the point selected the river was 2100 feet wide, 90 feet deep and had a rise and fall of four feet. This bridge was built in eight hours."[4] And our artillery commander should have added, many hands make light work. As each Union Corps crossed, it was hurried on to Petersburg in an effort to reach there and overpower the small garrison of Confederates before the arrival of our main army.

During our march to Petersburg on the 17th, down near the Bermuda Hundred line, we found the enemy in possession of some of General Beauregard's trenches, which were abandoned when he fell back to the relief of Petersburg. The Texans and 3rd Arkansas under the command of Brigadier General Gregg, and our brigade, being in front, were formed in line of battle with our two Georgia brigades as supports. Pickett's division of Virginians formed on our left.

Both divisions charged and retook the works without much difficulty, the enemy hastily retreating to a second line. The men all dropped down in the trenches, awaiting further orders. Several, officers principally, standing a few paces in rear of the regiment, quietly conversing, were suddenly attracted by a most unearthly yell. Both brigades were over the parapet, running, yelling and firing, and never hesitated until they reached and captured the second line of works, accomplishing the work before the officers could recover their wits.

At the time we were not aware that General Lee nor any of his staff were present, but I learned from Colonel Venable that General Lee tented on the south side of the James, near Drewry's Bluff on the 15th. Of this little affair, Colonel Venable says:

> On the 16th and 17th, his troops coming up, he superintended personally the recapture of Beauregard's Bermuda Hundred line . . . On the 17th a very pretty thing occurred, in these lines, of which I was an eyewitness, and which evinced the high spirit of Lee's men . . . After the left of Beauregard's evacuated line had been taken up, there remained a portion, the approach to which was more formidable. The order had been issued to General Anderson commanding the Corps to retake this portion of the lines by a joint assault of Pickett's and Field's divisions. Soon afterward the engineers, upon a careful reconnaissance, decided that a good line could be occupied without the loss of life which might result from this recapture. The order to attack was therefore withdrawn by General Lee. This rescinding order reached Field but did not reach Pickett. Pickett's division began its assault under the first order. The men of Field's division, hearing the firing and seeing Pickett's men engaged, leaped from their trenches—first the men, then the officers and flagbearers—rushed forward and were soon in the formidable trenches.[5]

Of course, this is the correct version of this minor affair, but as we saw only what was directly in our front, and were not in General Lee's confidence, we regarded it in an entirely different light. It was our firm conviction that we, and not Pickett, initiated the movement against the second line, nor did we know that any orders had been given to assault, and afterward rescinded. We really believed that the men of our two front brigades, on their own volition, charged and Pickett's men joined in—the very reverse of what actually occurred.

Very early the next morning (18th), we were hurried off to the defense of Petersburg, leaving Pickett's men to hold the Bermuda Hundred line. After reaching there we saw in a Richmond paper the copy of a dispatch sent to the War Office by General Lee, in which he facetiously said: "We tried very hard to keep Pickett's men from taking the enemy's breastworks but couldn't do it."[6] We, ignorant of the facts, thought it very strange that General Lee should give Pickett's men credit for work accomplished by other troops. Colonel Venable has made the matter clear and satisfactory to our minds, and at the same time given the men of Law and Gregg full credit for their sudden and unexpected charge.

We found, on reaching Petersburg and taking our position in the trenches, that General Beauregard's little force had bravely and successfully held its position against a heavy force of the enemy until the arrival of the advance of General Lee's troops. The battle had been on since the 15th, and many more of Grant's troops were numbered among his list of casualties, with slight loss on the part of the Confederates. The breastworks were ready for our reception, and a completed zig-zag trench was in rear of the regiment. It was before noon when General Lee, with our division and Kershaw's, reached our entrenchments, the first of his army to reach the Petersburg lines, which had been so stubbornly held by General Beauregard's forces.[7]

The enemy made an attack on our lines shortly after we occupied the trenches, but were easily driven back to their works, which were only a short distance in our front. When a soldier showed his head the least above the parapet he was sure to draw the fire of a Union sharpshooter. "K" Company had been very unfortunate in captains, having lost six either killed or permanently disabled. That office in this company had remained vacant for some time, when Aleck Murray of the company was appointed to that position while we were here. The day after he received his commission he was going to the rear in our narrow zig-zag, and having exposed his head while permitting a comrade to pass him, he, too, was killed, increasing the number to seven.

General Lee allowed a few of the men each evening to pass out to stretch their limbs, bathe in the Appomattox or visit Petersburg, if they wished. He prohibited anyone in the city from selling to the soldiers anything intoxicating, but by paying five dollars for a common cigar, a drink of whiskey was donated by the generous proprietor. Although shells were frequently thrown by the enemy into the city, ice cream could be procured almost any evening.

On that part of the line occupied by the 4th Alabama the enemy were protected in the same manner, about one hundred yards in our front; if anything, their works were stronger.

Our rations were, of course, cooked in the rear and brought into the trenches once a day. As they consisted almost wholly of cornbread, the weather being warm, it soon soured and became full of mould, unless, which was frequently done, and with but very little effort, some would consume the whole of their twenty-four hours meal as soon as received in the trenches. It was quite warm, dry and dusty during this and the preceding month that the regiment held this position. The small quantity of bacon issued was frequently cooked down in the trenches, with a handful of fuel picked up in the rear, the least breeze blowing in a full complement of sand and dust down into our frying pans.

All during the day the men took turns at sharpshooting. At night we were kept awake by the detestable mortar shells thrown into our trenches. Although these did only occasional damage, it was always doubtful in our minds for whom each one of those hurling, shrieking monsters, accompanied with whirling, lighted fuses, were intended, and was imagined by everyone to be descending on his own devoted head.

General Grant had sufficient reserves to not only operate on his flanks, but to relieve the forces in our front and give his men a respite. With our weak, thin line, daily made weaker and longer by the foe extending the flanks, and continual fighting, we had none for that purpose. Of reserves we had none. Generally a division which we termed the "Military Foot Ball" was kept constantly on the double quick, being "kicked" from one end of the line to the other to either defend or retake some part of it. Until the close of the month of July, the 4th Alabama was frequently ordered out of the trenches and hurried to different parts of the line.

At Petersburg, on the night of the 29th of July, the regiment was lying in the trenches just to the right of what was known on our line as Elliott's Salient. General Gregg came in person and whispered to Colonel Scruggs, commanding the regiment, that a large force of the enemy was crossing to the north side of the James River, and that he was ordered to take our two brigades out of the trenches and march to meet it before dawn on the 30th. General Grant had sent his cavalry and one corps to the north side, evidently for the purpose of drawing away from Petersburg a part of our forces, and if possible [to] capture Richmond, while he kept a large force to spring a surprise on General Lee, and capture Petersburg.[8]

The 4th Alabama moved out of the trenches some time before daybreak and falling in with the Texans and 3rd Arkansas took up a rapid march down the Telegraph Road, in direction of Richmond. General Lee had, the day before, sent a force to the north side and Pickett's division was still where we left it on the 18th. Only three divisions were left to defend our Petersburg lines.

Early in the morning after getting well on our way, an incessant infantry fire and furious cannonading was heard back at Petersburg, and in a short time a courier came dashing by to the front of our column, bearing orders to General Gregg to hasten back to Petersburg. Crossing the Appomattox bridge on our return, we were informed that the enemy had blown up Elliott's Salient. As we hurried forward to the trenches the negro prisoners, escorted by a guard, passed, going to the rear, many with shattered arms and bloody heads.[9]

On reaching the trenches we found that the wide gap in our lines made by the explosion had been recovered by Mahone's division of Virginians, Georgians and Alabamians. The mine, when completed, contained four tons of powder placed directly under one of our batteries, Haygood's[10] brigade of South Carolinians occupying the trenches on its right and left, when the explosion occurred, about five o'clock that morning. The battery was completely buried and two hundred of the South Carolinians were buried alive, while lying asleep. After about six hours of desperate fighting the enemy was driven out of the crater and our lines re-established. The next day (July 31st) General Lee permitted the enemy under flag of truce to bury his dead, which, according to the official reports, amounted to 504. There were 1881 wounded, and we captured 1413. Our entire loss was less than 1000.[11]

Some time after this fiasco the 4th Alabama was sent to the north side. There it remained in the trenches until the middle of August, when it was ordered with the rest of the brigade and some other commands to resist a force sent by General Grant from Petersburg, which had been sent to the north side, consisting of Hancock's Corps and a division of cavalry. This engagement has been, by different writers, called Darby Town Road, Fussell's Mill and Deep Bottom. It was an affair in which our troops were badly worsted, having lost six pieces of artillery and some prisoners. I was not with the regiment in this battle, being confined on the sick list in Richmond, at Howard Grove Hospital, when it occurred, and my only recollection of anything connected with it was seeing Colonel Lowther[12] of the 15th Alabama brought in seriously wounded and placed on a cot near my own. Sivly[13] and Zahn[14] of the 4th Alabama were also brought in the hospital wounded.[15]

On the 25th the regiment, having been ordered to the extreme right of the army on the south side, supported Mahone's division in an attack on the enemy tearing up the Weldon Railroad, in which the Confederates came off victors.[16] We remained on the south side until the 28th of September, when hurried orders were received to repair to the north side to reinforce Gregg's and Benning's brigades. The next day, en route to join our comrades, we heard heavy firing in their direction and hastened our march, reaching their position on the evening of the 29th.

We found them on the right and left and within a small redoubt which we knew as Fort Gilmer, to the left of a much larger and stronger one—Fort Harrison—down in the vicinity of Chaffin's Bluff, on the James River. The two little Confederate brigades had been all day resisting attacks made on them by white troops of Butler's Army of the James. We ran into, and on the flanks of the redoubt, and the old 4th Alabama never in all its existence received such a royal welcome. Cheer after cheer went up time and again from our hard-pressed comrades. They had been anxiously looking for our coming all day, fearing our works would be stormed and taken before re-enforcements would reach them.

Soon after our arrival a desperate assault was made on our line by a heavy column of Butler's negroes.[17] Although a terrific fire with rifles, aided by our artillery, was poured into the rapidly advancing column, it continued to rush forward until reaching and leaping into the moat, which was seven or eight feet deep. The negroes, urged on by their white officers, assisted each other in their attempts to reach the top of the parapet. When a wooly head appeared it was instantly pierced with one or more bullets. It was soon discovered from their actions and words, during our appeals to them to surrender, that they were gloriously drunk.

Finally our artillerists threw over into the moat shells with short lighted fuses, which soon caused them to capitulate, and they were then marched through a culvert into our works. Several of the captives' canteens contained more or less whiskey with a mixture of gunpowder. I don't suppose there ever was a Southern boy who has not been informed in his childhood days, by some wise old darkey, "Jes take a dram er whiskey an power and it will sure make you brave."

Several writers giving a description, usually in their Recollections, of these assaults on our lines, have contended that Law's brigade, having been at the time in the trenches at Petersburg, was not engaged in this fight. It is true we were late in reaching there but were in time to be with our almost exhausted comrades in the last and most determined assault of the enemy that evening. In order to clear this matter up, and dispel any doubts as to our being there, I will take the trouble to quote from the "Diary of the First Corps, C.S.A.," which can be found in the Official Records, which says: "In the afternoon Field arrives with Law's brigade just in time to aid Gregg's and Benning's brigades in repulsing a most violent assault on Fort Gilmer. Many negroes were killed in the ditch."

Fort Harrison, somewhat in advance and to the right of Fort Gilmer, having had only a very small garrison to defend it, was captured by a sudden assault of the enemy.[18] On the next day (September 30th) General Lee came over from the south side, determined to make an effort to retake from "those people" the Fort. Five brigades, the 4th Alabama included, were taken from the works to make the hazardous attempt. After losing about two thousand good men and officers and meeting with a bloody repulse, we returned to our trenches, and no effort was afterwards made by General Lee to retake it.[19] A strong new fortified line was made in rear of the Fort and connected right and left with our main line, on which no impression was made by the enemy during the entire siege.

Before the movement began against Fort Harrison, the 4th Alabama, still being at Fort Gilmer, J. S.[20] and J. W. Thompson[21] of C Company, both good and tried soldiers, were detailed before daylight of the 30th to go over the works on a scouting expedition. During their absence the regiment had been taken out of the works and ordered to join the forces which were getting into position to assault and attempt to retake Fort Harrison. When J. S. and J. W., on their return from scouting, approached the works at Fort Gilmer, not finding the regiment in the works, discovered instead of the familiar faces they expected to see, a line apparently dressed out in comfortable blue overcoats, which leveled its guns on them with orders to throw down their arms and come in. They immediately held a hasty consultation. J. W., who had on a new, warm, comfortable jacket, but recently received from the good folks at home, which he prized more highly than all the rest of his worldly possessions, said: "I would, in the event we are compelled to surrender, dislike very much to give up my new jacket." "Yes," said J. S., "and I am very much afraid, from the number of dead negroes lying around us here, which we killed yesterday evening, the devils will retaliate." Finding no possible way of escape, they finally threw down their arms and climbed over among their supposed enemy. They rejoiced to find that the regiment had moved and a battalion of the "Richmond Reserves" had been placed on that part of the line. The Reserves were a well-organized command under General Ewell, composed of the employees from the different departments in Richmond, and were only called out in cases of emergency. They wore very dark grey suits and were in a position to present a very much better and neater appearance then "we regulars."[22]

After this abortive struggle and heavy loss on our part in an attempt to retake Fort Harrison, the 4th Alabama still remained on the north side defending Richmond. Our scouts having discovered that Kautz's[23] Federal cavalry division was in our front in an exposed and partially entrenched position on the Darby Town Road, General Lee determined to attack him with our division.[24]

The 4th Alabama joined General Gary's[25] South Carolina mounted infantry. The next morning, as soon as the other regiments of the division which were to take part in the attack came up, the assault was made, and a gloriously successful one it was to our arms. The men went yelling, running and firing right through horses, wagons, cannon and camp, troopers fleeing in every direction. It was a regular picnic for the boys. Major Robbins cried out, "Look boys, I've at last found a prize worth fighting for." Holding aloft a frying pan with a good long handle and waving it in lieu of his sword, he cheered and urged the men forward, and appeared to value his capture immensely, until a bullet from one of Kautz's repeating Spencer rifles, with a "ping," went through the bottom of it, and it was doubtless a more severe wound than the brave and gallant old soldier received in the Wilderness. Throwing it down and looking at it with sadness, he exclaimed: "Yes, it was ever thus; from childhood's hour I've seen my fondest hopes decay."

Bob Tribble[26] of F Company and Steve Miller[27] of C Company captured two fine horses; one, a splendid saddle animal, was retained by Lieutenant Colonel Scruggs and was named in honor of General Gregg, who was killed in this battle leading the troops engaged. He had been a citizen of Texas since 1852, born in Lawrence County, Alabama, in 1828. The fact of his being an Alabamian, having married a most estimable lady, Miss Mollie Garth of Decatur, and being personally known to some of the 4th Alabamians from North Alabama, he had become endeared to many of the regiment, and his death was greatly deplored by the whole division.[28]

In this attack on the cavalry we captured several prisoners and horses, nine cannon and ten caissons and brought off a large quantity of entrenching tools, which were quite an acquisition. After the defeat of General Kautz and our signal success, we were so elated we began to look around for other worlds to conquer. Through tangled underbrush and through an almost impenetrable swamp we marched until we found the enemy's infantry, in large force, strongly fortified, on the New Market Heights Road. After a consultation of our officers, it was the conclusion that discretion was the better part of valor, and we were immediately drawn off and returned to our safe entrenchments.

It was some time during this month that General Longstreet returned, after his long absence caused from the severe wound received while fighting in the Wilderness, relieving General Richard Anderson of command of our Corps.[29]

On the 27th of October the regiment, with others of the division, was engaged, under his leadership, with a large number of General Ben Butler's troops down on the Williamsburg Road, in which we defeated them, inflicting a loss of about one thousand.[30] This proved to be, as usual on the part of the enemy, a demonstration against General Lee's forces on the north side, while General Grant was making an effort to extend his lines and correspondingly stretch ours still further beyond Petersburg down the Weldon Railroad. He had by this time, by his incessant hammering, wrested from us a sufficient number of miles of this railroad to place it beyond our reach, thereby depriving our army of one of its main arteries of procuring supplies, principally from Wilmington, the only importing depot of the South for our blockade-runners.

I have only stated in this sketch the most important of the marches, countermarches, engagements and skirmishes in which the 4th Alabama participated, from Cold Harbor, June 3rd, to the close of the 1864 Campaign. It is remarkable that we passed through so many dangers with so few casualties, which were two officers and eight men killed and two officers and thirty-two men wounded, total forty-four.

During the months of November and December 1864 the 4th Alabama continued on the north side defending Richmond. At this time General Grant confined his operations in front of Richmond and Petersburg to the defense and extension of his lines and to offensive movements for crippling General Lee's lines of communication (Weldon and South Side Railroads) and to prevent General Lee from detaching any considerable force to send to the aid of General Joseph E. Johnston, who was falling back through Georgia followed by Sherman.

It was also during these two winter months that General Lee—although I never could understand how he could afford, with his long, thin line, to run the risk—granted to those of his officers and men whose homes were not too remote and were accessible, a limited number of "furloughs of indulgence" for thirty days. As the homes of four companies from North Alabama of the regiment were in the hands of the enemy, they were deprived of that pleasure. General Hood, our former division commander, who had superseded General Joseph E. Johnston in command of the Army of Tennessee, having cut loose from in front of General Sherman, was then at or near Florence, Alabama, or perhaps had advanced into Tennessee as far as Columbia. In fact we of the Army of Northern Virginia were perfectly ignorant of his movements.

About the middle of November Lieutenant Colonel Scruggs visited Richmond and there met Colonel Lawson Clay (brother of Senator C. C. Clay) of Adjutant General Cooper's Department, who told Colonel Scruggs in perfect confidence that Huntsville would soon be uncovered by General Hood, who was then advancing on Nashville. Scruggs returned to camp that evening in high glee over the good news Colonel Clay had imparted, and told me privately to write applications for both of us to visit our homes in Huntsville. As it would be more expeditious to take them through than to send them, as customary, through the regular channels, Colonel Scruggs determined the next morning to mount his horse and take them through brigade, division and Corps headquarters, at all of which he was successful. He then had to ride to Petersburg to get them approved by General Lee.

Arriving at Petersburg, with fear and trembling as to the final result of fond anticipations, he handed the Commander-in-Chief the applications. General Lee examined them and remarked, "You and Adjutant Coles can't reach your homes." To secure the furlough being uppermost in Colonel Scrugg's mind, he quickly said: "Oh, yes we can, General, General Hood is expected to advance on Nashville and our homes will soon be uncovered." General Lee, in a very stern and positive manner inquired: "Colonel, who was your informant?" "For God's sake, don't force me to tell you, General," exclaimed Scruggs. The General's manner immediately changed, and he then very feelingly spoke of his soldiers whose homes were so remote from Richmond, and how he regretted they could not be permitted to visit them. Knowing full well that it would be impossible for a North Alabama soldier to visit his home and return in thirty days, he, however, approved the applications for the allotted time, with instructions to report to him in person on our return.

The possibility of reaching our homes after such a long separation from our mothers and sisters was hard to realize and there was very little sleep for the two fortunates that night. The venture was a severe and hazardous one, clothed in much uncertainty. Sherman was on his devastating march in the heart of the Confederacy and transportation facilities were almost completely worn out. To give a detailed account of our trials in surmounting the difficulties encountered on the homeward trip, and the return to the old regiment, would occupy too much space in this little volume. Before we reached Huntsville the bloody battle of Nashville, which occurred on the 15th and 16th of December, was fought, ending in defeat to our arms. Of course this cut our visit very short, and we were compelled to hasten our departure. We had consumed the whole of our precious thirty days in our efforts to reach home, and had scarcely gotten there before we had to leave.

For fear the enemy would send a detachment of cavalry, immediately after the defeat of General Hood, to Huntsville, Colonel Scruggs and I remained with a friend a few miles from the city, concealed, for two or three days, until a mount was sent me and our clothes brought out to us by Colonel Scruggs' sisters. Colonel Scruggs having secured a horse from an old darkey, we turned our faces toward Florence, so as to intercept General Hood, as we believed he would cross the Tennessee somewhere above that point.

On the 25th of December we reached General Hood at Bainbridge, as he was laying his pontoons across the river at that point. It was a pathetic scene to see those emaciated, worn-out soldiers, and it was hard to believe they were the same fine-looking, active, strong-limbed men we met at Chickamauga in 1863.

General Hood welcomed and treated us most cordially. The next day he put us across the pontoon as soon as the last plank was placed, as he said he wished to get us ahead of his camp followers. From there we rode to Greensboro and sold our mounts for $2500, hiring a conveyance to take us to Marion. There we found many of our friends refugeeing from Huntsville. We visited Selma and Montgomery, and at the latter place found Captain George Clark of Eutaw, Assistant Adjutant General of Sanders'[31] brigade, like ourselves returning to Virginia. He accompanied us all the way back to Richmond. On our way we stopped over for a day or two in the historic old city of Charleston, as this was our first chance to do so.

From there we proceeded by rail to Richmond, where Colonel Scruggs and I found the old 4th Alabama still in the same old trenches down below Richmond. Colonel Bowles left on leave of absence soon after our return and never came to us afterwards. We never knew until some time after the close of the war that he had been appointed Brigadier General a few days before General Lee surrendered. He was in command of our brigade in all the fights below Richmond during Colonel Perry's absence on leave, which occurred after our Fort Gilmer battle of September 29, 1864. After receiving his appointment as Brigadier General he was ordered to report to General Joseph E. Johnston and assigned to a brigade in General Stewart's Corps.[32]

About the last of January and first of February 1865 the weather was intensely cold and there was great suffering in the trenches. General Lee at this time wrote, in part, to the Richmond authorities: "Under these circumstances, heightened by assaults and fire of the enemy, some of the men had been without meat for three days, and all were suffering from reduced rations and scant clothing, exposed to battle, cold, hail and sleet ... The physical strength of the men, if their courage survives, must fail under this treatment."[33] This earnest appeal had the effect of spurring our Commissary Department at Richmond to renewed energies, which caused a decided improvement in our rations over the previous month. The officers were required to make monthly settlements with the Commissary Sergeant and generally would be in arrears. The result was that the officers, whose pay exceeded many times that of the men, were in the same condition, the men being furnished free of charge.

By the end of this month General Grant had extended his flanking movement, after many hard knocks and reverses inflicted on his troops by General A. P. Hill, beyond Petersburg, as far as Hicksford, a station on the Weldon Railroad.[34]

Until the last of March comparative quiet prevailed in our front. As soon as General Sheridan[35] reached General Grant with his cavalry, on the 27th of March, after defeating our forces in the Valley under General Early, the latter immediately issued instructions for a general movement against General Lee's lines on the 29th of March. From this time until the 2nd of April the death grapple continued.

On the 2nd General Grant hurled immense masses of infantry and cavalry against our inferior numbers until four o'clock that evening, when our line was at last broken on our extreme right.[36]

The 4th Alabama was hurried from the north side to Petersburg and arrived late in the evening, amid shot and shell. Our loss in killed, wounded and missing in Hill's Corps and Pickett's division was very heavy, General Hill being among the dead.[37] In the heroic defense of the Confederate Capital, our great leader and his noble army had accomplished everything except the impossible, and our only alternative was retreat. General Lee remarked to one of his staff that evening: "This, Colonel, is bad business. It has happened as I told them at Richmond it would happen. The line has been stretched until it has broken."[38]

21

Petersburg to Appomattox
April 2 to 11, 1865

It was about sunset on the evening of the 2nd of April when the 4th Alabama was withdrawn from the trenches and started in direction of Amelia Court House, where General Lee had ordered supplies to be concentrated for the army. Our Corps marched out first, followed by General John B. Gordon with his own and the remnant of the lamented A. P. Hill's. On arriving at Amelia Court House, having marched all night over muddy roads, we found no supplies awaiting the Army, and the two days lost in collecting them was fatal to us and could not be retrieved.

The enemy were constantly hovering on our flanks and rear. At Sayler's Creek, before reaching Farmville, our troops under General Ewell were surrounded and captured, depleting our forces by about 8,000.[1] While changing, under orders from General Lee, on the 7th, our Corps to the rear and that of General Gordon to the front, I stopped as we passed our wagon train to get some papers out of my desk, fearing they would be either captured or burned. Before I could secure them the alarm was given that the enemy's cavalry was threatening the train. A lot of sleepy, hungry stragglers were quickly collected behind the wagons just in time to meet a charge of Sheridan's troopers. We kept up such a racket that the enemy imagined there was a strong guard concealed under cover of the wagons, and hastily retired. It was very little sleep we obtained, and when we were allowed a few hours to rest, pickets had to be placed on our front, rear and flank.

I remember after passing Farmville and continuing our march, after one of these little rests, Colonel Scruggs and I being somewhat in advance of the regiment, when we suddenly came upon Jim Thompson and Adkins,[2] both of C Company. They were sitting on the side of the road, the advance pickets of the night before, waiting for the regiment, and were two of the most innocent-looking fellows I ever saw as they sat there, each one picking the feathers from the big plump turkeys which were lying across their laps. The Colonel, knowing the turkeys were stolen property without being told, turned to me and said: "Take those men back to Captain Robbins and tell him to make each one of them carry an extra gun." After getting well away from Scruggs, who continued on to the front, I said: "You boys can wait here until the regiment comes up, a turkey is heavier to carry anyhow than an extra rifle." I then left them sitting by the roadside making the feathers fly.

There was no possible way to secure subsistence except to pick it up along our march. The men, from hunger and loss of sleep, were becoming desperate and hard to control. Tom McCalley, now living in Birmingham, one of Forrest's troopers, had been exchanged and sent via City Point to Richmond. Having nothing to carry, he loaded himself with a large ham from the supplies we were compelled to leave at Petersburg, and came on behind the regiment, overtaking it after we passed Farmville. As long as it lasted, he kindly shared his ham with me, for which I have ever held him in grateful remembrance.

On the 8th of April the 4th Alabama was protecting a battalion of artillery of our Corps from the enemy on our flanks, as we slowly marched. On the morning of the 9th, having marched all night, we had halted, waiting on Gordon, who was fighting desperately in our front in his efforts to cut a pathway through the enemy, who by this time had enveloped what was left of our army, on both flanks, front and rear. Both Gordon and the rear of our Corps were pushing the enemy back, drifting our forces farther and farther apart. General Gordon had broken the line in our front, and was still driving the enemy, and we were expecting every moment to be ordered forward, being only a short distance in his rear. Finally quiet prevailed both in front and rear.

It was no doubt plainly evident to our general officers that our end was near at hand, but we of the line never had the remotest idea of a surrender. We knew we were surrounded by many times our number. Still we believed and hoped that General Lee, knowing so well his aggressiveness, would mass the troops he had left to him and break through the enemy's lines. Then rumors were whispered among the men, which had reached our ears from the front, that flags of truce were being exchanged, and this so much foreboded surrender that every man in the regiment was so overcome with disappointment and grief, that they either fell down or leaned against some support and wept.

At this very moment General Gordon was going forward under flag of truce with a note to General Grant from General Lee, to meet General Sheridan. General Gordon relates an incident which occurred when Sheridan was approaching him, in which he says, "As General Sheridan was approaching, I noticed one of my sharpshooters drawing his rifle down upon him. I at once called to him: 'Put down your gun, sir; this is a flag of truce.' But he simply settled it to his shoulder and was drawing a bead on Sheridan, when I leaned forward and jerked his gun. He struggled with me, but I finally raised it. I then loosed it, and he started to aim again. I caught it again, when he turned his stern, white face, all broken with grief and streaming with tears, up to me and said: 'Well, General, then let him keep on his own side.'"[3]

While the above scene was being enacted the 4th Alabama was ordered a short distance to the front. While making the movement General Lee rode by going to the front, and just as he reached the head of the regiment the report of a rifle rang out above the rear of the regiment. Quickly reining up Old Traveler, he inquired: "Who fired that gun?" When told it was only one of the men who wished to clean out his rifle, General Lee remarked that he did not wish any more firing and continued on to the front. He was then on his way to Appomattox Court House to meet General Grant. This was the last time the 4th Alabama saw him.

Late that evening the report was confirmed that General Lee had really surrendered.[4] Though young in years, yet old in war's terrible experience, through which few have passed, these ragged, half-starved, grim-visaged veterans were almost heart broken. Orderly Sergeant Jim Franklin[5] discovered that a member of the regiment had fortunately picked up a battle flag the last time we passed through Richmond and deposited it in his knapsack. This we substituted for our old bullet torn one which had waved over us continually from Seven Pines to Appomattox, and placed it on the flag staff to be surrendered. At the same time we tore into small pieces our precious old rag and divided it among the men. Our pangs of hunger were very much reduced on account of our grief-stricken condition. The mortification of having to march up and stack arms in front of a host of men, whom we had every right to consider, man for man, that we were their superiors, from past experience on many battlefields, was most galling to our proud spirits.

On the 10th we were busily engaged in making out our paroles, and on the 11th the immortal old 4th Alabama for the last time shouldered their rifles and marched out in front of a Yankee regiment awaiting to receive them.[6] Brave old Tom Norton,[7] as he stepped back into line after depositing his gun in the stack brought forth a smile from some of us near him on the right of the regiment, when he remarked to the Yankees facing our line only four or five paces distant: "Don't you make any demonstration over this, d——n you." The men and officers then returned to our bivouac and the career of the regiment was ended.[8]

It has been a source of pleasure and recreation during my occasional leisure moments to follow with my pen those old heroes with whom I was closely associated for four long years, to the end of a cause, though lost, we believed to be just.

Together in sunshine and shadow we fought, marched, slept and suffered, and for them and their descendants my humble efforts have been solely a work of the most ardent love and intense devotion which I have, and ever shall entertain for them.

22

Our Return Home

Our paroles under the agreement between Generals Lee and Grant permitted us to return to our homes, not to be disturbed by United States authority so long as we observed our paroles and the laws in force where we resided. General Lee, before we left for our homes, sent to each regiment his farewell address, General Order No. 9, which was read to the men by their respective Adjutants.[1]

All the members of the regiment concluded to return to their homes in Alabama over the most direct route, except Lieutenant Colonel Scruggs, Captain Karsner, myself and Major Robbins. The Major returned to his people in North Carolina. Scruggs, Karsner and myself, and Dr. J. J. Dement, whose home was also in North Alabama, joined us. The Doctor was the Surgeon of Thomas'[2] brigade of Heth's division, A. P. Hill's Corps. Also under the agreement General Grant allowed free transportation over all military roads and transports.[3] Knowing we would be delayed in reaching our homes to go via Lynchburg, in consequence of having to walk the greater distance, we determined, though almost penniless, to risk a Northern tour.

As we had nothing, our preparations for our departure were soon made. Colonel Scruggs turned his horse over to the little North Alabama squad to help them on their long walk. The Major, the first to leave, mounted on his old horse, and with tears streaming down his face, rode among us and bade us all an affectionate farewell. His parting words were: "God has, certainly for some good purpose, passed us safely through all the trials and danger which for four years we have encountered." One of the most vivid recollections I have of parting with my comrades on that eventful day was seeing that brave, pious and patriotic old soldier for the last time as he rode with bowed head out of view.

The squad I accompanied retraced its steps to Petersburg, arriving there on the 16th. While sitting on the platform waiting to take passage to City Point on a freight train, with a heavy heart, we learned of the death of Mr. Lincoln. We reached the Point late that evening and took passage on a transport for Baltimore. The lower deck was crowded with United States officers' horses, and the upper with officers. With music and whiskey, they were having a merry time, holding high revelry among themselves over the surrender of General Lee's little army. We were not permitted to go up into the cabin, having had a bayonet thrust in our faces when we made the attempt. The only recourse left our proud little squad was to wedge ourselves in among the closely crowded, restless horses, and there stand throughout the entire night.

We arrived the next morning in Baltimore, finding the whole city draped in mourning. The Colonel, Captain and I looked quite rough, but the Doctor appeared gorgeous, as we walked up from the wharf that early morning in April 1865. We three were dressed in dark grey jeans, with no insignia of office, a donation from kind friends of Marion, Alabama. The Doctor sported a new untarnished suit of cadet grey, his Major's stars showing conspicuously on his collar. As we wended our way to the Barnum, the most popular hotel in the city in those days, we observed an old gentleman standing in the doorway of Hortsman Brothers. As we were passing, he stepped back so as to conceal himself from the street and beckoned to us to enter. He informed us that a city ordinance had been passed since the death of Mr. Lincoln positively prohibiting a Confederate soldier wearing in public his uniform. We were taken back to the rear of the establishment, and each one was presented with a linen duster by our kind old friend.

We met many sympathizers, but on account of the manner of Mr. Lincoln's death, the citizens had to be very guarded in showing a Confederate any attention whatever. After reaching the hotel and taking a bath, which we very much needed, we repaired to the dining room, as it then was about breakfast time, the Doctor paying for our tickets.

After enjoying something we had not been accustomed to for years—a good meal—we were accosted as we emerged from the dining room by a fatherly looking old gentleman (whom we afterwards learned was the proprietor), who inquired if we had paid for our meals. Captain Karsner, thinking the old man imagined we were a lot of dead-beats, replied in a very emphatic manner: "Yes, sir, we have." Putting his hand gently on Karsner's shoulder, he replied almost in a whisper: "Oh, I meant no offense, my desire was, that if you had paid to have it returned to you." Of course we refused to accept his kindness. At his earnest request, we finally accepted a room free of charge until we could communicate with our friends. We were perfectly ignorant of how far north military roads extended.

Dr. Dement went down on St. Paul Street to seek relief from friends, while Captain Karsner and I repaired to the Transportation Office, leaving Colonel Scruggs in our room to entertain our friends, who were secretly and continually calling, we being the first of General Lee's army to reach there. The excitement over the martyred President ran so high no one dared speak to a Confederate on the street.

Failing to accomplish anything in the way of transportation, Karsner and I returned to the hotel. On our way there, we overtook a lady, who, when we approached quite near, without looking back, said in a low voice: "Don't walk up by my side, I wish to inquire if General Lomax[4] is safe." Being told that he was, she replied: "Thank God; he is my brother."

On reaching our room we found Dr. Dement had returned, accompanied by two big policemen. He stated that when he reached St. Paul Street a fanatical old lawyer ran out and violently accosted him for wearing his uniform on the street and became so boisterous that in a few moments a large mob was collected around him. We were particular, when on the street, to keep our dusters closely buttoned, but with all our precaution, it appeared, from the constant appeals from women and girls for just one brass button, that this did not prevent everyone knowing from where we hailed. We had no other clothes, the enemy having destroyed our baggage, as Dr. Dement informed the belligerent old lawyer.

The Doctor then appealed to the policemen to conduct him to his hotel, which they very willingly did. Mr. Robert Herstein, who had formerly been a merchant in North Alabama, and a friend of Colonel Scruggs and myself, was at that time in Baltimore and hearing of the disturbance, hastened to the hotel to discover if any of his friends were in trouble. Finding we were there, he came to our room and offered to advance our party all the funds we needed, which we very gratefully accepted, and left for our homes that night, reaching there several days before the other members, whose homes were in North Alabama.[5]

Appendix A

Letter of Captain Edward D. Tracy
Regarding Battle of First Manassas Battlefield—
In Camp, Six Miles from Manassas, July 24th, 1861

While at Winchester, there came an order to purge my Company of all men who could not stand a long, hard, forced march; which order being thrice repeated, we received the order to march at sunset on the 18th. We marched all that night, and the next day, and arrived at Piedmont after night of the 19th, broken down and starved. Throwing ourselves down on the ground, we promised ourselves a soldier's sweet sleep of a few hours, unlulled except for sweet memories, and unrocked except by dire fatigue. I fell down at the head of my company as soon as I gave orders to stack and *break*, and after thinking a moment of the dear ones, fell into a dead sleep. In an hour, the rain came down in torrents, but all too weak to awaken me. After I was floating off, some of my men pulled me up, and I got under a rude shed which they had made of rails and straw, and slept again till 1 A.M., of the 20th, when we took the cars. As soon as we were on board, and my men *seated*, I lay down on the floor of the car and *slept* again. Don't you think I was sleepy?

We arrived at the Junction, nearly dead with rain and hunger, about 10 o'clock of that day, and marched out about two miles into the woods, where we spent the day and night, having received some food and a little more rain. Of course, we had no tents. You may imagine that we were not very sprightly. I was ill with fever and other camp diseases, my tongue furred, etc., and hardly able to walk. But, on the 21st, we received the order that all who were able to march, should fall into ranks. I was no longer sick, my company numbered, rank and file, about seventy, and we started in double quick time, and marched, God knows how far, some eight or ten miles, until, at last, we got near where we are now encamped, when we were told to load as we went, and that the enemy were right before us. We marched up a hill in an open field, and, just at the brow, were ordered to lie down, fire and load, fire and load, etc.

The enemy were entrenched right before us, not more than 100 yards off, and the battle began. There were opposed to our regiment, as Kirby Smith informed me, yesterday (thank God! Smith is not dead, nor likely, in my opinion to die, though shot through the upper portion of the breast with a grapeshot—he said he would go to Lynchburg to-day), nearly the entire force of the enemy. Our brigade was on the extreme left, and there the battle raged hottest. For an hour and three-quarters, we stayed there in that open field, exposed to fire from front and the right flank, and I may say to you, I hope, without fear of misapprehension, that I did my devoir. I stood up in the front rank, rallying my men when the troops were lying down. I saw man after man of my company fall dead by my side, and others wounded. Our position was a most hazardous one, but well did we maintain it. At last, we were flanked on the left, and then, from three sides came the murderous fire. We fell back, our men falling as we retired.

Poor Col. Jones, who sat upon his horse as calm as a statue, during the whole fire, until the horse was shot from under him, fell as we retired from the field, shot twice, once through each thigh. I did not hear of it, until we rallied about half a mile back, when I called for volunteers to bring his body off, to which a portion of my command responded. Not having strength enough to bring Jones off, after going several hundred yards back with my little corps, and not being joined by others, I desisted, and proceeded to rejoin the regiment, which, under the galling and tremendous fire from the left, had again fallen back.

As I was bringing up the rear, our Major, Scott (Charley Scott, of California), fell right before me, shot through the leg. With the assistance of Spragins and one or two others, we brought him out of the fire, but were compelled to leave him in a wood near by. Our Lieut. Colonel, Law, was then shot, and his arm broken, and he was compelled to leave the field, and the regiment, or the fragment that remained unkilled, unwounded, or undispersed, were left like sheep without a shepherd.

The whole was terrible: the dead men, the wounded, the dying, the bursting of bombshells among us, all combined to make a scene wild and grand. The most excruciating torture was the intolerable, insatiable, and burning thirst for water. On all sides, from wounded and unwounded, the cry went up, 'water, water, water.'

It would be impossible to describe the events of the day in detail. Gen. Bee fell, mortally wounded, leading our regiment (which was his pet and pride), the balance of his brigade being dispersed. Our regimental loss, in killed and wounded, was about 200, out of 650 in the action.

We got Jones and Scott after the battle. Thank God! there is a good prospect of the recovery of the first—the recovery of the latter is hardly doubtful.

We have won a glorious victory, and the Fourth Alabama Regiment has won a name.

Captain Edward D. Tracy [*Huntsville Democrat*, August 7, 1861]

Appendix B

Incidents and Personal Experiences on the Battlefield at Gettysburg

Address by Capt. W. C. Ward, a private of Company G, Fourth Alabama Regiment, Law's Brigade, on Saturday, May 5, 1900, to Camp Hardee, in Birmingham, Alabama

Commander and Comrades: I was once young, vigorous, and of strong will. Thirty-seven years ago General Lee, in command of 63,000 infantry and artillery, crossed the Potomac at Williamsport, Md. Gen. J. E. B. Stuart, in command of the Cavalry Corps, had crossed the river below Harpers Ferry, and moved eastward through Maryland toward Winchester, near Baltimore. When Hood's Division reached the Potomac, the river was found to be swollen and almost half a mile in width. Without regard to order, the men dropped from the banks into the swiftly-flowing stream. Our cartridge boxes had been placed about the shoulders to protect them from the water, and in this condition we waded the river. The rain was falling quite steadily; so we were thoroughly wet all over. At Williamsport, a pretty little Maryland town, we were halted, and fires were built that we might dry our clothing. The rain still falling, the Commissary Department, with whiskey that cost the Confederacy nothing, undertook to wet the inside of the tired, hungry, and wet soldiers by distributing about one-half gill to each man. It was good whiskey, as we had not had any for many months. Knowing how good such a stimulant was at the end of a hard day's march, this private soldier attempted to do a prudent thing. Instead of pouring his whiskey into his stomach, he turned it into his canteen.

The march was resumed; and after moving rapidly northward for about one hour, the division was halted to rest. All lay down on the roadside, wet though it was; and when we arose again to resume the march, the canteen into which the whiskey had been so carefully poured had been reversed and all that soldier's good spirits lost. The loss produced a painful impression, and in all the years that have since gone he has remembered that loss with keen regret. All the good things that have ever come to him since have not compensated for the loss of that whiskey.

When the division reached a point just south of Greencastle, Pa., the men were halted and went into camp. Guns were stacked, and every preparation made for a good night. Near the bivouac there was a large spring, affording abundance of water for the weary soldiers. Many of the men went into the country foraging, returning—some, with chickens; some, with honey; some with butter and whatever else that was edible on which their hands could be laid. It was quite dark; and while the spring could be found, its topography could not be well observed. A member of Company K, from Scottsboro, Ala., going to the spring with his camp kettle for water, reached out into the spring and filled his kettle; but as he was thin from light diet, in drawing the full kettle toward him, he staggered, and his cap, saturated with the dirt and perspiration of a long service, fell into the water and disappeared from his sight. He returned to the camp capless. Shortly afterwards Jack Stewart, a tall member of Company G, six feet six inches high, and of the thickness of a fishing pole, went to the same spring with his kettle to procure water. Reaching out the full length of his arm, he drew in his kettle filled with water. Returning to the bivouac, he put the ration of beef for his mess into the kettle, and left it to boil over a slow fire, while the men, tired out, dropped off to sleep. Next morning at daybreak we were aroused to hastily prepare for the onward march into the land of our enemies. As rapidly as it could be done, the boiled meat was taken from the kettles and fairly divided among each mess. As this process was going on, there was heard a guttural muttering from Jack Stewart expressive of intense disgust and disappointment. It was: "——— ———— ——— ———, boys! Just look here!" All eyes were turned on Jack Stewart. The fingers of his left hand were spread out in his right. He held a forked stick, on which was suspended the well-boiled cap of Company K. The broth in the kettle was well colored with the dirt and perspiration of the cap, and the mass in the kettle was disgusting. Poor Jack and his messmates had to go without meat.

We were a joyous crowd. Marching rapidly northward, we soon entered Greencastle. Leaning over a fence that enclosed a cottage was a man with two ladies. They appeared to be absorbed looking at us; and while we were looking at them, [a man of] Company K, bareheaded, his shock of hair waving in the sunlight, went rapidly up to where the man and the ladies were standing. Not a word spoke he, not a motion made he, until he was within arm's length of the man; and then, without bow or other recognition of their presence, he simply lifted the man's hat and transferred it to his own head. The last we saw of that man and his companions he was scratching his naked head and the women were laughing at him. We were a merry lot. Entering the one long street of Greencastle, we found the people not at all afraid of us, as might have been expected. John Young, a private of Company I, of Huntsville, Ala., a man so bow-legged that he took in all sides of the street, remembering the wrongs that Huntsville had suffered at the hands of the Yankees, went up to an old gentleman standing in the presence of some ladies at the foot of a stairway that ascended immediately from the street, and lifted from the gentleman's head a beautiful new felt hat, at the same time carelessly dropping his own well-worn Confederate wool covering. The old gentleman seemed dazed. Rubbing his hands through his thin hair, he realized the situation, and was overheard to say: "I really believe that soldier has taken my hat."

While going through Greencastle, the fife and drum of the Forty-Eighth Alabama Regiment played "The Bonnie Blue Flag." The doors of the houses were all closed, but there was evidence of life in the upper stories. Back in the shadow of one of the upper rooms, while the fife was screaming out, I saw a young woman singing with all her might, and with great seriousness, "The Bonnie Blue Flag," keeping perfect time, from the motion of her lips, with the drum band.

We never halted. Marching through fields, over newly-planted corn and waving wheat, through orchards and currant bushes, we reached Chambersburg about noon. It was a beautiful town. Everything was fresh, indicating prosperity, and no signs of war. The stores were all closed, and the men, bareheaded, were standing in front. To our laughing inquiry, "Where are your hats?" they replied, laughing: "We have had some experience." There was nothing to indicate from the deportment of the citizens that their country was being invaded by a hostile army. Passing out of Chambersburg by the northeast pike, as we went through a gateway under a hill, crowned with a beautiful residence, we observed many ladies, well dressed, bearing on their bosoms the Union flag and making an ostentatious display of the Stars and Stripes. We took all of this in great good humor, neither giving nor taking offense. It was here that an incident occurred that has become famous. One of the young ladies, bolder than all the others, made a somewhat conspicuous and aggressive display of her flags and herself, accompanied by remarks. A bold Texan (and the

Texans of that division were always bold) said to the brave young woman: "Madam, you are doing a very dangerous thing waving that flag at Confederate soldiers." She inquired, with spirit: "Why, sir, am I doing a dangerous thing?" His reply was: "We rebels never see that flag flying over breastworks without charging them." The young woman made no reply, but her companions had a good laugh at her expense. The Texan shouldered his Springfield and went on his way as if regretting there were no orders to charge.

The division was bivouacked in a beautiful wood just north of Chambersburg, and there remained two or three days. It was a delightful rest. There we wrote our last letters to the loved ones at home. We had left the war-wasted and battle-riven Old Dominion, and had come to the land of corn and wine, flowing with milk and honey. Everything indicated prosperity and abundance. It was at a season of the year when the trees drooped with ripening cherries, and in every direction you could see these trees filled with Confederate soldiers helping themselves to that most luscious fruit. For a few miles around the camp the men had liberty to observe the country, always under instructions to do no mischief. Just how far they observed instructions is not known. A comrade had a negro servant named Ned that was a good fellow and very much attached to "Marse Joe," for whom he cared as a father might care for a son. Having a black skin, we thought the people would like to do something for Ned, and so he was sent out with as many canteens as he could carry and such other means of foraging as we had. Ned returned late in the afternoon with every canteen full of milk. These canteens had been captured, as well as our muskets, from the Federal Army; in fact, Lee's Army appeared to be equipped from the Federal Army. One canteen filled with skimmed milk was turned up to the mouth of this private soldier, who never stopped to breathe until the entire contents—three pints—had passed into his stomach; and then, with a sigh of satisfaction, he was ready to go to sleep.

It was on Tuesday morning, the first day of July, that Law's Brigade was ordered to the east and south to New Guilford as a corps of observation. We bivouacked in a most delightful little valley. The white, fat Chester pigs were too great a temptation for men tired of poor beef, and they fell on the Chester pigs, and it was not long before the mess had boiled hog's head and spareribs and newly-baked wheat bread for the haversacks. We went to sleep that night with the information that we were to march at 2 o'clock the next morning.

Promptly we were aroused, and began the most fatiguing march of the war. At daylight we were ascending the mountains; and, without halting, we went over the crest and down into the valley at Cashtown.

Then we began to realize what this march meant. Passing rapidly to the rear were hundreds of Federal prisoners taken in the battle of July 1, when Ewell's corps had crushed the corps of General Reynolds, of the Federal Army. It was then said, and many times repeated since, that if Ewell had only advanced without waiting for supports he could have occupied Cemetery Ridge and the long crest of Little Round Top. Hood's line of march carried him to the neighborhood of General Lee's left. Approaching the line of battle, we filed shortly to the right, and moved rapidly southward, weary as we were. The roads were the roughest and the long, sloping hills the steepest. The day was hot, and we were thirsty and had not stopped to rest or drink. We had already marched twenty-four miles, and were still marching two or three miles farther in view of the Federal Army crouching along the mountain ridge.

Apprehending that we would be immediately ordered into battle, water details were sent out, each man carrying a dozen canteens. After making a wide detour, the only water we could find was a little pond, where there was gathered at a water gap water quite hot and greenish, remaining from the spring rains. With this the canteens were filled, and we began making a double-quick to catch up with the marching army. Did you ever undertake to catch up with men moving away from you? This was found to be a very difficult undertaking. At last our places were reached. The canteens were distributed and our guns returned to us. Gasping and faint with weariness, we still moved to the right of the army.

At last the division was halted on the first foothill west of Little Round Top, and immediately the men lay down in line. From this position the hill declined rapidly into the valley along the foot of the mountain, which was densely wooded. From this position on the right we could see occasionally puffs of white smoke in both sides of the valley as pickets engaged in desultory firing. In front of us no living thing was to be seen. There was a small, low-roofed cottage near the foot of Round Top, and adjoining it there was a picket garden. Near by was a stone fence about four feet high. Through this little valley slowly ran a stream of water that spread out some yards in width, which, like all the other water we had seen that day, was quite warm. How vividly the whole picture comes back! As we lay there making these mental notes, the soldiers overheard a comrade say: "Boys, we are going to have a battle. There is old Fairfax, Longstreet's fighting Adjutant, and we never see him that we do not have a fight." Looking over the shoulder to the rear, one saw a tall, very handsomely-dressed officer in full uniform, mounted on a magnificent horse. In front of him there were gathered the Division Generals and the Brigade Generals, with members of their several staffs, making quite a company. This man was seen pointing in the direction of Little Round Top and to the right of it and along the ridge, as if giving the position of the enemy.

And who was old Fairfax, Longstreet's fighting Adjutant? And how was such a title acquired? John Walter Fairfax was a Virginia gentleman whose home, in Loudoun County, had been the home of James Monroe, once President of the United States; the descendant of one Thomas Fairfax, who, in the seventeenth century, had removed from England and settled in the State of Maryland. Colonel Fairfax had been opposed to secession, was a man of great wealth, living in elegant splendor. Having made provision for his family during the time he expected the war to continue, he cast his fortunes with the South and took a position as Volunteer Aid on the staff of General Longstreet, maintaining himself while serving in the army. In 1862, at the battle of Frazier's Farm [Glendale], there happened an incident that brought him to the notice of General Lee. He was sent with a message to the commander of the left brigade of Longstreet's Corps. That brigade was lying under the cover of a wood in front of a long line of Federal breastworks. There was a low, dropping fire of skirmishers. While delivering his message to the Brigade Commander, suddenly the left regiment of the brigade, from some cause never known, in line of battle sprang out from the woods, with colors flying, charged toward the Federal breastworks. The Brigade Commander, quivering with excitement, called out: "My God, Fairfax, look at that regiment! It is going to destruction! What must I do?" Without replying, grasping the desperate situation, Fairfax turned his horse, and, putting spurs to the animal, dashed down between the two lines of battle, thundering like a very god of war as he rode across the volleys of cannon and musketry, uttering with every bound his steed the command: "Charge, charge, charge!" Catching the inspiration of his great soul, the brave Confederates, without any command, dashed forward against and over the breastworks of the enemy, sweeping the Federals from the fields. On the day after the battle of Malvern Hill, while General Lee had McClellan's army cowering under the protection of the gunboats, at the headquarters of the Commanding General, which were at the residence of a private gentleman, before breakfast was served, General Lee was walking in the flower garden; and, meeting Mr. Fairfax, he plucked and handed him a rose, addressing him as Major, saying: "This is in recognition of your gallantry in battle. Before night your commission will be received." So ever afterwards John Walter Fairfax distinguished himself in battle. It was his custom before going into battle to dress himself in his best uniform, and while in battle to be mounted upon a most magnificent horse.

This was the man now giving directions to General Hood and his Brigade Commanders.

Immediately the pioneer corps of Law's Brigade passed in front of the Fourth Alabama, and with their axes attacked a body of timber just in front of the right of the Fifth Texas. As soon as the timber began to fall, a Federal battery over on the mountain, and apparently near what was called the "Devil's Den," opened fire on our line of battle. The second or third shell, bursting in the right company of the Fifth Texas, killed three men. A battery serving with Hood's Division immediately occupied the cleared space, and began to reply to the Federal battery. At this time Adj. Gen. Lee Terrell, of Law's Brigade, rode in front of the Fourth Alabama Regiment and commanded: "Attention, Fourth Alabamians!" The men sprang to their feet, their guns at an order. The thought that passed through the mind of the soldier was: "O God, just for a half hour's rest!" As soon as we were at attention, the command was, "Shoulder arms!" and then, "Right shoulder; shift arms!" and then, "Forward; guide center; march!" Then arose that wild, indescribable battle yell that no one having heard ever forgot. The men sprang forward as if at a game of ball.

The air was full of sound. A long line of Federal skirmishers, protected by a stone wall, immediately opened fire. Grape and canister from the Federal battery hurtled over us as we descended the hill into the valley. We rushed through our own battery while it was firing and receiving the fire from the enemy's guns. Men were falling, stricken to death. This soldier received on the left thigh a blow from a minie ball that was exceedingly painful, but for which he did not halt. The younger officers made themselves conspicuous by rushing to the front, commanding and urging the men to come on, while Adjutant General Terrell was doing what he could to restrain the impetuosity of the Fourth Alabama, calling on the men to observe the Fifth Texas—how orderly they were marching to the charge. In the din of battle we could hear the charges of canister passing over us with the noise of partridges in flight. Immediately to the right, Taylor Darwin, Orderly Sergeant of Company I, suddenly stopped, quivered, and sank to the earth dead, a ball having passed through his brain. There was Rube Franks, of the same company, just returned from his home in Alabama, his new uniform bright with color, the envy of all his comrades, his gladsome face beaming as if his sweetheart's kiss had materialized on his lips, calling to his comrades; "Come on, boys; come on! The Fifth Texas will get there before the Fourth! Come on, boys; come on!" He shortly afterwards met the fatal shot. There was Billy Marshall, running neck and neck with this private soldier, each striving to be first at the stone fence, behind which lay protected the Federal line of skirmishers, firing into the faces of the advancing Confederates. As we dashed into the slow-running water, Billy stooped, supporting himself on his left hand, without kneeling, holding his musket in his right hand, and drank as an animal might have done. I never saw him afterwards. His body was never found, and no one has ever heard of Billy Marshall since that day. Without doubt, he was killed before he reached the mountain.

Rushing up to the fence, dropping on the left knee, fixing bayonets, and springing over the wall, expecting to be riddled with bullets, was the act of a moment, not minutes. Looking around, this soldier saw his comrades quickly coming over the wall and forming into line of battle. The enemy had retreated up the sides of the mountain. The dead, fallen chestnut timber formed a natural abatis, through which passage was difficult. As soon as the line was formed, each man giving command to his fellow, the march through the abatis up the mountain side began at a quick step. There was a long line of large bowlders cropping out on the mountain side, forming a natural breastwork. Over and through this the line had to mount. The line had become broken because of the timber, and those of us in the front line, as soon as we were uncovered, received the first fire of the hidden Federals. A long line of us went down, three of us close together. There was a sharp, electric pain in the lower part of the body, and then a sinking sensation to the earth; and, falling, all things growing dark, the one and last idea passing through the mind was: "This is the last of earth."

Over their fallen comrades the men rushed up the mountain side, and soon struck the main line of the enemy, for there was a clash of musketry at close range. Minie balls were falling through the leaves like hail in a thunderstorm. Consciousness had returned. Dragging himself along the stony earth, as a wounded snake might have done, this soldier took shelter under a bowlder four or five feet in height, and there he ascertained the character of the injury. A private of Company A passed by, asking that he might give succor, and was told to go to the front, that he could do no service. The man went, and was severely wounded in the chest. Another, of Company E, stopping, was asked what he was doing in the rear. He replied that his gun was useless. The wounded soldier, pointing to his own musket, said: "Take mine; it is in good condition, and in my hands can never again be of service." While lying there weltering in his blood, another crouched behind the same rock as if for protection. The soldier asked, when he saw it was one of his messmates: "What are you doing here, John?" He replied, sick and exhausted: "I have fallen behind. What can I do for you?" He was told: "You can do nothing. Your place is with our company. Do you not hear that they have joined battle with the enemy?"

Without more [ado], John Mosely, going forward to his company, then engaged in the last great struggle of the day, went to his death, falling mortally wounded. Later the line of battle fell back to where the soldier was lying, and he heard one of his comrades say: "Halt here, boys, and let us make a stand at this place!" Soon they came to him, placed him on a stretcher, and carried him to the rear, where he would be safe, comparatively, feeling certain the battle would be renewed. In the meantime the field surgeon had administered a stimulant and morphine. All night in agony he lay, until about 3 o'clock in the morning, when he, with two others, was placed in an ambulance and carried to the Plank Farm Hospital, just in rear of the line of battle. The wounded of the division were gathered there, those most severely wounded receiving surgical aid first. Under the influence of a powerful opiate, sleep came, and for a few hours there was forgetfulness. When he awoke, he felt the craving of hunger; and, feeling for his haversack, he found that it, with the good rations prepared the day before, was gone. Some rascal, supposing him dead, had carried away the provisions he needed to save life.

Here his attention was arrested by a cannonading such as earth never before heard. The one hundred and twenty-five pieces of artillery of Lee's Army replied to one hundred and twenty-five of the Federal Army. Shot and shell passed in midair, and there was elemental war such as could only be where an army of demons contended with an army of demons, shot and shell shrieking in midair as lost souls might shriek and as wildest animals might shriek when engaged in death battles.

Lying under this fearful war of shot and shell lay Pickett's Division prone on the earth, awaiting the dread command, nerves strung and minds intent. At last there was a pause in the dreadful artillery duel, and then rang out the clear bugle note, calling the men to attention. Then sprang to life from Mother Earth eight thousand Virginians. Better men never went to battle and to death. To make grander men, God must create a new world. Down they descended into the valley of death, marching elbow to elbow as if on parade; up they ascended the hill of death, gathering into their breasts the fearful shot of the enemy, protected by earth works, rocks, and the advantages of ground. To the right and left of this forlorn hope, led by the brave Pickett, were his supports. They were present so that when Pickett pierced the center line they might attack and drive back the foe to the right and left of him. Over the earthworks went the brave Virginians, but they had attempted more than human bravery could accomplish. They were hurled back. On the retreat they still looked back on the foe they could not conquer. The supports went substantially as far to the front as Pickett himself went, for human valor never accomplished more than they accomplished. From the point where they started to the enemy's line the ground was strewn with the dead and dying. Three of the Brigade Generals had fallen; Pickett's Division had been destroyed. From Gettysburg he went back to Richmond with the remnant of his division to recruit. They did not win the battle but they won immortality as soldiers, and, as a division, left to the survivors and to the loved ones at home a fame imperishable and undying.

O God, that I were young again! I never hear the sound of martial music or see the brave array of men clothed in the habiliments of war that I do not say: "O that I were young again and in the long line, charging on the enemy's guns!" But it cannot be. The spirit of war still warms within me, but the chill of age has crept into my blood.

This terrible, disastrous charge substantially ended the battle of Gettysburg. On July 5 we heard the retreating tramp of comrades passing through the apple orchard where we lay holding our breath; and we knew that General Lee had retreated, though in good order. Three of my mess went down in that battle—one, to rise no more; two, to linger through many years, always with something to remind them of Gettysburg. Then began a battle grim and great—Skeleton Death against Skeleton Soldier. The little we had to eat scarcely kept life in our emaciated bodies—broth from poor boiled beef, unsalted, and broth again from the same boiled beef, and then the same unsalted, twice-boiled beef; and when at last the Federal officers took knowledge of us, they gave us as delicacies, suited to pain-racked frames and fever-burned bodies, hard-tack and pickled pork. Great green flies in swarms of millions gathered in the camp, grown unnaturally large, fattened on human blood, and contended with us for the hard-tack and pickled pork. Fever-smitten, pain-racked, there came to us another terror: we were to be devoured while living by maggots—creeping, doubling, crawling in among the nerves and devouring the soldier while yet alive. A comrade from Marion, Ala., who lay on his back on the ground until great sores had eaten into his body, discovered one day that he was bleeding very rapidly from the wound. A surgeon was summoned. The femoral artery had sloughed, and he was bleeding to death. To stay the bleeding, a tourniquet was placed over the artery, and this every movement of the body displaced. Whenever he would find himself bleeding, he would call out, "Quick, quick!" and his wounded comrade would roll over, place his thumb and finger on the bleeding artery, and cry for help. For forty-eight hours this struggle went on, the one wounded man staying the flow of the life current from the other. The blood had accumulated in a pool from the point of his hip to his heel, and in that blood at the end of the forty-eight hours the maggots were rioting in their gory feast and reveling in the poor fellow's wound. The noise they made, as they doubled and twisted, crept and crawled, was that of hogs eating corn. Lying on his stomach (because he could not sit up), the soldier dipped away, by the aid of a spoon [with] which he fed himself, a half gallon of these terrible insects. The surgeons at last did something: they ligated the artery, and saved the man. The brave fellow still lives, and has served his generation well in Marion, Ala.

Notwithstanding these terrible dark days, some things occurred that meant light in the gloom. Not long after the retreat of General Lee—one sad, terrible day as we lay under the tent fly—the shadow of a woman fell over us; and, looking up, we saw a handsome young woman, whose kind and intelligent face expressed gentleness and sympathy. She called to a sister, who was not far off and who rapidly came to where we lay. We soon knew them as Misses Mary and Sally Witherrow, whose home was in Gettysburg. They had heard that out in the fields, behind the line of battle, a large number of Confederate wounded were lying. Miss Mary Witherrow, with different young women at different times, came out to see us, sometimes bringing little delicacies; and one time she brought a bottle marked "Madeira Wine," and with it there was some cut-loaf sugar. When my comrade, Smith, had bled so nearly to death and looked like the pale marble emblem of death, I gave him quite freely of that bottle of whiskey. Whatever else I may forget, I will remember that bottle marked "Madeira Wine." In January, 1898, repenting of long years of ingratitude, I wrote to this young woman, directing the letter: "To Miss Mary Witherrow, who in July, 1863, lived in Gettysburg." When I had almost forgotten that I had written the letter, I received a warm, friendly letter from Mrs. Mary Witherrow Tanner, Washington, D.C. She was a Republican woman, but a Christian.

I cannot forbear to mention one other incident. When all had been removed but the helpless, three grand, Christian women from Baltimore came out to the field hospital where the badly wounded of Hood's Division had been gathered and erected a tent just outside of the ground whereon the wounded lay. In all the years that have gone since that fearful time their names have remained like the memory of sweet odors—Miss Melissa Baker, Mrs. J. L. Warfield, and Mrs. John Converse—names ever dear and never to be forgotten. They were refined, cultivated, elegant women. They came there to minister, and ministered unto the wounded prisoners. They were entitled to that commendation, the highest ever given to mortals: "I was sick, and ye visited me; I was in prison, and ye came unto me." They knelt by the pallet of straw on which the dying soldier lay and gave him such consolation as the word of God read by them could afford to the dying. There was no minister of the gospel in that land of the enemy who sought us out and offered comfort. These women, like Sisters of Mercy, held up the light to illumine the dark road on which the dying soldiers traveled into the great beyond. In all the years that have passed I have not heard from them, but—blessed be their names!—their good deeds have long since followed after them.

For this soldier this was the end of Gettysburg. In October, 1898, he had information from the battlefield which lifted his spirit into the very empyrean of the loftiest patriotism. To him his old company commander then, and now a Commissioner of the Battlefield of Gettysburg, wrote, saying: "The rock behind which you crawled on Little Round Top when wounded stands near Tullane avenue. On it with chisel I carved your name, the simple letters 'W-a-r-d.'" Comrades, this is my epitaph and that my monument. In the future people to whom I am unknown and never will be known will find that rock bearing that name, and may ask the questions, "Who was he? Whence came he? And what was his end?" and there will be no answer. Comrades, the end will soon come to us all. We go the way of all the earth. Our history can never be written as it ought to have been. They who fell never knew the degradation and sorrow through which we have passed. [CV, 8:345–49]

Appendix C

ANNALS OF THE WAR

CHAPTERS OF UNWRITTEN HISTORY

BATTLE OF THE WILDERNESS

**The Fourth Alabama Regiment
in the Slaughter Pen on May 6, 1884.**

DEATH OF WADSWORTH

How Lee Said: "Go In, My Brave Alabamians,
and Drive Them Back."

By P. D. Bowles,
Formerly Brigadier General Commanding in C.S.A.

We had come out of our winter quarters in East Tennessee and by easy stages on cars and marches reached Gordonsville, at the junction of the Virginia Central and Alexandria Railroads. We there spent several days in regimental and brigade drill. In the meantime the men had received new uniforms and our ranks had been doubled by the late furloughed men coming in. General Hoke had just captured Plymouth, N.C., and a good supply of rations had been sent to us fresh from Uncle Sam's commissariat. [On May] 3 the sun rose clear and after inspection in the morning the brigade was ordered out for drill, which lasted something over one hour, when we were marched back to camp. It being a warm day, both officers and men had disrobed themselves, when to our surprise orders came to prepare three days' rations and be ready to march in one hour. A part of the rations was sixty rounds of cartridges.

Marching Toward the Wilderness

We left Gordonsville about 3 P.M. not knowing in the least in what direction we were to go. But after marching out and halting in the edge of a large plain, we saw that the whole corps was in motion. General Longstreet and staff soon came in sight across the field and slowly rode down the road leading in the direction of Spotsylvania, which we afterwards found was called the Catharpin road. It was night before we came to the main line or road, and only went a short distance further before we bivouacked. The 4th was spent in going at a slow pace in the same direction, and at night we bivouacked in a grove near the road we had marched during the day. We quit camp at sunrise the next morning and still marched slowly as on the day before, until about 1 P.M., when we heard distant artillery firing on our front, which seemed to grow nearer as we continued to advance.

Evidences of Battle

After going a few miles further we met a squad of about thirty Yankee prisoners. In the squad was a captured colonel. From the officer in charge of those prisoners we learned that a brigade of Federal cavalry had come into our lines and that our cavalry was in hot pursuit. Every few hundred yards we would pass a house with from two to five wounded or dead Federal soldiers. We also passed a squad of Confederates digging a grave to bury one of their comrades, who, they said, had only joined them that morning and was killed in the first charge.

Cheers and Music

It was about this time that the news was passed down the line that General A. P. Hill was at that time engaged in a pitched battle with General Grant in the Wilderness. Further on we learned that Hill had driven the Federals several miles and had taken six thousand prisoners. This caused loud cheers for Hill and seemed to revive the spirits of the tired men, who marched on as if they had been imbued with new life. We halted about 10 P.M. and slept until 2 in the morning of the 6th, when we were awakened by the sweet notes of the Palmetto Sharpshooter's Band serenading General M. Jenkins. I never could find out why they should have been chosen that inopportune hour for music, unless they had some kind of a presentiment that it would be the last time they would ever have the chance, as he was killed the same day.

Forward at Double Quick

The band was cheered and in a few minutes orders came to break camp, and we continued our march down the Catharpin road, which was nearly parallel with the Wilderness plank road. At this point every few minutes orders came to quicken our steps, and we were not long in coming in full hearing of Hill's musketry on our left front. After going in this direction for a mile or two our head of column diverged to the left. I saw that we were making a bee line for the heavy firing, when a dashing courier came in sight, with orders for me to bring the command up at double-quick. So on we went over dew-wet fields, across branches and creeks, until our proximity to the firing suggested that we, too, had better prepare for action. So the column was halted and ordered to load, and then march on to the plank road.

At the Edge of the Maelstrom

The command had to pass through Hill's field hospital, where we saw hundreds of men who had been wounded the night before and that morning, and the reader may imagine that these hideous sights, fractured limbs and bloody clothing, did not add much to our courage. At this time there was also a continuous stream of wounded meeting us as we advanced, and each one was eagerly questioned as to how the fight was progressing. If it was a private who was questioned, he would say, "They are sorter driving us back." If it was an officer he would say: "Well, it's about a stand on both sides." We continued to move, expecting every moment to be hotly engaged, while the men were busy destroying letters and playing cards. Many of the former were tender missives from loved ones far away, which they determined should not run any risk of falling into the hands of either friend or foe. So in a very short time the line of march was strewn with bits of paper.

Signs of Desperate Fighting

The increased nearness of the firing and the long faces of the wounded were having a dampening influence upon "Old Bull's" (General Longstreet's) boys, but the change was not long in coming. We soon met a private holding up his wounded hand with a smile on his face, who almost hallooed it out: "Longstreet's boys are driving them like sheep." Then came such an expression of joy to the men's faces that I could see it at once. The whole line moved off at a quick step and soon passed out of the thick woods into the edge of an old field to the left of the plank road. Here we saw signs of desperate fighting all around.

Lee Warmed Up for Battle

General Lee was riding his horse up and down the columns and calling out to the men: "Go on, my brave Alabamians, and drive them back." This is the memorable time at which it is said he offered to lead Hood's old Texas Brigade in person, but was prevented by some of the Fifth Texas taking his horse by the bridle and leading him to the rear against the protest of the General. At this time, the Fifteenth Alabama Regiment, under the command of the gallant W. C. Oates, present member of Congress from the Third Alabama district, was just in my front, and there was a corpulent captain (the old hero, Captain Hatcher) of the regiment some fifteen paces in the rear of his company and trying to get up at a good run, and when he passed General Lee the latter called out: "Go on, my brave Alabama captain, and drive them back!" I must confess that this was one of the times that I thought things were getting a little squally.

Into the Chaparral

After passing General Lee something over two hundred yards we came to the crest of the hill, where we were halted and ordered to form line right forward. By the time this was done General Field came down the line in person and called out to me to throw forward a good skirmish line, and at the word "advance" to place the right of my regiment on the plank road and keep it there. During this time wounded Texans were coming out of the wood, while my skirmishers were halted at the edge of the dense undergrowth, which was so thick that you could not see ten feet in front of you. Soon the whole line was ordered to advance. The Fourth Alabama went forward at a double-quick, my right still resting on the plank road, and as my skirmish line was fired upon before they had gone fifty steps in the wood, they halted until my main line came up.

A Breastwork Taken

By this time the first or advance line of the enemy opened fire on us, and without a halt I ordered a charge, which was responded to by the whole line. On advancing some seventy-five or a hundred yards we came upon a breastwork, which consisted of logs piled up here and there sufficiently arranged to satisfy me that the enemy had just reached it and were hastily erecting it from logs lying indiscriminately in the woods. At the time of reaching this point we could see a few retreating Federals in front. So I ordered the command to lie down and sent forward a few videttes, who kept firing for some time only a short distance in my front. The Forty-Seventh Alabama was supporting me on the left and was under my supervision, the colonel being absent. I knew these were Confederate troops on the right of the plank road by the heavy firing, and that they were well up with their portion of the line. For a while, then, these few scattered logs constituted my outer line.

Attack and Repulse

Soon the Federals began firing and driving in my scouts, while they slowly advanced. When they came in sight I ordered my command to fire, which stopped the onward movement for a short time. Soon, however, the enemy began to advance the second time and in larger numbers than before, and as they advanced they fired very low, so that their shots were having a very perceptible effect on my line. I then ordered a charge over our low works, which was obeyed with alacrity, and the column continued to advance until we came to their second line of works, which was well built and some three feet high, the Federals retiring slowly as we came up. The Confederates at once took a sheltered position behind the same and opened a fire to the front, which the enemy slowly returned.

Retiring to the First Line

After remaining in this position some ten or fifteen minutes, I discovered by the balls coming from the right of the plank road that we had passed beyond our supports and were receiving a flank fire. I discovered, also, that the Forty-Seventh Alabama had fallen back in a few minutes after we had reached the second line of the enemy's defenses. It was also reported that a large body of the Federals was on our left. So I at once ordered the command to fall back to our first line. The enemy saw all this immediately and began to shower their leaden hail upon us just as we began the retrograde move, but the retreat was made in good order and continued until we reached our first line of works, when we turned and opened fire upon their advancing lines. My wounded were then taken to the rear.

Forward and Backward

In the meantime the enemy were continuing to advance through the thick underbrush until they came within about thirty yards of my line, when I ordered a second charge and again the hillsides echoed to the valleys the "rebel yell," and for the second time the Federals were driven beyond their second line of works. At this time the Twentieth Georgia came up and took position on my right, but parallel and facing the plank road. The loud commands of the Federal officers could be heard above the din of the musketry. It was a terrible moment. The Union lines began another advance. On they came, again and again, to meet a fearful slaughter and to be hurled back upon their supports with terrible loss, while their ranks were decimated at every advance.

Death of Wadsworth

During this time a Federal officer came dashing up almost to my right. Whether this was a mere act of bravado or because he could not manage his horse I do not know, but just as he reached the opening on the plank road and was near a large tree, one of the men in my command shot him off his horse. General Wadsworth was found mortally wounded at this point that night after the fight and properly cared for by the direction of General Lee.

Hot Work All Around

We discovered soon that we were opposed at this point by a valorous foe—one every way worthy of our steel. They continued their advance, firing as they came, while my men were falling by the dozens before their well-directed aim. It was here that Major W. M. Robbins (late Congressman from the Seventh North Carolina district) was by my side and my Adjutant, R. T. Coles, called out that Major Robbins was dead. Turning around I saw that the Major had fallen upon his face. On being turned over he opened his eyes and asked to be taken to the rear, but I well knew that to grant his request was to have two or three men riddled with bullets, and it was discovered that the Major only had a severe but not dangerous scalp wound.

Back to the Old Position

The Georgians during the time had retreated back to our first line and for some cause the enemy had ceased to fire, so I took advantage of the brief lull in hostilities to get the wounded off the field and at the same time ordered a retreat to our first line. When we began to fall back the Federals fired several volleys after us, but did not follow. On reforming I found that my command had suffered terribly. The gallant Captain Baylis Brown, of Company B, and his no less heroic comrade, Lieutenant Coonsy, were among the killed. Lieutenant J. S. Stearnes, of Company E, and Major Robbins were wounded. The enemy did not follow and seemed to be satisfied. So, after forming and waiting for some time, General Field came up and ordered me to march my regiment by the left flank, while Rodes' Alabama Brigade took our old position on the plank road. My command moved to where I found the remainder of the Alabama troops building works. We assisted at this work until about 3 P.M.

Supporting Perry

For some time no enemy appeared in our front, but very heavy firing could be heard on both our right and left most of the time. At this time Colonel Perry, of the Forty-Fourth Alabama Regiment, was commanding the brigade and ordered the command to advance by regiments in echelon—the Fourth, being on the right, was naturally in the rear some distance. This move was to support Brigadier General Perry's Florida Brigade, which was being hard pushed in our front. Our left front did not advance very far before they came up with the Floridians, who were retreating slowly. We were soon hotly engaged and had arrived just in time to prevent a disaster on that part of the field, as General Perry was certainly outnumbered by the Federals. The General and some of his color-bearers had just passed around my right, calling out that they were out of ammunition.

An Act of Heroism

There were two or three claybanks or roots of trees that had been torn up by the wind in my front behind which two or three Floridians were stationed and firing at the enemy at a distance of not more than forty steps. Finally they left this ambush and had not gone more than a few steps when one of them fell, shot in the leg. His comrade deliberately walked back, squatted down and the wounded man put his arms around his neck while he walked off with him before the whole Federal line, and if a single hostile shot was aimed at the two it passed wide of its mark and the wounded man was carried in safety from the field. It was one of the most heroic acts I ever witnessed.

Breasting the Storm

Here for a short time we were as hotly engaged as we had been at an earlier hour in the day. Every shot from the Federal lines seemed to tell on my already badly thinned ranks. The air was full of leaden hail, and why the whole of my line was not swept away seems a miracle. I had determined, however, to breast the storm until I saw one regiment of the brigade on the left had marched to the rear, leaving a gap in the line to which the Federals were moving forward to occupy and thus cut off our retreat.

A Brink Retreat

It was then stay and be captured or go. We went. As soon as we had ceased firing, the line in my immediate front charged. We moved off to the right, the enemy following rapidly and calling out at every breath: "Halt! halt! halt!" Their guns were either empty or their supply of cartridges was exhausted, as they fired only a few shots at our retreating lines. Looking back I saw a Federal officer with a long duster on and not less than one hundred sergeants and corporals, each one trying to capture a prisoner, for which they were promoted, as will be seen in my description of Spotsylvania hereafter.

Some Incidents

We soon came out of the wood and marched slowly up the hill in an old field, some three hundred yards from where we had formed in the morning. After forming with the remainder of the brigade in line, with the right front to the enemy, I went over to talk to Colonel Oates. He pointed out to me one of his men who was lying down by a Federal soldier and said: "You see that fellow over there by that wounded Yankee? Well, he has just brought him out of the woods on his back so as to get his boots as soon as he dies." Just about this time we heard three loud huzzas from the Federals in our front, but their joy was soon turned to grief by General Davis' Mississippi Brigade firing into them from the rear, when off they went like frightened sheep to the right, throwing away guns, hats, blankets and knapsacks by the hundreds.

In the Woods Next Day

We then marched over the same ground from which we had been driven only a short time before and took a position several hundred yards in front and remained until night awaiting the enemy, who failed to advance again. After dark we marched by the right flank across the plank road and took up a position about four hundred yards to the right and spent the night in building log works. The time passed quietly until morning, when I walked over the field and on the right of the plank road, where General McLaws' [division] had been engaged the previous day. I stepped seventy yards square in two or three paces and counted ten dead Federals to one dead Confederate, and on the left where our brigade had been engaged I counted six dead Federals to one Confederate. I also counted twenty-seven bullet marks on one small hickory bush. On the morning before the fight it was impossible to see twenty yards in any one direction, but then I could see for two hundred yards and leap my horse with ease.

The Fourth Alabama went in on the morning of the 6th with two hundred muskets and seventeen commissioned officers. During the day ninety men and ten officers were disabled, among the number Captain James Brown, Company I, and Lieutenants Jones and Newsom, and others whose names I do not remember, but I know that many a gallant soul on both sides went out on that awful day. [*Philadelphia Weekly Times*, October 4, 1884]

Notes

Abbreviations

B&L   Johnson, Robert V., and Clarence C. Buel, eds. *Battles and Leaders of the Civil War,* 4 vols. (New York: Thomas Yoseloff, 1956)

CSR   Compiled Service Records of Confederate Soldiers Who Served in Organizations from the State of Alabama, War Record Group 109, National Archives, Washington, D.C. Name of specified individual follows CSR in citation.

CV   *Confederate Veteran,* 40 vols. (Nashville, 1897–1932; rpt., Wilmington, N.C.: Broadfoot Publishing Company, 1987)

OR   U.S. War Dept., *The War of the Rebellion: A Compilation of the Official Records of the Union and Confederate Armies,* 128 vols. (Washington, D.C.: U.S. Government Printing Office, 1880–1901). Unless otherwise indicated, all citations to the *Official Records* refer to series 1.

Editor's Note

1. Kenneth W. Jones, "The Fourth Alabama Infantry: First Blood," *Alabama Historical Quarterly* 36, no. 1 (Spring 1974): 36–37.
2. Donald B. Dodd, "The Free State of Winston," *Alabama Heritage* 28 (Spring 1993): 10.
3. Ibid., 10, 11.
4. CSR, Robert T. Coles; CV, 33:102; *Huntsville* (Ala.) *Daily Times,* Feb. 15, 1925.

Introduction

1. James C. Brandon, a student residing in Huntsville, Ala., enlisted as a third corporal in Company I on Apr. 26, 1861. On Sept. 17, 1861, Brandon was transferred to the 7th Alabama Infantry Regiment. CSR, James C. Brandon.
2. Fielding Bradford, an unmarried student from Huntsville, Ala., enlisted in

Company I on Apr. 26, 1861, as a private. He was wounded at the First Battle of Manassas on July 21, 1861, and died on Aug. 5, 1861. CSR, Fielding Bradford.

Chapter 1. Company Sketches

1. Thomas J. Goldsby (1831–1884) was a native of Dallas County, Ala. A prewar graduate of Princeton University, he became a prosperous planter. He was elected captain of Company A of the 4th Alabama on Apr. 26, 1861, and was promoted to lieutenant colonel of the regiment on Nov. 8, 1861. He resigned when the regiment was reorganized in Apr. 1862. Robert K. Krick, *Lee's Colonels* (Dayton, Ohio: Press of Morningside Bookshop, 1979), 160.
2. Egbert J. Jones (1820–1861) was born in Limestone County, Ala. After graduating from the University of Virginia, he returned to Alabama, where he practiced law. He was tall, reputedly six feet and three inches. Prior to the Civil War, he served in the Alabama Legislature and on the board of trustees of the University of Alabama. Jones was elected colonel of the 4th Alabama on May 7, 1861. He was wounded in both hips at the First Battle of Manassas and died in Orange Court House on Sept. 3, 1861. Krick, *Lee's Colonels*, 213.
3. Jason M. West, a 28-year-old merchant, enlisted in Company A on Apr. 26, 1861, and was elected second lieutenant. He was elected captain on Apr. 22, 1862, and served in this rank throughout the rest of the war. West was wounded twice during the war—on Sept. 14, 1862, at the Battle of South Mountain, and on May 25, 1864, at the Battle of Hanover Junction. West surrendered with his company on Apr. 9, 1865. CSR, Jason M. West.
4. Tennent Lomax (1820–1862), a native South Carolinian, was a newspaper editor in Georgia prior to the Civil War. A veteran of the Mexican War, Lomax was appointed lieutenant colonel of the 3rd Alabama on Apr. 28, 1861, and was promoted to full colonel of the regiment on July 31, 1861. He was killed at the Battle of Seven Pines on June 1, 1862. Krick, *Lee's Colonels*, 242.
5. Evander McIvor Law (1836–1920) was born in Darlington, S.C. He graduated from South Carolina Military Academy in 1856 and joined the staff of the academy as assistant professor of history and belles lettres in 1857. He served as professor of history and belles lettres at Kings Mountain Military Academy in Yorkville from 1858 to 1860. He then moved to Tuskegee, Ala., where he cofounded and taught at the Military High School of Tuskegee, Ala. Company B of the 4th Alabama, the Tuskegee Zouaves, was raised by Evander Law and was composed largely of his students. After joining the 4th Alabama at Pensacola, Law was promoted to the rank of lieutenant colonel; he became a full colonel in Oct. 1861 and took command of the brigade just prior to the Battle of Seven Pines on May 31, 1862. Promoted to brigadier general on Oct. 15, 1862, he commanded the brigade with distinction through the Overland campaign of May and June 1864 and was severely wounded at the Battle of Cold Harbor on June 3, 1864. After recovering, he was sent to South Carolina to command a cavalry brigade. Law was commissioned as major general on Mar. 29, 1865, upon the recommendations of Gens. Joseph E. Johnston and Wade Hampton. He

was paroled in North Carolina in May 1865. After the war, Law organized the Alabama Grange in 1872 and again was associated with the Kings Mountain Military Academy until it closed in 1881. He then moved to Florida, where, in 1894, he founded the Southern Florida Military Institute at Bartow, which he headed until he resigned in 1903. He then worked as editor of the *Bartow Courier-Informant* in 1905-15, served as trustee of the Sumerlin Institute in 1905-12, and was a member of the Polk County Board of Education from 1912 until his death on Oct. 30, 1920, in Bartow, Fla. Evander Law was the last major general of the Confederacy to die. William C. Davis, ed., *The Confederate General*, 6 vols. (Harrisburg, Pa.: National Historical Society, 1991), 4:22-25.

6. Thomas B. Dryer, a 30-year-old merchant from Tuskegee, Ala., enlisted on Apr. 28, 1862, in Company B in Tuskegee. His initial rank was second lieutenant. Dryer was promoted to captain on May 3, 1861. He was wounded at the Battle of First Manassas on July 21, 1861. Dryer resigned his commission on Apr. 21, 1862, and left the regiment. CSR, Thomas B. Dryer.

7. E. Jones Glass enlisted in Company B on Apr. 28, 1861, in Tuskegee, Ala. He was elected captain on Apr. 21, 1862. Wounded by a musket ball in his knee on July 1, 1862, at the Battle of Malvern Hill, he was so incapacitated by this wound that he was unable to walk normally by Mar. 1863. His formal resignation from the regiment occurred on Mar. 16, 1863. CSR, E. Jones Glass.

8. Baylis E. Brown enlisted in Company B in Tuskegee, Ala., on Apr. 28, 1861. He was elected sergeant of his company on that date and second lieutenant on Apr. 21, 1862. Brown was promoted to first lieutenant on Feb. 20, 1863, and captain on Mar. 21, 1863. He served with Company B until his death on May 6, 1864, at the Battle of the Wilderness. CSR, Baylis E. Brown.

9. John P. Breedlove, a native of Tuskegee, Ala., was 21 years old when he enlisted in the Tuskegee Zouaves in Apr. 1861. He was a senior at Oglethorpe University in Georgia at the time of his enlistment. When the Tuskegee Zouaves were integrated into the 4th Alabama and designated as Company B, Breedlove was made 4th sergeant. At the reorganization of the regiment in spring 1862, Breedlove was elected 3rd lieutenant. He fought with the 4th Alabama in the Battle of First Manassas and in the Peninsula, Second Manassas, Maryland, Fredericksburg, Suffolk, and Gettysburg campaigns. At the Battle of Gettysburg, he was severely wounded when he was shot through the stomach on July 2, 1863, and was captured. He remained in a field hospital in Gettysburg for six weeks and was then transferred to the prison camps of Fort McHenry and Fort Delaware. Breedlove was exchanged in Dec. 1864, but due to his harsh imprisonment and the effects of his wound, he was no longer fit to take the field. After the war, he farmed outside Tuskegee and served as a representative in the Alabama Legislature. Jedediah Hotchkiss, in Clement A. Evans, ed., *Confederate Military History* (Atlanta: Confederate Publishing Co., 1899), 8:488-89.

10. N. H. R. Dawson, a native of South Carolina, was a 32-year-old attorney in Selma, Ala., at the outbreak of the Civil War. On Apr. 26, 1861, Dawson enlisted as a captain in Company C. He served with the regiment until it was reorganized on Apr. 21, 1862, when he resigned from the service. CSR, N. H. R. Dawson.

11. Alfred Price, a 24-year-old lawyer from Selma, enlisted as a second sergeant

in Company C on Apr. 26, 1861. Wounded at the First Battle of Manassas on July 21, 1861, he recovered quickly and was promoted to first sergeant of his company on Nov. 13, 1861. Price was elected captain on Apr. 21, 1862. He was wounded on June 27, 1862, at the Battle of Gaines' Mill, and died on July 7, 1862. CSR, Alfred C. Price.

12. Maj. Dowell Sterrett (1840–1919) was born in Shelby County, Ala. He attended Howard College in Elyton, Ala., and the University of Virginia, and studied medicine in Selma from 1859 to 1860. He joined Company C of the 4th Alabama in Selma on Apr. 10, 1861, as a private. He was elected first lieutenant of his company in the reorganization of the 4th Alabama after its initial 12-month service. Sterrett was promoted to captain on June 27, 1862, and was then elevated to the rank of major of the regiment on Sept. 17, 1862. In the Battle of Antietam (called "Sharpsburg" by southerners), Sterrett was wounded severely in his right leg, leading to its amputation. He was then transferred to the 4th Congressional District of Alabama and made quartermaster, where he was stationed throughout the remainder of the war. While serving as quartermaster, he was licensed to practice medicine by the Shelby County Medical Board in 1864. After the war, he graduated as valedictorian of his class at the Atlanta Medical College in 1866. CV, 18:430.

13. Frank C. Robbins, a native North Carolinian, was a teacher in Alabama when he enlisted on Apr. 26, 1861, in Company C. Elected second lieutenant on Apr. 21, 1862, Robbins was promoted to first lieutenant on July 12, 1862, and captain of Company C on July 24, 1863. Robbins was wounded at the Battle of Chickamauga on Sept. 19, 1863, and was wounded and captured on Nov. 25, 1863, in the fighting outside Knoxville. He was imprisoned in Camp Chase, Ohio, and Fort Delaware, Del., until being exchanged on Oct. 11, 1864. Robbins returned to duty with his company and surrendered with his men on Apr. 9, 1865. CSR, Frank C. Robbins.

14. Richard Clarke, a 47-year-old physician in Madison County, Ala., enlisted on May 23, 1861, in Huntsville, and was elected captain of Company D. He resigned on Apr. 25, 1862, due to his age. CSR, Richard Clarke.

15. Thomas K. Coleman was a 25-year-old farmer in Uniontown, Ala., when he enlisted on Apr. 25, 1861. He was elected first lieutenant of Company D. On Apr. 25, 1862, Coleman was promoted to captain. He was officially elevated to the rank of major on Oct. 3, 1863, which was also the date on which Coleman died of wounds that he received at Chickamauga. CSR, Thomas K. Coleman.

16. James T. Jones, a 27-year-old attorney from Demopolis, Ala., enlisted in Company D on Apr. 26, 1861. Elected first lieutenant on Apr. 21, 1862, Jones served with the regiment through the Peninsula, Second Manassas, and Maryland campaigns and was promoted to captain on Oct. 3, 1862. He remained with his company until Aug. 1864, when he was detached to serve with the Confederate War Department. CSR, James T. Jones.

17. Charles L. Scott (1827–1889) was born in Richmond, Va. He graduated in 1846 from William and Mary College in Williamsburg, Va., and was admitted to the Bar in the Commonwealth of Virginia in 1847. However, in 1849, bitten by the gold bug, he moved to California and in 1851 resumed the practice of law in Sonora, Calif. He was elected to the California Assembly for 1854–56 and then to Congress, on the Democratic ticket, for

1857–61. Scott became major of the 4th Alabama on May 7, 1861. He was wounded in the right leg in the Battle of First Manassas, which forced him to tender his resignation on July 23, 1862. In his letter of resignation to Samuel Cooper, adjutant general of the Confederacy, dated July 23, 1862, Scott stated that his wound was "ruptured by overexertion" while charging on the double quick upon the enemy's breastworks at the Battle of Seven Pines, rendering him "totally unfit for duty." After the war, he was a farmer in Wilcox, Ala., and also worked as a journalist. In Aug. 1885, he was appointed by President Grover Cleveland as U.S. minister to Venezuela, a position in which he served until Mar. 8, 1889. Scott died on Apr. 30, 1899, in Monroe County, Ala. Krick, *Lee's Colonels*, 336; *Biographical Dictionary of the United States Congress, 1774–1961* (Washington, D.C.: U.S. Government Printing Office, 1961), 572; and CSR, Charles L. Scott.

18. Pinckney Downie Bowles (1835–1910) was born in South Carolina. He attended the South Carolina Military Academy prior to the war. He was elected captain of the Conecuh Guards, which became Company E of the 4th Alabama on Apr. 1, 1861. Bowles was promoted to major of the 4th Alabama on Aug. 22, 1862; to lieutenant colonel on Sept. 30, 1862; and to colonel on Oct. 3, 1862. He fought with great gallantry and distinction throughout the war. After the war, he graduated from the University of Virginia and served as a judge in Alabama. Krick, *Lee's Colonels*, 63.

19. William Lee, an unmarried 26-year-old attorney, enlisted in Company E on Apr. 25, 1861, in Sparta, Ala. He was slightly wounded in the battles of Gaines' Mill on June 27, 1862, and of Malvern Hill on July 1, 1862, but remained in the ranks. Promoted to captain in Sept. 1862, he was wounded at Gettysburg on July 2, 1863, and died on July 3, 1863. CSR, William Lee.

20. Archibald D. McInnis, a native of Canada, was a 21-year-old telegraph operator in Evergreen, Ala., who enlisted in Company E in Sparta on Apr. 25, 1861. He was appointed first sergeant on July 22, 1861, despite suffering the effects of being wounded in his leg the day before at the Battle of First Manassas. McInnis was promoted to second lieutenant on Oct. 9, 1862, and to first lieutenant on June 1, 1863. He was wounded at Gettysburg on July 2, 1863, and was elevated to the position of captain of his company on July 3, 1863. He retired due to disability on Jan. 20, 1865. CSR, Archibald D. McInnis.

21. James W. Darby, a 21-year-old clerk, enlisted in Company E on Apr. 25, 1861. He was promoted to sergeant on Aug. 8, 1862; to second lieutenant on June 8, 1863; and to captain on Feb. 8, 1864. He surrendered with his company on Apr. 9, 1865. CSR, James W. Darby.

22. Gustavus B. Mastin (1838–1862), an attorney before the war, was a native of Huntsville, Ala. He enlisted on Apr. 26, 1861, in Company F of the 4th Alabama and was elected first lieutenant. He was promoted to captain on May 2, 1861, when Egbert Jones was elevated to colonel. Captain Mastin was killed in action on May 31, 1862, at the Battle of Seven Pines. *Northern Alabama Historical and Biographical* (Birmingham, Ala.: Smith and Deland, 1888), 280.

23. William W. Leftwich (1840–1863) was born in Alabama, the son of Jabez Leftwich, a Virginia-born tinner. Before the war William was a druggist. He enlisted as a sergeant in Company F of the 4th Alabama on Apr. 26, 1861. He was appointed first sergeant on Aug. 1, 1861, and was elected first lieutenant on Apr. 21, 1862, at the reorganization of the regiment. Finally

he was promoted to captain of Company F on May 31, 1862. Leftwich was wounded at the Battle of Gettysburg on July 2, 1863, and died on July 3, 1863, at Hood's division's hospital on the J. E. Plank farm on the bank of Willoughby Run just outside the town of Gettysburg. CSR, William W. Leftwich; Gregory Coco, *Wasted Valor* (Gettysburg, Pa.: Thomas Publications, 1988), 46.

24. James H. Brown was born in Alabama in 1838. A mechanic, he enlisted on Apr. 26, 1861, as first corporal in Company F. He was elected second lieutenant on Apr. 21, 1862. Brown was promoted to first lieutenant on Aug. 24, 1862, and to captain on July 3, 1863, replacing William Leftwich. He was captured on Apr. 3, 1865, in the Jackson Hospital in Richmond, Va., where he was convalescing from an illness. CSR, James H. Brown.
25. Henry H. Moseley was a single 19-year-old student who enlisted on Apr. 24, 1861, in Company G. Promoted from private to second lieutenant on Mar. 3, 1863, Moseley took command of Company G with the rank of captain on Oct. 3, 1863. Severely wounded and captured at the Battle of Knoxville on Nov. 25, 1863, he spent one year in Union prison camps. Exchanged in Dec. 1864, Moseley surrendered on Apr. 9, 1865. CSR, Henry H. Moseley.
26. Mordecai M. Cooke enlisted as a sergeant in Company G on Apr. 26, 1861. Cooke was wounded at the Battle of First Manassas on July 21, 1861. Promoted to the rank of orderly sergeant on Jan. 1, 1862, Cooke served with the regiment until he was severely wounded on Sept. 19, 1863, at the Battle of Chickamauga. Due to this wound and sickness, he was absent until late 1864, when he rejoined the 4th Alabama outside Petersburg. CSR, Mordecai M. Cooke.
27. Robert McFarland, aged 24, was elected captain of Company H on Apr. 28, 1861. He was a native of Ireland who was working as a lawyer in Florence, Ala. McFarland resigned on Apr. 21, 1862. CSR, Robert McFarland.
28. Heslop Armistead was a 24-year-old doctor from Florence, Ala., who enlisted in Company H on Apr. 28, 1861. He was elected third lieutenant on Aug. 6, 1861, and captain on Apr. 21, 1862. Armistead was killed at the Battle of Gaines' Mill on June 27, 1862. CSR, Heslop Armistead.
29. William F. Karsner, a farmer from Florence, Ala., enlisted in Company H on Apr. 28, 1861, and was elected third lieutenant. Appointed second lieutenant on Aug. 6, 1861, Karsner was then elected first lieutenant on Apr. 21, 1862. He was promoted to captain on June 27, 1862, and he led Company H until he surrendered on Apr. 9, 1865. CSR, William F. Karsner.
30. Edward D. Tracy (1833–1863) was born in Macon, Ga. He graduated at the age of 17 with a law degree from the University of Georgia, and practiced law in Macon and in Huntsville, Ala., prior to the Civil War. He raised what would later become Company I of the 4th Alabama, which was mustered in on May 2, 1861; he became its captain. He was appointed major of the 12th Alabama in July 1861 but declined that position. He was promoted to major of the 4th Alabama on July 17, 1861. On Oct. 12, 1861, Tracy was appointed lieutenant colonel of the 19th Alabama and was ordered to Mobile. He fought in several battles in the western campaigns in Maj. Gen. Edmund Kirby Smith's Army of East Tennessee and was promoted to brigadier general on Aug. 16, 1862. He was killed on May 1,

1863, at the Battle of Port Gibson in the Vicksburg campaign and was buried in Macon County, Ga. Davis, *Confederate General*, 6:54–57.
31. Charles C. Sale enlisted in Company I of the 4th Alabama on Apr. 26, 1861, and was elected second lieutenant. After the promotion of Captain Tracy, Sale was promoted to captain on Aug. 1, 1861. He died in Sept. 1861 from typhoid fever. CSR, Charles C. Sale.
32. Lawrence H. Scruggs was born on June 13, 1836, in Jackson County, Ala. Prior to the war, he was a cotton merchant in Huntsville, Ala. He enlisted as a private in Company I of the 4th Alabama on Apr. 26, 1861. He was elected major of the regiment on Sept. 30, 1862, and was promoted to lieutenant colonel on Oct. 3, 1862. He served with the 4th Alabama throughout the war, being wounded at the battles of Malvern Hill and Chickamauga, and he surrendered with the regiment at Appomattox. Krick, *Lee's Colonels*, 337; CSR, Lawrence H. Scruggs.
33. Watkins Harris, a student, enlisted as a private in Company I of the 4th Alabama on Apr. 26, 1861. He was elected first lieutenant on Apr. 21, 1862, at the reorganization of the regiment. When Lawrence H. Scruggs was promoted, Harris was elected captain on Oct. 1, 1862. After the Gettysburg campaign, he entered a hospital at Culpeper Court House on July 28, 1863, and was carried as sick on the company rolls until he was dropped on June 6, 1864. The rolls indicate that in Sept.–Oct. 1863 he was treated for chronic hepatitis. A letter from an examining surgeon, dated Oct. 14, 1864, noted that Harris was being treated for a "scrofulous disease of the spinal column which was developed by the hardship incident to camp life during the Pennsylvania Campaign." He was requested to resign in Nov. 1864. CSR, Watkins Harris.
34. Daniel H. Turner (1840–1921), a native of Huntsville, Ala., enlisted in Company I on Apr. 26, 1861, as a private. He was elected fourth sergeant on Aug. 1, 1861, replacing William T. Landman, who was killed at the Battle of First Manassas. In May 1862, he was elected first sergeant, and he was made second lieutenant on Oct. 1, 1862. On July 2, 1863, he was wounded in the Battle of Gettysburg and received a 40-day furlough on Aug. 12, 1863. Turner spent the rest of the war with the Quartermaster Department and surrendered with Gen. Joseph E. Johnston's army. CV, 30:27; and CSR, Daniel H. Turner.
35. Stephen J. Murphy was a 25-year-old clerk who enlisted in Company I on Apr. 26, 1861. He was appointed first sergeant on July 1, 1864. On Sept. 24, 1864, Murphy was wounded in the foot, but he recovered in time to surrender with his company on Apr. 9, 1865. CSR, Stephen J. Murphy.
36. Lewis E. Lindsay was a 41-year-old farmer who was elected captain of Company K on Apr. 27, 1861. He was killed on July 21, 1861, at the Battle of First Manassas. CSR, Lewis E. Lindsay.
37. James H. Young, a native of Kentucky, was a 36-year-old mechanic from Larkinsville, Ala., when he was elected a first lieutenant in Company K on Apr. 27, 1861. He was promoted to captain on July 30, 1861, and served in this rank until Apr. 20, 1862, when he resigned upon the expiration of his initial one-year term of service. CSR, James H. Young.
38. William H. Robinson, an unmarried 28-year-old attorney, enlisted in Company K on Oct. 23, 1861, in Larkinsville, Ala. Elected captain of Company K on Apr. 20, 1862, his leg was amputated after he was wounded

at the Battle of Gaines' Mill. No longer physically able to serve, Robinson resigned his commission on Aug. 21, 1862. CSR, William H. Robinson.

39. A native of Ireland, James Sullivan was a 28-year-old grocer who enlisted as a first sergeant in Company K on Apr. 27, 1861. He was promoted to the rank of second lieutenant on July 30, 1861, and to captain on Aug. 21, 1862. Sullivan was killed at the Battle of Antietam on Sept. 17, 1862. CSR, James Sullivan.

40. James H. Keith, a native of Tennessee, was a 35-year-old married mechanic when he enlisted as a private in Company K on Apr. 27, 1861. Keith was promoted to third sergeant on Aug. 1, 1861; to second lieutenant on Apr. 21, 1862; to first lieutenant on Aug. 10, 1862; and to captain on Sept. 17, 1862. He was killed on Dec. 13, 1862, at the Battle of Fredericksburg. CSR, James H. Keith.

41. John D. Ogilvie, a 26-year-old farmer, joined Company K on Apr. 27, 1861, and was named a corporal. He was promoted to second lieutenant on Apr. 20, 1862; and to captain on Dec. 19, 1862. He was wounded on Sept. 20, 1863, at the Battle of Chickamauga and died of disease on Feb. 29, 1864. CSR, John D. Ogilvie.

42. Alexander C. Murray was a 26-year-old merchant from Larkinsville, Ala., who enlisted as a drummer in Company K on Apr. 27, 1861. Murray was wounded on June 27, 1862, at the Battle of Gaines' Mill. After returning to his company, he was promoted to second lieutenant on Aug. 25, 1862. He suffered a fractured clavicle from a gunshot wound on Aug. 29, 1862, at the Battle of Second Manassas and again was in the hospital for several months. On Dec. 13, 1862, shortly after his return to duty, Murray was promoted to first lieutenant. Promoted to captain on Feb. 29, 1864, Murray led Company K until his death in action on July 28, 1864, in the Petersburg campaign. CSR, Alexander C. Murray.

43. Robert P. Jones formerly had been a member of the 2nd Alabama. Leaving that regiment, this 28-year-old teacher from Larkinsville enlisted as a private in Company K of the 4th Alabama on Nov. 25, 1862. Jones was promoted to second lieutenant on Jan. 29, 1863; to first lieutenant on July 3, 1863; and to captain on July 28, 1864. By the last date, however, Jones was in the hospital, as he had been severely wounded in both legs at the Battle of the Wilderness on May 6, 1864. His wounds forced his resignation on Mar. 29, 1865. CSR, Robert P. Jones.

44. George H. Newbill, a 20-year-old student from Pulaski, Tenn., enlisted as a private in Company K on May 23, 1861, at Harpers Ferry, Va. Newbill served with the 4th Alabama throughout the war and was wounded in the shoulder on June 3, 1864, at the Battle of Cold Harbor. He was promoted on Aug. 3, 1864, to second lieutenant, the rank he held when he surrendered with the remnants of his company on Apr. 9, 1865. CSR, George H. Newbill.

45. Rufus Hollis was an 18-year-old farmer from Larkinsville, Ala., who enlisted as a private in Company K on Apr. 27, 1861. Hollis was wounded at the Battle of Gaines' Mill on June 27, 1862, and was captured on Aug. 12, 1862. He escaped on Nov. 25, 1862, and rejoined the regiment. Promoted to corporal on June 1, 1863, Hollis spent most of the rest of his service with the litterbearers of the regiment. Hollis was promoted to sergeant in Jan. 1865 and surrendered on Apr. 9, 1865. CSR, Rufus Hollis.

Chapter 2. The First Manassas Campaign

1. James G. Hudson, a 39-year-old married merchant who was serving as a private in Company D of the 4th Alabama, told a different story concerning the loyalties of the citizens of Winchester when he wrote in his diary:

    When [our] army entered Winchester a large number of conspicuous secession flags were suspended across main street, beside a large number that were raised on public and private buildings about the town. On the Tuesday night, above mentioned [July 16, 1861], while our army was drawn up in line of battle, ready to defend the inhabitants of the city, and protect their lives and property from their northern foes, by some means or other, almost every one of the flags disappeared. What the object was in removing them, whether for the better security of the town, should [Maj. Gen. Robert] Patterson get possession, or whether to prevent the Northern army from securing the flags themselves the writer does not know. (James G. Hudson, "A Story of Company D, 4th Alabama Infantry Regiment, C.S.A," *Alabama Historical Quarterly* 23, nos. 1–2 (Spring 1961): 164; and CSR, James G. Hudson)

2. Joseph E. Johnston (1807–1891), an 1829 graduate of West Point, fought in the Seminole and Mexican wars and suffered wounds in both. He served in the prewar army, attaining the rank of brigadier general, until he resigned in Apr. 1861 to follow the fortunes of his native Virginia. He was appointed brigadier general in the Confederate Army on May 14, 1861, and sent to command the Confederate units, including the 4th Alabama, that were gathering at Harpers Ferry, Va. At the Battle of First Manassas, Johnston commanded the Confederate Army of the Shenandoah. After the victory at First Manassas, Johnston was promoted to full general on Aug. 31, 1861. He commanded the Confederate Army in the East, later known as the Army of Northern Virginia, until his severe wounding on May 31, 1862, at the Battle of Seven Pines. Returning to duty in Nov. 1862, Johnston was sent by President Davis to command Confederate armies in the western campaigns, where he served throughout the rest of the war. Davis, *Confederate General*, 3:193–97.

3. Union Maj. Gen. Robert Patterson, 69 years old at the time of the battle, commanded an army of 18,000 men, whose orders were to move into the Shenandoah Valley and pin down General Johnston's army, to prevent Johnston from reinforcing General Beauregard's army at Manassas Junction. General Patterson badly bungled his mission, which led directly to the Confederate victory at the Battle of First Manassas. John J. Hennessy, *The First Battle of Manassas: An End to Innocence, July 18–21, 1861* (Lynchburg, Va.: H. E. Howard, 1989), 5, 124.

4. Hudson also described this crossing in his diary:

    The order was given to, "forward march," when all hands were required to strip and wade the river, in some places waist deep. It was a novel sight, and one which afforded a vast amount of fun and merriment, to see thousands of soldiers, with nothing but their shirts on, and these tucked up under their arms, plunging into the river and breasting the swift current. Occasionally, bursts of laughter, and shouts, long and loud, would rend the air, as some officer or soldier would miss his foothold and plunge headlong into the water and disappear from sight. (Hudson, "A Story," 165)

5. Barnard E. Bee (1824–1861), a native of South Carolina, was an 1845 graduate of West Point who had served gallantly in the Mexican War and had attained the rank of captain in the prewar U.S. Army. He resigned his commission on Mar. 3, 1861, and went south. He was promoted to brigadier general in the Confederate Army on June 17, 1861, and commanded the 3rd Brigade of the Army of the Shenandoah at the Battle of First Manassas. This brigade consisted of the 4th Alabama, the 2nd and 11th Mississippi, and the 6th North Carolina regiments, and John Imboden's Staunton Artillery. Bee was wounded in the fighting and died on July 22, 1861. Davis, *Confederate General*, 1:94–95; Hennessy, *First Battle of Manassas*, 135.
6. Arnold Elzey (1816–1871), a native of Maryland, graduated from West Point in 1837 and fought in the Seminole and Mexican wars. A captain in the Second Artillery Regiment in the prewar army stationed in Augusta, Ga., he resigned his commission with the outbreak of the war and joined the Confederate Army. He was made colonel of the First Maryland Infantry Regiment, which was assigned to the Confederate forces forming at Harpers Ferry, Va. General Johnston put him in command of a brigade consisting of the 1st Maryland, the 10th and 13th Virginia, and the 3rd Tennessee regiments. When his brigade was transported to Manassas Junction, Brig. Gen. Kirby Smith attached himself to Elzey's unit and supplanted him in command of the brigade at the Battle of First Manassas. When Smith was severely wounded, Elzey resumed command of the brigade and led a dramatic counterattack which helped to turn the tide of the fighting. He was promoted to brigadier general to date from July 21, 1861, in recognition of his bravery. Elzey fought in the Valley campaign of 1862 and in the beginning of the Peninsula campaign, but he suffered a severe facial wound in the Battle of Gaines' Mill on June 27, 1862. After his return to duty in Dec. 1862, he was promoted to major general and assigned to the Department of Southern Virginia and North Carolina. In Apr. 1863, he was put in command of the Department of Richmond. His failing health due to his severe wound kept Elzey out of active field command for the remainder of the war. Davis, *Confederate General*, 2:98–103.
7. Edmund Kirby Smith (1824–1893) was a native of Florida who graduated from West Point in 1845 and fought in the Mexican War. After the war, he remained in the army, even teaching for a time at West Point. In Mar. 1861, he resigned as major of the 2nd U.S. Cavalry Regiment and joined the Confederate Army. He was promoted to brigadier general on June 17, 1861, and commanded Elzey's brigade at the First Battle of Manassas, where he was severely wounded in both shoulders. In recognition of his service, he was promoted to major general on Oct. 11, 1861. In Mar. 1862, he was assigned to the command of the Department of East Tennessee. In Oct. 1862, Smith was promoted to the rank of lieutenant general and given command of the Trans-Mississippi Department, which he led for the rest of the war. Davis, *Confederate General*, 5:163–67.
8. Francis S. Bartow (1816–1861) served in the Georgia Legislature before the war. He was elected colonel of the 8th Georgia Infantry Regiment on June 1, 1861, and was killed in action at the Battle of First Manassas. Krick, *Lee's Colonels*, 47.
9. Several false alarms took place in June and July, 1861, as the Confederates stationed in the Shenandoah Valley thought they were about to be attacked

by General Patterson's army. No such attacks took place. Hudson, "A Story," 151–60.
10. John D. Imboden (1823–1895), a native of Virginia, taught school and served as a representative in the Virginia Legislature prior to the Civil War. With the outbreak of the war, he organized the Staunton Artillery battery, which he commanded as a captain at the Battle of First Manassas. For the remainder of the war, Imboden served as a cavalry commander, eventually being promoted to the rank of brigadier general on Apr. 13, 1863. Davis, *Confederate General*, 3:137–41.
11. OR, vol. 2, pt. 2, p. 474.
12. Nathan G. Evans (1824–1868) graduated from West Point in 1848. He fought the Plains Indians in the prewar army, eventually attaining the rank of captain of the 2nd U.S. Cavalry Regiment. A native South Carolinian, Evans resigned his commission in the army when South Carolina seceded from the Union and joined the Confederate forces. He was commissioned colonel of the 4th South Carolina Infantry Regiment. At the Battle of First Manassas, Evans fought with great gallantry as a colonel in charge of a small brigade consisting of the 1st Special Louisiana Infantry Battalion, the 4th South Carolina Infantry, and two troops of the 30th Virginia Cavalry. After another successful engagement with Union forces at the Battle of Ball's Bluff in Oct. 1861, Evans was promoted to brigadier general. Despite his courage and ability to command, Evans was kept from higher rank during the rest of the war by a drinking problem. Davis, *Confederate General*, 2:107–8; Hennessy, *First Battle of Manassas*, 134.
13. Chatham Roberdeau Wheat (1826–1862) was a native of Virginia who graduated from the University of Nashville in 1845. Prior to the Civil War, he practiced law in New Orleans and served in the Louisiana Legislature. At the Battle of First Manassas, he was a major in command of the First Louisiana Special Battalion, out of which grew the famous "Louisiana Tigers." Wheat, a very brave and aggressive fighter, was killed leading his men in an attack on the Union lines at the Battle of Gaines' Mill on June 27, 1862. Krick, *Lee's Colonels*, 391.
14. Pierre G. T. Beauregard (1818–1893) was born in Louisiana and graduated from West Point in 1838. An engineer, he fought with great bravery in the Mexican War. After the war, he worked as a military engineer in New Orleans and served four days as superintendent of the U.S. Military Academy at West Point. When Louisiana seceded from the Union, Beauregard resigned his commission and joined the Confederate Army, becoming a brigadier general on Mar. 1, 1861. Stationed in Charleston, S.C., he accepted the surrender of Fort Sumter in Apr. 1861, becoming one of the South's first heroes. At the Battle of First Manassas, he commanded the Confederate Army of the Potomac in its overwhelming victory. In consequence, he was promoted to full general on Aug. 13, 1861. Personality problems developed between Beauregard and Jefferson Davis, who transferred the general to the West in winter 1861–62. For the rest of the war, he served in the Department of South Carolina and Georgia, the Department of North Carolina, and at Petersburg, Va. Davis, *Confederate General*, 1:85–90.
15. Irwin McDowell (1818–1885) was an 1838 graduate of West Point who served in the Mexican War. Until the outbreak of the Civil War, he was assigned to the office of the adjutant general of the U.S. Army. He was

appointed brigadier general in the Regular Army on May 14, 1861, and led the Union Army to its disastrous defeat at the Battle of First Manassas. After the battle, President Lincoln relieved McDowell of his command and replaced him with Maj. Gen. George B. McClellan. In Mar. 1862, McDowell was named a major general of volunteers and placed in command of a corps in the Army of the Potomac. In the campaign of Second Manassas, McDowell commanded the Third Corps of John Pope's Army of Virginia, which was disastrously defeated in the battle. McDowell again was relieved of his command, being assigned in July 1864 to head the Department of the Pacific. Ezra Warner, *Generals in Blue* (Baton Rouge: Louisiana State Univ. Press, 1864), 297–99.

16. David Hunter (1802–1886) graduated from West Point in 1822, and, as a major in the U.S. Army, was a guest of Lincoln on the Inaugural Train. As a colonel, he commanded the 2nd Division of the Union Army at the Battle of First Manassas, where he was wounded. Later Hunter fought unsuccessfully in the Shenandoah Valley but kept his rank due to important political connections in the Republican party. After the war, he presided over the trial of the conspirators in the Lincoln assassination. Warner, *Generals in Blue*, 244.

17. Samuel P. Heintzelman (1805–1880) was an 1826 graduate of West Point, served in the Mexican War, and, being a colonel, commanded the 3rd Division of the Union Army at the Battle of First Manassas, where he was wounded. As a major general, he later commanded the Third Corps of the Army of the Potomac in the Peninsula campaign. Relieved after the campaign of Second Manassas, he held minor posts in Washington throughout the rest of the war. Warner, *Generals in Blue*, 227–28.

18. Ambrose E. Burnside (1824–1881) was an 1847 graduate of West Point, but resigned from the army in 1853 to go into business. At the outbreak of the Civil War, he organized the 1st Rhode Island Infantry, a three-months regiment. At the Battle of First Manassas, he commanded the Second Brigade in Hunter's division. His later Civil War career was marked by blunders and disasters, including his ill-fated assaults on the heights behind Fredericksburg in his position as Commander of the Army of the Potomac. Warner, *Generals in Blue*, 57–58.

19. Andrew Porter (1820–1872) fought in the Mexican War and remained in the U.S. Army. In the Battle of First Manassas, he commanded the 1st Brigade in Hunter's division, consisting of all the Regular Army troops that were on the field and other volunteer units. After Hunter was wounded, Porter took command of the division. During the Peninsula campaign, he served as the provost marshal general of the Army of the Potomac. Plagued by poor health, he resigned from the army in Apr. 1864. Warner, *Generals in Blue*, 377–78.

20. The 4th Alabama had advanced to the crest of Buck Hill. Hennessy, *First Battle of Manassas*, 55.

21. James Hudson of Company D later described this advance, and the 4th Alabama's initial contact with the Union forces:

> The regiment were ordered out of a piece of timber, in which they were concealed, into an open cornfield, within a short distance of Sherman's celebrated battery, and within 200 yards of the thousand of the enemy. Our regiment had scarcely emerged from the timber, before a murderous fire was

opened upon them by the Yankeys who were posted on a hill behind a picket fence. Our brave boys marched steadily forward in the face of the shower of bullets, falling around them, until they had ascended some distance up the hill, when they were ordered to halt and lie down. It was a critical moment, and a fearful position for a handful of men (between six and seven hundred) to occupy; with nothing to shelter them from the fearful storm of bullets, and almost entirely unable to return the fire, from the position of the enemy, and the nature of the ground. (Hudson, "A Story," 166–67)

22. John Fowler, a 30-year-old brickmason from Uniontown, Ala., serving as a private in Company D of the 4th Alabama, in a letter home dated Aug. 17, 1861, described this first fire: "I am proud to say that I fired the first shot, that was fired in the ranks of the 'Cane-break rifles.' Lieutenant Coleman was by my side when I fired, and remarked 'that I should not have shot.' I waited until I saw him good, that is, till I saw his body down to his hips. I drew as fine a bede on him as any one can with a rifle, and pulled trigger, and down went the stars and stripes." CSR, John D. Fowler; David M. Sullivan, ed., "Fowler the Soldier, Fowler the Marine," *Civil War Times Illustrated* 26 (Feb. 1988): 30.
23. Thomas J. "Stonewall" Jackson (1824–1863) was an 1846 graduate of West Point who served with great distinction in the Mexican War. He resigned from the U.S. Army in 1851 and became a professor at the Virginia Military Institute. When Virginia seceded from the Union, Jackson followed her fortunes. At the time of the Battle of First Manassas, in which Jackson earned his immortal nickname, he was commanding the 1st Brigade of the Confederate Army of the Shenandoah. He went on to become one of the two most famous corps commanders of the Army of Northern Virginia, until being mortally wounded by his own men at the Battle of Chancellorsville. Davis, *Confederate General*, 3:150–52.
24. Wade Hampton (1818–1902) a native of South Carolina, was the head of one of the wealthiest families in the South prior to the Civil War. At the Battle of First Manassas, Hampton commanded Hampton's South Carolina Legion and suffered a slight wound in the head. He went on to fight with great honor in the Cavalry Corps of the Army of Northern Virginia, suffering several wounds. Hampton eventually rose to the command of the Cavalry Corps. Transferred to lead the cavalry opposing Sherman's march through South Carolina, he was promoted to the rank of lieutenant general. Davis, *Confederate General*, 3:50–52.
25. One man, Joe Angell, a 23-year-old private in Company F of the 4th Alabama, remained with Colonel Jones after he fell. He tried to remove Colonel Jones, who was a large man, from the field, but was unable to do so. He then ran after the retreating 4th Alabama to get help. As he was running, he was caught in a crossfire and fell to the ground to find cover. As he was lying there, his knapsack was struck by a cannonball, which stunned him and threw the contents of his knapsack all over the field. As Angell lay stunned, an advancing Federal soldier, who apparently thought he was dead, stole his personal equipment. Finally, as the tide of battle turned, Angell returned to the field where Colonel Jones lay helpless and removed him to a field hospital. CV, 18:133.
26. James Hudson also described the 4th Alabama's first retreat: "The regiment retreated to the piece of timber, which it had left, under a shower of bullets

poured upon it from the front, right and left, followed by the Yankees themselves. It was a matter of perfect astonishment, to all, that a single man of the regiment escaped alive, and nothing but the protecting power of an overruling Providence could have saved them." Hudson, "A Story," 167.

27. Hudson described the disastrous mistake of the 4th Alabama: "In a few moments a large body of troops were discovered just up the branch drawn up in close order. These our officers and men took for friends, thinking they were the Georgia and Mississippi Regiments belonging to their brigade, which had been stationed in the woods as a reserve. Many of the men contended that they were Yanks, and raised their guns to fire at them. The officers ordered the guns down assuring the men that they were friends. They were however speedily undeceived by a shower of bullets, that was poured upon them by their supposed friends." Hudson, "A Story," 168.

28. J. A. Chapman of Company B in the 4th Alabama also wrote of this meeting with General Johnston: "While the Captains of the regiment were holding a brief counsel of war to determine who should take command, General Johnston came up, and learning the situation, said to our flagbearer, Robert Sinclair: 'Sergeant, hand me your flag.' The noble boy replied: 'General, I cannot give up my flag, but I will put it wherever you command.'" CV, 30:197.

29. OR, vol. 2, pt. 2, p. 492, which is paraphrased by Coles.

30. Ibid., 481.

31. Porter King, aged 37 at the time of his enlistment in Apr. 1861, was elected captain of Company G on Apr. 24, 1861. He resigned from the army on Apr. 24, 1862, when he was not re-elected captain of the company. CSR, Porter King.

32. Hudson remembered General Bee's words differently: "While the 4th Regiment was recovering from the temporary excitement, caused by the deception which had been practiced upon them, General Bee rode up and asked who, in the regiment would follow him to the conflict. Every man rose up, raised a shout and replied, we will follow you to the death. General Bee then led off in the direction of the house on the hill where the old lady was killed, and near where Sherman's Battery was taken." Hudson, "A Story," 169.

33. William M. Robbins, who later became major of the 4th Alabama, described this scene in a postwar article:

> It was just at this moment our Brigadier-General Bee came galloping to the Fourth Alabama and said: "My brigade is scattered over the field, and you are all of it now at hand. Men, can you make a charge of bayonets?" Those poor, battered, and bloody-nosed Alabamians, inspired by the lion like bearing of that heroic officer, responded promptly, "Yes, General, we will go wherever you lead, and do whatever you say." Bee then said, pointing towards where Jackson and his men were so valiantly battling about a quarter of a mile to the west and left of us, "*Yonder stands Jackson like a stone wall. Let us go to his assistance.*" Saying this, he dismounted, placed himself at the left of the Fourth Alabama, and led the regiment (what remained of them) to Jackson's position and joined them on to his right . . . It is not true that General Bee said "rally behind the Virginians," or behind anybody else. It is not true that he was rallying his men at all, for they were not retiring. The glory of the Stonewall Brigade does not need to be enhanced by any depreciation of the equal firmness and heroism of other men on that historic field. (William M.

Robbins, "The Sobriquet 'Stonewall': How It Was Acquired," *Southern Historical Society Papers* 19 (1891):166–67)

34. John Pelham (1838–1863), born in Calhoun County, Ala., resigned from West Point in 1861, prior to his graduation. At the time of the Battle of First Manassas, Pelham was a lieutenant with Capt. E. G. Alburtis' four-gun battery. He was named captain of Pelham's Battery of Horse Artillery in what was to become part of the Cavalry Corps of the Army of Northern Virginia on Mar. 23, 1862. He was promoted to major on Aug. 9, 1862, and to lieutenant colonel on Apr. 4, 1863, due to his great bravery and gallantry in all the battles of the Army of Northern Virginia. Pelham won the praise of Robert E. Lee himself for his conduct at the Battle of Fredericksburg. Pelham was killed at an engagement at Kelly's Ford, Va., on Mar. 17, 1863, and his body was shipped to Alabama, amid great ceremony, for burial. Krick, *Lee's Colonels*, 302.

35. Again, Hudson has left a description of the 4th Alabama's second advance:

> As the Regiment was marching up a narrow road through a pine thicket, [Alburtis'] Battery, which had been driven from its position, came dashing down the road under full headway. The men were compelled to file right and left into the thicket, to prevent being run over. The larger portion of the regiment filed off to the left, the remainder, including 20 members of the Canebrake Rifle Guards, filed to the right. Thus, the regiment was separated. After the road became clear of [Alburtis'] Battery and train, all of the 4th Alabama that General Bee could find, was the twenty members of the Canebrake Rifle Guards, and a few others that had fallen in with them. General Bee at the head of these led on to where the battle was raging hottest, immediately in front of Sherman's battery and not more than 200 yards distant from it. They soon reached a point where the bullets fell like hail around them. Just here while General Bee was riding in front of his men, cheering them onward to victory and inspiring them with fresh courage and heroism, [he] fell mortally wounded. Orderly Sergeant W. O. Hudson, and I, Warren Hudson bore him in their arms to a shade nearby where they made his situation as comfortable as possible. At the request of General Bee, P. Warren Hudson remained by his side, administering to his wants, and then took charge of his body, carrying it safely back to Manassas. Orderly Sergeant Hudson returned to the fight. (Hudson, "A Story," 169–70)

36. According to a modern study, Jackson had two guns of Standard's Thomas Artillery, three guns from Imboden's battery, four guns from the Rockbridge Artillery, four guns from Pelham's battery, and five guns from the Washington Artillery. Hennessy, *First Battle of Manassas*, 70.

37. Jubal A. Early (1816–1894) was an 1837 graduate of West Point who served during the Mexican War. He later resigned from the army and became a successful attorney in Virginia. At the Battle of First Manassas, Early was a colonel in command of the 6th Brigade of the Confederate Army of the Potomac; he won great glory by his conduct in this battle. During the course of the war, Early rose through the ranks to become a lieutenant general in charge of one of the corps of the Army of Northern Virginia. By 1864, Early was known to be one of the finest combat officers in the Army of Northern Virginia, but his irascible temper and disposition led Robert E. Lee to call him "my bad old man." Davis, *Confederate General*, 2:89–90.

38. This was Jefferson Davis, president of the Confederate States of America during the entire time of its existence.
39. According to an Alabama newspaper, Evander Law had his arm broken by a shot and was forced to leave the field. Fortunately for Law, his arm did not have to be amputated. *Huntsville* (Ala.) *Democrat*, Aug. 7, 1861.
40. See OR, vol. 2, pt. 2, p. 570, for Confederate casualties.
41. General Heintzelman's report is found in ibid., 402–4 and 410.
42. William R. Oakley enlisted as a private in Company G on Apr. 24, 1861. Promoted to sergeant on Apr. 21, 1862, Oakley was named colorbearer of the regiment in June 1862. He was killed at the Battle of Gaines' Mill on June 27, 1862. CSR, William R. Oakley.
43. Michael Corcoran (1827–1863) was a native of Ireland who emigrated to the U.S. in 1849. After settling in New York City, he entered a prewar militia regiment, the 69th New York, as a private. He quickly rose through the ranks to become its colonel. The 69th New York Militia, which was not mustered into Federal service, fought at the Battle of First Manassas as part of the 3rd Brigade of the 1st Division of the Union Army. The brigade was commanded by Col. William T. Sherman. During the battle, Corcoran was wounded and captured. He was exchanged in Aug. 1862 and was promoted to Brigadier General of Volunteers. He died when his horse fell on him on Dec. 22, 1863. Warner, *Generals in Blue*, 93–94.
44. William T. Sherman (1820–1891) became one of the famous Union generals during the Civil War. A native of Ohio, Sherman graduated from West Point in 1840 and served in California during the Mexican War. He resigned from the army in 1853 and worked in banking and law, with indifferent results. The outbreak of the war found Sherman working as the superintendent of the Louisiana State Seminary of Learning and Military Academy (presently Louisiana State University). He rejoined the U.S. Army as a colonel in the 13th U.S. Infantry in May 1861. At the Battle of First Manassas, Sherman commanded a brigade composed of the 13th, 69th, and 79th New York Regiments, the 2nd Wisconsin, and Company E, 5th U.S. Artillery. Promoted to brigadier general on Aug. 7, 1861, Sherman was transferred to the West, where he gained fame as a great commander. He ended the war with the rank of major general and in 1869 was promoted to full general and commander of all the Armies of the U.S. Warner, *Generals in Blue*, 441–44; Hennessy, *First Battle of Manassas*, 130.
45. Daniel Tyler (1799–1882) was an 1819 graduate of West Point. He was president of a railroad company in Georgia prior to the Civil War. With the onset of the war, Tyler was named a brigadier general of Connecticut volunteers. At the Battle of First Manassas, he commanded the 1st Division of the Union Army. He later served in Mississippi and commanded minor posts until his resignation in Apr. 1864. Warner, *Generals in Blue*, 514.
46. See n. 35 for different information on the men who carried General Bee off the field.
47. George T. Anderson, a student, enlisted in Company I on Apr. 26, 1861. He was killed in the fighting on July 21, 1861. CSR, George T. Anderson.
48. Zachariah C. Deas (1819–1882) was born in South Carolina but moved to Alabama at the age of 16 and became a prosperous cotton broker. In the Battle of First Manassas, Deas was attached to the staff of General Johnston. After the battle, he raised the 22nd Alabama Infantry and was

elected its colonel. At the Battle of Shiloh, Deas took command of the brigade to which the 22nd Alabama was attached and fought bravely. He was promoted to brigadier general on Dec. 20, 1862, and put in the command of a brigade of five Alabama regiments. Deas fought in all the major battles of the western campaigns, in the Atlanta campaign, and in resisting Sherman's "March to the Sea." Davis, *Confederate General*, 2:60–61.
49. OR, vol. 2, pt. 2, p. 868.
50. P. Turner Vaughan, a 20-year-old unmarried farmer, enlisted as a private in Company C on Apr. 26, 1861. He was appointed third sergeant on Sept. 3, 1861; second sergeant on Apr. 21, 1862; and second lieutenant on Jan. 29, 1863. Vaughan resigned his commission on Dec. 20, 1864. CSR, P. Turner Vaughan.
51. Joseph Hardie was a 26-year-old married banker who joined Company A on Apr. 26, 1861, and was elected first lieutenant. He was appointed regimental adjutant on May 2, 1861. Hardie resigned as adjutant on Apr. 26, 1862, and was replaced by Robert T. Coles. CSR, Joseph Hardie.
52. Eugene Carter, a lieutenant with the 8th U.S. Infantry Regiment, recorded in his journal his encounter with Colonel Jones, lying mortally wounded on the field: "As we got to the edge of the wood we observed a white flag upon a sword, held by someone lying down. We went to the spot and found Colonel Jones of one of the Alabama regiments mortally wounded. He asked for a drink of water, which we gave to him. He asked what we intended to do, and we told him to whip them. He said, 'Gentlemen, you have got me, but a hundred thousand more await you!'" Robert G. Carter, *Four Brothers in Blue* (Austin: Univ. of Texas Press, 1978), 13.
53. P. T. Vaughan, "Memories of the Civil War," undated newspaper clipping, Smith Papers, Scrapbook 3, Bowling Library, Judson College, Marion, Ala.
54. In the Battle of First Manassas, the 7th Georgia lost 19 killed and 134 wounded, the 8th Georgia lost 41 killed and 159 wounded, and the 27th Virginia lost 19 killed and 122 wounded. Hennessy, *First Battle of Manassas*, 135.
55. John B. Hood (1831–1879), a native of Kentucky, was an 1853 graduate of West Point. He resigned his position as first lieutenant of the 2nd U.S. Cavalry Regiment to join the Confederacy on Apr. 16, 1861, and was immediately named colonel of the 4th Texas Infantry Regiment. On Mar. 6, 1862, he was promoted to brigadier general, to command what would later be known as "Hood's Texas Brigade." He was elevated to the rank of major general on Oct. 11, 1862, and was named to command a division in what was to be the First Corps of the Army of Northern Virginia. The 4th Alabama would serve in this division for the rest of the war. Hood, after recuperating from a severe left arm wound received at Gettysburg, and the amputation of his right leg after being wounded at Chickamauga, was promoted to lieutenant general and eventually given command of the Army of Tennessee. He was disastrously defeated by General Schofield in the battles of Franklin and Nashville and, at his request, was relieved of his command in Jan. 1865. He never again held an active post in the Confederate Army. Davis, *Confederate General*, 3:121–27.
56. Joseph E. Johnston, "Responsibilities of the First Bull Run," B&L, 1:248.
57. OR, vol. 2, pt. 2, p. 403.

Chapter 3. From Manassas to the Peninsula Campaign

1. Some of the victorious Confederates went to the battlefield as tourists and wrote to their loved ones about what they saw. Otis Smith, a private in the 6th Alabama, in a letter dated Aug. 18, 1861, wrote:

   > Driven here by overwhelming numbers, our forces retreated into a maple grove some quarter of a mile distant in a southeast course where they again made a stand. Here [we saw] abundant evidences of War's devastating hand—the ground plowed up by shot, trees shattered and cut to pieces, fragments of shell and every now and then a little hillock of fresh earth marking a dead soldier's hasty grave . . .
   > The marks of the deadly carnage are on every hand. At least three hundred graves meet your eye and the long trench shows where they fell so thick that a single grave could not be allotted to each.
   > Here lie the carcasses of at least seventy-five horses rotting in the sun and rain, principally artillery horses. On the right of the house, going down to the creek about 200 yards, fell General Bee, marked by a post set up. To the left fell Colonel [C. F.] Fisher [of the 6th North Carolina], just in front was the terrible charge of the Louisiana Tigers and Hampton's Legion. Here the enemies batteries were taken, including Sherman's celebrated one. The graves of the enemy could be distinguished from ours by the manner of burial. The enemy were buried by throwing dirt upon them just as they fell, sufficient to cover them, while ours were put in graves and generally marked by some means of recognition.
   > The severe rains had washed the dirt from many of the lightly covered bodies, exposing protruding limbs and grinning skulls to view in all their horror. All over this field could be seen the print of tramping horses, the heavy artillery, the ploughing ball, the shower of bullets. Here were shreds of torn garments, empty cartridges, broken canteens, torn haversacks, all telling the terrible work of destruction. (Otis D. Smith to "Mrs. Allen," Aug. 18, 1861, typescript copy courtesy of Manassas National Military Park)

2. W. H. C. Whiting (1824–1865) graduated from West Point in 1845 with the highest grades ever attained by a cadet until Douglas MacArthur graduated from the academy in 1903. Whiting served in the prewar U.S. Army, reaching the rank of captain. Born in Mississippi and raised in Massachusetts, he resigned his commission on Feb. 20, 1861, and joined the Confederacy. As chief engineer for the Confederate Army of the Shenandoah, he was responsible for the movement of General Johnston's troops to Manassas Junction on July 19–21, 1861. This move turned the tide of battle in the Confederates' favor. In recognition of this service, on July 21, 1861, he received a battlefield promotion from President Jefferson Davis to the rank of brigadier general. Whiting took over command of General Bee's brigade after Bee's death. Whiting later commanded the division to which the 4th Alabama was assigned, until, in Nov. 1862, General Hood was promoted into his place and Whiting was transferred to a different department. Whiting was wounded in the Union attack on Fort Fisher in mid-Jan. 1865 and died Mar. 10, 1865, of diarrhea while a prisoner of war. Davis, *Confederate General*, 6:132–33.

3. Benjamin Allston was an 1853 graduate of West Point and a lieutenant in the prewar U.S. Army. With the rank of major, Allston held several

commands with the Provisional Army of the Confederate States until he was assigned to command the 4th Alabama in fall 1861. Promoted to the rank of colonel and assistant inspector general of the Confederate Army in May 1862, he fought in the western campaigns during the remainder of the war. Krick, *Lee's Colonels*, 33.
4. Owen K. McLemore (1835–1862) was born in LaFayette, Ala. He graduated from West Point in 1856 and served as a second lieutenant in the 8th and 6th U.S. Infantry Regiments from 1856 to 1861. He resigned from the army after the firing on Fort Sumter and returned to Alabama. Upon reaching home, his first duty was to enlist men for the 4th Alabama. He was then sent to Manassas Junction and appointed a lieutenant of artillery; he saw service in the Battle of First Manassas. He was appointed major of the 14th Alabama on Nov. 20, 1861, and transferred to the 4th Alabama on May 2, 1862, with a promotion to the rank of lieutenant colonel. McLemore was wounded at the Battle of Gaines' Mill on June 27, 1862, and was mortally wounded in the right shoulder at the Battle of South Mountain on Sept. 14, 1862. He died in Winchester, Va., on Sept. 30, 1862. CV, 10:367–68; Krick, *Lee's Colonels*, 255.
5. William J. Kennedy was a 27-year-old editor from Selma, Ala., who enlisted as a private in Company A on Apr. 26, 1861. Promoted to quartermaster sergeant on May 19, 1861, Kennedy was discharged on Oct. 19, 1861, due to chronic inflammation of the liver. CSR, William J. Kennedy.
6. William C. Oates (1833–1910) was a native of Alabama who began the Civil War as captain of Company G of the 15th Alabama. He acted as colonel of the 15th Alabama from Apr. 28, 1863, but his appointment was never confirmed by the Confederate Congress, and Oates' official rank from that date was major. He was promoted to lieutenant colonel on Dec. 7, 1864, after being severely wounded in the Petersburg campaign. His work, *The War between the Union and the Confederacy* (1905; Dayton, Ohio: Press of Morningside Bookshop, 1985), is one of the finest records of service in the Army of Northern Virginia and is cited frequently by Coles. Krick, *Lee's Colonels*, 292.
7. Oates, *War between the Union*, 775.
8. The "Texans" were the 1st, 4th, and 5th Texas Infantry Regiments, which became three of the best infantry regiments in the Army of Northern Virginia.
9. Gustavus W. Smith (1821–1896), a native of Kentucky, was an 1842 graduate of West Point. He fought in the Mexican War and was posted back to West Point afterwards. He taught there until he resigned in 1854 to pursue a career in civil engineering. At the outbreak of the Civil War, he was the Street Commissioner in New York City. He joined the Confederacy and was made a major general by President Jefferson Davis on Sept. 19, 1861. President Davis assigned him to General Johnston's army, where he became a senior division commander and eventually wing commander. When Johnston was seriously wounded at the Battle of Seven Pines on May 31, 1862, Smith assumed command of the army, and continued the battle on June 1, 1862. However, President Davis personally discovered that Smith was incapable—physically or mentally or both—of acting as army commander and replaced him with Gen. Robert E. Lee. This ended Smith's association with what was to become the Army of Northern Virginia; he

never again held field command and ended the war as a major general in the Georgia State Militia. Davis, *Confederate General*, 5:173–75.
10. George B. McClellan (1826–1885) graduated from West Point in 1846 and served with great honor in the Mexican War. He resigned his commission as captain in the 1st U.S. Cavalry Regiment in 1857 to enter civilian life. Prior to the Civil War, McClellan became president of the Ohio and Mississippi Railroad. After the debacle at the Battle of First Manassas, President Lincoln called McClellan to Washington and promoted him to the rank of major general in the Regular Army, in recognition for a small brilliant campaign in western Virginia, which McClellan had led. He was responsible for the formation and training of the Army of the Potomac and led it through its unsuccessful Peninsula campaign. He was placed in limbo during the Second Manassas campaign, but Lincoln restored him to command after that disaster. McClellan commanded the Army of the Potomac in the Maryland campaign in the fall of 1862. He was relieved by Lincoln on Nov. 7, 1862, and never again had an active command in the Civil War. Among the soldiers, he was the most popular commander that the Army of the Potomac ever had. He ran unsuccessfully against Lincoln as the Democratic candidate for president in 1864. After the war, McClellan served as governor of New Jersey. Warner, *Generals in Blue*, 292–98.
11. Col. Egbert Jones died at 1 A.M. on Sept. 3, 1861. His remains were transported to Huntsville, Ala., arriving there on Sept. 6, 1861. A very large and impressive funeral was held, and the funeral procession included judges and lawyers of Huntsville. *Huntsville* (Ala.) *Democrat*, Sept. 11, 1861.
12. Regarding the return of Colonel Law to command, a member of Company D of the 4th Alabama wrote, "On Saturday the 25th of Oct., while at Camp Fisher, an election was held for Colonel of the Regiment, which resulted in the almost unanimous vote for Lieutenant Colonel Law, he having received every vote cast, *except four*, which were thrown for acting Colonel Allston. This vote was highly complimentary to Colonel Law, and showed his popularity, and the high appreciation of his qualities both as a gentlemen and brave and gallant officer. Indeed Colonel Law is the *idol* of the 4th Alabama." Hudson, "A Story," 178.
13. Elias C. Spragins, an unmarried farmer from Huntsville, Ala., enlisted as a third lieutenant in Company I on Apr. 26, 1861. On Sept. 1, 1861, he was promoted to the rank of first lieutenant. Spragins resigned on Apr. 20, 1862. CSR, Elias C. Spragins.
14. Samuel Moore, an unmarried student from Huntsville, Ala., enlisted as a private in Company I on Apr. 26, 1861. He left the 4th Alabama on May 10, 1862, when he was promoted to first sergeant in the 26th Alabama. CSR, Samuel Moore.
15. As previously stated, Major Scott's letter of resignation was dated July 23, 1862.
16. William B. Bradley was a student from Huntsville, Ala., when he enlisted in Company I on Apr. 26, 1861, with the rank of corporal. Reduced to private for some unnamed offense in Dec. 1861, he served with the regiment until his capture on Oct. 29, 1863. CSR, William B. Bradley.
17. William O. Hudson, a native Virginian, was a 39-year-old married merchant when he enlisted in Company D on Apr. 25, 1861. He was discharged due to illness on Nov. 14, 1861. CSR, William O. Hudson.
18. Another member of the 4th Alabama felt similarly toward Captain Clarke:

"Captain Clarke is noted throughout the whole regiment for his kindness, care, attention and watchfulness which he manifests towards his men. Such is his popularity, not only with nearly all the members of his own Company, but with the Regiment, that hundreds of them would defend him to the last, and follow him into the most imminent danger." Hudson, "A Story," 156–57.

19. S. Newton McCraw, a 22-year-old lawyer from Selma, Ala., enlisted as a second lieutenant in Company C on Apr. 26, 1861. He resigned in the reorganization of the regiment on Apr. 21, 1862. CSR, S. Newton McCraw.
20. Dr. Duryee has not been identified in the service records of the 4th Alabama.
21. Hugh Bradley, a 26-year-old physician, enlisted in Company C on Apr. 26, 1861. He was immediately assigned as assistant surgeon of the 4th Alabama but spent most of his service in various hospitals for assorted physical maladies of his own. Bradley was discharged from the service for disability secondary to a double inguinal hernia on Dec. 9, 1862. CSR, Hugh Bradley.
22. E. John Kirksey was a 24-year-old physician residing in Marion, Ala., when he enlisted as a private in Company G on Apr. 24, 1861. He served as assistant surgeon of the 4th Alabama from May 9, 1861, to July 1862, when he was made assistant surgeon of the 18th Alabama. CSR, E. John Kirksey.
23. John R. Slaughter enlisted as a private in Company I on Apr. 26, 1861. Appointed assistant surgeon on Apr. 27, 1861, Slaughter resigned on Dec. 31, 1861. CSR, John R. Slaughter.
24. The 4th Alabama, like many other Confederate regiments, originally had enlisted for 12 months. When the soldiers' terms of service expired either at the end of 1861 or in the spring of 1862, a frantic effort was made by the Confederate government to re-enlist them for the duration of the war, or a maximum of three years. The solution hit upon by the Confederate government was the Furlough and Bounty Act, enacted on Dec. 11, 1861, which gave each enlisted man or non-commissioned officer a bounty of $50 and a furlough of 60 days for his re-enlistment. The law also enabled any soldier who wished to change his company or even his branch of service to do so, and gave the men the right to elect their own company and field officers; a great crisis in the Confederate command ensued. For more information regarding this act and the reorganization of the Confederate Army at this time, see Douglas Southall Freeman, *Lee's Lieutenants* (New York: Charles Scribner's Sons, 1970), 1:130–34.
25. A typical article in an Alabama newspaper at the time read as follows: "Captain L. H. Scruggs, Corporal H. B. Roper, and Private T. T. Patton, of the 'North Alabamians,' and Captain G. B. Mastin, Corporal A. H. Simpson and Private James B. White, of the 'Huntsville Guards,' returned home to recruit for their respective companies. Our fine looking friend, Lieutenant W. B. Rison, has also arrived. We are glad to find our Manassas hero friends in good health and learn that the health of their noble regiment is excellent. It is proposed to fill up the regiment to the full quota and reorganize for the war. We wish the recruiting officers the greatest success. It would be a crying shame for such a regiment, the special pride of our State, to disband, or to be deficient in the full number of men." *Huntsville* (Ala.) *Democrat,* Mar. 12, 1862.
26. Many of the Union regiments who fought at the Battle of First Manassas

had enlisted for a period of ninety days. Thereafter, most Union regiments enlisted for a period of three years.
27. OR, vol. 2, pt. 2, p. 325.

Chapter 4. Peninsula Campaign and Battle of Seven Pines

1. Richard S. Ewell (1817–1872) was an 1840 graduate of West Point and served in the prewar U.S. Army. A native of Virginia, he resigned to join the Confederate Army in Apr. 1861. Ewell was named a brigadier general on June 17, 1861, and commanded a brigade in the Confederate Army of the Potomac at the Battle of First Manassas. One of the army's "quaintest" characters, he became a major general on Jan. 24, 1862, and commanded a division which was assigned to Stonewall Jackson's small Army of the Valley and participated in the famous Valley campaign in spring 1862. Ewell was severely wounded on Aug. 28, 1862, in the Second Manassas campaign, losing his lower left leg. After a long recuperation, he returned to the Army of Northern Virginia and was promoted to the rank of lieutenant general. In the reorganization of the army which took place after General Jackson's death, Ewell was assigned to command the Second Corps of the Army of Northern Virginia, which he led from the Gettysburg campaign in summer 1863 to the end of May 1864, when he was relieved of his command due to persistent health problems. For the remainder of the war, Ewell commanded the defenses in the Department of Richmond. Davis, *Confederate General*, 2:111–12.
2. George E. Pickett (1825–1875) is one of the most famous soldiers of the Army of Northern Virginia. Pickett was an 1846 graduate of West Point— one who, despite poor academic achievement, fought with great bravery and honor in the Mexican War and in the western campaigns against the Indians. A native of Virginia, he resigned from the U.S. Army on June 25, 1861. In the Confederate Army, he was promoted from colonel in the Virginia Provisional Force to brigadier general and brigade commander on Feb. 28, 1862. He was wounded on June 27, 1862, while leading his brigade at the Battle of Gaines' Mill, and, while recuperating, missed the Second Manassas and Maryland campaigns. Upon his return to the army, he was elevated to the rank of major general on Oct. 11, 1862, and commanded a division composed of one South Carolina and four Virginia brigades. It was in this capacity that he "led" three of his Virginia brigades in the famous "Pickett's Charge" at the Battle of Gettysburg on July 3, 1863. Although he retained division command, the rest of his wartime career was undistinguished. Davis, *Confederate General*, 55:29–34.
3. Among other items lost to the Confederate army by this retreat were more than one million pounds of meat, greatly needed by the troops in the coming months. For more information regarding this retreat, and the dispute that arose between General Johnston and the Confederate government (principally President Davis), see Freeman, *Lee's Lieutenants*, 1:137–47.
4. John B. Magruder (1807–1871) was an 1830 graduate of West Point. He served with valor in the Mexican War, commanding a battery that contained, among other officers, Lt. Thomas J. Jackson. A native Virginian, Magruder resigned from the prewar U.S. Army on Apr. 20, 1861, and

joined the Confederate Army. He was promoted to brigadier general on June 17, 1861, and to major general on Oct. 7, 1861. At this time, General Magruder commanded the Confederate forces stationed on the Virginia Peninsula. Leading what later was known as the Army of Northern Virginia through the end of the Seven Days' battles, which ended the Peninsula campaign, he achieved markedly indifferent results. In fact, he was accused by some observers of being drunk at several key moments. After the Peninsula campaign, General Magruder was transferred to the Department of the Trans-Mississippi, where he served the remainder of the war. Davis, *Confederate General*, 4:138–41.

5. Benjamin Huger (1805–1877), a native South Carolinian, was an 1825 graduate of West Point. He served in the Mexican War and the prewar U.S. Army, from which he resigned on Apr. 22, 1861. He was appointed brigadier general in the Confederate Army on June 17, 1861, and was made major general on Oct. 7, 1861. He commanded a division in the Peninsula campaign. Huger was harshly criticized for his tardiness in this campaign and was removed from command by Gen. Robert E. Lee. After his removal, Huger served the Confederate Army as inspector of artillery and ordinance, and in the Trans-Mississippi Department. Davis, *Confederate General*, 3:128–29.

6. William M. Robbins (1828–1905) was a prewar lawyer in Alabama who was elected lieutenant of Company G of the 4th Alabama on Apr. 24, 1861. Promoted to captain on Apr. 21, 1862, Robbins fought with the regiment throughout the war, winning promotion to major on Oct. 3, 1863. He was wounded at the Battle of the Wilderness on May 6, 1864, and surrendered with the remainder of the regiment on Apr. 9, 1865, at Appomattox. After the war, he served in Congress in 1873–79 and, to the everlasting gratitude of Civil War enthusiasts everywhere, as the sole former Confederate on the three-man Gettysburg Battlefield Commission. In this position, Robbins was responsible for writing and putting up most of the markers signifying the locations of Confederate brigades on that battlefield. Krick, *Lee's Colonels*, 322.

7. William B. Franklin (1823–1903) was an 1843 graduate of West Point. He served in the Mexican War and in the prewar U.S. Army. Just prior to the Civil War, Franklin was in charge of constructing the new Capitol dome in Washington, D.C. He commanded a brigade in Samuel Heintzelman's division at First Manassas, a division in the Army of the Potomac during the Peninsula campaign, and eventually the Sixth Corps in the Army of the Potomac. At Fredericksburg he led the army's left wing. After being replaced as commander of the left wing in Jan. 1863, Franklin served in the Union army in the western campaigns. Warner, *Generals in Blue*, 159–60.

8. The Battle of Williamsburg, which took place on May 5, 1862, was fought between Confederates principally under the command of Maj. Gen. James Longstreet, and elements of the Union Third and Sixth Corps. For more information regarding this battle, as seen from the Confederate point of view, see Freeman, *Lee's Lieutenants*, 1:174–92.

9. James J. Archer (1817–1864), although not a West Point graduate, served as an officer in the Mexican War and rose to the rank of captain prior to the Civil War. He resigned his commission in Apr. 1861 and joined the Confederacy. Although a Maryland native, he was commissioned colonel of the 5th Texas Infantry on Oct. 2, 1861. For a time he served as temporary

commander of what was later to be called the Texas Brigade, until he was replaced by Gen. John Hood. Archer was promoted to brigadier general on June 3, 1862, and commanded his brigade with gallantry until he was captured at the Battle of Gettysburg. He was the first general officer of the Army of Northern Virginia to be captured in the war. He later was exchanged but died as a result of broken health due to his harsh treatment in prison. Davis, *Confederate General*, 1:37–38.

10. The Battle of Eltham's Landing, which took place on May 6, 1862, primarily involved the 1st, 4th, and 5th Texas, the 18th Georgia, and elements of the Sixth Corps of the Army of the Potomac, which had landed on the York River near Eltham's Landing in an effort to attack the rear of General Johnston's retreating army. For more information regarding this battle, see Col. Harold B. Simpson, *Hood's Texas Brigade: Lee's Grenadier Guard* (Dallas, Tex.: Alcor Publishing Co., 1983), 97–103.

11. William Hartley, a native of New Haven, Conn., enlisted as a private in Company B on Apr. 26, 1861. Hartley was working as a surveyor in Huntsville when the Civil War broke out. Appointed first sergeant in Aug. 1861, Hartley was killed on May 6, 1862. CSR, William Hartley.

12. John Cussons was an Englishman who cast his lot with the Confederacy. He rose to the rank of captain and served on General Law's staff. He was captured at the Battle of Gettysburg but later escaped from confinement at the notorious Fort Delaware prison. Oates, *War between the Union*, 78.

13. Anthony B. Shelby, a student from Huntsville, Ala., enlisted as a private in Company I on Apr. 26, 1861. He fought with the regiment until Aug. 1, 1862, when he was discharged for being underage. CSR, Anthony B. Shelby.

14. The Battle of Seven Pines took place on May 31 and June 1, 1862, when General Johnston, under pressure from the Confederate authorities at Richmond, launched a furious assault on the Third and Fourth Corps of the Army of the Potomac, who were on the southern bank of the Chickahominy River, isolated from the rest of the Army of the Potomac. After some initial success, the Confederate assault failed in its purpose—to destroy this portion of the Union army—due to some incredibly bad planning on Johnston's part. For more information on the confusion, see Freeman, *Lee's Lieutenants*, 1:225–43.

15. Porterfield Graham was a 20-year-old student who enlisted in Company G on Apr. 24, 1862. He was killed by lightning on May 31, 1862. CSR, Porterfield Graham.

16. This camp had been occupied by Brig. Gen. Silas Casey's division of the Fourth Corps of the Army of the Potomac, which had been surprised by the Confederate assault and forced to retreat after a short fight. For more information on the initial fighting, see Steven H. Newton, *The Battle of Seven Pines* (Lynchburg, Va.: H. E. Howard, 1993), 37–55.

17. This was Capt. James Brady's Pennsylvania Battery, composed of four 10-pounder Parrott rifles. The battery later was reinforced by Lt. Edmund Kirby's Company I, 1st U.S. Artillery, composed of five 12-pounder Napoleon cannons. Stephen W. Sears, *To the Gates of Richmond* (New York: Ticknor and Fields, 1992), 135–36.

18. General Johnston had been shot in the right shoulder by a musket ball, a relatively minor wound, but then, several minutes later, he was struck in the chest by a shell fragment and knocked off his horse. This wound was severe,

and Johnston was physically incapable of continuing in command of the army. Newton, *Battle of Seven Pines*, 83.
19. Milton E. Croxton, a 27-year-old druggist from Huntsville, Ala., enlisted as a private in Company F on Apr. 26, 1861. Elected first sergeant of Company F on Apr. 20, 1862, Croxton was killed on May 31, 1862. CSR, Milton E. Croxton.
20. This was a counterattack by seven regiments of the Union Second Corps, recently arrived on the field. Newton, *Battle of Seven Pines*, 81.
21. Robert E. Lee (1807–1870), son of the famous "Light Horse Harry" Lee of Revolutionary War fame, was a Virginia native who graduated from West Point in 1825. He served as an engineer in the prewar U.S. Army and on the staff of Maj. Gen. Winfield Scott in the Mexican War, where he won many honors for his bravery and gallant conduct. After the war, he remained in the army, eventually becoming colonel in the 2nd U.S. Cavalry Regiment. It was under Lee's command that a Marine detachment captured John Brown in Harpers Ferry, Va., in 1859, ending Brown's famous raid. Offered the command of the principal Union Army at the outbreak of the Civil War, Lee refused and offered his services to his native state when Virginia seceded from the Union in Apr. 1861. Lee was commissioned a brigadier general in the Regular Army of the Confederacy in May 1861 and was made a full general in Aug. 1861. He commanded Confederate forces in a disastrous campaign in western Virginia in summer and autumn 1861 and was serving as military advisor to President Jefferson Davis when, on June 1, 1862, Davis named him to command the Confederate army defending Richmond. This force he named the Army of Northern Virginia. Lee led this army with great brilliance throughout the rest of the war. After its close, Lee served as president of Washington College, now called Washington and Lee University. Davis, *Confederate General*, 4:45–57.
22. These reinforcements had come primarily from the Carolina and Georgia coastlines.

Chapter 5. Seven Days Battle

1. Prior to the Civil War, Nathaniel P. Banks (1816–1894) served in the Massachusetts Legislature, as governor of Massachusetts, and as Speaker of the U.S. House of Representatives. Due to his important political connections, Lincoln appointed Banks as major general of volunteers in the U.S. Army at the outbreak of the war. Stonewall Jackson soundly whipped Banks in the famous Valley campaign of 1862, and Banks earned a nickname as Jackson's "commissary general." While commanding a corps in Pope's Army of Virginia, Banks again was defeated by Jackson at the Battle of Cedar Mountain on Aug. 9, 1862. He later commanded Union troops in the Port Hudson and Red River campaigns and served as a postwar congressman. Warner, *Generals in Blue*, 17–18.
2. John C. Fremont (1813–1890) was a politician and a famous explorer of the western frontier prior to the Civil War. His strong abolitionist views, combined with his great personal popularity, led Lincoln to appoint him as major general in the Regular Army on May 14, 1861. Fremont's bungling, however, combined with Jackson's brilliance, resulted in a series of Confederate victories in the Valley campaign of 1862. At his own request,

Fremont was then relieved of command. As an Independent, he was a candidate for president in summer 1864. Warner, *Generals in Blue*, 160–61.
3. James Shields (1810–1879), despite not being a graduate of West Point, served as an officer in the Mexican War. He later was elected a senator from Illinois and then from Minnesota prior to the Civil War. Lincoln named him a brigadier general of volunteers on Aug. 19, 1861. He too was defeated by Stonewall Jackson in the Valley campaign of 1862. On Mar. 28, 1863, Shields resigned from the Union Army. Warner, *Generals in Blue*, 444–45.
4. This was the brilliant campaign waged by Stonewall Jackson and his small Army of the Valley in spring 1862. Jackson confounded several Union armies designed to destroy him, winning worldwide acclaim for himself and his men. A fine description of this campaign and of its effect on the successful defense of Richmond during the Peninsula campaign of 1862 is found in Freeman, *Lee's Lieutenants*, 1:303–488.
5. Alexander R. Lawton (1818–1896) was an 1839 graduate of West Point. He was a railroad president and politician in Georgia prior to the Civil War. On Feb. 17, 1861, he was one of the first men named brigadier general by President Davis. Lawton at that time commanded a brigade consisting of the 13th, 26th, 31st, 60th, and 61st Georgia Volunteer Infantry Regiments, assigned to Jackson's Army of the Valley. He rose to the command of a division in Jackson's wing of the Army of Northern Virginia, and was wounded at the Battle of Antietam on Sept. 17, 1862. Lawton later served as quartermaster general of the Confederacy. Davis, *Confederate General*, 4:27–28.
6. Lawton's brigade of Georgians was one of the major reinforcements supplied to the Army of Northern Virginia after General Lee took command, being transferred from the Georgia coastline defenses to Virginia.
7. Brig. Gen. Irvin McDowell, the Union commander at the disastrous defeat at the Battle of First Manassas, was replaced by General McClellan. McDowell was now in command of what would later become the First Corps of the Army of the Potomac.
8. Fitz John Porter (1822–1901) was an 1845 graduate of West Point and fought in the Mexican War. He remained in the Federal army and was named brigadier general of volunteers on Aug. 7, 1861. He was one of General McClellan's closest confidantes in the Army of the Potomac. Porter rose to command the Fifth Corps in the Army of the Potomac, which he led with brilliance in the Peninsula campaign in spring and summer 1862. Due to his actions/inactions at the Battle of Second Manassas, he was relieved of his command and cashiered. He became the subject of one of the most famous court-martials in American military history. Warner, *Generals in Blue*, 378–80.
9. James Reilly (1822–1894), a native of Ireland, fought in the Mexican War and served in the U.S. Army prior to the Civil War. He was named a lieutenant in the Ellis Light Artillery of North Carolina on May 31, 1861, and was promoted to captain of the Rowan Artillery from North Carolina on June 28, 1861. It is in this capacity that his battery served with Law's brigade. Krick, *Lee's Colonels*, 317.
10. Captain W. L. Balthis was the commander of the Staunton Virginia Artillery battery, which had been led by John Imboden at the Battle of First Manassas. B&L, 2:315.

11. The Reverend Doctor R. L. Dabney was serving as major and chief of staff in Stonewall Jackson's Army of the Valley. He became one of Jackson's early biographers after the war. Dabney also frequently acted as clergyman, conducting religious services for Jackson's troops.
12. Ambrose P. Hill (1825–1865), a native of Virginia, was an 1847 graduate of West Point. He resigned from the U.S. Army in Mar. 1861 and joined the Confederacy as colonel of the 13th Virginia Infantry. He was promoted to brigadier general on Feb. 26, 1862. Hill served as a brigade commander at the Battle of Williamsburg on May 5, 1862. On May 26, 1862, he was made major general and placed in command of the six brigades which formed the famous "Light" Division, the largest division in the Army of Northern Virginia until its reorganization in May 1863. He was promoted to the rank of lieutenant general in May 1863 and took command of the newly formed Third Corps of the Army of Northern Virginia. On Apr. 2, 1865, Hill was killed in the final days of the war outside Petersburg, Va. Davis, *Confederate General*, 3:96–98.
13. The Battle of Mechanicsville (Ellerson's Mill), fought on June 26, 1862, resulted when Gen. A. P. Hill, despite strict instructions from General Lee to await the arrival of Jackson and his command, became impatient when not hearing from Jackson and launched a series of disastrous attacks with his division across the creek. Confederate casualties in Hill's division—reinforced by one of Gen. D. H. Hill's five brigades—were extremely heavy, while Union losses were light. However, by the morning of June 27, 1862, the Union forces had retreated from their positions east of the creek to an even stronger position around Gaines' Mill. For more information regarding General Lee's plan of battle and the fighting at Mechanicsville, see Clifford Dowdey, *The Seven Days: The Emergence of Robert E. Lee* (Wilmington, N.C.: Broadfoot Publishing Co., 1988), 148–92.
14. William F. Parker, an unmarried 26-year-old bookkeeper from Enterprise, Ala., enlisted as a private in Company D on Mar. 4, 1862. Promoted to orderly sergeant in Nov. 1862, Parker was wounded by a musket ball in the thigh on July 2, 1863, at the Battle of Gettysburg, and was captured. Exchanged in Sept. 1863, Parker was captured again on Apr. 3, 1865, and imprisoned at Point Lookout, Md., until he took the Oath of Allegiance on July 25, 1865. Parker received the high compliment of being labeled in his service record a "gallant and meritorious" soldier. CSR, William F. Parker.
15. With his division leading the Confederate pursuit, Gen. A. P. Hill discovered the Union Fifth Corps in its new position around Gaines' Mill and launched his six brigades in a series of attacks on the Union positions, which were repulsed with much bloodshed. Sears, *To the Gates of Richmond*, 223–26.
16. Law's brigade attacked the portion of the Union lines held by the left of the brigade of Brig. Gen. Charles Griffin and by the right of the brigade of Brig. Gen. John Martindale. Sears, *To the Gates of Richmond*, 231, 241.
17. A modern author has described the Union position thus: "Across his whole front Porter had placed his infantry in three tiers on the hillside, behind hastily built lines of logs and loose earth packed in knapsacks. Porter's infantrymen were firing from stationary positions, which increased accuracy, and in solid alignment, which increased the density of the fire power." Dowdey, *Seven Days*, 224.
18. General Law later wrote: "The fringe of woods along the Federal line was

shrouded in smoke, and seemed fairly to vomit forth a leaden and iron hail." E. M. Law, "On the Confederate Right at Gaines' Mill," B&L, 2:363.

19. Charles W. Field (1828–1892), a native of Kentucky, was an 1849 graduate of West Point and served in the prewar U.S. Army until he resigned in Apr. 1861. He was named a brigadier general in the Confederate Army in Mar. 1862 and was assigned to command a brigade in A. P. Hill's "Light" Division. He was severely wounded in the Battle of Second Manassas on Aug. 30, 1862, and lost a leg. Upon his recovery, he was promoted to major general in Feb. 1864 and given command of Hood's division, which he led throughout the rest of the war. Davis, *Confederate General*, 2:124–25.

20. General Law wrote:

> Passing over the scattering line of Confederates on the ridge in front, the whole division broke into a trot down the slope towards the Federal works. Men fell like leaves in an autumn wind, the Federal artillery tore gaps in the ranks at every step, the ground in rear of the advancing column was strewn thickly with the dead and wounded; not a gun was fired in reply; there was no confusion, and not a step faltered as the two gray lines swept swiftly and silently on; the pace became more rapid every moment; when the men were within 30 yards of the ravine, and could see the desperate nature of the work in hand, a wild yell answered the roar of Federal musketry, and they rushed for the works. The Confederates were within ten paces of them when the Federals in the front line broke cover, and, leaving their log breastworks, swarmed up the hill in the rear, carrying away their second line with them in their rout. Then we had our "innings." As the blue mass surged up the hill in our front, the Confederate fire was poured into it with terrible effect. The target was a large one, the range short, and scarcely a shot fired into that living mass could fail of its errand. The debt of blood contracted but a few moments before was paid, and with interest. (E. M. Law, "On the Confederate Right at Gaines' Mill," B&L 2:363)

21. OR, vol. 11, pt. 2, p. 556.
22. James Harrison, a 37-year old married merchant, enlisted for one year in Company D on July 21, 1861, just after the Battle of First Manassas. He fought with the 4th Alabama until his term of service ended, and he officially left the regiment on July 25, 1862. CSR, James Harrison.
23. The full account of Private Harrison's heroism was described in the *Selma* (Ala.) *Daily Reporter*, Aug. 13, 1862.
24. The Confederates had inflicted approximately 6,900 casualties on the reinforced Union Fifth Corps, including more than 2,800 prisoners taken, and captured 22 guns. Sears, *To the Gates of Richmond*, 249.
25. All too common in Alabama newspapers after this battle and all other campaigns in the war, were notices such as the following: "Another of Alabama's brave sons has laid down his life, a sacrifice on the shrine of Southern independence. The lifeless form of Thomas Elijah Robbins now lies in the cold narrow home of the dead. . . . Through the Battle of Seven Pines Elijah passed without receiving any injury; and was in the first of those series of battles before Richmond, in which he received a wound through the shoulder which proved fatal." *Southwestern Baptist* (Tuskeegee, Ala.), Sept. 6, 1862.
26. The Battle of Malvern Hill, fought on July 1, 1862, was a disastrous defeat for the Army of Northern Virginia, which lost some 5,000 men attacking

the Army of the Potomac, strongly posted at the crest of Malvern Hill. For a detailed description of this fighting, see Dowdey, *Seven Days*, 309–46.

27. Daniel H. Hill (1821–1889) graduated from West Point in 1842 and saw heavy fighting in the Mexican War. He resigned from the U.S. Army in 1849 and taught at Washington College, Davidson College, and the North Carolina Military Institute. Hill was elected colonel of the 1st North Carolina Volunteers and fought at the first engagement of the Civil War at Big Bethel, Va., on June 10, 1861. Gaining fame as a result of this battle, he was promoted to brigadier general on July 10, 1861. He was elevated to major general on Mar. 26, 1862, and was placed in command of a Confederate division in the trenches at Yorktown. Hill led his division with great personal gallantry in the Peninsula campaign. After the Maryland campaign of Sept. 1862, he was blamed for the loss of Robert E. Lee's Special Order 191, which gave General McClellan Lee's plans for the campaign. He served with the Army of Northern Virginia until after the Battle of Fredericksburg on Dec. 13, 1862, when he was transferred to the Department of North Carolina. Hill's harsh personality alienated many in the Army of Northern Virginia, including Robert E. Lee himself. However, he was one of the finest combat officers in the Confederate Army throughout the war. Davis, *Confederate General*, 3:102–5.

28. James M. Jordan, a 21-year-old Georgia native, was working as a carpenter in Summerfield, Ala., when he enlisted as a private in Company C on Apr. 26, 1861. He was killed in action on July 1, 1862. CSR, James M. Jordan.

29. Thomas J. Patton was a student from Huntsville, Ala., who joined Company I as a private on Apr. 26, 1861. He was killed at the Battle of Malvern Hill on July 1, 1862. CSR, Thomas J. Patton.

30. James Longstreet (1821–1904) was a native of South Carolina who graduated from West Point in 1842. He was wounded in the Mexican War and served in the prewar U.S. Army, attaining the rank of major in the Paymaster's Department. He resigned from the army on June 1, 1861, and joined the Confederates. On June 17, 1861, Longstreet was commissioned brigadier general in the Confederate Army. In recognition of his gallant fighting at the First Battle of Manassas, he was promoted on Oct. 7, 1861, to the rank of major general. Longstreet fought in what was to become the Army of Northern Virginia in the great campaigns in the eastern theater, commanding the right wing of the army. Nicknamed "Lee's Warhorse," Longstreet was promoted to lieutenant general on Oct. 9, 1862, and named commander of the First Corps of the Army of Northern Virginia. He served as corps commander through the remainder of the war, being severely wounded on May 6, 1864, at the Battle of the Wilderness. Upon his return to duty on Oct. 19, 1864, Longstreet fought with the Army of Northern Virginia until its surrender at Appomattox. In the postwar years, Longstreet earned the enmity of surviving Confederates by accepting Republican governmental appointments from his prewar friend, President U. S. Grant, and by attacking Gen. Robert E. Lee in print. Davis, *Confederate General*, 4:91–95.

Chapter 6. The Second Battle of Manassas

1. John Pope (1822–1892) graduated from West Point in 1842 and served in

the prewar U.S. Army. He was appointed brigadier general of volunteers on June 14, 1861, and fought in the early western campaigns with distinction, culminating with his victory at the Battle of Island No. 10 in Apr. 1862. Based on this success, President Lincoln gave him command of the newly-formed Army of Virginia in June 1862. Pope issued an infamous series of orders designed to bring the war to the civilian population of the Commonwealth of Virginia, for which he was named a "miscreant" by Gen. Robert E. Lee. After his disastrous defeat at the Battle of Second Manassas, Lincoln transferred him back to the West, where he spent the rest of the war fighting Sioux Indians. Warner, *Generals in Blue*, 376–77.

2. The Army of Virginia, commanded by General Pope, was composed of the First Army Corps under the command of Maj. Gen. Franz Sigel, the Second Army Corps under the command of Maj. Gen. Nathaniel Banks, and the Third Army Corps under the command of Maj. Gen. Irvin McDowell. B&L, 2:497.
3. The Battle of Cedar Mountain, fought on Aug. 9, 1862, took place between three divisions in General Jackson's command and General Banks' Second Corps of the Army of Virginia, supported at the end of the battle by elements of McDowell's corps. After some initial success, Banks was soundly defeated by General Jackson and forced to retreat. For this battle, see Freeman, *Lee's Lieutenants*, 2:16–51.
4. On Aug. 4, 1862, General McClellan was ordered by his superiors in Washington to move his Army of the Potomac to reinforce General Pope. John J. Hennessy, *Return to Bull Run* (New York: Simon and Schuster, 1993), 27.
5. John Freid, a native of Virginia, enlisted in Company B on Apr. 28, 1861. He was an unmarried 19-year-old student at that time. Freid served as a musician with the 4th Alabama throughout the war and surrendered with the regiment on Apr. 9, 1865. CSR, John Freid.
6. George Thomas Fogarty, 20 years old at the outbreak of the Civil War, enlisted on Apr. 28, 1861, in Company B. Named chief musician of the 4th Alabama, he served with the regiment until his capture at Gettysburg on July 4, 1863. Fogarty was held as a prisoner at Fort Delaware until his exchange sometime in 1864 and then rejoined the regiment. He surrendered on Apr. 9, 1865. CSR, George Thomas Fogarty.
7. James Hickey, also known as Morgan R. Scullin, a 20-year-old unmarried student from Tuskegee, enlisted in Company B on Apr. 28, 1861. He was promoted to principal musician on May 3, 1861, and served in this post until he resigned in Jan., 1864, and returned to the ranks of the regiment. Scullin surrendered with the 4th Alabama on Apr. 9, 1865. CSR, James Hickey/Morgan Scullin.
8. Isaac R. Trimble (1802–1888), a Maryland native, was an 1822 graduate of West Point. He resigned from the army in 1832 and became very successful in railroad engineering. Trimble was appointed a brigadier general in the Confederate Army on Aug. 9, 1861. In Stonewall Jackson's Army of the Valley, he commanded an infantry brigade in the Valley campaign of 1862. In the Second Manassas campaign, Trimble's brigade consisted of the 15th Alabama, the 12th and 21st Georgia, and the 21st North Carolina. Trimble was severely wounded in the leg on Aug. 29, 1862, during the fighting at Second Manassas. After a long period of recuperation, he returned to the Army of Northern Virginia in time for the Gettysburg campaign in summer

1863. On July 3, 1863, he took command of two small brigades in "Pickett's Charge" and was shot in the same leg that previously had been wounded, leading to its amputation. He was taken prisoner by the Federal forces and was not exchanged until Mar. 1865. Davis, *Confederate General*, 6:60–61.
9. This small skirmish, involving Confederates of Hood's, Law's, and Trimble's brigades, and Union soldiers from General Sigel's First Corps of the Army of Virginia, was described by General Trimble in his report: "Our men boldly advanced with enthusiastic cheers and drove the opposing forces into the river and across it in great disorder, to seek protection in General Sigel's camp and under his guns, which opened a furious discharge against us without serious injury. Our men pursued them closely and slaughtered great numbers as they waded the river or climbed up the opposite bank. The water was literally covered with dead and wounded. Over 100 prisoners were captured, and among the dead was found one colonel." Gen. Henry Bohlen, a Union brigade commander, was killed in this fighting. OR, vol. 12, pt. 2, p. 719; Hennessy, *Return to Bull Run*, 69–70.
10. This was Jackson's famous flank march around General Pope's army, which took place from Aug. 25–28, 1862. Jackson, leading his wing on a forced march of more than 50 miles around Pope's right flank, captured Pope's supply depot at Manassas Junction early on the morning of Aug. 27, 1862. The best description of this march and its results are found in Hennessy, *Return to Bull Run*, 96–137.
11. G. F. R. Henderson, *Stonewall Jackson and the American Civil War* (New York: Longmans, Green and Co., 1936), 490.
12. Thomas L. Christian, a native of Virginia, was a 23-year-old single clerk when he enlisted in Company D on Apr. 25, 1861. Appointed orderly sergeant on Feb. 1, 1862, Christian was elected second lieutenant on Nov. 4, 1862, and was then appointed assistant inspector general on General Law's staff. He was captured at Gettysburg and taken to the prison camp at Johnson's Island, Ohio, and then sent to a prison in Baltimore, remaining there until his exchange on Mar. 17, 1864. Christian returned to a position on the brigade staff, where he served for the remainder of the war. CSR, Thomas L. Christian.
13. Coles's original appendix has not been found.
14. Daniel R. Jones (1825–1863) was an 1846 graduate of West Point. He served in the Mexican War and in the Department of the West in the prewar U.S. Army. A native of South Carolina, Jones resigned from the Federal army on Feb. 15, 1861, and joined the Confederates, being commissioned in the rank of major. He was promoted to brigadier general on June 17, 1861, and commanded a brigade in P. T. Beauregard's Army of the Potomac in the Battle of First Manassas. He was promoted to major general, to rank from Mar. 16, 1862, and served as commander of a division in the Peninsula campaign. He also participated in the Second Manassas campaign and in the Maryland campaign in fall 1862. He suffered a heart attack in mid-Oct. 1862, and his heart condition caused his death on Jan. 15, 1863. Davis, *Confederate General*, 3:200–201.
15. General Law later described this climb: "Here we were confronted by a natural wall of rock, which seemed impassable. Men were sent out on both sides to search for some opening through which we might pass, and a crevice was soon found several feet above our level, where the men could get through one at a time, the first being lifted up by those behind, and each

man as he got up lending a helping hand to the next." E. M. Law, "The Virginia Campaign of 1862," *Philadelphia Weekly Press*, Oct. 26 and Nov. 2, 1887.
16. Cadmus M. Wilcox (1824–1890), an 1846 graduate of West Point, served in the Mexican War and in the prewar U.S. Army. With the outbreak of the Civil War, he resigned his commission and became colonel of the 9th Alabama Infantry on July 9, 1861. Promoted to brigadier general on Oct. 21, 1861, Wilcox commanded a brigade of Alabama troops in the Army of Northern Virginia that became famous for hard fighting. In the Second Manassas campaign, Wilcox also assumed command of two other brigades, those commanded by W. S. Featherston and Roger Pryor. Wilcox served with distinction throughout the war, finally winning promotion to the rank of major general on Aug. 13, 1863. He later became commander of a division in the Third Corps and served until the surrender at Appomattox. Davis, *Confederate General*, 6:138–41.
17. OR, vol. 12, pt. 2, p. 564.
18. This was the battle of Brawner's Farm, which took place on the late afternoon and evening of Aug. 28, 1862. Jackson launched two divisions against one and a half brigades of Pope's army. The battle, a classic stand-up fight of approximately three hours, ended in a bloody draw. Hennessy, *Return to Bull Run*, 164–91.
19. Jasper Stinson, a 21-year-old single student from Sparta, Ala., enlisted as a private in Company E on Apr. 25, 1861. He was killed on Aug. 30, 1862. CSR, Jasper Stinson.
20. Bradley T. Johnson (1829–1903) was a native of Maryland who before the war held various political positions, including that of chairman of the Maryland Democratic party. He was elected major of the 1st Maryland Confederate Infantry Regiment in June 1861 and fought at the Battle of First Manassas. He then was promoted to lieutenant colonel and assumed command of the regiment in spring 1862. The 1st Maryland served in Jackson's famous Valley campaign of 1862 but was disbanded on Aug. 17, 1862. At that time, Jackson assigned Johnson to the temporary command of Brig. Gen. John R. Jones's brigade, which consisted of the 21st, 42nd, and 48th Virginia Regiments and the 1st Virginia Battalion. Johnson led the brigade in the Second Manassas campaign. After that battle, Johnson had various postings with the infantry and cavalry and served on several military administrative boards in Richmond. He was promoted to brigadier general on June 28, 1864, and assigned command of a brigade in the Cavalry Corps of the Army of Northern Virginia. After the failure of Early's Valley campaign in 1864, Johnson was named to command the Confederate prison camp at Salisbury, N.C., where he served until the end of the war. Davis, *Confederate General*, 3:172–78.
21. The Union artillery was Capt. George A. Gerrish's 1st Battery, New Hampshire Light Artillery, consisting of four guns; the infantry were skirmishers of the 2nd U.S. Sharpshooters and two companies of the 56th Pennsylvania Regiment. Hennessy, *Return to Bull Run*, 291, 292, and 298.
22. Sgt. W. H. Proctor of the 2nd U.S. Sharpshooters described the fighting between the 4th Alabama and his regiment on the evening of Aug. 29, 1862:

> We went down the pike at double quick, Gen. Hatch riding with the skirmish line and constantly calling out, "Hurry up, hurry up." . . . As we broke over a ridge there lay a line of battle six rods away. We delivered our fire, the enemy rose and returned it, so that the line of barrels were leveled in our faces. We went to grass literally, and the storm passed overhead. Our bugles sounded a recall. The skirmish line went backwards to the right and left, the infantry tried to deploy into line under a heavy fire from the advancing enemy, but not a single regiment made a complete success of the maneuver. Most of them were penned up and forced back in a helpless mass, a fine target for the volleys poured into them. (Proctor, Account, p. 3, typescript copy courtesy of Manassas National Military Park, Manassas, Va.)

23. John P. Hatch (1822–1901), an 1845 graduate of West Point, served in the Mexican War and in the prewar U.S. Army. He was commissioned brigadier general of volunteers on Sept. 28, 1861. He was named commander of the cavalry of General Banks's command in the Shenandoah Valley, but Gen. John Pope later relieved him of this assignment and put him in charge of an infantry brigade in time to fight in the Second Manassas campaign. He was badly wounded in the Battle of South Mountain on Sept. 14, 1862, in which he was commanding a division in the First Corps of the Army of the Potomac. After his recovery, he served in administrative and garrison positions for the rest of the war. Warner, *Generals in Blue*, 216–17.
24. Given the short duration of the fight and the small number of men involved on the Union side, Jackson's casualties were very heavy. A modern study of the battle estimates that Jackson lost more than 1,250 men. Alan Gaff, *Brave Men's Tears: The Iron Brigade at Brawner's Farm* (Dayton, Ohio: Press of Morningside Bookshop, 1985), 160.
25. John M. Stone (1830–1900), born in Tennessee, lived in Mississippi before the war. He was elected captain of Company K of the 2nd Mississippi on May 1, 1861, and was named colonel of the same regiment on Apr. 16, 1862. At this time, he was the senior colonel in Law's brigade. Krick, *Lee's Colonels*, 360.
26. On General Pope's plans regarding "pursuing" the "retreating" Army of Northern Virginia, see Hennessy, *Return to Bull Run*, 309–13 and 325–31.
27. George W. Morell (1815–1883) was an 1835 graduate of West Point. He resigned from the prewar U.S. Army in 1837 and became a lawyer. At the outbreak of the Civil War, he joined the New York militia and was made a brigadier general of volunteers on Aug. 9, 1861. He was promoted to the position of division commander in May 1862 and served in the Fifth Corps of the Army of the Potomac. Morell fought in the Peninsula campaign and at the Battles of Second Manassas and Antietam. After the Battle of Antietam, Morell held no further active field command for the remainder of the war. Warner, *Generals in Blue*, 330–31.
28. This was the assault of the Union Fifth Corps of the Army of the Potomac, commanded by Maj. Gen. Fitz John Porter, which was made on Jackson's lines hidden behind the railroad embankment at approximately 3 P.M. on Aug. 30, 1862. The best description of this attack is found in Hennessy, *Return to Bull Run*, 339–61.
29. Stephen D. Lee (1833–1908) graduated from West Point in 1854. He served in the prewar U.S. Army and saw combat in Florida in the Third Seminole War. He resigned from the army when South Carolina seceded

from the Union and joined the Confederacy. By the time of the Second Manassas campaign, Lee was colonel in charge of a battalion of artillery in General Longstreet's wing. It was the artillery fire of his command that helped to repel the attack of Porter's Fifth Corps on Aug. 30, 1862, which was reinforcing the initial assault wave. Lee and his 18 guns kept the corps from advancing to the point of initial breakthrough in the Confederate lines. Lee rose through the ranks, being promoted to the rank of lieutenant general in the Confederate service by the end of the war. Davis, *Confederate General*, 4:58–63.

30. This was a famous incident in which men of the 1st Louisiana Regiment, who had run out of ammunition, resorted to throwing stones from their position in the railroad embankment, trying to resist the overwhelming Union onslaught of Porter's Fifth Corps.
31. OR, vol. 12, pt. 2, p. 666.
32. Only General Longstreet's wing led the initial counterattack, as Jackson's men did not move forward for more than an hour. Hennessy, *Return to Bull Run*, 382.
33. The men of Law's brigade almost immediately swept away the 45th New York and then were counterattacked by the 2nd and 7th Wisconsin Regiments in the Dogan Orchard. Hennessy, *Return to Bull Run*, 426.
34. The Union battery was Capt. Hubert Dilger's Company K, 1st Ohio Light Artillery. Hennessy, *Return to Bull Run*, 426.
35. Turner Ashby (1828–1862), a Virginia farmer, was one of the South's finest cavalrymen in the early days of the Civil War. When Virginia seceded from the Union, Ashby formed a cavalry company, which became part of the 7th Virginia Cavalry. Originally a captain, he was promoted to the rank of lieutenant colonel on July 23, 1861. He fought with Jackson in the famous Valley Campaign of 1862, in which he earned promotion to brigadier general. However, on June 6, 1862, while fighting in the Valley, he was killed. Davis, *Confederate General* 1:47–48.

Chapter 7. Maryland Campaign

1. The capture of General Pope's supplies at Manassas Junction on Aug. 27, 1862, referred to in the previous chapter.
2. Thomas L. Samuels, born in Mississippi, was an unmarried 19-year-old clerk living in Selma, Ala., when he enlisted in Company A on Apr. 26, 1861. He was appointed second sergeant of his company on Oct. 26, 1861, and first sergeant on Apr. 22, 1862. As Coles states, Samuels was captured on Aug. 29, 1862, but escaped. Detailed to General Law's staff in Mar. 1864, he was severely wounded on June 3, 1864, which forced his resignation from active service on Dec. 20, 1864. CSR, Thomas L. Samuels.
3. Franz Sigel (1824–1902), born in Baden, Germany, graduated from a German military academy and served in the army of Grand Duke Leopold. After the Revolution of 1848, Sigel fled to America, where initially he settled in New York and later moved to St. Louis, Mo. He was named brigadier general of volunteers by President Lincoln on Aug. 7, 1861, and was promoted to major general on Mar. 22, 1862. His immense popularity among German immigrants in the U.S., together with his Republican friends, protected Sigel's high rank despite his obvious military

incompetence. He commanded a corps in Pope's Army of Virginia, which was predominately composed of either German-Americans or immigrant Germans. This corps later became the Eleventh Corps of the Army of the Potomac and was referred to as a "Dutch" corps. Sigel ended the war in the rank of major general. Warner, *Generals in Blue*, 447–48.
4. William Z. Sterling, an unmarried 18-year-old farmer from Tuskegee, Ala., enlisted as a private in Company B on Apr. 28, 1861. Promoted to corporal on Apr. 21, 1862, Sterling was present in all the battles in which the 4th Alabama participated. He surrendered on Apr. 9, 1865. CSR, William Z. Sterling.
5. In an attempt to outflank General Pope's retreating army after the Battle of Second Manassas, General Lee sent Stonewall Jackson on another flank march. The resulting Battle of Chantilly, Va., fought in a driving thunderstorm on Sept. 1, 1862, ended in a tactical draw. On Chantilly, see Freeman, *Lee's Lieutenants*, 2:130–35.
6. Philip Kearny (1815–1862) served as an officer in the U.S. Army prior to the Mexican War. He fought with great distinction in that war, where he lost his left arm. He resigned from the army in 1851 and, as he was independently wealthy, traveled around the world. Eventually he enlisted as an officer in the French Army in 1859. With the onset of the Civil War, Kearny returned home and was appointed brigadier general of volunteers on Aug. 7, 1861. He was assigned to command a New Jersey brigade in what ultimately became a unit in the Sixth Corps of the Army of the Potomac. Due to his leadership and magnetism, Kearny was assigned to divisional command in the Third Corps of the Army of the Potomac and was promoted to the rank of major general on July 4, 1862. After fighting gallantly in the Battle of Second Manassas, Kearny was killed in the Battle of Chantilly on Sept. 1, 1862. Warner, *Generals in Blue*, 258–59.
7. James J. Hager, listed in the records as being 6 feet, 5 inches tall, joined Company I on Sept. 14, 1862. In the Gettysburg campaign, Hager went absent without leave and was captured near Hagerstown, Md., his home, on June 29, 1863. Transferred to Fort Delaware, he was held as a prisoner until June 14, 1865, when he took the Oath of Allegiance. CSR, James J. Hager.
8. On Sept. 2, 1862, President Lincoln relieved General Pope of his command and reinstated General McClellan as commander of all the Union forces defending Washington, including both his Army of the Potomac and Pope's former Army of Virginia, which now was merged with the Army of the Potomac. Stephen W. Sears, *Landscape Turned Red* (New Haven: Ticknor and Fields, 1983), 15.
9. General Lee's famous "Lost Order," Special Order No. 191, found on Sept. 13, 1862, by members of the 27th Indiana Regiment, did indeed reveal to General McClellan all of General Lee's plans and the deployment of his forces to carry out these plans. The mystery of how this important document came to be left at an abandoned Confederate campsite never has been solved. See Sears, *Landscape Turned Red*, 110–13.
10. Gen. D. H. Hill, with his small division of 5,000 men, was entrusted with the key mission of holding Fox's and Turner's Gaps in the South Mountain range, until Confederate reinforcements could arrive. Had the Army of the Potomac succeeded in driving back Hill's men and crossing South Mountain, the Army of Northern Virginia could have been split in two and possibly destroyed.

11. Thomas F. Drayton (1808–1891) was a South Carolina native who graduated from West Point in 1828. He resigned from the U.S. Army in 1836 and became a planter at his family's plantation and president of a railroad in South Carolina. He joined the Confederate Army and was appointed brigadier general on Sept. 25, 1861, by President Davis, a personal friend. In the Second Manassas and Maryland campaigns, he commanded a brigade composed of the 50th and 51st Georgia, the 15th South Carolina, and Phillip's Georgia Legion. Drayton saw no further active field command with the Army of Northern Virginia after the Battle of Antietam, being assigned to the Department of Trans-Mississippi. Davis, *Confederate General*, 2:76–77.
12. William T. Wofford (1824–1884) practiced law and served in the Georgia House of Representatives prior to the Civil War. With the outbreak of the Civil War, he was elected colonel of the 18th Georgia Infantry Regiment, which was assigned to Hood's Texas Brigade. Wofford commanded the brigade in the Maryland campaign. He was promoted to brigadier general on Apr. 23, 1863, and became one of the great brigade commanders of the Army of Northern Virginia. He was transferred to Georgia to take over an independent command in Jan. 1865. Wofford surrendered in Georgia on May 12, 1865. Davis, *Confederate General*, 6:156–57.
13. OR, vol. 19, pt. 1, p. 922.
14. Hood's division had counterattacked advancing elements of the Union Ninth Corps, spearheaded by Brig. Gen. Isaac Rodman's division. Sears, *Landscape Turned Red*, 138.
15. Early on the evening of Sept. 16, 1862, General McClellan ordered General Hooker's First Corps of the Army of the Potomac to cross Antietam Creek and form for its intended daybreak assault on the left flank of the Confederate lines. Sears, *Landscape Turned Red*, 176.
16. This was Lt. William Elliott's Brooks South Carolina Artillery, composed of two 10-pounder and two 20-pounder guns. John M. Priest, *Antietam: The Soldiers' Battle* (Shippensburg, Pa.: White Mane Publishing Co., 1989), 324.
17. James A. Walker (1832–1901), as a cadet at Virginia Military Institute prior to the Civil War, was expelled after a disciplinary altercation with Professor Thomas J. Jackson, later famous as "Stonewall" Jackson. The boy then attempted to kill Jackson by hitting him with a brick but, fortunately for the future Confederacy, failed. Walker practiced law before the Civil War and, when Virginia seceded, became captain of Company C of the 4th Virginia Infantry. Walker then was promoted to lieutenant colonel of the 13th Virginia Infantry on May 17, 1861, and to colonel of the same unit in Apr. 1862. He fought with Jackson in his famous Valley campaign and in the Peninsula campaign in 1862. In the Maryland campaign of 1862, Walker commanded the brigade that had been led by Brig. Gen. Isaac Trimble prior to his wounding at the Battle of Second Manassas. The brigade was composed of the 15th Alabama, 12th and 21st Georgia, and 21st North Carolina. Walker was wounded in the Battle of Antietam, when he was struck by a shell. He later rose to the rank of brigadier general and served throughout the rest of the war. Davis, *Confederate General*, 6:86–87.
18. On Sept. 15, 1862, Stonewall Jackson and the six divisions assigned to him as part of General Lee's Special Order Number 191 forced the surrender of the Union forces bottled up in Harpers Ferry, taking more than 11,000

prisoners, 13,000 small arms, 200 wagons, and 73 pieces of artillery. Sears, *Landscape Turned Red*, 153.
19. Lafayette McLaws (1821–1897) was a Georgia native who graduated from West Point in 1842. He served in the Mexican War and in the prewar U.S. Army. When Georgia seceded from the Union, he joined the Confederacy and was commissioned colonel in command of the 10th Georgia Infantry Regiment on June 17, 1861. He was promoted to brigadier general on Sept. 25, 1861, and to major general on May 23, 1862. McLaws was placed in the command of a division in what was to become Longstreet's First Corps of the Army of Northern Virginia. McLaws led his division for more than two years, fighting in all the campaigns of the Army of Northern Virginia during that period, until he became involved in a court-martial controversy with General Longstreet during winter 1863–64. To resolve the controversy, McLaws was transferred to Savannah, Ga., where he ended the war in obscurity. Davis, *Confederate General*, 4:129–31.
20. James H. Stewart, a merchant from Summit, Ala., enlisted in Company I on Apr. 26, 1861. He was elected third lieutenant of his company on Apr. 20, 1862, and first lieutenant in Nov. 1862. Stewart was wounded on Nov. 25, 1863. The last entry in his service records shows him absent without leave since Apr. 1864. CSR, James H. Stewart.
21. Joseph B. Frame enlisted on Apr. 26, 1861, in Company I of the 4th Alabama. No wonder it was said that he could whip any three men; he was 6 feet, 2 inches tall when he enlisted. He was captured at Hog Mountain, Tenn., on Oct. 29, 1863, and held as a prisoner until June 14, 1865. CSR, Joseph B. Frame.
22. The alignment of the brigade was, from left to right, 2nd Mississippi, 11th Mississippi, 6th North Carolina, and 4th Alabama. Priest, *Antietam*, 55.
23. OR, vol. 19, pt. 1, pp. 937–38.
24. The full description of this action, as seen from the position of the 10th Maine, is found in John M. Gould, *History of the 1st-10th-29th Maine Regiment* (Portland, Me.: Stephen Berry, 1871), 232–53.
25. A modern study of the Texas Brigade puts the losses of the 1st Texas at 186 out of 226 engaged, or 82.3%. Simpson, *Hood's Texas Brigade*, 176.
26. Alfred H. Colquitt (1824–1894) practiced law and represented Georgia in Congress prior to the Civil War. When Georgia seceded from the Union, he left Congress and was elected colonel of the 6th Georgia Infantry Regiment. In June 1862, Colquitt was placed in command of a brigade in Maj. Gen. D. H. Hill's division. Colquitt was promoted to the rank of brigadier general on Sept. 2, 1862, for his performance in the Peninsula campaign. During the Maryland campaign, his brigade was composed of the 6th, 23rd, 27th, and 28th Georgia, and the 13th Alabama Infantry Regiments. After the Maryland campaign, Colquitt led his brigade in the Fredericksburg and Chancellorsville campaigns. He was then transferred to North Carolina and later to the Department of Florida. Colquitt returned to the Army of Northern Virginia during the Petersburg campaign and ended the war in North Carolina, where he surrendered. Davis, *Confederate General*, 2:9–10.
27. William M. Arnold enlisted as a captain in Company A of the 6th Georgia on Apr. 22, 1861. He was promoted to major of the regiment on June 16, 1863, and to lieutenant colonel on Jan. 20, 1864. Arnold was wounded at

Malvern Hill, Antietam, and Chancellorsville, and was killed at Petersburg on July 7, 1864. Krick, *Lee's Colonels*, 38.
28. Roswell S. Ripley (1823–1887) was an 1843 graduate of West Point. He served in the Mexican War and the Third Seminole War in Florida, but in 1853 he resigned to join his wife in South Carolina and pursue a business career. Though a native of Ohio, Ripley joined the Confederate forces, being appointed brigadier general on Aug. 15, 1861. In the Maryland campaign, he commanded a brigade in Gen. D. H. Hill's division, composed of the 4th and 44th Georgia and the 1st and 3rd North Carolina Infantry Regiments. Ripley was wounded in the throat in the Battle of Antietam and never returned to the Army of Northern Virginia, being placed in command of the First Military District of South Carolina. Davis, *Confederate General*, 5:89–90.
29. The Confederate regiment to the right of the 4th Alabama in the East Woods was the 21st Georgia, which was a part of the brigade commanded by Col. James Walker. Priest, *Antietam*, 73.
30. George S. Greene (1801–1899) was an 1823 graduate of West Point. He resigned from the U.S. Army in 1836 and became a civil engineer. Greene was elected colonel of the 60th New York Infantry in Jan. 1862. He was promoted to brigadier general of volunteers on Apr. 28, 1862, and became one of the oldest field commanders in service. His troops coined the nickname of "Pap" for him. In the Battle of Antietam, he commanded a division in the Twelfth Corps of the Army of the Potomac, which made a deep and temporarily successful penetration of the Confederate lines around the Dunker Church. He later fought with great success at the Battle of Gettysburg and in the western campaigns, where he was severely wounded in Oct. 1863. When he died, he was the oldest living graduate of West Point. Warner, *Generals in Blue*, 186–87.
31. David B. King, an unmarried 19-year-old farmer from Whitesburg, Ala., enlisted as a private in Company F on Sept. 1, 1861, when the 4th Alabama was stationed at Camp Law, Va. King was promoted to second lieutenant on Aug. 30, 1862, and was wounded at the Battle of Antietam on Sept. 17, 1862. Left on the field, he was captured and, while in Union hands, died of his wounds. CSR, David B. King.
32. OR, vol. 19, pt. 1, p. 923.

Chapter 8. From Sharpsburg to Fredericksburg

1. This was the Battle of Shepherdstown, Va., fought on Sept. 20, 1862, when Confederate forces under the command of Gen. A. P. Hill disastrously repulsed a Union reconnaissance in force made by regiments of the Fifth Corps of the Army of the Potomac. For this Union debacle, see Freeman, *Lee's Lieutenants*, 2:226–35.
2. Braxton Bragg (1817–1876) was a native North Carolinian who graduated from West Point in 1837 and fought in the Mexican War. He resigned from the prewar U.S. Army in 1856 and moved to Louisiana. After Louisiana seceded from the Union, he was commissioned a brigadier general in the Confederate Army on Mar. 7, 1861. Bragg was appointed major general on Sept. 12, 1861, and promoted to general on Apr. 12, 1862, in part because of his long friendship with President Davis. Bragg commanded

the Confederate Army of Tennessee in the western campaigns with little success; his ill-fated invasion of Kentucky took place in fall 1862. Because of his unpleasant personality and military failures, Bragg was one of the most hated men in all of the Confederacy; he was finally relieved of field command after the crushing Confederate defeat on Missionary Ridge on Nov. 25, 1863. Davis, *Confederate General*, 1:113–15.
3. Maj. Gen. Ambrose Burnside replaced Gen. George McClellan as commander of the Army of the Potomac on Nov. 7, 1862, at the behest of President Abraham Lincoln. Sears, *Landscape Turned Red*, 340–41.
4. The advance elements of the Army of the Potomac, comprised of the Second and Ninth Corps under the command of General Sumner, had arrived opposite Fredericksburg on Nov. 19, 1862, but delayed crossing the river to wait for pontoon bridges to arrive. The delay caused the subsequent disaster.

Chapter 9. Fredericksburg

1. William T. Turner was an unmarried 22-year-old bookkeeper when he enlisted in Company D on Apr. 26, 1861. He was elected second lieutenant on Apr. 21, 1862, and first lieutenant on Nov. 3, 1862. Described in the regiment's records as "gallant and meritorious," he was mortally wounded at the Battle of the Wilderness on May 6, 1864. CSR, William T. Turner.
2. On Nov. 6, 1862, the Army of Northern Virginia was officially divided into two corps. The First was commanded by General Longstreet and the Second by General Jackson. The 4th Alabama, a part of General Hood's division, was assigned to the First Corps. Freeman, *Lee's Lieutenants*, 2:269.
3. William Barksdale (1821–1863), a prewar Mississippi Congressman, ardently advocated southern states' rights in the U.S. Congress from 1852 to 1861. When Mississippi seceded from the Union, he left Congress and became colonel of the 13th Mississippi on May 14, 1861. He assumed command of the Mississippi Brigade, composed of the 13th, 17th, 18th, and 21st Mississippi Regiments, on June 29, 1862, when its previous commander was killed at the Battle of Savage's Station. Barksdale was promoted to brigadier general on Aug. 12, 1862, and saw heavy action in the Second Manassas and Maryland campaigns. Barksdale's brigade, and units of Perry's Florida Brigade, fought brilliantly against heavy odds on Dec. 11, 1862, when the Army of the Potomac tried to force a crossing of the Rappahannock River into the town of Fredericksburg. Barksdale's men withdrew from the town only on the express orders of General McLaws, their division commander. Barksdale later was mortally wounded on July 2, 1863, while leading his brigade in its gallant charge at the Battle of Gettysburg. Davis, *Confederate General*, 1:58–59.
4. Henry J. Hunt (1819–1889) was an 1839 graduate of West Point and a veteran of the Mexican War. His specialty was artillery. General McClellan placed him in charge of training the artillery reserve of the Army of the Potomac in winter 1861–62. Hunt commanded the artillery of the Army of the Potomac during the Peninsula campaign of 1862 and was named brigadier general of volunteers on Sept. 15, 1862, in recognition of his great skill and bravery in battle. He remained chief of artillery until June 1864, when General Grant placed him in charge of all Petersburg siege operations. Warner, *Generals in Blue*, 242–43.

5. Stafford Heights was a commanding Union position across the Rappahannock River from the town of Fredericksburg and served as an excellent location for many artillery batteries of the Army of the Potomac during the Battle of Fredericksburg.
6. William Swinton, *Campaigns of the Army of the Potomac* (New York: Charles Scribner's Sons, 1882), 240.
7. The first two Union regiments to cross into Fredericksburg by boat were the 19th Massachusetts and the 7th Michigan, followed soon after by the 20th Massachusetts. Swinton, *Campaigns*, 241.
8. Richard Jones was 23 years old, single, and working as a merchant in Mobile, Ala., when he joined Company D at Camp Law, Va., on Sept. 24, 1861. He was wounded in his left side on Sept. 17, 1862, and returned to the regiment on July 6, 1863. Wounded again on Sept. 19, 1863, at the Battle of Chickamauga, by a musket ball passing through his left groin to his right side, Jones recovered to rejoin the 4th Alabama and surrender on Apr. 9, 1865. CSR, Richard Jones.
9. One of General Burnside's innovations, upon taking command of the Army of the Potomac, was forming his army into "Grand Divisions." The Right Grand Division was commanded by Maj. Gen. Edwin Sumner and was composed of the Second and Ninth Army Corps. The Center Grand Division was commanded by Maj. Gen. Joseph Hooker and was composed of the Third and Fifth Army Corps. The Left Grand Division was commanded by Maj. Gen. William Franklin and was composed of the First and Sixth Army Corps. On Jan. 21, 1863, when General Hooker took command of the Army of the Potomac, he abolished the concept of "Grand Divisions." B&L, 3:143–45.
10. Edwin V. Sumner (1797–1863) had served continuously in the U.S. Army since 1819. He fought in Mexico and against the Indians in the West, and he served as colonel of the 1st U.S. Cavalry Regiment from 1855 until the outbreak of the Civil War. He was promoted to brigadier general in the Regular Army in 1861. When General McClellan formed the Army of the Potomac into corps commands, Sumner was promoted to lead what was to become the Second Corps of the Army of the Potomac. He was elevated to the rank of major general in the Regular Army on May 31, 1862. As noted above, he commanded the Right Grand Division during the Fredericksburg campaign. When General Hooker took command of the Army of the Potomac, Sumner was relieved at his own request and died soon after. Warner, *Generals in Blue*, 489–90.
11. Joseph Hooker (1814–1879) graduated from West Point in 1837 and fought in the Mexican War. He resigned from the army in 1853 and became a farmer in California. With the outbreak of the Civil War, he tendered his services to President Lincoln and on Aug. 6, 1861, was commissioned a brigadier general of volunteers. He led a division in the Third Corps of the Army of the Potomac in the Peninsula campaign and fought with great dash. Hooker was beloved by the common soldiers and lived up to his nickname, "Fighting Joe," with his conduct in the Peninsula, Second Manassas, and Maryland campaigns. During the Fredericksburg campaign, Hooker commanded the Center Grand Division. After Burnside's bungling, Hooker was named to replace him in command of the Army of the Potomac on Jan. 21, 1863. He led the army to one of its bitterest defeats in the Chancellorsville campaign of Apr.-May 1863. Hooker resigned from

command of the Army of the Potomac on June 27, 1863, and was replaced by George Meade. Hooker served out the remainder of the Civil War in the western campaigns. Warner, *Generals in Blue*, 233–35.

12. Richard H. Anderson (1821–1879) was a South Carolina native who graduated from West Point in 1842 and served in the prewar U.S. Army in the Mexican, Mormon, and Indian wars. He resigned from the army on Feb. 15, 1861, and gave his allegiance to his native state. He was promoted to brigadier general in the Confederate Army on July 19, 1861, and served in Florida for the rest of the year. Anderson was transferred to what later was called the Army of Northern Virginia on Jan. 31, 1862, and assigned to command a brigade composed of five South Carolina regiments. During the fighting in the Peninsula campaign, his inspired leadership marked him as one of the most promising brigadier generals in the army. He became known as "Fighting Dick." He was promoted to major general on July 14, 1862, and took over the command of a division. Anderson fought in all the battles of the Army of Northern Virginia during the remainder of the war, being promoted to lieutenant general on June 1, 1864, in recognition of the fact that he had replaced the wounded Lieutenant General Longstreet in command of the First Corps on May 7, 1864. Davis, *Confederate General*, 1:28–29.

13. Howell Cobb (1815–1868) was a Georgia lawyer and politician who had served in the U.S. Congress and in the cabinet of President James Buchanan. He was one of the original southern "fire-eaters" who called for the secession of Georgia from the Union and the formation of a Southern Confederacy. When the Confederacy came into being, Cobb enlisted as colonel of the 16th Georgia Infantry Regiment on July 15, 1861. At the same time, Cobb also served as a representative in the Confederate Congress from Georgia. Due to his political connections, he was promoted to brigadier general on Feb. 13, 1862, and assigned to brigade command. He fought in the Peninsula campaign and in the Maryland campaign, where his brigade fell apart under his less than inspired leadership. He was then replaced by his brother, Thomas R. R. Cobb, who led the brigade at the Battle of Fredericksburg. Howell Cobb later served in the District of Florida and in the Atlanta campaign with the rank of major general. Davis, *Confederate General*, 1:207–9.

14. William B. Taliaferro (1822–1898) was a Virginia native who fought as an officer in the Mexican War. When Virginia seceded from the Union, Taliaferro was appointed colonel of the 23rd Virginia Infantry Regiment. Promoted to brigadier general on Mar. 6, 1862, he was assigned to command a brigade under Gen. Stonewall Jackson. Despite the fact that Jackson and he did not get along, he fought in Jackson's command in the famous Valley campaign of 1862 and in the Peninsula campaign. By seniority, when its former commander was killed on Aug. 9, 1862, at the Battle of Cedar Mountain, Taliaferro assumed command of Jackson's former division. On Aug. 28, 1862, he was seriously wounded at the Battle of Brawner's Farm and had to take a leave of absence to recuperate. By the time of the Fredericksburg campaign, Taliaferro had returned to the command of his division. After this battle, when Taliaferro was not promoted to the rank of major general, he requested and received a transfer out of the Army of Northern Virginia. Taliaferro served out the war in posts

in South Carolina, Florida, and North Carolina; in North Carolina, he finally surrendered on May 2, 1865. Davis, *Confederate General*, 6:25.
15. James E. B. "Jeb" Stuart (1833–1864) was one of the most flamboyant cavalry commanders the U.S. ever produced. An 1854 graduate of West Point, he served in the 1st U.S. Cavalry Regiment. While in this posting, he assisted Lt. Col. Robert E. Lee in the capture of John Brown, ending Brown's raid on Harpers Ferry, Va., in Oct. 1859. When Virginia seceded from the Union, Stuart, as a native son, resigned from the army on May 3, 1861. He was appointed lieutenant colonel in the Provisional Army of Virginia and took command of the 1st Virginia Cavalry Regiment on July 16, 1861. Due to his brilliant cavalry command at the Battle of First Manassas, Stuart was promoted to brigadier general on Sept. 24, 1861, and took charge of the cavalry of what was to become the Army of Northern Virginia, eventually being promoted to the rank of major general. Stuart's cavalry became the scourge of the Army of the Potomac, and he gained worldwide recognition for his flamboyant exploits and skilled leadership. Stuart was wounded at the Battle of Yellow Tavern on May 11, 1864, and died the next day. Davis, *Confederate General*, 6:19–23.
16. John W. Young, a printer from Huntsville, Ala., enlisted as a private in Company I in May 1862. He was wounded in the arm on June 27, 1862, at the Battle of Gaines' Mill but remained on duty until he was shot and lost three fingers on his right hand on July 2, 1863. He served on the staff of the brigade commissary and as a hospital clerk with the 4th Alabama until his surrender on Apr. 9, 1865. CSR, John W. Young.
17. As previously stated, Thomas Coleman's service records indicate that his date of promotion was Oct. 3, 1863.
18. Elements of the Union First Corps in Franklin's Grand Division had achieved a temporary break in Jackson's line, but the penetration was quickly sealed by reinforcements from Jubal Early's and A. P. Hill's divisions, and the Union forces were forced to retreat. See Freeman, *Lee's Lieutenants*, 2:338–58.
19. William H. French (1815–1881) was an 1837 graduate of West Point who fought in the Mexican and Seminole wars. With the outbreak of the Civil War, he was promoted to the rank of brigadier general of volunteers on Sept. 28, 1861, and assigned to command a brigade in what would become the Second Corps of the Army of the Potomac. He fought in the Peninsula campaign as a brigade commander and in the Maryland campaign as a division commander in the same corps. He was promoted to major general on Nov. 29, 1862, and continued as division commander in the Second Corps in the Fredericksburg campaign. French commanded the Department of Harpers Ferry in the Gettysburg campaign and served in the Army of the Potomac in the Mine Run campaign of late 1863, after which he was relieved of his command for slowness in exploiting a possibly favorable situation. He served on various military administrative boards for the rest of the war. Warner, *Generals in Blue*, 161–62.
20. Thomas R. R. Cobb (1823–1862), a wealthy planter and lawyer in Georgia, was a fervent advocate of slavery and states' rights and served as a delegate to the Georgia Secession Convention. He was commissioned colonel of Cobb's Legion on Aug. 28, 1861. Cobb served in the Peninsula campaign but missed the Maryland campaign because he was home in Georgia on furlough. On Nov. 1, 1862, he was promoted to the rank of brigadier

general and replaced his brother, Howell Cobb, in command of a Georgia brigade consisting of the 16th, 18th, and 24th Georgia, as well as Cobb's and Phillip's legions. The brigade held the Sunken Road position at the base of Marye's Heights during the Battle of Fredericksburg, which unquestionably was the key Confederate position during the battle. It repulsed at least nine separate assaults by Burnside's men. Cobb, however, was not to savor this great victory. He was mortally wounded when a piece of shrapnel struck him in the left leg and severed his femoral artery, causing his death in minutes. Davis, *Confederate General*, 2:2–3.

21. Joseph B. Kershaw (1822–1894), a Mexican War veteran, was a prosperous prewar South Carolina lawyer and member of the South Carolina Legislature. Named colonel of the 2nd South Carolina Infantry Regiment on Apr. 9, 1861, he fought in the Battle of First Manassas and was promoted to brigadier general on Feb. 13, 1862. He took command of a brigade composed of Orr's Rifles and the 2nd, 3rd, 7th, 8th, and 15th South Carolina Regiments. Kershaw fought with his brigade in the Peninsula, Maryland, and Fredericksburg campaigns. Kershaw's brigade reinforced Cobb's brigade in the Sunken Road position at the base of Marye's Heights in the Battle of Fredericksburg. In recognition of his continued competence, Kershaw was promoted to major general and placed in command of McLaws' division in winter 1863–64. He fought as a division commander for the remainder of the war. On Apr. 6, 1865, Kershaw was taken prisoner at the Battle of Sayler's Creek. Davis, *Confederate General*, 4:11–13.
22. Winfield S. Hancock (1824–1886) was one of the ablest and most famous commanders on the Union side during the Civil War. An 1844 graduate of West Point, Hancock fought gallantly in the Mexican War. He remained in the U.S. Army and served on the western frontier. With the outbreak of the Civil War, he was promoted to brigadier general of volunteers on Sept. 23, 1861, and assigned to brigade command in what would become the Sixth Corps of the Army of the Potomac. He fought in the Peninsula campaign and took command of a division in the Second Corps at the Battle of Antietam when its former commander was mortally wounded. He was promoted to the rank of major general on Nov. 29, 1862, and led his division in its ferocious assaults on the stone wall at the base of Marye's Heights in the Battle of Fredericksburg. Hancock continued in division command during the Chancellorsville campaign, being promoted to the command of the Second Corps of the Army of the Potomac after the campaign. It was his brilliant achievements and gallant conduct during the Battle of Gettysburg that won Hancock lasting fame. After being severely wounded in the groin at the Battle of Gettysburg on July 3, 1863, Hancock left the Army of the Potomac for a long period of recuperation but returned in time for the spring campaign of 1864. He never fully recovered from his wound, however. After the war, he ran for president on the Democratic ticket in 1880 but lost to James Garfield. Warner, *Generals in Blue*, 202–4.
23. James B. Walton (1813–1885) was a native of New Orleans. He entered Confederate service as major of the famous Washington Artillery Battalion of Louisiana and was promoted to colonel in command of the battalion on Mar. 26, 1862. Krick, *Lee's Colonels*, 386.
24. Andrew A. Humphreys (1810–1883) was a native Pennsylvanian who graduated from West Point in 1831 and served as an engineer in the prewar U.S. Army. With the outbreak of the Civil War, he became an aide to

General McClellan and was promoted to brigadier general of volunteers in Apr. 1862. He served as the Army of the Potomac's chief topographical engineer in the Peninsula campaign. In Sept. 1862, he was promoted to command a division of Pennsylvanians in the Fifth Corps of the Army of the Potomac, which Humphreys led in a gallant, doomed charge in the Battle of Fredericksburg. By the end of the war, after serving as chief of staff of the Army of the Potomac, Humphreys had been promoted to command of the Second Corps. Warner, *Generals in Blue*, 240–42.
25. Samuel S. Sturgis (1822–1889) graduated from West Point in 1846 and fought in the Mexican War, where he briefly was captured. After that war, he served in the U.S. Army in its campaigns against the Plains Indians. With the outbreak of the Civil War, Sturgis was promoted to brigadier general on Aug. 10, 1861, to recognize his gallantry in the Battle of Wilson's Creek. In the Battle of Fredericksburg, Sturgis commanded a division in the Ninth Corps of the Army of the Potomac. After the battle, Sturgis served in the western campaigns for the rest of the war. Warner, *Generals in Blue*, 486–87.
26. Swinton, *Campaigns*, 252.
27. OR, vol. 21, p. 451.
28. The fleeing Confederate regiment was the 16th North Carolina, which had been attacked by a New Jersey brigade of the Union Sixth Corps. Joseph G. Bilby, *Three Rousing Cheers* (Hightstown, N.J.: Longstreet House, 1993), 37.
29. Joseph W. Latimer (1843–1863) was a Virginia native who attended the Virginia Military Institute prior to the Civil War. He was elected lieutenant of the Courtney Artillery battery on Sept. 15, 1861. Latimer was made captain in summer 1862 and was named acting chief of artillery of General Ewell's division in Dec. 1862. He later was promoted to major on Mar. 2, 1863, and became known in the ranks of the Army of Northern Virginia as the "Boy Major." While directing his guns at the Battle of Gettysburg, Latimer was mortally wounded on July 2, 1863, and died on Aug. 1, 1863. Krick, *Lee's Colonels*, 231.
30. Virginius Smith, an unmarried 19-year-old clerk, a native of Virginia, enlisted in Company G on Apr. 24, 1861. Detailed to serve at brigade headquarters on Feb. 3, 1862, Smith was killed on Dec. 13, 1862. CSR, Virginius Smith.
31. In his official report, General Law wrote of Private Smith, "It is with deep sorrow that I report the death of V. S. Smith, of the 4th Alabama Regiment, an acting officer on my staff. Alabama never bore a braver son, and our country's cause has never received a sacrifice of a manlier spirit. He fell where the hour of danger always found him—at his post." OR, vol. 21, p. 624.
32. William H. Ware was a 20-year-old student from Uniontown, Ala., who joined Company D as a private on Apr. 25, 1861. Wounded on June 27, 1862, Ware was recognized in the records of the 4th Alabama as a "gallant and meritorious" solder. He was killed on Dec. 13, 1862. CSR, William H. Ware.
33. William A. Caldwell, a student from Huntsville, Ala., enlisted in Company I on Apr. 26, 1861. He served in all the battles in which the 4th Alabama fought until he was killed on Dec. 13, 1862. CSR, William A. Caldwell.
34. Gilchrist R. Bouleware was an unmarried student when he enlisted in Company E as a private on Apr. 25, 1861. He was promoted to colorbearer

and third sergeant on June 8, 1863. His records indicate that he was wounded on Dec. 13, 1862, and was forced to retire from the regiment due to disability on Feb. 1, 1864. CSR, Gilchrist R. Bouleware.
35. Henry Benjamin Love, an unmarried 22-year-old farmer, enlisted in Company F on Apr. 26, 1861. Love was wounded slightly in the face at the Battle of First Manassas on July 21, 1861, and lost a finger on Dec. 13, 1862. In the fighting around Spotsylvania, he was wounded slightly on May 8, 1864, and then was wounded severely in the foot. Upon his recovery from these wounds, he transferred to the 4th Alabama Cavalry. CSR, Henry B. Love.
36. William O. Newsome enlisted as a private in Company H on July 26, 1861. He was promoted to first sergeant of his company on Apr. 21, 1862, and to second lieutenant on July 10, 1863. He died on May 27, 1864, from a wound received at the Battle of the Wilderness on May 6, 1864. CSR, William O. Newsome.
37. Reuben F. Nix, an unmarried 21-year-old student from Marion, Ala., enlisted in Company G on Apr. 24, 1861. He served with the 4th Alabama until his discharge on Aug. 13, 1864, when he became a second lieutenant in Company C, 31st Alabama Infantry. CSR, Reuben F. Nix.
38. The Army of the Potomac lost 1,284 killed, 9,600 wounded, and 1,769 missing or captured; while the Army of Northern Virginia lost 608 killed, 4,116 wounded, and 653 missing or captured. B&L, 3:145–47.
39. Steptoe P. Chapman was an unmarried 22-year-old student who joined Company F on Sept. 21, 1861, at Camp Law, Va. As Coles states, Chapman's records indicate that he served on detached duty on General Longstreet's staff. CSR, Steptoe P. Chapman.
40. For more on this incident, and on why General Jackson did not launch a counterattack on the defeated Union Army, see Freeman, *Lee's Lieutenants*, 2:369–73.
41. Albert Sidney Johnston (1803–1863) was an 1826 graduate of West Point and an outstanding soldier in the prewar U.S. Army. A native of Kentucky, he aligned himself with the Confederacy and served in its armies in the West. He was killed at the Battle of Shiloh on Apr. 6, 1862. Davis, *Confederate General*, 3:188–89.
42. This was the Battle of Cedar Mountain, fought on Aug. 9, 1862.
43. As previously stated, the three Texas regiments in the Army of Northern Virginia were the 1st, 4th, and 5th Texas.
44. Henry L. Benning (1814–1875) was a native of Georgia who earned his living as a lawyer and a judge. He was elected colonel of the 17th Georgia Infantry Regiment on Aug. 29, 1861, and led that unit in the Peninsula, Second Manassas, and Maryland campaigns. When Gen. Robert Toombs resigned as commander of the brigade, Benning replaced him and was promoted to brigadier general, ranking from Jan. 17, 1863. The brigade consisted of the 2nd, 15th, 17th, and 20th Georgia Regiments. He served as a brigade commander with the Army of Northern Virginia for the rest of the war and surrendered at Appomattox Court House. Davis, *Confederate General*, 1:100–101.
45. George T. Anderson (1824–1901) was a native of Georgia who fought in the Mexican War and served for a time after the war in the U.S. Army. With the outbreak of the Civil War, he was elected colonel of the 11th Georgia Infantry Regiment on July 2, 1861. He was commissioned brigadier

general on Nov. 1, 1862, in recognition of the great leadership qualities he demonstrated in the brigade, which he had led as its senior colonel through the Peninsula, Second Manassas, and Maryland campaigns. This brigade was composed of the 7th, 8th, 9th, 11th, and 59th Georgia Regiments and was commanded by Anderson during the remainder of the war. Davis, *Confederate General* 1:20–21.

Chapter 10. The Siege of Suffolk

1. Maj. Gen. Joseph Hooker replaced Maj. Gen. Ambrose Burnside as commander of the Army of the Potomac on Jan. 25, 1863. Freeman, *Lee's Lieutenants*, 2:429.
2. William Duncan was named an assistant surgeon of the 4th Alabama on Jan. 11, 1863. He suffered from smallpox from the beginning of Feb. 1863 until Sept. 1863. Duncan was transferred to duty at the Howard Grove Hospital in Richmond on June 17, 1864. CSR, William Duncan.
3. This man could not be sufficiently identified in the records of the 4th Alabama.
4. "Bombproof positions" were those posts held by so-called rear-rank soldiers—those who did not have to face combat conditions and were, therefore, both envied and ridiculed by front-line troops.
5. Roger A. Pryor (1828–1919) was a Virginia native who worked as a lawyer, newspaper editor, and congressman prior to the Civil War. An ardent secessionist, he was named colonel of the 3rd Virginia Infantry Regiment upon the outbreak of the Civil War. Pryor was promoted to brigadier general on Apr. 16, 1862, and served with distinction in the Peninsula campaign. Pryor's brigade fought in the Second Manassas and Maryland campaigns, sustaining such heavy losses that the brigade was disbanded. He was then assigned to command a brigade south of the James River in Nov. 1862. Longstreet relieved Pryor of his command on Mar. 9, 1863, and he resigned his brigadier's commission on Aug. 8, 1863. Davis, *Confederate General*, 5:64–65.
6. Samuel B. McCalley, a native of Virginia, was a student living in Huntsville, Ala., when he enlisted on Apr. 26, 1861, in Company I. He served with the 4th Alabama throughout the war and surrendered on Apr. 9, 1865. CSR, Samuel B. McCalley.
7. One of the main purposes of this expedition was to gather supplies for the Confederacy. Freeman, *Lee's Lieutenants*, 2:476–77.
8. E. F. DeGraffenreid joined the 4th Alabama as an assistant surgeon in Mar. 1863. He served with the regiment until he was captured on July 13, 1863, at Williamsport, Md.; he was held as a prisoner at Forts McHenry and Lafayette. The last notation in his service records indicates that DeGraffenreid was admitted to a hospital in Baltimore on Aug. 4, 1863, suffering from acute diarrhea. CSR, E. F. DeGraffenreid.
9. Charles F. Taliaferro, an unmarried 26-year-old physician from Brooklyn, Ala., enlisted as a private in Company E on Apr. 25, 1861. He was promoted to second lieutenant on Apr. 9, 1862, and to first lieutenant on Aug. 22, 1862. Taliaferro was named an assistant surgeon of the 4th Alabama on Aug. 13, 1862, and served in this position for the rest of the war. CSR, Charles F. Taliaferro.

10. This incident is described in Oates, *War between the Union*, 176–78.
11. Leigh R. Terrell (1835–1864) was a lawyer in Uniontown, Ala. Originally enlisting in the 4th Alabama, he was promoted to the rank of captain and assistant adjutant general on the staff of Brigadier General Law on Oct. 14, 1862. While serving as lieutenant colonel of the 47th Alabama, Terrell was mortally wounded on Oct. 13, 1864. Krick, *Lee's Colonels*, 369.
12. John K. Connally (1839–1904) was born in Tennessee but was residing in North Carolina prior to the Civil War. He was elected colonel of the 55th North Carolina on May 19, 1862, and served with the regiment until he was wounded and captured at the Battle of Gettysburg on July 1, 1863. Krick, *Lee's Colonels*, 97.
13. On Apr. 19, 1863, 5 guns and more than 130 Confederate soldiers were captured in a surprise Union night attack on Fort Huger. Neither General Law nor Colonel Connally had placed pickets on the Nansemond River. Freeman, *Lee's Lieutenants*, 2:486.
14. Alfred H. Belo (1839–1901) was a native of North Carolina who enlisted as a captain in the 21st North Carolina on May 22, 1861. He was elected captain of the 55th North Carolina on Nov. 1, 1862. Belo was promoted to major of the 55th in May 1863 and was named lieutenant colonel of the regiment on July 3, 1863, a position in which he served for the rest of the war. Krick, *Lee's Colonels*, 50–51.
15. For Major Belo's description of this highly unusual occurrence, see Stuart Wright, ed., *Memoirs of Alfred Horatio Belo* (Gaithersburg, Md.: Olde Soldiers Books, 1991), 16–17.
16. While engaged in a night scouting expedition in advance of his own lines, General Jackson was shot and mortally wounded by men of the 18th North Carolina on May 2, 1863. He died on May 10, 1863.
17. The garrison of Suffolk was composed of some 15,000 Union troops; none of them were battle-hardened veterans like the troops of the Army of the Potomac. Freeman, *Lee's Lieutenants*, 2:494.

Chapter 11. Incidents on the Rappahannock and Rapidan

1. In the Chancellorsville campaign, which lasted from Apr. 29, 1862, to May 6, 1863, the Army of Northern Virginia, facing heavy odds, soundly defeated General Hooker's Army of the Potomac, which was forced to retire to its encampments around Stafford Heights. Chancellorsville has been recognized by many Civil War historians as Lee's greatest triumph.
2. OR, vol. 25, pt. 2, p. 793.
3. Due to Stonewall Jackson's death, General Lee felt it necessary to reorganize the Army of Northern Virginia. General Ewell was promoted to lieutenant general and given command of Jackson's old Second Corps on May 23, 1863; and on May 24, 1863, General Hill similarly was promoted and given command of the newly formed Third Corps. Freeman, *Lee's Lieutenants*, 2:695–96.
4. The Battle of Kelly's Ford, although only an engagement, resulted in the death of John Pelham.
5. On June 9, 1863, the great cavalry battle of Brandy Station, Va., was fought. It was in this engagement that the cavalry of the Army of the

Potomac finally came of age, as they fought Jeb Stuart's Confederate cavalry to a standstill. On this battle, see Freeman, *Lee's Lieutenants*, 3:1–19.
6. OR, vol. 27, pt. 1, p. 39.

Chapter 12. Gettysburg Campaign

1. P. Turner Vaughan of Company C of the 4th Alabama described this march in his diary: "The day has been excessively warm. I have seen more men faint today than ever before. It is said that several have died." P. Turner Vaughan, "Diary of Turner Vaughan, Company C, 4th Alabama Regiment, C.S.A., Commenced Mar. 4, 1863, and Ending Feb. 12, 1864," *Alabama Historical Quarterly* 18, no. 4 (Winter 1956): 585.
2. Robert E. Rodes (1829–1864) was a native Virginian and a graduate of Virginia Military Institute. He worked as a civil engineer prior to the Civil War in Texas, North Carolina, Missouri, and Alabama. With the coming of the war, Rodes enlisted as a captain in the 5th Alabama and was commissioned colonel on May 11, 1861. He was promoted to brigadier general on Oct. 21, 1861. His brigade of Alabama troops fought with great distinction in all the battles of the Army of Northern Virginia. In recognition of his gallantry at the Battle of Chancellorsville, where Rodes acted as division commander, he was commissioned major general to rank from May 2, 1863, and was given permanent command of a division in the Second Corps of the Army of Northern Virginia. He led this division, with indifferent results, for the remainder of his life. Rodes was killed on Sept. 19, 1864, in the Third Battle of Winchester in General Early's Valley campaign of 1864. Davis, *Confederate General*, 5:107–9.
3. Although Berryville was captured on June 13, 1863, most of the Union garrison escaped, due to poor coordination between the Confederate infantry and cavalry. Edwin B. Coddington, *The Gettysburg Campaign: A Study in Command* (New York: Charles Scribner's Sons, 1968), 90.
4. Gen. Jeb Stuart took three brigades of the cavalry corps of the Army of Northern Virginia on an ill-fated ride around the Army of the Potomac, which was following the Army of Northern Virginia northward into Maryland and Pennsylvania. Stuart was out of contact with General Lee and the Army of Northern Virginia for several key days, depriving Lee of his "eyes and ears." On Stuart and his crucial role in the Gettysburg campaign, see Coddington, *Gettysburg Campaign*, 108–13, 198–206.
5. Again, although Rodes captured Martinsburg on June 14, 1863, most of the Union garrison escaped. Coddington, *Gettysburg Campaign*, 90.
6. For the complete text of General Lee's order, titled General Order No. 72, see OR, vol. 27, pt. 3, pp. 912–13.
7. Coles either was not paying attention or chose to ignore the extent of the plundering that the Army of Northern Virginia did during the Gettysburg campaign. In his diary entry for June 28, 1863, Turner Vaughan wrote, "Our boys have been foraging all over the neighboring country. No one has committed any outrage upon the people that I have heard of, though they have perhaps taken from them more than they should have done of chickens, turkeys, ducks, etc. Stringent orders have been issued against such conduct by our generals, though it is rather a hard matter to restrain our troops when they remember the devastated plains of Virginia and the

conduct of the Federals in other portions of our country especially in New Orleans and the northern part of Alabama." Vaughan, "Diary," 588.
8. Harrison was a spy whose true identity still has not been discovered, although several theories have been propounded. On Harrison and his role in the Gettysburg campaign, see Coddington, *Gettysburg Campaign*, 180–81, 188–89.
9. George G. Meade (1815–1872), though born in Spain, was a native Pennsylvanian who graduated from West Point in 1835, served in the Mexican War, and was a military engineer in the prewar U.S. Army. With the outbreak of the Civil War, Meade was made a brigadier general of volunteers and given the command of an excellent brigade of Pennsylvanians in the future Fifth Corps of the Army of the Potomac. Meade fought in the Peninsula campaign, where he was wounded at the Battle of Glendale on June 30, 1862. After his recuperation, he fought in the Maryland campaign, and in the battles of Fredericksburg and Chancellorsville. In the latter, Meade led the Fifth Corps of the Army of the Potomac with the rank of major general. When General Hooker, by direct order of the President, resigned on June 28, 1863, Meade was promoted to command the Army of the Potomac, which he led during the rest of the war. Warner, *Generals in Blue*, 315–17.
10. The Alabama Brigade has never received the praise that it deserved for its march on the morning of July 2, 1863, from New Guilford to the battlefield of Gettysburg. This march, estimated at between 20 and 28 miles, took place in nine to ten hours and was made in scorching July heat and humidity. The column was enveloped in vast dust clouds, and the men very early ran out of water. The men in the brigade were veterans, however, and accomplished their assigned task in time to participate in the fighting on the afternoon of July 2, 1863. An excellent description of this march is found in Coddington, *Gettysburg Campaign*, 369.
11. The fighting which took place on July 1, 1863, on the rolling hills north and west of the town of Gettysburg, was between most of the Second and Third Corps of the Army of Northern Virginia and the First and Eleventh Corps of the Army of the Potomac. It ended in a victory for the Confederates, and the remnants of the two Union corps retreated through Gettysburg to new positions on the hills south of town. General Ewell failed to order his Second Corps to assault the new Union positions on the late afternoon and early evening of July 1, 1863, enabling the rest of the Union Army of the Potomac to concentrate in these positions, which then were assaulted by the Confederates on July 2–3, 1863.
12. When the attack began, the alignment of the brigade, from left to right, was the 4th Alabama, 47th Alabama, 15th Alabama, 44th Alabama, and 48th Alabama. Harry W. Pfanz, *Gettysburg: The Second Day* (Chapel Hill: Univ. of North Carolina Press, 1987), 159.
13. This was Little Round Top.
14. This was the 4th New York Battery, commanded by Capt. James E. Smith, composed of six 10-pounder Parrott rifles. Four guns in the battery were positioned facing west on Houck's Ridge atop Devil's Den, and the remaining two guns were placed in Plum Run Valley, northeast of the other four pieces. Pfanz, *Gettysburg*, 127.
15. These were skirmishers of the 2nd U.S. Sharpshooters Regiment. Pfanz, *Gettysburg*, 168.

16. A member of the 2nd U.S. Sharpshooters described the initial onslaught of the Alabama Brigade: "They came yelling and firing and struggling over fences and through the timber. Just in front of where I was, the land was open and, as they were mostly dressed in butternut-colored clothes they had the appearance of a plowed field being closed in mass formation until they got within good fighting distance to our line, when they broke into line of battle formation three lines deep." Russell C. White, ed., *The Civil War Diary of Wyman S. White* (Baltimore, Md.: Butternut and Blue, 1991), 164.
17. This man has not been identified in the service records of men who served in the 4th Alabama.
18. On July 2, 1863, Professor Michael Jacobs of Pennsylvania College recorded the temperature as 81 degrees. *Gettysburg Star and Sentinel,* July 30, 1885.
19. Charles F. Halsey, an unmarried 27-year-old mechanic from Huntsville, Ala., enlisted in Company F on Apr. 26, 1861. The records indicate that Halsey served at least part of his service as a musician and that he deserted on Feb. 18, 1865. CSR, Charles F. Halsey.
20. The Union regiment being attacked by the 4th Alabama was the 83rd Pennsylvania, a sturdy veteran outfit in a brigade commanded by Col. Strong Vincent, in the Fifth Corps of the Army of the Potomac. From the position of the 83rd Pennsylvania, the attack of the 4th Alabama was described as follows: "On came the enemy, running and yelling like fiends. . . . They soon neared our position, and our skirmishers were driven in, the enemy following closely in their rear. They at once attacked the whole line, but threw the weight of their force against the centre where lay the 83rd and 44th [New York]. In an instant a sheet of smoke and flame burst from our whole line, which made the enemy reel and stagger, and fall back in confusion. But soon rallying they advanced again to the assault. Taking position behind the rocks, they poured in a deadly fire upon our troops. Hundreds of them approached even within fifteen yards of our line, but they approached only to be shot down or hurled back covered with gaping wounds." Amos M. Judson, *History of the Eighty-Third Regiment Pennsylvania Volunteers* (Dayton, Ohio: Press of Morningside Bookshop, 1986), 126-27.
21. Of this failure, Major Robbins of the 4th Alabama later wrote: "I have always believed we would have taken [Little Round Top] if we had not been so fagged out by our long, forced march on that broiling July day, and, moreover, we had to climb over the steep and ragged spur of Big Round Top before reaching the foot of Little Round Top, on the summit of which was the enemy's main line. When we arrived there many of our poor fellows were fainting and falling, overcome with heat and weariness, and in spite of exhortations from their officers, the men in line felt that they must lay down and rest awhile before making the second climb and storming the enemy's position on the crest. Thus our line stopped its advance, lay down among the rocks and boulders, and simply returned the fire of the enemy." CV, 8:168.
22. OR, vol. 27, pt. 2, p. 391.
23. Ibid., 358.
24. James L. Sheffield (1819-1892) was a native of Huntsville, Ala., who served in the Alabama Legislature prior to the Civil War. He was appointed colonel of the 48th Alabama on May 13, 1862, and was wounded at the Battle of Cedar Mountain on Aug. 9, 1862. Sheffield returned to command

the regiment at the Battle of Gettysburg. He resigned his commission on May 31, 1864. Krick, *Lee's Colonels*, 340.
25. William F. Perry (1823–1901) was a native of Alabama who served as a college president prior to the Civil War. He joined the 44th Alabama as a private on May 6, 1862, and quickly was appointed major on May 16, 1862. He became lieutenant colonel on Sept. 1, 1862, and assumed command of the 44th Alabama on Sept. 17, 1862, when its colonel was killed at the Battle of Antietam. Perry, with the rank of colonel, commanded the 44th Alabama at the Battle of Gettysburg and led the Alabama Brigade in the campaigns in the West in fall and winter 1863 and in the Overland campaign of 1864. When Law returned to brigade command at the end of May 1864, Perry resumed command of the 44th Alabama. When Law was wounded at the Battle of Cold Harbor in June 1864, Perry again took over the brigade until he was wounded in the Petersburg campaign in Aug. 1864. Perry finally was promoted to brigadier general, to rank from Feb. 21, 1865, and surrendered the Alabama Brigade at Appomattox Court House. Davis, *Confederate General*, 5:22–23.
26. Michael J. Bulger (1806–1900) was a native of Alabama who served in the Alabama Legislature prior to the war. He was elected captain of Company A of the 47th Alabama on Mar. 20, 1862, and was promoted to major on Aug. 23, 1862. After the Second Manassas campaign, he was promoted to the rank of lieutenant colonel on Sept. 13, 1862. Bulger was wounded and captured at the Battle of Gettysburg. Krick, *Lee's Colonels*, 76.
27. Jerome B. Robertson (1815–1891) was a native of Texas who earned his living as a physician and as a member of the Texas Legislature prior to the Civil War. When Texas seceded from the Union, Robertson raised the future Company I of the 5th Texas Infantry Regiment. He was appointed lieutenant colonel of the regiment on Oct. 10, 1861, and was promoted to colonel on June 3, 1862, when Col. James Archer was made brigadier general. Robertson commanded the regiment in the Peninsula, Second Manassas, and Maryland campaigns. He was wounded at the Battle of Gaines' Mill on June 27, 1862, and at Second Manassas on Aug. 30, 1862. In recognition of his bravery, he was promoted to brigadier general on Nov. 1, 1862, and took command of the Texas Brigade, which he led at the Battle of Gettysburg. During the Gettysburg campaign, the Texas Brigade was composed of 1st, 4th, and 5th Texas and 3rd Arkansas. In the controversy that arose between General Longstreet and some of his brigade commanders in late 1863 and early 1864, Robertson was relieved of his command and returned to Texas, where he took command of the reserve forces of that state until the end of the war. Davis, *Confederate General*, 5:102–3.
28. The brigades of Generals Benning and Anderson of General Hood's division supported the Alabama and Texas brigades. General Kershaw's South Carolina Brigade was formed to the left of the Texas Brigade. Pfanz, *Gettysburg*, 159–60.
29. Houck's Ridge and its southern end, Devil's Den, are not part of Little Round Top, but are approximately 500 yards southwest of the crest of Little Round Top.
30. Paul J. Semmes (1815–1863), a native of Georgia, was one of the wealthiest men in that state prior to the Civil War. With its onset, Semmes was appointed quartermaster general of Georgia. On May 2, 1861, he was

elected colonel of the 2nd Georgia Infantry Regiment. Appointed brigadier general on Mar. 18, 1862, Semmes led his brigade in the Peninsula, Maryland, Fredericksburg, and Chancellorsville campaigns. In the Gettysburg campaign, Semmes's brigade was composed of the 10th, 50th, 51st, and 53rd Georgia Regiments. He was wounded at the Battle of Gettysburg on July 2, 1863, and died on July 10, 1863. Davis, *Confederate General*, 5:138–39.

31. Daniel E. Sickles (1819–1914) was a prewar New York City politician who served in the U.S. Congress in 1857–61. Appointed brigadier general of volunteers by President Lincoln on Sept. 3, 1861, he took command of the Excelsior Brigade from New York, which was assigned to what became the Third Corps of the Army of the Potomac. Sickles fought in the Peninsula campaign and was promoted to major general, ranking from Nov. 29, 1862. Commanding a division in the Third Corps in the Fredericksburg campaign, Sickles was elevated to command of the Third Corps by the time of the Battle of Chancellorsville. In the Battle of Gettysburg, he was severely wounded and lost his right leg. After losing his leg, Sickles never again held an active field command during the war. Warner, *Generals in Blue*, 446–47.

32. General Sickles, against the orders of General Meade, moved his Third Corps of the Army of the Potomac in advance of the main line of the Union Army, so that his corps formed a salient, with its center based around the Peach Orchard. On this movement and its consequences for the Army of the Potomac in the Battle of Gettysburg, see Pfanz, *Gettysburg*, 124–48.

33. Gouverneur K. Warren (1830–1882) was a New York native who graduated from West Point in 1850. He served the prewar U.S. Army as an engineer; with the outbreak of war, he was appointed lieutenant colonel of the 5th New York Regiment on Mar. 14, 1861. In Aug. 1861 he was promoted to colonel. In the Peninsula campaign, despite being only a colonel, Warren commanded a brigade in the Fifth Corps of the Army of the Potomac and continued in brigade command in the Second Manassas and Maryland campaigns. He was promoted to brigadier general of volunteers on Sept. 26, 1862, in recognition of his excellent service. At the Battle of Gettysburg, he served as chief engineer of the Army of the Potomac. Through his astute recognition of the strategic significance of Little Round Top and by rushing troops to that point, Warren is credited with saving the Little Round Top position for the Union Army and thus, possibly, winning the battle. After the battle, he was promoted to major general and assigned to corps command. Warren was assigned to permanent command of the Fifth Corps and led the corps until he was relieved of his command by General Sheridan on Apr. 1, 1865, after the Battle of Five Forks. Warner, *Generals in Blue*, 541–42.

34. These three guns were from Captain Smith's 4th New York Light Battery and were captured by portions of the 1st Texas and 20th Georgia. Pfanz, *Gettysburg*, 195.

35. Oates, *War between the Union*, 210.
36. Ibid., 219.
37. Ibid., 227.
38. OR, vol. 27, pt. 2, p. 330.
39. Oates, *War between the Union*, 776.

40. Diaries and letters from members of Law's Alabama Brigade rated this their hardest fight. In a letter to his family dated July 9, 1863, Capt. Reuben V. Kidd of Company A, 4th Alabama, wrote, "We attacked them on the 2nd of this month, in one of the strongest natural positions that I ever saw . . . our loss, I think, was much heavier than in any battle ever fought by this army." Alice V. D. Pierrepont, *Reuben Vaughan Kidd: Soldier of the Confederacy* (Petersburg, Va.: 1947), 328.
41. Richard B. Garnett (1817–1863), an 1841 graduate of West Point, saw fighting in the Third Seminole War and remained in the prewar army for twenty years until Virginia's secession led to his resignation. Initially he was a major in the Confederate Regular Army. Garnett was promoted to brigadier general on Nov. 14, 1861, and assigned to command Stonewall Jackson's old brigade. In Mar. 1862, at the Battle of Kernstown, Garnett withdrew his brigade without orders and was relieved of his command by Jackson. Held in limbo by a court-martial proceeding which never concluded, Garnett finally took command of a brigade in General Pickett's division. He led it on July 3, 1863, in "Pickett's Charge" and was killed. Davis, *Confederate General*, 2:168–69.
42. Lewis A. Armistead (1817–1863) was a member of a famous military family. Despite being expelled from West Point for fighting, Armistead served in the Mexican War and rose to the rank of captain in the prewar U.S. Army. He resigned on May 25, 1861, and was commissioned colonel in command of the 57th Virginia Infantry Regiment. On Apr. 1, 1862, Armistead was promoted to brigadier general in command of a brigade of Virginia troops that would be placed in General Pickett's division. Armistead was wounded and captured on July 3, 1863, and died on July 5, 1863. Davis, *Confederate General*, 1:40–41.
43. James L. Kemper (1823–1895), a Virginia native, served as a quartermaster in the Mexican War but saw no fighting. He earned his living as a lawyer in Virginia, and when that state seceded, Kemper was named colonel of the 7th Virginia. He fought at First Manassas and in the Peninsula campaign, winning promotion to brigadier general on June 2, 1862. Kemper commanded a small division in the Second Manassas campaign and a brigade again in the Maryland and Fredericksburg campaigns. Assigned to General Pickett's division in Oct., 1862, Kemper was severely wounded and captured on July 3, 1863. After his exchange in Sept. 1863, he saw no further field service during the war. Davis, *Confederate General*, 4:5–7.
44. James J. Pettigrew (1828–1863) was a native of North Carolina and a brilliant scholar. Despite having no military experience, he was named colonel of the 22nd North Carolina on July 21, 1861. Promoted to brigadier general on Feb. 26, 1862, Pettigrew was wounded and captured at the Battle of Seven Pines on May 31, 1862. Exchanged in Aug. 1862, Pettigrew took command of a brigade of North Carolinians. They saw fierce fighting on July 1, 1863, and were part of General Lee's grand assault on July 3, 1863. In this assault, Pettigrew was wounded in the right hand, but he retained his command. He was wounded in a skirmish at Falling Waters, Md., on July 14, 1863, and died on July 17, 1863. Davis, *Confederate General*, 5:24–25.
45. Rufus B. Franks, a student from Huntsville, Ala., enlisted in Company I on Apr. 26, 1861. He was mortally wounded on July 2, 1863, having fought

unscathed in all the previous actions in which the 4th Alabama participated. CSR, Rufus B. Franks.

46. Henry B. Roper, an unmarried clerk from Huntsville, Ala., enlisted as a private in Company I on Apr. 26, 1861. Appointed sergeant on Oct. 28, 1861, Roper was promoted to second lieutenant on Jan. 11, 1863. He was wounded by a musket ball passing through his left lung on July 2, 1863, and was left behind when the Army of Northern Virginia retreated from Gettysburg. Roper was taken prisoner on July 4, 1863, and held in hospitals in Gettysburg until Jan. 23, 1864, when he was transferred to the prison camp at Point Lookout, Md. Exchanged on Mar. 17, 1864, Roper was permanently disabled and officially resigned on Oct. 24, 1864. CSR, Henry B. Roper.

47. Capt. Amos Judson of the 83rd Pennsylvania wrote of the battle's pathetic aftermath, which he discovered when he went to succor the Alabamians who lay wounded in front of his regiment's position on the evening of July 2:

> Their wounds were torturing them, and attracted by their groans, I went towards the spot and found them lying upon their blankets in a pool of blood, their limbs shivering with the cool night air, and the young sergeant incapable of moving without wrenching his broken bone, so as to send a thrill of agony through his whole body. He was a manly young fellow, of finely moulded features, and well shaped limbs, apparently about twenty-one, and evidently descended of gentle blood. "Oh Sir," he exclaimed brokenly, "I am glad you have come to my assistance; will you please give me a drink of water and help me to turn over; I am lying on my broken limb, and cannot help myself." Fortunately I had a canteen of water by my side, and applied it to lips of these suffering men. I then went in search of help, for I could not lift them alone. Having found a soldier to assist me, we returned and did the best we could for them. We made a nice, soft bed of leaves, large enough for both and then bathed and bound up their wounds with our handkerchiefs. We then took one of the blankets of his comrade, which was not so bloody, and spread it upon the bed of leaves, and put their knapsacks at the head for pillows. As we took hold of the young man to lift him to his new bed, he shrieked in agony, "Oh, men, for God's sake, do be careful. Oh my Mother!" (Judson, *History of the Eighty-Third*, 135)

48. H. Judson Kilpatrick (1836–1881) was a native of New Jersey who graduated from West Point in 1861. He began the war as a captain in the 5th New York Infantry Regiment and, when he was shot at the Battle of Big Bethel in June 1861, became the first Regular Army officer wounded in the Civil War. He became lieutenant colonel of the 2nd New York Cavalry Regiment in Sept. 1861, was promoted to colonel of the regiment in Dec. 1862, and was made brigadier general on June 14, 1863. In the Gettysburg campaign, he commanded a division in the Cavalry Corps of the Army of the Potomac. In Apr. 1864, Kilpatrick was transferred to command a cavalry division in General Sherman's army and fought with Sherman for the rest of the war. Warner, *Generals in Blue*, 266–67.

49. Elon J. Farnsworth (1837–1863) was a Michigan native who enlisted in the 8th Illinois Cavalry Regiment at the onset of the Civil War. He was promoted from captain to brigadier general on June 29, 1863, and commanded a brigade in General Kilpatrick's division. Farnsworth was

killed leading a gallant but futile charge on the afternoon of July 3, 1863. Warner, *Generals in Blue*, 148–49.
50. Coles captures the essence of the heated verbal exchange between Kilpatrick and Farnsworth, which preceded Farnsworth's ill-fated charge into the heart of Hood's division.
51. The great cannonade of the afternoon of July 3, 1863, opened at approximately 1 P.M. and continued for approximately one and a half to two hours. Coddington, *Gettysburg Campaign*, 493, 502.
52. The six brigades from Gen. A. P. Hill's corps in the attack were commanded by Generals Davis, Lane, and Scales, and Colonels Marshall, Brockenbrough, and Fry. Coddington, *Gettysburg Campaign*, 490.
53. Birkett D. Fry (1822–1891) had been born in Virginia and earned his living as a cotton manufacturer and soldier of fortune prior to the Civil War. Fry raised the 13th Alabama Infantry Regiment, which elected him its colonel on July 19, 1861. Wounded at the Battle of Seven Pines on May 31, 1862, Fry commanded his regiment in the Maryland campaign and again was wounded at the Battle of Antietam on Sept. 17, 1862. He returned to his command in time to fight in the Chancellorsville campaign and at the Battle of Gettysburg, where he was wounded and captured on July 3, 1863. Held a prisoner until Apr. 1864, Fry returned to the army and was promoted to the rank of brigadier general on May 24, 1864. He was assigned to command the brigade containing the 13th Alabama. On June 28, 1864, Fry went on sick leave and permanently left the Army of Northern Virginia. He served through the rest of the war in the State of Georgia. Davis, *Confederate General*, 2:152–53.
54. The three Tennessee regiments were the 1st, 7th, and 14th Tennessee. Coddington, *Gettysburg Campaign*, 593.
55. In fact, Lieutenant Vaughan, in his diary entry for July 4, 1863, wrote:

> There was heavy fighting yesterday. The cannonade has been the most tremendous I have ever heard. I have been able to learn nothing of the battle in other parts of the line, but I suppose that the fight has gone against us. Benning's brigade being flanked our division has had to fall back.
> A cavalry charge on our right was repulsed with severe loss to the enemy. Our boys really enjoyed that part of the battle. (Vaughan, "Diary," 588–89)

56. Samuel Whitworth was a 28-year-old teacher living in Madison Station, Ala., when he enlisted as a private in Company F on Aug. 16, 1861, while the 4th Alabama was stationed at Camp Jones, Va. He fought with the regiment in all its battles from that time until June 4, 1864, when he was severely wounded in the breast. This wound precluded any further active service. CSR, Samuel Whitworth.
57. Farnsworth's cavalry brigade was composed of the 5th New York, the 18th Pennsylvania, the 1st Vermont, and the 1st West Virginia Cavalry Regiments. Coddington, *Gettysburg Campaign*, 586.
58. Of this advance, General Law later wrote, "I saw a ragged Confederate battle flag fluttering among the trees at the foot of the opposite ridge, and the men with it soon after appeared, running out into the open ground on the farther side of the valley. It was the 4th Alabama Regiment, Law's Brigade, which had been taken from the main line and sent down by Lieutenant Wade. The men opened fire as they ran. The course of the

cavalry was abruptly checked and saddles were rapidly emptied." E. M. Law, "The Struggle for Round Top," B&L, 3:329.
59. Capt. William W. Leftwich of Company F died at Hood's division's hospital on J. E. Plank's farm on the bank of Willoughby Run, just outside the town of Gettysburg. Coco, *Wasted Valor*, 46.
60. William C. Ward, a 25-year-old teacher from Marion, Ala., enlisted as a private in Company G on Apr. 24, 1861. Appointed second corporal of his company on Sept. 1, 1861, Ward served with the 4th Alabama until being severely wounded by a musket ball in his thigh on July 2, 1863. When the Army of Northern Virginia retreated from Gettysburg, Ward was left behind and captured. He was held as a prisoner in Camp Letterman, a hospital complex outside the town of Gettysburg, until his exchange in Oct. 1863. Ward's wound was such that the resulting disability kept him from further service with the regiment. CSR, William C. Ward.
61. The order of the Confederate retreat from Gettysburg had Gen. A. P. Hill's Third Corps leading, followed by General Longstreet's First Corps, and concluding with General Ewell's Second Corps. Coddington, *Gettysburg Campaign*, 538.
62. A modern study of the Gettysburg campaign has put Meade's reinforcements after the Battle of Gettysburg at between 11,000 and 14,000, and 6 batteries. Coddington, *Gettysburg Campaign*, 560.
63. OR, vol. 27, pt. 2, p. 301.
64. Thomas H. Carter (1831–1908) was a native Virginian who began the war as captain of the King William Artillery of Virginia. He rose through the ranks to become lieutenant colonel commanding an artillery battalion attached to Gen. Robert Rodes's division of the Second Corps of the Army of Northern Virginia. Krick, *Lee's Colonels*, 86.
65. This was the Alabama battery known as the Jeff Davis Artillery, commanded by Capt. W. J. Reese. B&L, 3:438.
66. In his diary entry for July 14, 1863, Turner Vaughan remembered the taking down of the pontoon bridge differently: "As the bridge was cut loose and swinging around to the Virginia banks some dozen or more of our skirmish line appeared on the other side. They were a few minutes too late for the bridge and throwing down their guns they wrung their hands with the most agonized expressions. We soon relieved them by sending over a boat and bringing them across. The Yankees fired a few shells and their skirmishers shot at us a little but did no damage." Vaughan, "Diary," 590.
67. John W. Moseley was an unmarried 24-year-old merchant when he enlisted in Company G on Apr. 24, 1861. Promoted to third sergeant of his company in Jan. 1862, Moseley survived all the battles in which the 4th Alabama fought until he was mortally wounded on July 2, 1863. Left behind when the Army of Northern Virginia retreated, Moseley died in Union hands on July 5, 1863. CSR, John W. Moseley.

Chapter 13. From Falling Waters to Fredericksburg

1. During this time, a member of the 4th Alabama noted in his diary the effect of two years' service on the men: "On the march today we have found plenty of apples and some good peaches. When we first entered the service, in passing through an orchard, no man was allowed to pluck an apple or peach.

In fact most of us thought it wrong and would not enter an orchard without permission of the owner. But two years of living on bread and bacon and no vegetables has wrought a change. The soldier's system cries out for a change of diet—and now in passing an orchard he doesn't hesitate to get all the fruit he can." Vaughan, "Diary," 594.
2. The divisions of Generals Hood and McLaws and the artillery battalion of the First Corps were transferred westward and attached to General Bragg's Army of Tennessee in Sept. 1863. On this transfer, see Freeman, *Lee's Lieutenants*, 3:219, 3:228.

Chapter 14. Chickamauga Campaign

1. William S. Rosecrans (1819–1902) was a native of Ohio who graduated from West Point in 1842 and remained in the U.S. Army until his resignation in 1854. With the onset of the Civil War, he returned to the army and was promoted to brigadier general in the Regular Army, to date from May 16, 1861. Rosecrans took command of the Union Army of the Cumberland (formerly the Army of the Ohio) on Oct. 27, 1862, with the rank of major general; he fought in the western campaigns until after the Union defeat at the Battle of Chickamauga, when he was replaced by Maj. Gen. George H. Thomas. He served out the war as the commander of the Department of Missouri. Warner, *Generals in Blue*, 410–11.
2. Micah Jenkins (1835–1864) was a native South Carolinian who graduated from the South Carolina Military Academy in 1854. He founded the Kings Mountain Military School in South Carolina, where he worked as a teacher and administrator prior to the outbreak of the Civil War. When South Carolina seceded from the Union, Jenkins was appointed colonel of the 5th South Carolina Infantry Regiment, which he led in the Battle of First Manassas. When the Confederate Army was reorganized in Apr. 1862, Jenkins, with the rank of colonel, took command of the Palmetto Sharpshooters and fought in the Peninsula campaign. In recognition of his bravery, Jenkins was promoted to brigadier general on July 22, 1862, and given command of a South Carolina brigade in the Army of Northern Virginia. He was severely wounded in the Battle of Second Manassas on Aug. 30, 1862, and did not return to the Army until Nov. 1862. He and his brigade were in reserve in the Fredericksburg campaign and missed the campaign of Chancellorsville and the Battle of Gettysburg. On Sept. 11, 1863, Jenkins and his brigade were assigned to Hood's division, which was transferred to the Confederate Army of the Tennessee. The brigade did not participate in the fighting at Chickamauga, but when Hood was seriously wounded, Jenkins took command of his division. Jenkins was later killed accidentally by his own men in the confused fighting at the Battle of the Wilderness on May 6, 1864. Davis, *Confederate General*, 3:165–67.
3. The nine brigades of the First Corps which were transferred to the Army of the Tennessee were those of Generals Kershaw, Wofford, Humphreys, Bryan, Jenkins, Law, Robertson, G. T. Anderson, and Benning. Of these, the brigades of Kershaw, Humphreys, Law, Robertson, and Benning were engaged at Chickamauga. B&L, 3:675.
4. Leonidas Polk (1806–1864) was a native of North Carolina who graduated from West Point in 1827 and almost immediately resigned from the U.S.

Army to attend the Virginia Theological Seminary. A devout Christian, he was a bishop in Louisiana prior to the war. When Louisiana seceded from the Union, Polk offered his military services to the Confederacy. President Davis, an old friend, accepted his services and commissioned Polk a major general on June 25, 1861. He fought in the western campaigns in General Johnston's and General Bragg's Army of Tennessee and was promoted to lieutenant general on Oct. 11, 1862. In the Battle of Chickamauga, Polk commanded the right wing of Bragg's Army, which consisted of five divisions. After the battle, he was relieved of his command by Bragg, who accused him of deliberately disregarding orders. Thanks to the intercession of his friend, President Davis, Polk later was restored to his command. Polk was killed in the Atlanta campaign on June 14, 1864. Davis, *Confederate General*, 5:45–47.

5. Nathan B. Forrest (1821–1877) was a native Tennesseean who before the war had been a successful slave trader and plantation owner. With the outbreak of the war, Forrest formed a cavalry battalion, which became the 3rd Tennessee Cavalry Regiment. He was elected its colonel on Apr. 2, 1862. Forrest was one of the greatest war leaders the Confederacy produced and has been lauded as a military genius. In recognition of his hard fighting in the western campaigns, he ended the war with the rank of lieutenant general, having earned the fear and respect of all his Union opponents. Davis, *Confederate General*, 2:139–44.

6. The Alabama Brigade had struck the Union infantry brigade commanded by Brig. Gen. Charles Cruft and composed of the 1st and 2nd Kentucky, the 31st Indiana, and the 90th Ohio Regiments. Peter Cozzens, *This Terrible Sound* (Chicago: Univ. of Illinois Press, 1992), 238–39.

7. This man (probably William F. Karsner) has not been identified in the service records of the 4th Alabama.

8. Lt. Gen. D. H. Hill, who was in command of a corps in General Polk's right wing in the battle, called it "the sparring of the amateur boxer, and not the crushing blows of the trained pugilist." Daniel H. Hill, "Chickamauga—The Great Battle of the West," B&L, 3:650–51.

9. Capt. Reuben V. Kidd had enlisted as first sergeant in Company A on Apr. 26, 1861. He was promoted to first lieutenant on Apr. 21, 1862, and captain on Nov. 1, 1862. He was killed in the fighting on Sept. 19, 1863, and was buried on the battlefield by members of his company and his servants. CSR, Reuben V. Kidd; Pierrepont, *Reuben Vaughan Kidd*, 336.

10. For the Confederate plan of attack on the morning of Sept. 20, 1863, and General Polk's role in this attack, see Cozzens, *This Terrible Sound*, 299–308.

11. The Texas Brigade and the Alabama Brigade were in the third line of assault. Cozzens, *This Terrible Sound*, 368.

12. The Alabama Brigade was confronting breastworks held by Col. John Connell's Union brigade, composed of the 17th and 31st Iowa, and by the 82nd Indiana Infantry Regiment, supported by Company D, First Michigan Light Artillery, which at the time of the Battle of Chickamauga was equipped with six guns. Cozzens, *This Terrible Sound*, 371.

13. Stephen D. Quinley, a 44-year-old farmer from Evergreen, Ala., enlisted as a private in Company E on Feb. 7, 1863. He fought with the 4th Alabama for the rest of the war, suffering only a slight wound in his chest on May 6, 1864, and surrendered with the regiment on Apr. 9, 1865. CSR, Stephen D. Quinley.

14. The Alabama Brigade captured only three of the six guns of Company D, First Michigan Light Artillery, in this fighting. Cozzens, *This Terrible Sound*, 371.
15. General Hood's right leg was amputated at the hip, but eventually he recovered physically. Davis, *Confederate General*, 3:121.
16. Benjamin G. Humphreys (1808–1882), a native of Mississippi, was a wealthy plantation owner prior to the Civil War. When war started, he organized what became Company I of the 21st Mississippi and entered the Confederate service as its captain. He was promoted to colonel of the regiment on Sept. 11, 1861, and served with the regiment in Barksdale's Mississippi Brigade in all of the campaigns of the Army of Northern Virginia. When Barksdale was killed at the Battle of Gettysburg on July 2, 1863, Humphreys, as senior colonel, took command of the brigade. He was promoted to brigadier general on Aug. 12, 1863, and led the brigade until he was severely wounded on Sept. 3, 1864. After his recuperation, Humphreys ended the war in the Department of Mississippi. Davis, *Confederate General*, 3:132–33.
17. OR, vol. 30, pt. 2, p. 288.
18. Ulysses S. Grant, *Personal Memoirs of U. S. Grant* (New York: C. L. Webster and Co., 1886), 2:9.
19. Bushrod Jones, a 24-year-old attorney from Uniontown, Ala., enlisted as a private in Company D on Apr. 25, 1861. Elected second lieutenant on Aug. 2, 1861, Jones resigned from the 4th Alabama in Apr. 1862, and later joined the 58th Alabama. CSR, Bushrod Jones.
20. George D. Johnston (1832–1910), an Alabama lawyer and politician, joined Company G of the 4th Alabama as a second lieutenant and fought with the regiment in the Battle of First Manassas. He was appointed major of the 25th Alabama in Jan. 1862 and thereafter fought in the western campaigns. Promoted to brigadier general on July 26, 1864, Johnston was wounded in the Atlanta campaign but recovered in time to attempt to withstand General Sherman's army in its "March to the Sea." Davis, *Confederate General*, 3:191.
21. For a more detailed look at the Confederate high command's reaction to their victory, see Cozzens, *This Terrible Sound*, 517–20.
22. James Longstreet, *From Manassas to Appomattox: Memoirs of the Civil War in America* (Philadelphia: J. B. Lippincott, 1896), 437.

Chapter 15. Our Campaign in Lookout Valley

1. A man in the 4th Alabama, in his diary entry of Oct. 2, 1863, wrote: "Nothing of any interest has transpired since the battle. Our line of battle now touches the river on the extreme right and left enclosing Chattanooga and its host of yankees. They make the air noisy day and night with the sound of busy axes, picks, and shovels. We advanced our picket line several nights ago and dug our rifle pits within a few hundred yards of the Yankee breast works. The next morning a Yank cried out 'Hello boys! What did you dig them holes for?' 'Come over,' said a rebel, 'and see, and now tell us what you have thrown up all that dirt and piled all those logs for.' 'Oh', said he, 'we did that for a shade.'" Vaughan, "Diary," 597.
2. This was Barret's Missouri Battery, which was part of the reserve artillery of the Army of the Tennessee. B&L, 3:675.
3. Another man of the 4th Alabama described this action: "The companies on

picket have done considerable execution—stopped the wagon train and killed a number of mules. The drivers left their teams and took to the woods as soon as the firing commenced. The road is very narrow and the wagons could not be turned around so they have been standing still since morning, the mules being exposed to a continuous fire from our picket lines." Vaughan, "Diary," 598.

4. Ulysses S. Grant (1822–1885) graduated from West Point in 1843. Having fought with great bravery in the Mexican War, Grant failed to live up to his initial military success, in part due to his fondness for alcohol, and resigned from the U.S. Army on July 31, 1854. He failed at a succession of low-level jobs in Missouri prior to the Civil War. When the war began, Grant was appointed colonel of the 21st Illinois and, through important political connections, was promoted to brigadier general in Aug. 1861. He achieved a series of successes in the western battles, culminating with the capture of the fortress of Vicksburg on July 4, 1863. He then was promoted to the rank of major general in the Regular Army. In Oct. 1863, Grant was placed in command of the Division of the Mississippi. Promoted to lieutenant general in Mar. 1864, Grant was given command of all the U.S. armies. He transferred his headquarters to the East and, from that time on, campaigned exclusively with the Army of the Potomac. When the Civil War ended, Congress recognized his leadership ability by making him a full general—the first since General Washington. Elected U.S. president in 1868 and 1872, he presided over administrations marked by much corruption. In the last years of his life, while suffering from throat cancer, Grant penned his memoirs, which proved a great literary and financial success. Warner, *Generals in Blue*, 183–86.

5. George H. Thomas (1816–1870) was a native Virginian who graduated from West Point in 1840. He fought in the Mexican War and served on the western frontier in the prewar U.S. Army. After Virginia's secession from the Union, Thomas became a so-called "renegade Virginian," in that he remained loyal to the Union. He served as a colonel in Maj. Gen. Robert Patterson's army in and around Harpers Ferry in July 1861 and was promoted to brigadier general on Aug. 17, 1861, and transferred to the western theater. Elevated to the rank of major general of volunteers on Apr. 25, 1862, Thomas rendered distinguished service in all the battles in the western campaigns. Thomas's brilliant performance at the Battle of Chickamauga earned him the *nom de guerre* "Rock of Chickamauga." He replaced General Rosecrans in command of the Army of the Cumberland in the Chattanooga campaign. Thomas served under the command of Gen. William T. Sherman in the latter's famous Atlanta campaign, and in Sept. 1864 he was sent to Tennessee. On Dec. 15–16, 1864, troops under his command defeated the Confederates at Nashville. Warner, *Generals in Blue*, 500–502.

6. Grant, *Personal Memoirs*, 2:3–4.

7. Basil W. Duke (1838–1916) was a Kentucky native who was active in the pro-secession movement in Missouri. With the outbreak of the Civil War, he joined the Confederacy and initially served in a Kentucky infantry regiment. He was made a lieutenant colonel in the 2nd Kentucky Cavalry Regiment and fought in the Battle of Shiloh in Apr. 1862, where he was wounded. Duke went on to become one of the leading Confederate cavalry commanders, arousing terror in Union ranks in all the western campaigns.

However, it was not Duke who informed Colonel Oates of the Union reinforcements at this time, as Duke had been captured in July 1863 and taken to a Union prison camp. He finally was exchanged in summer 1864. Promoted to the rank of brigadier general on Sept. 15, 1864, Duke took command of Morgan's cavalry, which he led for the rest of the war. Davis, *Confederate General*, 2:80–82.
8. The Morgan referred to was John H. Morgan (1825–1864), a native of Kentucky who, as a colonel, formed and commanded the 2nd Kentucky Cavalry Regiment for the Confederacy. He was promoted to brigadier general on Dec. 11, 1862, and led several famous cavalry raids into Union territory. In one of these raids, in July 1863, Morgan was captured and imprisoned in Ohio. He escaped from the Ohio State Penitentiary in Nov. 1863 and returned to the Confederacy. Morgan was killed on Sept. 3, 1864, in a skirmish at Greeneville, Tenn. Davis, *Confederate General*, 4:184–89.
9. On Sept. 24, 1863, after the Union disaster at Chickamauga, under orders from Secretary of War Stanton, the Eleventh and Twelfth Corps of the Army of the Potomac were transferred to the western theater and attached to the Army of the Cumberland. In winter 1863–64, these two corps were combined and redesignated the Twentieth Corps and were placed under the command of Gen. Joseph Hooker, former commander of the Army of the Potomac, who had resigned his command just prior to the Battle of Gettysburg. Warner, *Generals in Blue*, 234.
10. See Oates, *War between the Union*, 271–82.
11. Ibid., 280–81.
12. Francis M. Sampey, an unmarried 18-year-old student from Belleville, Ala., enlisted as a private in Company E on Apr. 25, 1861. His service records indicate that he suffered a slight wound on June 27, 1862, and was captured on Sept. 14, 1862. However, Sampey was paroled on Sept. 27, 1862, and returned to duty with the 4th Alabama, with which he served until he surrendered on Apr. 9, 1865. CSR, Francis M. Sampey.
13. Oates was shot in the right hip and thigh and returned home to Alabama to recuperate. He resumed active duty in Mar. 1864. Oates, *War between the Union*, 227, 337–38.
14. OR, vol. 31, pt. 1, p. 79.
15. William B. Hazen (1830–1887) was a native Vermonter who served in the prewar U.S. Army in its campaigns against the western Indians. At the beginning of the Civil War, he became colonel of the 41st Ohio Infantry Regiment and fought in the western campaigns. He was promoted to brigadier general in Apr. 1863 and led a brigade of the 3rd Division in the Army of the Cumberland in the Chattanooga campaign. Hazen then fought in the Atlanta campaign and with General Sherman in his famous "March to the Sea." He won promotion to major general in Apr. 1865. Warner, *Generals in Blue*, 225–26.
16. John B. Turchin (1822–1901) was the only Russian-born general on either side in the Civil War. After graduating from the Imperial Military School in St. Petersburg, Russia, he fought in the Crimean War. He emigrated to the U.S. in 1856 and lived in Illinois. When the Civil War began, Turchin was commissioned colonel of the 19th Illinois Infantry Regiment. In May 1862, he was recommended for dismissal from the service after a court-martial ruled that he was responsible for the actions of his men who plundered Athens, Ala. Reinstated by President Lincoln, he was promoted

to the rank of brigadier general of volunteers on July 17, 1862. He fought in the Battle of Chickamauga and in the Chattanooga campaign as brigade commander in the 3rd Division of the Fourteenth Corps. On Oct. 4, 1864, due to ill health, Turchin resigned from the army. Warner, *Generals in Blue*, 511–12.
17. OR, vol. 31, pt. 1, p. 93.
18. John Bratton (1831–1898) was a successful planter and physician in South Carolina before the Civil War. He joined the Confederates as a lieutenant in the 6th South Carolina Infantry Regiment and was promoted to colonel of the regiment when the Confederate Army reorganized in Apr. 1862. On May 31, 1862, he was wounded and captured in the battle of Seven Pines but was exchanged and returned to the Army of Northern Virginia in time to fight with his regiment in the Fredericksburg campaign in Dec. 1862. The 6th South Carolina was not with the Army of Northern Virginia in the Chancellorsville and Gettysburg campaigns, having been transferred to the West with the rest of General Jenkins's brigade in Sept. 1863. When Jenkins replaced Hood in command of the division, Bratton took command of the South Carolina Brigade. When Longstreet's corps was transferred back to Virginia, Bratton and his men fought in the Overland campaign in spring 1864. His gallantry there won him a commission as brigadier general on June 9, 1864. He later fought in the Petersburg campaign and surrendered at Appomattox on Apr. 9, 1865. Davis, *Confederate General*, 1:124–25.
19. Howard's corps formerly had been the Eleventh Corps of the Army of the Potomac, which, as previously stated, had been transferred to the West.
20. E. Porter Alexander (1835–1910) was a native of Georgia who graduated from West Point in 1857. He became one of the brilliant artillery officers of the Confederacy. When Georgia seceded from the Union, Alexander resigned from the U.S. Army and was commissioned a captain of engineers in the Confederate States Service. He served as chief signal officer for Gen. P. G. T. Beauregard during the First Manassas campaign and, until the end of the Maryland campaign in Sept. 1862, remained on the headquarters staff of what became the Army of Northern Virginia. Promoted to lieutenant colonel of artillery on July 17, 1862, Alexander was given command of a battalion of artillery in Longstreet's First Corps in Nov. 1862. In recognition of his service, Alexander was promoted to the rank of colonel on Mar. 3, 1863. He led his command brilliantly in the Fredericksburg, Chancellorsville, and Gettysburg campaigns. In the Battle of Gettysburg, he was given personal charge of the artillery of Longstreet's corps for the "Great Cannonade" on July 3, 1863, which preceded "Pickett's Charge." He fought with the First Corps in the western campaigns of 1863 and early 1864. Alexander finally was promoted to brigadier general on Mar. 1, 1864, and elevated to chief of artillery of the First Corps on Mar. 19, 1864. He surrendered at Appomattox Court House with the remnants of the Army of Northern Virginia on Apr. 9, 1865. Davis, *Confederate General*, 1:11–12.
21. See OR, vol. 31, pt. 1, pp. 224–28, for General Law's report, here paraphrased.
22. See OR, vol. 31, pt. 1, pp. 524–31, for General Jenkins's report, which is paraphrased here.
23. The Confederate attack principally had been made on Brig. Gen. John Geary's division of the Union Twelfth Corps. B&L, 3:728.

24. John W. Geary (1819–1873) was a native Pennsylvanian who fought in the Mexican War. After that war, he served as the first mayor of San Francisco and as a governor of Kansas Territory. With the outbreak of the Civil War, he was elected colonel of the 28th Pennsylvania Infantry Regiment. Geary was promoted to brigadier general on Apr. 25, 1862, and commanded a brigade in what was to become the Twelfth Corps of the Army of the Potomac. He was wounded at the Battle of Cedar Mountain on Aug. 9, 1862. Upon his recovery, Geary served as a division commander in the Twelfth Corps in the Chancellorsville, Gettysburg, Chattanooga, and Atlanta campaigns. Warner, *Generals in Blue*, 169–70.
25. OR, vol. 31, pt. 1, p. 95.
26. On this fighting, see Ulysses S. Grant, "Chattanooga," B&L, 3:690.
27. George H. Anderson was 21 years old, earning his living as a farmer in Sparta, Ala., when he joined Company E as a private on Aug. 31, 1861. He fought with the 4th Alabama until his death in action on Oct. 28, 1863. CSR, George H. Anderson.

Chapter 16. Knoxville Campaign

1. These Confederate movements are described in Freeman, *Lee's Lieutenants*, 3:285–89.
2. This was the same Gen. Ambrose Burnside who had commanded the Union's Army of the Potomac in the Fredericksburg campaign and had been relieved in Jan. 1863. He was now in command of the Union Army of the Ohio. Warner, *Generals in Blue*, 58.
3. For more information on the conflicts among Generals Longstreet, McLaws, Jenkins, and Law, a recurring theme over the next two chapters, see Freeman, *Lee's Lieutenants*, 3:280–314.
4. OR, vol. 31, pt. 1, pp. 498–99, which is paraphrased by Coles.
5. Fort Loudon was the Confederate name for the place that the Union soldiers called Fort Sanders.
6. Alexander stated: "We also rigged up an old flat-boat and made a ferry with some telegraph wire, by which we carried Parker's rifle-guns to the south side of the river and established a battery on a commanding hill, from which we could enfilade the western front of the fort at a range of 2,600 yards." E. Porter Alexander, "Longstreet at Knoxville," B&L, 3:748.
7. General Longstreet's plan of attack is discussed fully in Freeman, *Lee's Lieutenants*, 3:289–93.
8. This was the famous "Battle above the Clouds," in which Union forces under Gen. Joseph Hooker attacked and carried the Confederate positions on Lookout Mountain. The Union Army of the Cumberland followed this victory with its successful attack on Missionary Ridge on Nov. 25, 1863. After this defeat, President Davis relieved General Bragg of his command. On the Chattanooga campaign, see Grant, "Chattanooga," B&L, 3:679–711.
9. OR, vol. 31, pt. 1, p. 466.
10. A source on the Union side of the lines stated that the garrison of Fort Sanders consisted of four 20-pounder Parrotts, six 12-pounder Napoleons, and two 3-inch rifled guns, with 120 infantrymen from the 79th New York, 75 infantrymen of the 29th Massachusetts, 60 infantrymen of the 2nd

Michigan, 80 infantrymen of the 20th Michigan, and 40 skirmishers from the 2nd Michigan. Orlando Poe, "The Defense of Knoxville," B&L, 3:742.
11. General Grant had sent Maj. Gen. William T. Sherman with part of the Army of the Tennessee and a corps of the Army of the Cumberland to raise the siege at Knoxville. Grant, "Chattanooga," B&L, 3:711.
12. Bushrod R. Johnson (1817–1880) was an Ohio native who graduated from West Point in 1840. He served in the prewar U.S. Army and fought in the Mexican War. Johnson got caught in a profiteering scheme in Mexico after that war and was forced to resign from the army in 1847. He then taught at military institutes in Kentucky and Tennessee. With the outbreak of the Civil War, Johnson joined the Confederacy. He was promoted to brigadier general on Jan. 24, 1862, and fought in the western campaigns, but his appointment was not confirmed by the Confederate Congress for more than two years. Wounded at the Battle of Shiloh on Apr. 6, 1862, Johnson recovered and rose to command a division by the time of the Battle of Chickamauga. His division was attached to Longstreet's First Corps in the Knoxville campaign. Finally confirmed in the rank of brigadier general on Feb. 17, 1864, Johnson and his division were transferred to the defenses around Richmond, where they saw action in the Petersburg campaign. As major general, a rank to which he was promoted on May 21, 1864, Johnson was a key participant in the Confederate disaster at Sayler's Creek on Apr. 6, 1865, for which Gen. Robert E. Lee relieved him of his command. Davis, *Confederate General*, 3:181–85.
13. This was the battle of Bean's Station, fought on Dec. 15, 1863.
14. OR, vol. 31, pt. 1, p. 464.

Chapter 17. East Tennessee Campaign

1. Thomas L. Matthews was a 24-year-old mechanic at the time of his enlistment in Company K on Apr. 27, 1861. Matthews was promoted from private to fourth sergeant of his company on Dec. 7, 1862. Except for the Battle of the Wilderness on May 6, 1864, where he was slightly wounded in the leg, Matthews fought unscathed in all the battles in which the 4th Alabama participated. He was captured on Apr. 6, 1865. CSR, Thomas L. Matthews.
2. Batte O. Peterson, an unmarried 20-year-old student from Tuskegee, enlisted as a private in Company B on Apr. 28, 1861. Promoted to the rank of first sergeant on Apr. 21, 1862, he was elected second lieutenant on Mar. 16, 1863. Peterson was killed on Jan. 16, 1864. CSR, Batte O. Peterson.
3. John A. Jones (1831–1896) was a graduate of the University of Alabama. He was elected captain of Company B of the 44th Alabama on Mar. 15, 1862. He was promoted to major on Sept. 1, 1862, and, at the Battle of Antietam, to lieutenant colonel of the regiment on Sept. 17, 1862. Jones served in the latter capacity for the rest of the war. Krick, *Lee's Colonels*, 215.
4. On the bad feelings between Generals Longstreet and Law, see Freeman, *Lee's Lieutenants*, 3:303–5.
5. Simon B. Buckner (1823–1914) was a Kentuckian who graduated from West Point in 1844 and fought heroically in the Mexican War. After serving as an instructor at West Point and seeing active duty on the western frontier, he resigned from the U.S. Army in 1855 and returned to Kentucky.

Although owning no slaves and being antisecessionist in feeling, Buckner joined the Confederate forces on Sept. 11, 1861, and was appointed brigadier general on Sept. 14, 1861. He surrendered the Confederate garrison at Fort Donelson to General Grant on Feb. 16, 1862, and was held prisoner at Fort Warren in Boston Harbor until his exchange on Aug. 16, 1862. Upon his return to the Confederacy, Buckner was promoted to major general and fought the remainder of the war in the western campaigns. At this time, he commanded a division which was attached to Longstreet's First Corps in the Knoxville campaign. Davis, *Confederate General*, 1:139–41.

6. OR, vol. 31, pt. 1, p. 472.
7. A correspondent with the Alabama Brigade described the men's feelings regarding their return to Virginia: "The change is welcomed with rapture by our men; they are perfectly frantic with enthusiasm and joy; enthusiasm at being again in Virginia, with General Lee, and joy in the hope that one crushing blow on Grant will save the country, end the war, and give us a speedy and honorable peace, with independence." *Montgomery* (Ala.) *Daily Mail*, May 8, 1864.
8. Colonel Oates of the 15th Alabama, who had returned to the brigade in Mar. 1864 after recuperating from his wound, suggests General Longstreet's possible motive for transferring the Alabama Brigade from his command to that of General Buckner:

> The transfer of the brigade into Buckner's division just at a time when he knew that the old division was going back to Lee's army, was intended by Longstreet as a punishment to the brigade by leaving it in East Tennessee, just where none of us desired to be left. The effort to punish the men of that brigade to gratify his malice against Law, its commander, was too small a thing for a man of Longstreet's position to have stooped to perform. But he was brimful of malice. In his book, written many years after the war, he never mentioned Law's brigade in complimentary terms except slightly for its good marching at Gettysburg. He ignored it, though no brigade in his corps did better fighting or contributed more to his good reputation as a hard fighter than the officers and men of this brigade. He did injustice to them because he hated Law. (Oates, *War between the Union*, 339)

9. A letter in an Alabama newspaper from an unidentified correspondent in the Alabama Brigade described these hardships: "Law's Brigade is positively suffering for clothing, many of the men are about naked, and as a body they are more destitute now than they have been at any previous period of the war. We have received no clothing from the Quartermaster's Department for many, many months, and the only good clothing we have in camp is that brought back by those lately returned from furlough. . . . In conclusion, let me seriously say to the people of Alabama, that the brave boys of Law's Brigade—the heroes of Gettysburg and Chickamauga—have not the wherewithal to shelter them from the cold, or even to cover their nakedness." *Montgomery* (Ala.) *Daily Mail*, Apr. 27, 1864.

Chapter 18. Wilderness

1. When General Longstreet learned that General Law had been released from arrest, he wrote to Richmond: "If my efforts to maintain discipline, spirit, and zeal in the discharge of official duty are to be set aside by the return of General Law and his restoration to duty without trial, it cannot be well for me to remain in command. I cannot yield the authority of my position so long as I am responsible for the proper discharge of its functions. It is necessary, therefore, that General Law should be brought to trial upon the charges that have been preferred against him, or that I be relieved from duty in the Confederate States service." OR, vol. 31, pt. 1, p. 475. Upon receiving this ultimatum from General Longstreet, General Lee, fearful of losing his most dependable corps commander, recommended that General Law be relieved from duty until an investigation was held. General Law was not restored to his command until after the Battle of the Wilderness had been fought and the First Corps was on its march to Spotsylvania.
2. Colonel Oates described the brigade's feelings for General Law: "On the third of May we marched to and a little south of Gordonsville and camped. As the brigade passed Law, who stood in front of his tent, each regiment cheered him." Oates, *War between the Union*, 340.
3. OR, vol. 29, pt. 2, p. 749.
4. OR, vol. 29, pt. 1, p. 408.
5. This was the Bristoe Station campaign, which took place in mid-Oct. 1863. Here Gen. A. P. Hill and his Third Corps suffered a bloody rebuff at the hands of General Warren and the Second Corps of the Army of the Potomac.
6. In Mar. 1864, U. S. Grant was promoted to the rank of lieutenant general and named general-in-chief of all U.S. armies. On Mar. 17, 1864, Grant formally took command and established his headquarters with the Army of the Potomac, where he remained through the end of the war; however, the Army of the Potomac officially continued to be commanded by General Meade. Edward Steere, *The Wilderness Campaign* (Harrisburg, Pa.: Stackpole Co., 1960), 14.
7. Gen. Charles Field by now had recuperated from the loss of his leg in Aug. 1862 in the Second Manassas campaign and had assumed command of the division to which the 4th Alabama was assigned.
8. This was the emotional reunion between General Lee and the veterans of the First Corps of the Army of Northern Virginia, which took place at the great review of Apr. 29, 1864, near Gordonsville, Va. See Freeman, *Lee's Lieutenants*, 3:342–43.
9. Grant, *Personal Memoirs*, 2:188.
10. Generals Ewell and A. P. Hill had advanced on parallel roads toward the Army of the Potomac, which attempted to pass southeastward through the Wilderness after crossing the Rapidan River. General Ewell advanced his Second Corps eastward on the Orange Turnpike, while Gen. A. P. Hill led the Third Corps east down the Orange Plank Road. The two roads were, at various points, two to three miles apart. The fighting through May 5, 1864, was extremely chaotic and bloody. The terrain of the Wilderness, being very thickly wooded and almost without roads or clear fields, lent itself to the mass confusion and dreadful tactical mistakes which took place on both sides. On the fighting of May 5, 1864, as it related to the Army of

Northern Virginia, see Clifford Dowdey, *Lee's Last Campaign* (Wilmington, N.C.: Broadfoot Publishing Co., 1988), 83–136.
11. This was the attack of General Hancock's Second Corps of the Army of the Potomac, which was launched westward from the Brock Road on both sides of the Orange Plank Road, at 4:30 A.M. on May 6, 1864, and which rolled back two divisions of Gen. A. P. Hill's corps in confusion. For a description of this attack, see Steere, *Wilderness Campaign*, 328–38.
12. Henry Heth (1825–1899) was a Virginian who graduated from West Point in 1847 and fought on the western frontier in the prewar U.S. Army. When Virginia seceded from the Union, he organized the 45th Virginia Infantry Regiment, which he commanded with the rank of colonel in 1861. He was promoted to brigadier general on Jan. 6, 1862, and fought in western Virginia and Kentucky. In Jan. 1863, Heth was transferred to command a brigade in Gen. A. P. Hill's "Light" Division and fought in the Chancellorsville campaign. When Hill was wounded on May 2, 1863, in the Battle of Chancellorsville, Heth, as the senior brigadier, took command of the division. He was promoted to major general on May 23, 1863, and retained a division command in what was now A. P. Hill's Third Corps for the rest of the war. Davis, *Confederate General*, 3:89–90.
13. At this time, Cadmus Wilcox was commander of a division in Gen. A. P. Hill's Third Corps. B&L, 4:183.
14. James S. Wadsworth (1807–1864) was a wealthy New York landowner who served as a volunteer aide at the Battle of First Manassas. In recognition of his bravery, he was commissioned a brigadier general of volunteers on Aug. 9, 1861. He served as the military governor of the District of Columbia and ran unsuccessfully for governor of the State of New York in 1862. In late Dec. 1862, Wadsworth was assigned to command a division in the First Corps of the Army of the Potomac, which he led with great bravery at the Battle of Gettysburg in July 1863. When the Army of the Potomac was reorganized in spring 1864, Wadsworth was assigned to command a division in the Fifth Corps. He was mortally wounded in the Battle of the Wilderness on May 6, 1864. Warner, *Generals in Blue*, 532–33.
15. On the unpreparedness of the troops of Generals Heth and Wilcox to meet Hancock's attack on the morning of May 6, 1864, and the responsibility for that unpreparedness, see Freeman, *Lee's Lieutenants*, 3:353–55.
16. General Kershaw's division, led by his former South Carolina Brigade, was the first to counterattack the Federal advance on the south side of the Orange Plank Road. General Anderson's Georgia Brigade did lead the counterattack of General Field's division on the north side of the Orange Plank Road. Steere, *Wilderness Campaign*, 339–42.
17. John Gregg (1828–1864) was born in Alabama, where he earned his living as a lawyer. After several years of practice, he moved to Texas and served as a district judge. When Texas seceded from the Union in 1861, he organized the 7th Texas Infantry Regiment, which elected him colonel. He surrendered with the regiment at Fort Donelson in Feb. 1862. After being exchanged, Gregg was promoted to the rank of brigadier general on Aug. 29, 1862. He commanded a brigade in the western campaigns and was wounded at the Battle of Chickamauga on Sept. 20, 1863. Upon his recovery, General Longstreet placed him in command of the Texas Brigade in the Army of Northern Virginia, replacing General Robertson, whom Longstreet had arrested. Gregg commanded the Texas Brigade until he was

killed on Oct. 7, 1864, in the Petersburg campaign. Davis, *Confederate General*, 3:37–39.
18. Gen. William F. Perry, commander of the Alabama Brigade at this time, later described this scene: "As the column wheeled into line, it passed immediately by a large group of horsemen, consisting chiefly of the corps and division commanders and their officers of the staff. But the central figure of that group . . . was General Lee. The conception of his appearance in my mind to this day is of a grand equestrian statue, of colossal proportions. His countenance, usually so placid and benign, was blazing with martial ardor. The lamb in his nature had given place to the lion, and his spirit seemed transfused through every one who looked upon him. It was impossible not to feel that every man that passed him was, for the time being, a hero." William F. Perry, "Reminiscences of the Campaign of 1864 in Virginia," *Southern Historical Society Papers* 7 (1879): 52.
19. This dramatic incident took place after the famous "Lee to the Rear" episode involving the Texas Brigade. On this stirring moment, see Simpson, *Hood's Texas Brigade*, 396–98.
20. The Alabama Brigade had been fighting the famous "Iron Brigade," the 1st Brigade of the 4th Division of the Fifth Corps, one of the more famous units in the Army of the Potomac. Robert Garth Scott, *Into the Wilderness with the Army of the Potomac* (Bloomington: Indiana Univ. Press, 1985), 131–32.
21. The order suspending prisoner exchange was promulgated by the U.S. War Department and not General Grant. Although Grant took command some four months after the order was issued, Grant received "credit" for it.
22. Col. J. Howard Kitching commanded four battalions of "Heavy Artillery" men, who originally had enlisted to serve the guns in the forts around Washington. In May 1864, they were ordered by General Grant to join the Army of the Potomac and fight as infantry. Kitching's men, numbering approximately 2,400 muskets, were attached to the Fifth Corps of the Army of the Potomac. Steere, *Wilderness Campaign*, 296.
23. Grant's headquarters were in a field opposite the Lacy house, which was serving as headquarters of General Warren, the commander of the Fifth Corps of the Army of the Potomac. Steere, *Wilderness Campaign*, 96, 123.
24. The Alabama Brigade had repelled the advancing brigade of Brig. Gen. Alexander Webb of the Union Second Corps, which was spearheaded by the advance of the 20th Massachusetts directly down the Plank Road. Scott, *Into the Wilderness*, 133, 150–51.
25. General Wadsworth's horse had been frightened by a bursting shell and went within twenty feet of the front rank of the 4th Alabama. As the general's aide tried to get control over the horse and lead it and the general back to Union lines and safety, Wadsworth was shot in the back of the head and mortally wounded. Steere, *Wilderness Campaign*, 151.
26. Edward A. Perry (1831–1889) was born in Massachusetts, attended Yale University, and became an instructor at Greenville Academy in Alabama. He then practiced law in Alabama and Florida prior to the Civil War. Although a northerner by birth, with the secession of Florida from the Union, he raised a company of Floridians which was assigned to the 2nd Florida Infantry Regiment. In May 1862, Perry was elected colonel of the regiment, which fought in a brigade in General Longstreet's command in the Peninsula campaign. Perry was wounded while in command of the

regiment on June 30, 1862, at the Battle of Glendale. Upon recuperation from his wound, in recognition of his gallantry, Perry was promoted to brigadier general on Sept. 30, 1863, and placed in command of the newly formed Florida Brigade, consisting of the 2nd, 5th, and 8th Florida Infantry Regiments. He led this brigade in the Fredericksburg and Chancellorsville campaigns. However, he became ill with typhoid fever after Chancellorsville and missed the Gettysburg campaign. Perry returned to the brigade in time for the Battle of the Wilderness on May 5–6, 1864, in which he again was severely wounded. As a result of this wound, he never was physically fit to command his brigade. Davis, *Confederate General*, 5:20–21.

27. William Mahone (1826–1895), a native Virginian, was a railroad man in Virginia prior to the Civil War. He was elected colonel of the 6th Virginia Infantry Regiment on May 2, 1861, and served in the Department of Norfolk. He was promoted to brigadier general on Nov. 16, 1861, and placed in command of the brigade in which the 6th Virginia served. He and his brigade fought in the Peninsula campaign and in the campaign of Second Manassas, where he was wounded. He returned to his brigade in time to fight in the Fredericksburg, Chancellorsville, and Gettysburg campaigns, and he led the brigade in the indecisive maneuvering and fighting that took place in fall 1863. When the Army of Northern Virginia was reorganized in May 1863, Mahone and his brigade had been assigned from Longstreet's First Corps to A. P. Hill's Third Corps. In the counterattack on May 6, 1864, Mahone led his brigade and the brigades of William T. Wofford, Joseph Davis, and G. T. Anderson in their massive assault from the unfinished railroad at the southern end of the Wilderness battlefield, which disorganized Hancock's Second Corps of the Army of the Potomac. In recognition of his gallantry and hard fighting, Mahone was promoted; he ended the war as a major general and division commander in the Third Corps. Davis, *Confederate General*, 4:143–46.

28. Gilbert Moxley Sorrel (1838–1901) was a native of Georgia who worked for the Central Railroad in Georgia prior to the Civil War. With the outbreak of the war, Sorrel served as a volunteer aide to General Longstreet in the Battle of First Manassas. As a result of his conduct, he was appointed captain and assistant adjutant general in Longstreet's brigade on Sept. 11, 1861. He was promoted to major on May 5, 1862, and to lieutenant colonel on June 1, 1863. As a staff officer, he accompanied Mahone and his four brigades in the railroad cut attack on May 6, 1864, and some, including Sorrel himself, claimed that he led the assault. Sorrel was later promoted to brigadier general on Oct. 27, 1864, and commanded a Georgia brigade in A. P. Hill's Third Corps for the remainder of the war. Davis, *Confederate General*, 5:192–93.

29. G. Moxley Sorrel, *Recollections of a Confederate Staff Officer* (New York: Neale Publishing Co., 1905), 236.

30. Swinton, *Campaigns*, 434.

31. General Longstreet and his staff were fired on by men of the 41st Virginia of Mahone's brigade, who were on the north side of the Plank Road. When Mahone's men saw soldiers of the 12th Virginia approaching them from the south side of the Plank Road, due to the heavy foliage and undergrowth, they mistook them for Union soldiers and opened fire on them. George S. Bernard, *War Talks of Confederate Veterans* (Dayton, Ohio: Press of the Morningside Bookshop, 1981), 95.

32. Coles is referring to the mortal wounding of Stonewall Jackson by the 18th North Carolina Infantry Regiment, which took place on May 2, 1863.
33. Francis A. Walker, *History of the Second Corps in the Army of the Potomac* (New York: Charles Scribner's Sons, 1886), 428, which is paraphrased.
34. Perry, "Reminiscences of the Campaign," 7:59–60.
35. Oates, *War between the Union*, 349.
36. The Alabamians had run into the advance of General Burnside's Ninth Corps, which was attached to the Army of the Potomac as an independent command. Steere, *Wilderness Campaign*, 413–15.
37. George W. Cary, a native of LaGrange, Ala., had enlisted as a sergeant in the 10th Alabama. He was named captain of Company E, 44th Alabama, on May 16, 1862, and promoted to major of the regiment on June 18, 1863. Cary surrendered with the remnants of the 44th Alabama on Apr. 9, 1865. Krick, *Lee's Colonels*, 86.
38. The three Florida regiments were the 2nd, 5th, and 8th Florida, composing a brigade commanded by Brig. Gen. E. A. Perry in Anderson's division of Gen. A. P. Hill's Third Corps. Steere, *Wilderness Campaign*, 473.
39. General Perry later wrote of this sequence of events: "The ammunition of the men began to be exhausted. The direction of the firing to the left indicated that my worst apprehensions were likely to be soon realized. I hastened thither, and arrived in time to find the Forty-seventh doubling back and the enemy pouring round its flank. I endeavored to steady and reform it with its front so changed as to face them, but they were too near at hand and their momentum was too great. Nothing was left us but an inglorious retreat, executed in the shortest possible time and without regard to order. It was the first time since its organization, and, until it folded its colors forever at Appomattox, it was the last, that the brigade ever was broken on the battlefield." Perry, "Reminiscences of the Campaign," 7:61–62.
40. Thomas J. Melton, a 16-year-old farmer, enlisted in Company C on Apr. 26, 1861, as a third sergeant. Promoted to second sergeant on Mar. 6, 1862, and first sergeant on Jan. 21, 1863, Melton was wounded at the Battle of Gaines' Mill on June 27, 1862, and at the Battle of Chickamauga on Sept. 19, 1863. On May 6, 1864, he was severely wounded and never returned to active duty with the regiment. CSR, Thomas J. Melton.
41. The attack of Brig. Gen. John B. Gordon and his Georgia brigade of the Second Corps was made against the extreme right flank of the Union's Sixth Corps late on the evening of May 6, 1864. For this attack, see Steere, *Wilderness Campaign*, 431–55.
42. Longstreet's wound in the throat was quite severe and rendered his right arm partially useless. His recuperation lasted until Oct. 19, 1864, when he was able to return to duty with the Army of Northern Virginia. Davis, *Confederate General*, 4:94.
43. A study of the records of the 4th Alabama failed to reveal anything on this man's identity.
44. John E. Stearnes was a 16-year-old student from Sparta, Ala., when he enlisted as a corporal in Company E on Apr. 25, 1861. He had evidently lied about his age, as the records indicate that on Aug. 10, 1862, he was discharged for being under age. Undeterred, Stearnes reenlisted as a private in Company E in Feb. 1863. He was appointed orderly sergeant of his company on Sept. 8, 1863, and promoted to second lieutenant on Feb. 11,

1864. Stearnes was wounded severely in the neck on May 6, 1864, but recovered and returned to duty with the 4th Alabama, serving until he surrendered on Apr. 9, 1865. CSR, John S. Stearnes.
45. Henry S. Figures, an 18-year-old salesman from Huntsville, Ala., enlisted as a private in Company F on June 10, 1861, in Winchester, Va. Elected sergeant of his company on Apr. 21, 1862, he served with the 4th Alabama until he was named adjutant of the 48th Alabama in May 1863. CSR, Henry S. Figures.

Chapter 19. Spotsylvania Ridge to the James River

1. The First Corps of the Army of Northern Virginia began a night march, on a trace and through burning woods, from its position on the southern end of the Wilderness battlefield to the vital crossroads of Spotsylvania. The objectives were to reach Spotsylvania Court House before the arrival of the Army of the Potomac, and to keep the Army of Northern Virginia constantly interposed between the Army of the Potomac and Richmond. Freeman, *Lee's Lieutenants,* 3:380.
2. The South Carolina Brigade of the First Corps was now commanded by Col. John W. Henagan of the 8th South Carolina. General Kershaw, its former commander, had been promoted to division commander. William B. Matter, *If It Takes All Summer* (Chapel Hill: Univ. of North Carolina Press, 1988), 361.
3. For an excellent description of the delaying action fought by the Confederate cavalry, the arrival of the South Carolina Brigade, and its repulse of the attack of the leading elements of the Union Fifth Corps on Laurel Hill, the "Ridge" described by Coles, see Matter, *If It Takes All Summer,* 54–63.
4. On May 10, 1864, General Heth's division of the Confederate Third Corps attacked the Union Second Corps' positions south of the Po River and threw the Union troops back across the river. For more details on this fighting, see Matter, *If It Takes All Summer,* 141–48.
5. This assault was made by two brigades of the 4th Division of the Union Fifth Corps, which were very feebly supported by the remainder of the division. Matter, *If It Takes All Summer,* 151.
6. One of the Union attackers described the Confederate position: "This was perhaps the most formidable point along the enemy's whole front. Its densely wooded crest was crowned by earthworks, while the approach, which was swept by artillery and musketry fire, was rendered more difficult and hazardous by a heavy growth of low cedars, the long, bayonet-like branches of which interlaced." Rufus W. Dawes, *Service with the Sixth Wisconsin Volunteers* (Dayton, Ohio: Press of Morningside Bookshop, 1984), 264.
7. The Alabama Brigade was attacked by two brigades of the Union Fifth Corps which was commanded by Maj. Gen. Gouverneur Warren. Matter, *If It Takes All Summer,* 152.
8. An officer in the "Iron Brigade," which was involved in this attack, described it thus: "We came suddenly upon their works without being aware of their proximity, on account of the thick brush, and we received a very destructive enfilading fire. . . . The enemy poured over us a continual storm of bullets. We now saw the bodies of our soldiers burning in grass and

leaves which had been ignited by the musketry." Dawes, *Service with the Sixth*, 265–66.
9. An interesting description of this attack on the Texas Brigade by the 86th New York and 3rd Maine Regiments of the Union Fifth Corps is found in J. B. Polley, *Hood's Texas Brigade* (Dayton, Ohio: Press of Morningside Bookshop, 1976), 237–39.
10. For the rationale behind General Lee's decision to remove most of the Confederate artillery from the salient, see Matter, *If It Takes All Summer*, 174–79.
11. The initial attack on the Confederate position at the salient was made by all four divisions of the Union Second Corps, which numbered approximately 19,000 men at this time. Matter, *If It Takes All Summer*, 189.
12. John B. Gordon (1832–1904) was a native of Georgia who practiced law and worked in his father's coal-mining business prior to the Civil War. At the outbreak of the war, he raised a company for the 6th Alabama Infantry Regiment, which elected him major on May 14, 1861. He was promoted to lieutenant colonel on Dec. 26, 1861, and to colonel of the regiment on Apr. 1, 1862. The 6th Alabama fought in the Peninsula and Maryland campaigns of 1862. Gordon was severely wounded at the Battle of Antietam on Sept. 17, 1862, and did not rejoin the army until Mar. 30, 1863. He commanded a brigade of Georgians in the Chancellorsville and Gettysburg campaigns and was promoted to the rank of brigadier general on May 7, 1863. One of the best combat officers in the Army of Northern Virginia, Gordon was made major general on May 14, 1864, for his gallant leadership at the Battle of Spotsylvania, where he took command of a division. With the rest of the Second Corps of the Army of Northern Virginia, Gordon fought in the Shenandoah Valley campaign of 1864. When General Early was relieved of command of the Second Corps, Gordon was promoted to corps command. He led the last assault of the Army of Northern Virginia on Fort Stedman on Mar. 25, 1865, and surrendered with General Lee at Appomattox Court House. Gordon commanded the remnants of the Army of Northern Virginia at the surrender ceremonies on Apr. 12, 1865. After the war, he served in the U.S. Senate and commanded the United Confederate Veterans. Davis, *Confederate General*, 3:8–12.
13. This was the second famous "Lee to the Rear" episode of this campaign. For this action, see John B. Gordon, *Reminiscences of the Civil War* (New York: Charles Scribner's Sons, 1903), 278–79, which Coles paraphrases. For another description of the episode, see Matter, *If It Takes All Summer*, 201–2.
14. The Alabama Brigade once again was attacked by troops from the Union Fifth Corps, which launched several attacks in order to divert Confederate reinforcements from the fighting around the salient. Matter, *If It Takes All Summer*, 231–32.
15. For more information on this disastrous attack by the Union Second Corps on May 18, 1864, see Matter, *If It Takes All Summer*, 308–11.
16. OR, vol. 36, pt. 2, p. 628.
17. Fitzhugh Lee (1835–1905), a native of Virginia and the nephew of Robert E. Lee, graduated from West Point in 1856. He fought in the prewar U.S. Army and was wounded in a skirmish with Indians in 1859. When Virginia seceded from the Union, Lee cast his lot with his state and immediately was appointed lieutenant colonel of the 1st Virginia Cavalry Regiment. Promoted to colonel in command of the regiment on Apr. 23, 1862, he

fought in the Peninsula campaign. Lee was promoted to brigadier general on July 24, 1862, and elevated to major general in command of a division in the Cavalry Corps of the Army of Northern Virginia on Sept. 3, 1863. Lee held this rank for the remainder of the war, and, on May 11, 1864, he took command of the Confederate cavalry forces on the field at Yellow Tavern after Jeb Stuart suffered his mortal wound. Lee fought with the Confederate cavalry until he surrendered on Apr. 22, 1865. Davis, *Confederate General*, 4:36–39.

18. Maj. Gen. J. E. B. Stuart was mortally wounded at the Battle of Yellow Tavern, Va., on May 11, 1864, in a fight with Union cavalry. He died on the evening of May 12. Freeman, *Lee's Lieutenants*, 3:420–31.

19. According to the service records of the 4th Alabama, Ephraim F. Powell, a native of Georgia, was mortally wounded in the shoulder on June 3, 1864, at the Battle of Cold Harbor, and died on June 23, 1864. An unmarried 23-year-old mechanic who was living in Evergreen, Ala., when the war broke out, Powell enlisted in Company E on Apr. 25, 1861. He had fought unscathed in the battles in which the regiment had participated before his fatal wounding. CSR, Ephraim F. Powell.

20. General Law later wrote:

> On examining the line I found it bent sharply back at almost a right angle, the point of which rested upon a body of heavy woods. The works were in open ground and were ill adapted to resist an attack. The right face of the angle ran along a slope, with a small marshy stream behind and higher ground in front. The works had evidently been built where the troops found themselves at the close of the fight the previous evening.
>
> Convinced that under such assaults as we had sustained at Spotsylvania our line would be broken at that point, I proposed to cut off the angle by building a new line across its base, which would throw the marshy ground in our front and give us a clear sweep across it with our fire from the slope on the other side. This would not only strengthen but shorten the line considerably. (E. M. Law, "From the Wilderness to Cold Harbor," B&L 4:138–39)

Thus the higher leadership of the Army of Northern Virginia had learned the bitter lessons of Spotsylvania.

21. Joseph Finegan (1814–1885) was a native of Ireland who immigrated to the U.S. and settled in Florida in the 1830s. With the outbreak of the Civil War, after serving as a member of the Florida governor's staff, Finegan was commissioned a brigadier general on Apr. 5, 1862. He fought in Florida for the next two years in command of a brigade of Florida troops. In May 1864, at the request of Gen. Robert E. Lee, General Finegan and his brigade were transferred to the Virginia theater. For the remainder of the war, Finegan commanded a brigade consisting of the 2nd, 5th, 8th, 9th, 10th, and 11th Florida Infantry Regiments. Davis, *Confederate General*, 2:126–27.

22. General Law later wrote of this second assault: "On reaching the trenches, I found the men in fine spirits, laughing and talking as they fired. There, too, I could see more plainly the terrible havoc made in the ranks of the assaulting column. I had seen the dreadful carnage in front of Marye's Hill at Fredericksburg, and on the 'old railroad cut' where Jackson's men had held at the Second Manassas; but I had seen nothing to exceed this. It was not war; it was murder. When the fight ended, more than a thousand men

lay in front of our works either killed or too badly wounded to leave the field." E. M. Law, "From the Wilderness to Cold Harbor," B&L, 4:141.
23. Colonel Oates of the 15th Alabama wrote of this attack: "The charging column, which aimed to strike the 4th Alabama, received the most destructive fire I ever saw. It was subjected to a front and flank fire from the infantry, at short range, while my piece of artillery poured double charges of canister into them. The Georgians loaded for the Alabamians to fire. I could see the dust fog out of a man's clothing in two or three places at once where as many balls would strike him at the same moment." Oates, *War between the Union*, 367.
24. George J. Stannard (1820–1886) a native Vermonter, became colonel of the 4th Vermont Infantry Regiment at the outbreak of the Civil War. When the regiment was not sent immediately to the front, he became lieutenant colonel of the 2nd Vermont, which fought in the Peninsula campaign. He was elected colonel of the 9th Vermont in July 1862. Stannard and the 9th Vermont were captured in the surrender at Harpers Ferry in the Maryland campaign on Sept. 15, 1862. After Stannard was exchanged, he was promoted to brigadier general on Mar. 11, 1863. He commanded the Second Vermont Brigade in the First Corps of the Army of the Potomac and fought with great distinction in the Battle of Gettysburg on July 2 and 3, 1863, particularly in repelling the Pickett-Pettigrew charge on July 3, 1863. In the Overland campaign of May and June 1864, Stannard commanded a brigade in the Eighteenth Corps of the Army of the James, which was attached to the Army of the Potomac, and fought in the Battle of Cold Harbor, where he was wounded. In the fighting around Petersburg in 1864, Stannard lost his right arm. Warner, *Generals in Blue*, 471.
25. John H. Martindale (1815–1881) was born in New York. He graduated from West Point in 1835 but almost immediately resigned from the U.S. Army and practiced law in New York prior to the Civil War. With the coming of war, trained soldiers were needed, and Martindale was appointed brigadier general of volunteers on Aug. 9, 1861. He fought in the Peninsula campaign as a brigade commander in the Fifth Corps of the Army of the Potomac. He then served as the military governor of Washington, D.C., until spring 1864. In the Overland campaign of May and June 1864, Martindale led a division of the Eighteenth Corps. Due to ill health, Martindale resigned from the army on Sept. 13, 1864. Warner, *Generals in Blue*, 312–13.
26. William F. Smith (1824–1903) was an 1845 graduate of West Point. He served in the prewar U.S. Army and as an aide on the staff of General McDowell in the Battle of First Manassas. He was promoted to brigadier general of volunteers on Aug. 13, 1861, and led a division of the Sixth Corps in the Peninsula and Maryland campaigns. Promoted to major general on July 4, 1862, Smith commanded the Sixth Corps in the Fredericksburg campaign. After he was relieved of his command due to his personal attacks on General Burnside, who commanded the Army of the Potomac at that time, Smith was demoted to the rank of brigadier general and posted to the West. Here he served under Gen. U. S. Grant and won his respect and affection. Due to his contributions to the Union successes in the West, most notably at the opening of the Cracker Line in late Oct. 1863, Smith was reappointed to the rank of major general on Mar. 9, 1864, and given command of the Eighteenth Corps of the Army of the James.

This corps was attached to the Army of the Potomac in late May 1864 and fought in the Battle of Cold Harbor and the Petersburg campaign. On July 19, 1864, due to alleged incompetence in not taking Petersburg in an assault in mid-June 1864, Smith was relieved of his command. Warner, *Generals in Blue,* 462–63.
27. One of the Union soldiers facing the fire of the Alabama Brigade described it as "more like a volcanic blast than a battle." Noah Trudeau, *Bloody Roads South* (Boston: Little, Brown, 1989), 287.
28. Javez Harris was a married 21-year-old farmer at the time of his enlistment in Company A on Sept. 26, 1861, at Camp Law, Va. He was captured on Sept. 14, 1862, and held in the Fort Delaware prison camp until his exchange on Nov. 10, 1862. Harris was promoted to corporal on Dec. 31, 1862, and to first sergeant on May 19, 1863. The records do not indicate that he was wounded at all during his term of service. CSR, Javez Harris.
29. Joseph A. Zahm, a railroad worker living in Huntsville, Ala., was a native of Indiana who enlisted as a private in Company I on Apr. 26, 1861. He was severely wounded in the head and thigh on June 27, 1862. Appointed second sergeant of his company on May 1, 1863, Zahm was killed in action on June 4, 1864. CSR, Joseph A. Zahm.
30. Gen. Martin T. McMahon, "Cold Harbor," B&L, 4:218.
31. Francis Walker, *General Hancock* (New York: D. Appleton, 1894), 226.
32. On this nonsensical delay—attributed to General Grant's refusal to observe the niceties of military formality in asking properly for a truce—see Trudeau, *Bloody Roads South,* 302–9.
33. Benjamin F. Butler (1818–1893) was an influential prewar Massachusetts lawyer and politician who on May 16, 1861, became the first major general of volunteers appointed by President Lincoln. While serving as the military governor of New Orleans in 1862, his conduct toward the citizens of that city earned him the nickname of "Beast." He served as commander of the Army of the James in 1863 and 1864. When he failed to follow General Grant's orders in May and June 1864 and in the Dec. 1864 amphibious attack on Fort Fisher, N.C., Grant finally was able to relieve Butler, despite his political connections, and send him home. Warner, *Generals in Blue,* 60–61.
34. After over a week's stalemate in the fetid trenches around Cold Harbor, General Grant managed on June 12, 1864, to move his entire army across the James River to threaten the capture of the important city of Petersburg, without General Lee's discovering Grant's intentions. Trudeau, *Bloody Roads South,* 312–20.
35. John C. Breckinridge (1821–1875) was a Kentucky lawyer and politician who fought in the Mexican War and served as vice president in the administration of President James Buchanan. In 1860, he ran for president as the candidate of the southern wing of the Democratic party, finishing second to Abraham Lincoln in the electoral vote count. From the onset of the Civil War until fall 1861, Breckinridge served in the U.S. Senate. After his arrest for suspected disloyalty was ordered by U.S. government authorities, Breckinridge fled south and was commissioned a Confederate brigadier general by President Davis. He served in the western campaigns and was promoted to major general on Apr. 18, 1862. In Feb. 1864, Breckinridge held a post as an independent commander in the Department of Southwest Virginia; in May 1864 he defeated an invading Federal force

at the Battle of New Market, Va. In late May 1864, Breckinridge and his division were transferred eastward and attached to the Army of Northern Virginia, where he and his men served directly under the personal command of Gen. Robert E. Lee. After renewed fighting in the Shenandoah Valley in late 1864, President Davis named Breckinridge his last secretary of war. Davis, *Confederate General*, 1:126–27.

36. Robert F. Hoke (1837–1912) was a North Carolinian who had been educated at the Kentucky Military Institute. When the Civil War began, he initially served as a second lieutenant in the 1st North Carolina Infantry Regiment. He then was promoted to the rank of lieutenant colonel of the 33rd North Carolina, which was posted to a brigade in Gen. A. P. Hill's "Light" Division. Hoke commanded the regiment in the Peninsula, Cedar Mountain, Second Manassas, and Maryland campaigns. He then was promoted to full colonel and took command of the 21st North Carolina, which fought in the Battle of Fredericksburg. Hoke was elevated to brigadier general, ranking from Jan. 17, 1863, and took command of a North Carolina brigade in the Second Corps of the Army of Northern Virginia. He was wounded at the Battle of Chancellorsville. Upon his recovery, Hoke was assigned to command troops on the North Carolina coast. He was made major general on Apr. 20, 1864, and placed in charge of a division. Hoke's division served in the Confederate forces assigned to defend Petersburg in the Bermuda Hundred campaign of May 1864. Late that same month, the division was transferred to the Army of Northern Virginia to compensate for severe losses sustained in the battles of the preceding month. Hoke fought in the Siege of Petersburg until he was transferred to the Department of North Carolina in Nov. 1864. He surrendered in Apr. 1865. Davis, *Confederate General*, 3:114–15.

Chapter 20. Siege of Richmond and Petersburg

1. Charles S. Venable, "The Campaign from the Wilderness to Petersburg," *Southern Historical Society Papers* 14 (1886): 534.
2. Since Apr. 1864, Gen. P. G. T. Beauregard had been in command of the Confederate forces defending southern Virginia and North Carolina, including the Richmond and Petersburg lines. Freeman, *Lee's Lieutenants*, 3:450.
3. On General Lee's dilemma regarding General Grant's movement to Petersburg, see Dowdey, *Lee's Last Campaign*, 317–58.
4. This is a paraphrasing of Gary W. Gallagher, ed., *Fighting for the Confederacy: The Personal Recollections of General Edward Porter Alexander* (Chapel Hill: Univ. of North Carolina Press, 1989), 420.
5. Charles S. Venable, "General Lee and the Wilderness Campaign," B&L, 4:245–46.
6. Walter Harrison, *Pickett's Men* (Gaithersburg, Md.: Olde Soldier Books, 1987), 136.
7. The stand by General Beauregard and his men on June 15–18, 1864, prevented Grant and the Armies of the James and of the Potomac from taking Petersburg before General Lee and his Army of Northern Virginia could arrive in time to save it. For more on this stand, see Freeman, *Lee's Lieutenants*, 3:528–38.

8. Coles correctly states that General Grant sent the Second Corps of the Army of the Potomac and two divisions of cavalry north of the James River, to act as a diversion. Grant wanted General Lee to draw off some of his army to meet such a threat, while the real action took place south of the James River. There General Burnside's Ninth Corps exploded a mine under Elliott's Salient, which resulted in the Battle of the Crater. Michael A. Cavanaugh and William Marvel, *The Battle of the Crater: The Horrid Pit* (Lynchburg, Va.: H. E. Howard, 1989), 20–21.
9. The "Negro" prisoners were members of the 4th Division of the Ninth Corps, which was attached to the Army of the Potomac. They had attacked the Confederate positions after the explosion of the mine. Cavanaugh and Marvel, *Battle of the Crater*, 56.
10. The South Carolina Brigade actually was commanded by Brig. Gen. Stephen Elliott, who was wounded in the Battle of the Crater. Cavanaugh and Marvel, *Battle of the Crater*, 39, 43.
11. A modern study has verified Coles's figures of Union casualties in this fighting, but the Confederates lost approximately 1,500 men. Noah Trudeau, *The Last Citadel* (Boston: Little, Brown, 1991), 127.
12. Alexander Lowther was a native of Alabama, who was elected captain of Company A of the 15th Alabama on July 26, 1861. He was promoted to major on Jan. 25, 1862, and to colonel of the regiment on Apr. 28, 1863. He was frequently absent from the 15th Alabama, which was the reason that Colonel Oates commanded the regiment throughout many of its battles. When he finally returned to the regiment in 1864, Oates was transferred to the 48th Alabama. Colonel Lowther was wounded in the fighting at Deep Bottom on Aug. 16, 1864. Krick, *Lee's Colonels*, 244.
13. This man could not be identified by a search of the 4th Alabama's rolls in the National Archives.
14. The only "Zahn" or "Zahm" listed in the rolls of the 4th Alabama is Joseph A. Zahm, who, as previously discussed, was killed on June 4, 1864.
15. The fighting at Deep Bottom took place on Aug. 14–16, 1864. For an excellent description of this fighting, see Oates, *War between the Union*, 373–80. Oates was then in command of the 48th Alabama. He was severely wounded on Aug. 16, 1864. This wound resulted in the amputation of Oates's right arm.
16. A fine account of this fighting is found in Trudeau, *Last Citadel*, 171–91.
17. The assault was made by black troops from the 3rd Division of the Eighteenth Army Corps. The division was commanded by Brig. Gen. Charles J. Paine. Trudeau, *Last Citadel*, 209.
18. Fort Harrison was captured on Sept. 29, 1864, by an assault of the 1st Division of the Eighteenth Army Corps, commanded by Brig. Gen. George F. Stannard. Trudeau, *Last Citadel*, 210.
19. This unsuccessful Confederate attempt to retake Fort Harrison is described in Trudeau, *Last Citadel*, 213–17.
20. John S. Thompson, a 17-year-old farmer, had enlisted in Company C on Apr. 26, 1861. He served as a private in the ranks of the regiment throughout the entire war. CSR, John S. Thompson.
21. James W. Thompson, an 18-year-old farmer from Harpersville, Ala., enlisted as a private in Company C on Mar. 2, 1862. He was severely wounded at the Battle of Gettysburg on July 2, 1863, and did not return to duty with the regiment until May 1864. Thompson then remained on duty

with the 4th Alabama until he surrendered on Apr. 9, 1865. CSR, James W. Thompson.
22. By the end of May 1864, General Ewell's physical condition had deteriorated so drastically that he was unable to remain in command of the Second Corps of the Army of Northern Virginia. He was removed and given charge of the reserve troops in the Department of Richmond. Freeman, *Lee's Lieutenants*, 3:510.
23. August V. Kautz (1828–1895) was a native of Germany who immigrated to Ohio with his family in the late 1820s. He fought in the Mexican War as a private and later graduated from West Point in 1852. Kautz served in the prewar U.S. Army in the campaigns against the Plains Indians. With the outbreak of the Civil War, Kautz was named captain of the 6th Ohio Cavalry Regiment, and he fought bravely in the Peninsula campaign. Promoted to colonel of the 2nd Ohio Cavalry, Kautz was sent with the regiment to assignments in Ohio and Kentucky. In Apr. 1864, he was named commander of a division of cavalry in General Butler's Army of the James and was promoted to brigadier general on May 7, 1864. Kautz led his cavalry division in the Petersburg campaign until Mar. 1865, when he was named to command an infantry division of black troops, which he marched into Richmond when it fell on Apr. 3, 1865. Warner, *Generals in Blue*, 257–58.
24. This fighting took place north of the James River on Oct. 27, 1864. On this attack, see Trudeau, *Last Citadel*, 237–41, 247–48.
25. Martin W. Gary (1831–1881) was a South Carolina native who raised Company B of the Hampton Legion, which he led in the Battle of First Manassas. Elected lieutenant colonel of the Hampton Legion on June 16, 1862, Gary fought with the Army of Northern Virginia in the Peninsula, Second Manassas, and Maryland campaigns of 1862. Gary was promoted to colonel of the Hampton Legion on Dec. 12, 1862. When it was converted from infantry to cavalry in Mar. 1864, he was elevated to command the cavalry brigade of the Department of Richmond. Gary was promoted to brigadier general on July 3, 1864, and fought in the Petersburg campaign. Davis, *Confederate General*, 2:177–78.
26. Robert D. Tribble was a 19-year-old farmer from Madison Station, Ala., who enlisted as a private in Company F on Apr. 26, 1861. He was wounded on July 2, 1863, and on May 6, 1864, and surrendered on Apr. 9, 1865. CSR, Robert D. Tribble.
27. Stephen J. Miller, an 18-year-old farmer, enlisted as a private in Company C on Apr. 26, 1861. Promoted to second corporal on Dec. 1, 1862, he was reduced in rank back to private on Mar. 1, 1863, for some undescribed indiscretion. Wounded on Sept. 20, 1863, Miller returned to duty with the regiment and served until his surrender on Apr. 9, 1865. CSR, Stephen J. Miller.
28. Gen. John Gregg had been killed on Oct. 7, 1864, in the fighting north of Fort Harrison along the Charles City Road, south of Richmond. Davis, *Confederate General*, 3:38–39.
29. After recuperating from the wound he sustained in the Battle of the Wilderness on May 6, 1864, General Longstreet returned to his First Corps command on Oct. 19, 1864. Davis, *Confederate General*, 4:94.
30. The fighting on Oct. 27, 1864, is fully described in Trudeau, *Last Citadel*, 224–54.

31. John C. C. Sanders (1840–1864) was an Alabama native who, despite his youth, was elected captain of the 11th Alabama Infantry Regiment in 1861. His regiment, a part of Wilcox's Alabama Brigade, fought in the Peninsula campaign. Sanders was wounded on June 30, 1862, in the Battle of Glendale. Upon his recovery, Sanders participated in the Second Manassas and Maryland campaigns, where he again was wounded. In the Maryland campaign, Sanders served as colonel of the 11th Alabama. He was engaged in the Fredericksburg and Chancellorsville campaigns and at the Battle of Gettysburg, where he was seriously wounded. Sanders took command of the brigade on May 12, 1864, when his predecessor was killed in the Battle of Spotsylvania. Promoted to brigadier general on June 7, 1864, Sanders then was formally assigned to command the brigade. He was killed in the fighting at Globe Tavern in the Petersburg campaign on Aug. 21, 1864, but his brigade retained his name after his death. Davis, *Confederate General*, 5:126–27.
32. Pinckney Bowles ended the war as a colonel and was never appointed to the rank of brigadier general. Krick, *Lee's Colonels*, 63.
33. For a full description of the pitiful state of the Army of Northern Virginia at this time, see Freeman, *Lee's Lieutenants*, 3:619–23.
34. This was the Battle of Hatcher's Run on Feb. 5–7, 1865. See Trudeau, *Last Citadel*, 312–22.
35. Philip H. Sheridan (1831–1888) was a native New Yorker who became one of the most famous soldiers in the history of the U.S. Army. He graduated from West Point in 1853 and served in the prewar army on the western frontier. When the Civil War began, Sheridan first acted as chief quartermaster and commissary of the Army of Southwest Missouri. On May 25, 1862, he was appointed colonel of the 2nd Michigan Cavalry Regiment. In the fighting in the West, Sheridan won a reputation for great boldness and gallantry in action. He was promoted to brigadier general of volunteers on Sept. 13, 1862, and to major general on Mar. 16, 1863. On Sept. 20, 1863, at the Battle of Chickamauga, one of Sheridan's three infantry brigades helped to hold the line for the Union army, staving off complete disaster, while Sheridan and the other two brigades skedaddled. In the fighting at Chattanooga in Nov. 1863, Sheridan's men, without specific orders to do so, climbed Missionary Ridge and helped break the Confederate lines, thereby helping win the battle. When General Grant was promoted and brought east to command all the U.S. armies, he brought his friend Sheridan with him and named him chief of the Cavalry Corps of the Army of the Potomac. Sheridan infused the Union cavalry with his boldness and led it with distinction throughout the remainder of the war. He won great victories in the Valley campaign of 1864 and at the climactic Battle of Five Forks in Apr. 1865. It was Sheridan's leadership which won the Battle of Sayler's Creek, and Sheridan who, during the Appomattox campaign, placed his men in front of the Army of Northern Virginia, blocked its retreat, and finally compelled its surrender. After the war, Sheridan rose in the U.S. Army until he became its commanding general in 1884, upon the retirement of General Sherman. Warner, *Generals in Blue*, 437–39.
36. The Battle of Five Forks was fought on Apr. 1, 1865. In this engagement, Gen. Fitzhugh Lee's cavalry and General Pickett's infantry commands were overwhelmed by General Sheridan and his cavalry and by the Fifth Corps of the Army of the Potomac. See Freeman, *Lee's Lieutenants*, 3:655–74.

37. On Apr. 2, 1865, after the Confederate lines around Petersburg had been broken by a Union general assault, Gen. A. P. Hill, commander of the Third Corps of the Army of Northern Virginia, was killed by two Union soldiers from the 138th Pennsylvania Infantry Regiment. Trudeau, *Last Citadel*, 373–75.
38. John E. Cooke, *Wearing of the Gray* (Bloomington: Indiana Univ. Press, 1959), 447–48.

Chapter 21. Petersburg to Appomattox

1. The Battle of Sayler's Creek, fought on Apr. 6, 1865, resulted in approximately one-third of the remnants of the Army of Northern Virginia being either killed or captured. For more details on this battle, termed "the Black Day of the Army," see Freeman, *Lee's Lieutenants*, 3:698–711.
2. Agrippa Adkins was 18 years old when he enlisted as a private in Company C on Apr. 26, 1861. He fought unscathed in all of the 4th Alabama's battles, surrendering on Apr. 9, 1865. CSR, Agrippa Adkins.
3. This is a paraphrase of Gordon, *Reminiscences*, 440.
4. General Lee had surrendered the Army of Northern Virginia between 1:30 P.M. and 2:00 P.M. on Apr. 9, 1865, at the Wilmer McLean house in Appomattox Court House, Va. Frank P. Cauble, *The Surrender Proceedings* (Lynchburg, Va.: H. E. Howard, 1987), 47.
5. James H. Franklin, born in England, was a 21-year-old clerk in Selma, Ala., when he enlisted in Company A on Apr. 26, 1862. Promoted from private to fourth sergeant of his company on Dec. 4, 1862, Franklin served until he was wounded and captured at Gettysburg. He was held as a prisoner at Fort Delaware until his exchange in early 1864. Franklin was promoted to orderly sergeant on July 1, 1864, and surrendered on Apr. 9, 1865. CSR, James H. Franklin.
6. The 4th Alabama had only 202 officers and men on its rolls when it surrendered on Apr. 9, 1865. Clement A. Evans, *Confederate Military History*, 8:61.
7. Thomas J. Norton, a native of Ireland, was a 22-year-old grocer from McKinley, Ala., who enlisted as a private in Company D on Apr. 25, 1861. He served with the 4th Alabama throughout the war, suffering a wound on June 27, 1862, at the Battle of Gaines' Mill. Listed in the records as being a "gallant and meritorious" soldier, Norton surrendered on Apr. 9, 1865. CSR, Thomas J. Norton.
8. The best and most moving description of the formal surrender proceedings is found in Joshua Chamberlain, *The Passing of the Armies* (Dayton, Ohio: Press of Morningside Bookshop, 1982), 258–72. Chamberlain had the honor of commanding the surrender proceedings for the Army of the Potomac.

Chapter 22. Our Return Home

1. For the full text of General Order No. 9, see Cauble, *Surrender Proceedings*, 88; and OR, vol. 46, pt. 3, p. 744.
2. Edward L. Thomas (1825–1898), a native Georgian who fought in the Mexican War, was a planter in Georgia before the Civil War. On Oct. 15,

1861, Thomas was appointed colonel of the 35th Georgia Infantry Regiment. In recognition of his bravery in the Peninsula campaign, Thomas was given command of the brigade when his brigade commander was wounded, and he led it from then until the surrender at Appomattox. He was promoted to brigadier general, to rank from Nov. 1, 1862, and remained in this rank for the rest of the war. Davis, *Confederate General*, 6:45–47.
3. A full description of the terms of surrender given by General Grant to General Lee and his Army of Northern Virginia is found in Cauble, *Surrender Proceedings*, 52, 74.
4. Lunsford L. Lomax (1835–1913) graduated from West Point in 1856. A native of Virginia, he resigned his commission in the U.S. Army on Apr. 25, 1861, when Virginia seceded from the Union. Lomax served in various staff positions in the Confederate army in the West in 1861 and 1862. On Feb. 8, 1863, he was promoted to colonel and assigned to command the 11th Virginia Cavalry Regiment in the Army of Northern Virginia. In recognition of his gallantry in the Gettysburg campaign, he was promoted to brigadier general on July 30, 1863, and assigned to command a brigade in the Cavalry Corps. Lomax fought with the Army of Northern Virginia for the rest of the war, serving in the Overland campaign of May and June 1864 and in the Shenandoah Valley campaign in fall 1864. He was promoted to major general on Aug. 10, 1864. After the fall of Richmond, Lomax took his command to North Carolina, where he surrendered in spring 1865. Davis, *Confederate General*, 4:85.
5. As a final note, this article in an Alabama newspaper: "We see every day an officer of the old 4th Alabama Infantry, handling a trowel, others, privates, working with a will at their trades, others are raising a crop of corn, and a field officer putting up a saw mill. These men have been through tempests of shell, grape and minnie balls, now want peace and civil government, and have gone to work to recuperate exhausted means. Thousands of others are doing the same, and will be true as steel to their oaths. Those who have seen the most of the war are the fastest friends of peace, and grumble the least." *Southern Advocate* (Huntsville, Ala.), July 12, 1865.

Bibliography

Primary Sources

Manuscript Materials

Compiled Service Records of Confederate Soldiers Who Served in Organizations from the State of Alabama. War Record Group 109. National Archives, Washington, D.C.
Proctor, W. H. Account. Typescript. Manassas National Military Park, Manassas, Va.
Smith, Otis D. Letter to "Mrs. Allen." Aug. 18, 1861. Typescript of letter. Manassas National Battlefield Park, Manassas, Va.
Vaughan, P. T. "Memories of the Civil War." Undated newspaper clipping. Smith Papers, Scrapbook 3, Bowling Library, Judson College, Marion, Ala.

Newspapers and Periodicals

Confederate Veteran. 40 vols. 1895–1932. Nashville, 1897–1932. Rpt. Wilmington, N.C.: Broadfoot Publishing Company, 1987.
Gettysburg (Pa.) *Star and Sentinel*. 1885.
Huntsville (Ala.) *Daily Times*. 1925.
Huntsville (Ala.) *Democrat*. 1861–62.
Huntsville (Ala.) *Independent*. 1861.
Montgomery (Ala.) *Daily Mail*. 1864.
Philadelphia Weekly Press. 1887.
Philadelphia Weekly Times. 1884.
Selma (Ala.) *Daily Reporter*. 1862.
Southwestern Baptist. Tuskegee, Ala. 1862–64.
Southern Advocate. Huntsville, Ala. 1861–62. 1865.
Southern Historical Society Papers. 1876–1959.

Secondary Sources

Bernard, George S. *War Talks of Confederate Veterans.* Dayton, Ohio: Press of Morningside Bookshop, 1981.
Bilby, Joseph G. *Three Rousing Cheers.* Hightstown, N.J.: Longstreet House, 1993.
Biographical Dictionary of the United States Congress, 1774–1961. Washington, D.C.: U.S. Government Printing office, 1961.
Carter, Robert G. *Four Brothers in Blue.* Austin: Univ. of Texas Press, 1978.
Cauble, Frank P. *The Surrender Proceedings.* Lynchburg, Va.: H. E. Howard, 1987.
Cavanaugh, Michael A., and William Marvel. *The Battle of the Crater: The Horrid Pit.* Lynchburg, Va.: H. E. Howard, 1989.
Chamberlain, Joshua. *The Passing of the Armies.* Dayton, Ohio: Press of Morningside Bookshop, 1982.
Coco, Gregory. *Wasted Valor.* Gettysburg, Pa.: Thomas Publications, 1988.
Coddington, Edwin B. *The Gettysburg Campaign: A Study in Command.* New York: Charles Scribner's Sons, 1968.
Cooke, John E. *Wearing of the Gray.* Bloomington: Indiana Univ. Press, 1959.
Cozzens, Peter. *This Terrible Sound.* Chicago: Univ. of Illinois Press, 1992.
Davis, William C., ed. *The Confederate General.* 6 vols. Harrisburg, Pa.: National Historical Society, 1991.
Dawes, Rufus W. *Service with the Sixth Wisconsin Volunteers.* Dayton, Ohio: Press of Morningside Bookshop, 1984.
Dodd, Donald B. "The Free State of Winston." *Alabama Heritage* 28 (Spring 1993): 9–19.
Dowdey, Clifford. *Lee's Last Campaign.* Wilmington, N.C.: Broadfoot Publishing Company, 1988.
———. *The Seven Days: The Emergence of Robert E. Lee.* Wilmington, N.C.: Broadfoot Publishing Company, 1988.
Evans, Clement A., ed. *Confederate Military History.* 13 vols. Atlanta: Confederate Publishing Company, 1899.
Freeman, Douglas S. *Lee's Lieutenants.* 3 vols. New York: Charles Scribner's Sons, 1970.
Gaff, Alan. *Brave Men's Tears: The Iron Brigade at Brawner's Farm.* Dayton, Ohio: Press of Morningside Bookshop, 1985.
Gallagher, Gary W., ed. *Fighting for the Confederacy: The Personal Recollections of General Edward Porter Alexander.* Chapel Hill: Univ. of North Carolina Press, 1989.
Gordon, John B. *Reminiscences of the Civil War.* 1903. Rpt. New York: Charles Scribner's Sons, 1970.
Gould, John M. *History of the 1st–10th–29th Maine Regiment.* Portland, Me.: Stephen Berry, 1871.
Grant, Ulysses S. *Personal Memoirs of U. S. Grant.* 2 vols. New York: C. L. Webster and Company, 1886.
Harrison, Walter. *Pickett's Men.* Gaithersburg, Md.: Olde Soldier Books, 1987.
Henderson, G. F. R. *Stonewall Jackson and the American Civil War.* New York: Longmans, Green and Company, 1936.
Hennessy, John J. *The First Battle of Manassas: An End to Innocence, July 18–21, 1861.* Lynchburg, Va.: H. E. Howard, 1989.
———. *Return to Bull Run.* New York: Simon and Schuster, 1993.

Hudson, James G. "A Story of Company D, 4th Alabama Infantry Regiment, C.S.A." *Alabama Historical Quarterly* 23, nos. 1–2 (Spring 1961): 139–79.
Johnson, Robert V., and Clarence C. Buel, eds. *Battles and Leaders of the Civil War*. 4 vols. New York: Thomas Yoseloff, 1956.
Jones, Kenneth W. "The Fourth Alabama Infantry: First Blood." *Alabama Historical Quarterly* 36, no. 1 (Spring 1974): 36–37.
Judson, Amos M. *History of the Eighty-Third Regiment Pennsylvania Volunteers*. Dayton, Ohio: Press of Morningside Bookshop, 1986.
Krick, Robert K. *Lee's Colonels*. Dayton, Ohio: Press of Morningside Bookshop, 1979.
Longstreet, James. *From Manassas to Appomattox: Memoirs of the Civil War in America*. Philadelphia: J. B. Lippincott, 1896.
Matter, William B. *If It Takes All Summer*. Chapel Hill: Univ. of North Carolina Press, 1988.
Newton, Steven H. *The Battle of Seven Pines*. Lynchburg, Va.: H. E. Howard, 1993.
Northern Alabama Historical and Biographical. Birmingham, Ala.: Smith and Deland, 1888.
Oates, William C. *The War between the Union and the Confederacy*. 1905. Dayton, Ohio: Press of Morningside Bookshop, 1985.
Pfanz, Harry W. *Gettysburg: The Second Day*. Chapel Hill: Univ. of North Carolina Press, 1987.
Pierrepont, Alice V. D. *Reuben Vaughan Kidd: Soldier of the Confederacy*. Petersburg, Va.: privately published, 1947.
Polley, J. B. *Hood's Texas Brigade*. Dayton, Ohio: Press of Morningside Bookshop, 1976.
Priest, John M. *Antietam: The Soldiers' Battle*. Shippensburg, Pa.: White Mane Publishing Company, 1989.
Scott, Robert Garth. *Into the Wilderness with the Army of the Potomac*. Bloomington: Indiana Univ. Press, 1985.
Sears, Stephen W. *Landscape Turned Red*. New York: Ticknor and Fields, 1983.
———. *To the Gates of Richmond*. New York: Ticknor and Fields, 1992.
Simpson, Harold B. *Hood's Texas Brigade: Lee's Grenadier Guard*. Dallas, Tex.: Alcor Publishing Company, 1983.
Sorrell, G. Moxley. *Recollections of a Confederate Staff Officer*. New York: Neale Publishing Company, 1905.
Steere, Edward. *The Wilderness Campaign*. Harrisburg, Pa.: Stackpole Company, 1960.
Sullivan, David M., ed. "Fowler the Soldier, Fowler the Marine." *Civil War Times Illustrated* 26 (Feb. 1988): 28–35, 44–45.
Swinton, William. *Campaigns of the Army of the Potomac*. New York: Charles Scribner's Sons, 1882.
Trudeau, Noah. *Bloody Roads South*. Boston: Little, Brown, 1989.
———. *The Last Citadel*. Boston: Little, Brown, 1991.
U.S. War Dept. *War of the Rebellion: A Compilation of the Official Records of the Union and Confederate Armies*. 128 vols. Washington, D.C.: U.S. Government Printing Office, 1880–1901.
Vaughan, P. Turner. "Diary of Turner Vaughan, Company C, 4th Alabama, C.S.A., Commenced March 4, 1863, and Ending February 12, 1864." *Alabama Historical Quarterly* 18, no. 4 (Winter 1956): 573–604.
Walker, Francis A. *General Hancock*. New York: D. Appleton, 1894.

———. *History of the Second Corps in the Army of the Potomac.* New York: Charles Scribner's Sons, 1886.
Warner, Ezra. *Generals in Blue.* Baton Rouge: Louisiana State Univ. Press, 1964.
White, Russell C., ed. *The Civil War Diary of Wyman S. White.* Baltimore, Md.: Butternut and Blue, 1991.
Wright, Stuart, ed. *Memoirs of Alfred Horatio Belo.* Gaithersburg, Md.: Olde Soldiers Books, 1991.

Index

Adkins, Agrippa, 191–92, 302n
Adrian, Lt. (44th Ala.), 112
Alabama Secession Convention, xiv
Alabama troops, infantry
—3rd, 10, 224n
—6th, 240n, 294n
—13th, 16, 68, 110, 277n
—14th, 31, 39
—15th, 31, 87, 106–8, 131, 135, 139, 141–46, 164–66, 184, 217, 241n, 271n, 299n
—25th, 138, 281n
—44th, 87, 106–7, 112, 135, 140, 146, 154, 156, 165, 173–74, 220, 271n, 273n
—47th, 87, 106–7, 135, 140, 161–62, 165, 218, 271n, 292n
—48th, 87, 103, 106–7, 133–35, 140, 145, 164–66, 204, 271n, 299n
—58th, 138, 281n
—5th Battalion, 110
Alburtis's (Va.) Battery, 23, 237n
Alexander, E. Porter, 147, 150–51, 179, 284n–85n
Allston, Benjamin, 30–33, 240n–42n
Amelia Court House, Va., 191
Anderson, Archer, 63
Anderson, George H., 147, 285n
Anderson, George T. (Brig. Gen.), 87–88, 97, 106–8, 160–61, 174, 267n–68n, 273n, 279n, 289n, 291n
Anderson, George T. (Pvt.), 26, 238n

Anderson, Richard H., 79, 89, 96–97, 159, 163, 166, 178, 180, 187, 263n, 292n
Angell, Joseph, 235n
Antietam, Battle of. *See* Sharpsburg, Battle of
Appomattox Court House, Surrender at, xiv, 11–17, 25, 86–87, 192–95, 245n, 251n, 254n, 267n, 273n, 284n, 294n, 302n–3n
Archer, James, 40, 110, 245n–46n, 273n
Arkansas troops, infantry, 3rd, 81, 87, 103, 106–7, 135, 143–46, 150–51, 160, 168–69, 180, 183, 273n
Armistead, Heslop, 15, 25, 38, 48, 228n
Armistead, Lewis A., 108, 275n
Army of the Cumberland (Union), 279n, 282n–83n, 285n–86n
Army of the James (Union), 184, 296n–98n, 300n
Army of Northern Virginia (Conf.), 50, 68, 70, 76–77, 87, 96, 102, 114, 156–58, 172, 174, 179, 188, 231n, 235n, 237n, 239n, 244n–51n, 254n–55n, 257n–61n, 263n–64n, 266n–67n, 269n–71n, 276n–78n, 284n, 288n–89n, 291n–95n, 298n, 300n–303n
Army of the Ohio (Union), 285n
Army of the Potomac (Conf.), 20, 22, 24, 233n, 253n

Army of the Potomac (Union), 77, 89, 158, 234n, 242n, 246n, 248n, 251n–52n, 255n, 257n–58n, 260n–71n, 274n, 276n, 282n–83n, 285n, 288n–93n, 296n–99n, 301n–2n
Army of the Shenandoah (Conf.), 19–20, 24, 231n–32n, 235n, 240n
Army of the Tennessee (Conf.), 26, 133–34, 138, 156, 188, 239n, 261n, 279n–81n
Army of the Tennessee (Union), 286n
Army of the Valley (Conf.), 45, 244n, 248n–49n, 252n
Army of Virginia (Union), 50–51, 234n, 247n, 252n, 257n
Arnold, William M., 68, 259n–60n
Ashby, Turner, 59, 256n
Ashland, Va., 45, 89–90
Atlanta, Battle of, 280n–81n

Ball's Bluff, Battle of, 233n
Balthis, W. L., 45, 248n
Baltimore, Md., 196–97
Banks, Nathaniel P., 44, 50, 247n, 252n, 255n
Barksdale, William, 77–78, 106, 261n, 281n
Barret's (Mo.) Battery, 139, 143, 281n
Bartow, Francis S., 20, 22–23, 29, 97, 232n
Bean's Station, Tenn., 152, 286n
Beauregard, P. G. T., 19–20, 22–23, 179–81, 231n, 233n, 253n, 284n, 298n
Bee, Barnard E., 17, 19–25, 28–29, 201, 232n, 236n–38n, 240n
Belo, Alfred H., 93–94, 269n
Benning, Henry L., xiii, 87–88, 97, 106–8, 130–31, 134, 145, 160, 184–85, 267n, 273n, 277n, 279n
Bermuda Hundred Line, Attack on, 180–81
Berry, Randall, 27
Berry's Ford, Va., 100, 130
Berryville, Va., 98, 101, 270n
Big Bethel, Battle of, 251n, 276n
Blain's Crossroads, Tenn., 152
Bohlen, Henry, 253n
Boonsboro Gap. *See* Turner's Gap
Boulware, Gilchrist R., 83, 266n–67n
Bowles, Pinckney D., 14, 33, 38, 80, 84, 93, 154, 161–63, 170, 189, 214–22, 227n, 301n
Bradford, Fielding, 9, 223n–24n
Bradley, Hugh, 35, 243n
Bradley, William Barlow, 33–34, 242n
Brady, James (Pa.) Battery, 246n
Bragg, Braxton, 72, 132–35, 137–41, 144–45, 147–48, 150–51, 260n–61n, 279n–80n, 285n
Brandon, James C., 9, 223n
Brandy Station, Va., 97–98, 269n–70n
Bratton, John, 144–46, 148, 284n
Brawner's Farm, Battle of, 54, 254n–55n 263n
Breckinridge, John C., 178, 297n–98n
Breedlove, John P., 12, 113, 225n
Bridgeport, Tenn., 139–41, 144, 147
Bristoe Station, Va., 30, 32, 288n
Brockenbrough, John, 277n
Brown, Baylis E., 12, 166, 219, 225n
Brown, James H., 14, 166, 222, 228n
Brown, John, 247n, 264n
Brown's Ferry, 139, 141–47
Bryan, Goode, 279n
Buckner, Simon B., 155, 286n–87n
Bulger, Michael J., 106–7, 273n
Bull's Gap, Camp at, 155
Bunker Hill, Va., 130
Burnside, Ambrose E., 21, 74–75, 78–82, 85, 89, 149, 151, 234n, 261n–62n, 265n, 268n, 285n, 292n, 296n, 299n
Butler, Benjamin F., 178, 184, 187, 297n, 300n

Caldwell, William A., 83, 266n
Camp Chase, Ohio, 226n
Camp Letterman, Pa., 278n
Campbell's Station, Tenn., 148
Carlisle, Pa., 102
Carter, Eugene, 239n
Carter, Thomas H., 115, 278n
Cary, George W., 165, 173–74, 292n
Casey, Silas, 246n
Cashtown, Pa., 103, 205
Cedar Mountain, Battle of, 50, 87, 247n, 252n, 263n, 267n, 272n, 285n
Centreville, Va., 30, 37–38, 157
Chamberlain, Joshua, 302n
Chambersburg, Pa., 102–3, 204–5

Chancellorsville, Battle of, 94–96, 159, 235n, 260n, 262n, 269n–70n, 289n, 298n
Chantilly, Battle of, 61, 257n
Chapman, J. A., 236n
Chapman, Steptoe, 84–85, 267n
Chattanooga, Tenn., 133, 137–41, 143–44, 147, 150, 152, 157, 301n
Chester Gap, Va., 130
Chickamauga, Battle of, 13, 133–38, 141, 156, 163, 226n, 228n–30n, 239n, 262n, 279n–82n, 287n, 289n, 292n, 301n
Christian, Thomas L., 53, 109, 253n
Clarke, George, 189
Clarke, Richard, 13, 23, 27, 34, 226n, 242n–43n
Clay, Lawson, 188
Cobb, Howell, 79, 263n, 265n
Cobb, Thomas R. R., 81, 263n–65n
Cold Harbor, Battle of, 173–78, 224n, 230n, 273n, 295n–97n
Coleman, Thomas K., 13, 38, 80, 104–5, 109, 135, 137, 226n, 235n, 264n
Coles, Robert T., xiii–xvi, 9, 28, 49, 51–52, 58–59, 64, 66, 69–70, 73, 83–84, 92–93, 102, 104–5, 108–9, 111, 131, 140–42, 149, 154–55, 160–63, 165, 170, 175–76, 183–84, 188–89, 191–92, 195–97, 219
Colquitt, Alfred H., 68, 259n
Connell, John, 280n
Connelly, John, 93, 269n
Cooke, James H., 104
Cooke, Mordecai M., 15, 228n
Coonsey, Lt., 166, 219
Cooper, Samuel, 155, 188
Corcoran, Michael, 25, 238n
Crater, Battle of the, 183, 299n
Croxton, Milton E., 42, 247n
Cruft, Charles, 280n
Crutchfield Farm, Va., 171
Culpeper, Va., 30, 50–51, 74–75, 97–98, 100, 132, 257
Cussons, John, 40, 53, 55, 82, 93, 246n

Dabney, Rev. Dr. R. L., 45, 249n
Dalton, Ga., xiii, 11–14, 16, 41
Dandridge, Tenn., 154

Darby, James W., 14, 227n
Darby Town Road, Battle of, 183–84
Darwin, Taylor, 208
Davis, Jefferson, 24, 42–43, 97, 151, 231n, 233n, 238n, 240n–41n, 247n–48n, 258n, 260n, 280n, 285n, 297n–98n
Davis, Joseph, 221, 277n, 291n
Dawes, Rufus W., 293n–94n
Dawson, N. H. R., 12–13, 225n
Deas, Zachariah C., 26, 238n–39n
Deep Bottom, Battle of, 299n
DeGraffenreid, E. F., 92, 268n
Dement, J. J., 195–97
Dilger, Hubert Battery (Co. K, 1st Ohio Light Artillery), 256n
Drayton, Thomas F., 63, 258n
Dryer, Thomas B., 12, 225n
Duke, Basil W., 141, 282n–83n
Dumfries, Va., 32
Duncan, William, 89, 175–76, 268n
Duryee, Dr., 35, 243n

Early, Jubal A., 24, 79, 102, 190, 237n, 264n, 270n
Eighteenth Corps (Union), 296n, 299n
Eleventh Corps (Union), 60, 144–45, 157, 257n, 271n, 283n–84n
Elliott, Stephen, 299n
Elliott, William (Brooks South Carolina Artillery) Battery, 65, 258n
Eltham's Landing, Battle of, 40, 246n
Elzey, Arnold, 19, 24, 232n
Evans, Nathan G., 20–22, 29, 233n
Evergreen, Ala., 14
Ewell, Richard S., 37, 44, 46, 97–98, 100–103, 105, 114, 158–59, 167, 171, 185, 191, 206, 244n, 266n, 269n, 271n, 278n, 288n, 300n

Fairfax, John, 206–8
Falling Waters, Va., 113–14, 130, 275n
Farmville, Va., 191–92
Farnsworth, Elon J., 109–10, 112, 276n–77n
Fayetteville, Pa., 103
Featherston, W. S., 254n
Field, Charles W., 47, 155, 157–58, 161, 164, 180, 185, 217, 219, 250n, 288n–89n

Fifth Corps (Union), 72, 248n–49n, 255n–56n, 260n, 262n, 266n, 271n–72n, 274n, 289n–90n, 293n–94n, 296n, 301n
Figures, Henry S., 166, 293n
Finegan, Joseph, 174, 295n
First Corps (Conf.), 13, 49, 51–52, 74, 77, 79, 96–97, 100, 113, 133–34, 156, 159, 166–68, 171, 178, 185, 187, 191–92, 251n, 259n, 261n, 263n, 278n–79n, 284n, 286n–88n, 291n, 293n, 300n
First Corps (Union), 248n, 250n, 255n, 258n, 262n, 264n, 271n, 289n, 296n
Fisher, C. F., 240n
Five Forks, Battle of, 274n, 301n
Florence, Ala., 15, 188
Florida troops, infantry
—2nd, 291n–92n
—5th, 291n–92n
—8th, 291n–92n
Fogarty, George T., 51, 86, 252n
Forrest, Nathan B., 134, 192, 280n
Fort Delaware, 225n–26n, 246n, 252n, 257n, 297n, 302n
Fort Donelson, 287n, 289n
Fort Fisher, 76, 240n, 297n
Fort Gilmer, 184–85, 189
Fort Harrison, 184–86, 299n–300n
Fort Huger, 269n
Fort Lafayette, 268n
Fort Loudon, 150–51, 155, 285n–86n
Fort McHenry, 225n, 268n
Fort Monroe, 38
Fort Stedman, 294n
Fort Warren, 287n
Fourth Corps (Union), 246n
Fowler, John, 235n
Frame, Joseph B., 67, 259n
Franklin, Battle of, 239n
Franklin, James H., 193, 302n
Franklin, William B., 40–41, 79–82, 245n, 262n, 264n
Franks, Rufus B., 109, 208, 275n–76n
Frederick, Md., 61–62
Fredericksburg, Battle of, 16, 75, 77–85, 230n, 234n, 237n, 261n–67n, 285n, 295n
Fredericksburg, Va., Camp at, 76, 88, 132

Frederickshall Station, Va., 45
Freeman's Ford, Skirmish at, 52, 253n
Freid, John, 51, 86, 252n
Fremont, John C., 44, 50, 247n–48n
French, William H., 81, 264n
Fry, Birkett, 110, 277n
Furlough and Bounty Act, 243n

Gaines' Mill, Battle of, xiv, 13, 15–16, 25, 46–49, 172, 226n–28n, 230n, 232n–33n, 238n, 241n, 244n, 249n–50n, 264n, 273n, 292n, 302n
Gainesville, Va., 54
Garnett, Richard B., 108, 275n
Gary, Martin V., 186, 300n
Geary, John W., 147, 284n–85n
Georgia troops, infantry
—7th, 20, 22, 28–29, 88, 97, 239n
—8th, 20, 22, 28–29, 88, 97, 239n
—18th, 32, 40, 49, 54, 68, 87, 246n
—20th, 218–19, 274n
—21st, 260n
Gerrish, George (1st Battery, New Hampshire Light Artillery), 55, 254n
Gettysburg, Battle of, 12, 14, 103–15, 141, 202, 205–13, 225n, 227n–29n, 239n, 244n–46n, 249n, 252n–53n, 260n–61n, 265n–66n, 269n, 271n–78n, 281n, 283n–84n, 287n, 296n, 299n, 301n–2n
Glass, E. Jones., 12–13, 38, 80, 225n
Glendale, Battle of, 207, 271n, 291n, 301n
Globe Tavern, Battle of, 301n
Goldsby, Thomas J., 11, 23, 32–33, 224n
Gordon, John B., 166, 169, 191–93, 292n, 294n
Gordonsville, Va., 50–51, 156, 158, 214–15, 288n
Gould, John M., 68, 70
Graham, Porterfield, 41, 246n
Grant, Ulysses S., 137, 140, 147, 151–52, 157–59, 162–63, 166–72, 176–79, 181–83, 187, 190, 193, 195, 215, 251n, 261n, 282n, 286n–88n, 290n, 296n–99n, 301n, 303n
Greencastle, Pa., 102, 203–4
Greene, George S., 69–70, 260n
Greeneville, Tenn., 283n
Greenwood, Pa., 103

Gregg, John, 160, 180–86, 289n–90n, 300n
Griffin, Charles, 249n
Groveton, Va., 55–56, 58
Guild, Lafayette, 108

Hager, James J., 61, 257n
Hagerstown, Md., 61–62, 113
Halsey, Charles F., 104, 272n
Hampton, Wade, 22, 224n, 235n
Hampton's (S.C.) Legion, 22, 32, 40, 49, 54, 70, 87, 240n, 300n
Hancock, Winfield S., 81, 160, 163–64, 168–69, 172, 176, 183, 265n, 289n, 291n
Hanover Junction, Battle of, 224n
Hardie, Joseph, 27, 73, 239n
Harpers Ferry, Va., xiii, 19, 27, 29, 41, 62, 66–67, 70, 231n–32n, 258n–59n, 264n, 282n, 296n
Harris, Javez, 175, 297n
Harris, Watkins, 16, 229n
Harrisburg, Pa., 102
Harrison (Conf. spy), 102–3, 271n
Harrison, James, 47–48, 250n
Harrison's Landing, Va., 48, 50–51
Hartley, William, 40–41, 246n
Hatch, John P., 55, 255n
Hatcher, Capt. (15th Ala.), 217
Hatcher's Run, Battle of, 301n
Haygood's (S.C.) Brigade, 183
Hazel Ford, Skirmish at, 131
Hazen, William B., 143–44, 283n
Heintzelman, Samuel P., 21, 25, 29, 234n, 238n, 245n
Henagan, John W., 293n
Heth, Henry, 160, 166, 168, 172, 195, 289n, 293n
Hickey, James (aka Morgan R. Scullin), 51, 86, 252n
Hill, Ambrose P., 46–47, 50, 67, 72, 79, 82, 85, 97–98, 100–103, 110, 113–14, 130–31, 157–60, 163, 168, 174, 190–91, 195, 215–16, 249n–50n, 260n, 264n, 269n, 277n–78n, 288n–89n, 291n–92n, 298n, 302n
Hill, Daniel H., 48, 62–63, 68–69, 79, 85, 249n, 251n, 257n, 259n–60n, 280n
Hoke, Robert F., 178, 214, 298n
Hollis, Rufus, 17, 25, 230n

Hood, John B., 28, 32, 40, 45, 49, 51–52, 54–55, 58, 63, 67, 69–70, 73, 77, 84, 89, 97, 99, 102, 105–8, 133–34, 137–39, 156–57, 187–89, 202, 206, 208, 212, 217, 239n–40n, 246n, 250n, 253n, 258n, 261n, 273n, 277n–79n, 281n, 284n
Hooker, Joseph, 79–81, 83, 89, 98, 100, 102–3, 144, 147, 157, 258n, 262n–63n, 268n–69n, 271n, 283n, 285n
Howard, Oliver O., 145, 284n
Hudson, James G., 231n, 234n–37n, 242n–43n
Hudson, William O., 34, 59, 237n, 242n
Huger, Benjamin, 38, 245n
Humphreys, Andrew A., 81, 265n–66n
Humphreys, Benjamin, 137, 279n, 281n
Hundley's Corner, Va., 46
Hunt, Henry, 78, 261n
Hunter, David, 21, 234n
Huntsville, Ala., 9, 14, 16, 188–89, 242n

Imboden, John D. (Staunton Artillery Battery), 20–21, 23, 232n–33n, 237n, 248n
Indiana troops, infantry
—27th, 257n
—31st, 280n
—82nd, 280n
Iowa troops, infantry
—17th, 280n
—31st, 280n
Iron Brigade (Union), 290n

Jackson, Thomas J., 22–24, 26, 28, 37, 44–52, 54–57, 60–62, 66, 76, 79–82, 84–85, 94, 96–97, 235n–37n, 244n, 247n–49n, 252n–59n, 261n, 263n–64n, 267n, 269n, 275n, 292n
Jacobs, Michael, 272n
Jeff Davis (Ala.) Artillery Battery, 115, 278n
Jenkins, Micah, 133, 137, 141, 144–45, 147–48, 157, 164, 215–16, 279n, 284n–285n
Johnson, Bradley T., 55, 57, 254n
Johnson, Bushrod, 152, 286n
Johnson's Island, Ohio, 253n
Johnston, Albert S., 86, 267n

Johnston, George D., 138, 281n
Johnston, Joseph E., 18–20, 23–24, 27–30, 32, 37–39, 41–42, 187–89, 224n, 229n, 231n, 236n, 240n–41n, 244n, 246n–47n, 280n
Jones, Bushrod R., 138, 281n
Jones, Daniel R., 54, 253n
Jones, Egbert J., xiii, 11, 14, 20, 22, 26–27, 29, 32, 200–201, 224n, 235n, 239n, 242n
Jones, James T., 13, 48–49, 226n
Jones, John A., 154, 286n
Jones, Richard, 78, 262n
Jones, Robert P., 17, 166, 222, 230n
Jordan, James M., 48, 251n
Judson, Amos, 272n, 276n
Judson, J. A., 55

Karsner, William F., 15, 35–36, 69–70, 83, 86, 195–97, 228n, 280n
Kautz, August V., 186, 300n
Kearny, Philip, 61, 257n
Keith, James H., 16, 83, 230n
Kelly's Ford, Skirmish at, 98, 237n, 269n
Kemper, James L., 108, 275n
Kennedy, William J., 31, 241n
Kentucky troops, infantry
—1st, 280n
—2nd, 280n
Kernstown, Battle of, 275n
Kershaw, Joseph B., 81, 106, 137, 158–59, 167, 181, 265n, 273n, 279n, 289n, 293n
Kershaw, W. T., 135
Kidd, Reuben V., 136, 275n, 280n
Kilpatrick, H. Justin, 109, 276n–77n
King, David B., 69, 260n
King, Porter, 23, 27, 236n
Kirby, Edmund (Company I, 1st U.S. Artillery), 246n
Kirksey, E. John, 35, 243n
Kitching, J. Howard (U.S. Heavy Artillery Regiments), 162, 290n
Knoxville, Battle of, 148–50, 152, 155, 157, 226n, 228n, 285n–86n

LaGrange Military Academy, xiv, 9
Landman, William, 229n
Lane, James, 277n
Latimer, Joseph W., 82, 266n

Law, Evander M., xiii, 12–13, 22, 24, 32–33, 39, 43, 45, 49, 53, 55–56, 63, 65, 68, 87, 93, 106–8, 110–11, 130, 134–35, 137, 141–47, 151–52, 155–57, 167, 173, 175, 181, 184–85, 200, 205, 208, 224n–25n, 238n, 242n, 246n, 248n–50n, 253n–56n, 266n, 269n, 273n, 277n–79n, 284n–88n, 295n–96n
Lawton, Alexander R., 44, 67, 248n
Lee, Fitzhugh, 172, 294n–95n, 301n
Lee, Robert E., xiii, 43–44, 46, 48–53, 58, 61–62, 73–74, 76, 79–81, 83, 85, 89, 92, 94, 96–98, 100–103, 105, 113–15, 130, 132–33, 138, 155–60, 163–64, 166–69, 171–72, 177–83, 185–88, 190–93, 195, 202, 207, 212, 214, 217, 219, 237n, 241n, 245n, 247n–49n, 251n–52n, 257n–58n, 264n, 269n–70n, 275n, 286n–88n, 290n, 294n–99n, 302n–3n
Lee, Stephen D., 57–58, 65, 255n–56n
Lee, William, 14, 227n
Leftwich, William W., 14, 113, 227n–28n, 278n
Lenoir's Station, Tenn., 148
Lincoln, Abraham, 50, 74, 98, 113, 178, 196–97, 234n, 242n, 247n–48n, 252n, 257n, 261n, 274n, 283n, 297n
Lindsay, Lewis E., 16, 229n
Lomax, Lunsford L., 197, 303n
Lomax, Tennant, 12, 224n
Longstreet, James E., 49, 51, 54, 57–58, 85, 90, 92, 94–95, 97, 100, 102–3, 105–6, 114, 132–34, 136–39, 141, 144–45, 147–52, 155–56, 158–59, 163–64, 178, 187, 207, 215–16, 245n, 251n, 256n, 259n, 261n, 263n, 267n–68n, 273n, 278n, 284n–92n, 300n
Lookout Mountain, Tenn., 139, 143–44, 285n
Lookout Valley, Tenn., 139, 141–42, 144, 147, 155, 157, 281n–85n
Loudon, Tenn., 148
Louisiana troops, infantry
—1st, 256n
—Tigers, 20–21, 240n
Love, Henry Benjamin, 83, 267n
Lowther, Alexander, 184, 299n
Lynchburg, Va., xiii

Magruder, John B., 38–39, 244n–45n
Mahone, William, 163–64, 183–84, 291n
Maine troops, infantry
—3rd, 294n
—10th, 68, 70, 259n
Malvern Hill, Battle of, 48, 225n, 227n, 229n, 250n–51n, 260n
Manassas, First Battle of, 14, 16–17, 19–29, 88, 199–201, 224n–29n, 231n–40n, 243n–44n, 248n, 251n, 253n, 264n, 267n
Manassas, Second Battle of, xiv, 9, 54–59, 87, 230n, 234n, 244n, 248n, 250n–58n, 273n, 279n, 288n, 291n, 295n
Marion, Ala., 15, 189
Marshall, Billy, 208–9
Marshall, J. K., 277n
Martindale, John H., 175, 249n, 296n
Martinsburg, Va., 62, 72, 98, 101–2, 270n
Massachusetts troops, infantry
—19th, 262n
—20th, 262n, 290n
—23rd, 175
—25th, 175
—27th, 175
—29th, 151, 285n
Mastin, Gustavus B., 14, 38, 42, 227n, 243n
Matthews, Thomas L., 154, 286n
McCalley, Samuel Bolivar, 91–92, 268n
McCalley, Thomas, 192
McClellan, George B., 32, 37–39, 44–45, 48, 50–51, 62–64, 67, 72, 74, 234n, 242n, 248n, 251n–52n, 257n–58n, 261n–62n, 266n
McCraw, S. Newton, 35, 243n
McDowell, Irwin, 20, 36, 44, 50, 57, 233n–34n, 248n, 252n, 296n
McFarland, Robert, 15, 32, 228n
McInnis, Archibald D., 14, 55, 227n
McLaws, Lafayette, 67, 70, 75–76, 79, 89, 96, 105–6, 132–33, 137, 139, 144–45, 148–52, 155, 221, 259n, 261n, 265n, 279n, 285n
McLemore, Owen K., 31–32, 39, 47–48, 58, 64, 71, 241n
McMahon, Martin, 176–77
Meade, George G., 103, 113–14, 157–58, 263n, 271n, 274n, 278n, 288n
Mechanicsville, Va., 46, 172, 249n

Melton, Thomas J., 154, 166, 292n
Michigan troops, artillery, Company D, 1st Michigan Light, 281n
Michigan troops, infantry
—1st, 29
—2nd, 285n–86n
—7th, 262n
—20th, 151, 286n
Miller, Stephen J., 186, 300n
Minnesota troops, infantry, 1st, 29
Missionary Ridge, Battle of, 261n, 285n, 301n
Mississippi troops, infantry
—2nd, 19–20, 22, 29, 64, 86–87, 232n, 259n
—11th, 19–20, 22, 29, 65, 86–87, 232n, 259n
Montgomery, Ala., 11, 189
Moore, Samuel, 33, 242n
Morell, George W., 57, 255n
Morgan, John H., 15, 141, 283n
Morristown, Tenn., 152–55
Moseley, Henry H., 15, 228n
Moseley, John W., 115, 209–10, 278n
Murphy, Stephen J., 16, 173–74, 229n
Murray, Alexander C., 16, 181, 230n

Nashville, Battle of, 189, 239n, 282n
New Guilford, Pa., 103, 205, 271n
New York troops, cavalry, 5th, 277n
New York troops, infantry
—11th, 29
—27th, 22, 40
—44th, 272n
—45th, 256n
—69th, 25, 238n
—71st, 26
—79th, 151, 285n
—84th (14th Brooklyn), 29
—86th, 294n
Newbill, George H., 17, 175, 230n
Newsome, William O., 83–84, 134–35, 154–55, 166, 222, 267n
Ninth Corps (Union), 258n, 261n–62n, 266n, 292n, 299n
Nix, Reuben F., 84, 112, 267n
Norfolk, Va., 38
North Anna Campaign, 171–72
North Carolina troops, infantry
—6th, 19, 53, 55, 86, 232n, 240n, 259n

North Carolina troops, infantry, *continued*
—16th, 266n
—18th, 269n, 292n
—55th, 93
Norton, Thomas J., 193–94, 302n

Oakley, William R., 25, 238n
Oates, William C., 31, 93, 106–8, 131, 139, 141–43, 164–65, 217, 221, 241n, 283n, 287n–88n, 296n, 299n
Ogilvie, John D., 16, 230n
Ohio troops, infantry
—18th, 143
—90th, 280n
Orleans, Va., 53

Paine, Charles J., 299n
Panther Springs, Camp at, 154
Parker, William F., 46, 249n
Patterson, Robert, 18–20, 231n, 233n, 282n
Patton, Thomas J., 48, 243n, 251n
Pelham, John, 23, 31, 79, 98, 237n, 269n
Pennsylvania troops, cavalry, 18th, 277n
Pennsylvania troops, infantry
—5th Reserves, 66
—55th, 175
—56th, 254n
—83rd, 272n, 276n
—111th, 70
—138th, 302n
Pensacola, Fla., 12, 14
Perry, Edward A., 163, 165, 220, 261n, 290n–92n
Perry, William F., 106–7, 156, 164–66, 175, 189, 220, 273n, 290n, 292n
Petersburg, Va., 90, 94, 196
Petersburg, Va., Siege of, xiv, 16, 178–90, 230n, 241n, 249n, 260n–61n, 290n, 296n–302n
Peterson, Batte O., 154, 286n
Petrikin, Hardman P., 66
Pettigrew, James J., 108, 275n
Pickett, George E., 37, 79, 81, 89, 103, 105, 108, 110, 114, 157, 178, 180–81, 183, 190, 210–11, 244n, 275n, 301n
Piedmont, Va., 19
Point Lookout, Md., 249n, 276n

Polk, Leonidas, 134, 136, 279n–80n
Pope, John, 50–54, 56–57, 60, 62, 234n, 247n, 251n–57n
Port Gibson, Battle of, 16, 229n
Porter, Andrew, 21, 234n
Porter, Fitz John, 44, 46, 72, 248n–49n, 255n–56n
Powell, Ephraim F., 173, 295n
Price, Alfred, 13, 38, 48, 225n–26n
Proctor, William H., 254n–55n
Pryor, Roger A., 90, 254n, 268n

Quinley, Stephen D., 136–37, 163, 280n

Raccoon Ford, Camp at, 95, 97
Raccoon Mountain, 34, 139–43
Reilly, James (N.C.) Battery, 45, 103, 110–12, 248n
Reese, W. J., 115, 278n
Reynolds, John, 206
Richmond, Va., 51, 88–90, 186–87, 189, 298n, 300n
Ringgold, Ga., 133
Ripley, Roswell S., 69, 260n
Rison, W. B., 243n
Robbins, Frank C., 13, 226n
Robbins, Thomas E., 250n
Robbins, William M., 38, 47, 52, 66, 68, 70–71, 80, 149, 163, 186, 192, 195, 219, 236n–37n, 245n, 272n
Robertson, Jerome B., 106–8, 155, 273n, 279n, 289n
Robinson, William H., 16, 39, 229n–30n
Rockbridge (Va.) Artillery Battery, 237n
Rodes, Robert E., 101–2, 220, 270n, 278n
Rodman, Isaac, 258n
Rogersville, Tenn., 152
Roper, Henry B., 109, 113, 243n, 276n
Rosecrans, William S., 133–34, 136, 138, 140, 279n, 282n

Sale, Charles C., 16, 229n
Sampey, Francis M., 142, 283n
Samuels, Thomas L., 60, 175, 256n
Sanders, John C. C., 189, 301n
Savage's Station, Battle of, 261n
Sayler's Creek, Battle of, 191, 265n, 286n, 301n–2n

Scales, Alfred, 277n
Scott, Charles L., xiii, 14, 24–25, 27, 32–34, 39, 200–201, 226n–27n, 242n
Scruggs, Lawrence H., 16, 38, 48, 59, 64–65, 68, 84, 86, 90–92, 104–6, 110, 113, 115, 135, 145, 170, 173, 182, 186, 188–89, 191–92, 195–97, 229n, 243n
Second Corps (Conf.), 49, 52, 74, 77, 79, 87, 89, 96–98, 100, 103, 158, 167, 244n, 261n, 269n–71n, 278n, 288n, 292n, 294n, 298n, 300n
Second Corps (Union), 247n, 261n–62n, 264n–66n, 288n–91n, 293n–94n, 299n
Selma, Ala., 11, 189
Semmes, Paul J., 106, 273n–74n
Seven Pines, Battle of, 14, 41–43, 224n, 227n, 231n, 241n, 246n, 250n, 275n, 277n, 284n
Sharpsburg, Battle of, 16, 64–71, 226n, 230n, 248n, 258n–60n, 265n, 273n, 277n, 286n, 301n
Sheffield, James L., 106–7, 134–35, 145–46, 272n–73n, 294n
Shelby, Anthony B., 41, 246n
Shepherdstown, Va., 72, 102, 260n
Sheridan, Philip H., 190–91, 193, 274n, 301n
Sherman, William T., 25, 187–88, 234n–36n, 238n, 240n, 276n, 281n–83n, 286n, 301n
Shields, James, 44, 248n
Shiloh, Battle of, 239n, 267n, 282n, 286n
Sickles, Daniel E., 106–7, 274n
Sigel, Franz, 60, 252n–53n, 256n–57n
Simpson, A. H., 243n
Sinclair, Robert, 236n
Sivly, 184
Sixth Corps (Union), 176, 245n–46n, 257n, 262n, 265n–66n, 292n, 296n
Slaughter, John R., 35, 243n
Smith, E. Kirby, 20, 24, 200, 228n, 232n
Smith, Gustavus W., 32, 42–43, 241n–42n
Smith, James (4th N.Y. Battery), 271n, 274n
Smith, Otis, 240n
Smith, Virginius S., 82, 266n
Smith, William F., 175–76, 296n–97n

Snicker's Ferry, Va., 100–101
Sorrell, Gilbert Moxley, 163, 291n
South Carolina troops, infantry, 4th, 20–21
South Mountain, Battle of. *See* Turner's Gap, Battle of
Spotsylvania, Battle of, 166–71, 267n, 293n–94n, 301n
Spragins, Elias C., 33, 200, 242n
Stanley, Timothy, 143
Stannard, George J., 175, 296n, 299n
Stanton, Edwin, 283n
Stearnes, John E., 166, 219, 292n–93n
Stephenson, Tenn., 139–40
Sterling, William Z., 61, 90, 257n
Sterrett, Major Dowell, 13, 226n
Stewart, Jack, 203
Stewart, James H., 67, 259n
Stinson, Jasper, 55, 254n
Stone, John M., 56, 64, 255n
Stuart, J. E. B., 79–80, 97–98, 101–2, 158, 167, 172, 202, 264n, 270n, 295n
Sturgis, Samuel S., 81, 266n
Suffolk, Siege of, 90–95, 268n–69n
Sumner, Edwin V., 79, 261n–62n
Sweetwater, Tenn., 148

Taliaferro, Charles F., 92, 268n
Taliaferro, William B., 79, 263n–64n
Tennessee troops, infantry
—1st, 19, 277n
—7th, 277n
—14th, 277n
Terrell, Leigh R., 93, 208, 269n
Texas Brigade, 32, 40, 44–45, 49, 54, 68, 81, 87, 90, 103, 106–7, 135, 143–46, 150–51, 160, 168–69, 180, 183, 217, 239n, 241n, 246n, 258n–59n, 273n, 280n, 289n–90n, 294n
Texas troops, infantry
—1st, 68, 70, 107, 112, 146, 241n, 246n, 259n, 267n, 273n–74n
—4th, 108, 146, 241n, 246n, 267n, 273n
—5th, 40, 68, 103, 108, 208, 217, 241n, 246n, 267n, 273n
Third Corps (Conf.), 97, 100, 103, 113, 158, 166–67, 249n, 269n, 271n, 278n, 288n–89n, 291n–93n, 302n
Third Corps (Union), 106, 245n–46n,

Third Corps (Union), *continued*
  257n, 262n, 274n
Thomas (Va.) Artillery Battery, 237n
Thomas, Edward L., 195, 302n–3n
Thomas, George H., 140, 279n, 282n
Thompson, James W., 185, 191–92, 299n–300n
Thompson, John S., 185, 299n
Thoroughfare Gap, Skirmish at, 53–54, 253n–54n
Toombs, Robert, 267n
Tracy, Edward D., 16, 22, 199–201, 228n–29n
Tribble, Robert D., 186, 300n
Trimble, Isaac R., 52, 108, 252n–53n, 258n
Turchin, John B., 143–44, 283n–84n
Turner, Daniel H., 16, 69, 92–93, 229n
Turner, William T., 76, 131, 149, 261n
Turner's Gap, Battle of, 62–64, 224n, 241n, 255n, 257n–58n
Twelfth Corps (Union), 144, 157, 260n, 283n–85n
Tyler, Daniel, 25, 238n
Tyner's Station, Tenn., 148

Uniontown, Ala., 13
United States Sharpshooters, 2nd Regiment, 107, 254n–55n, 271n–72n
United States troops, infantry, 8th, 31, 48, 239n

Vaughan, P. Turner, 26–27, 111, 173–74, 239n, 270n–71n, 277n–79n, 281n–82n
Venable, Charles, 159, 179–81
Vermont troops, cavalry, 1st, 277n
Vincent, Strong, 272n
Virginia troops, infantry
—12th, 291n
—27th, 28, 239n
—41st, 291n

Wadsworth, James S., 160, 162–63, 219, 289n–90n
Walke, Sgt., 89
Walker, James A., 66, 258n, 260n
Walton, James B., 81, 265n

Ward, William C., 113, 202–13, 278n
Ware, William H., 82, 266n
Warren, Gouverneur K., 106, 169, 274n, 288n, 290n, 293n
Warrenton, Va., 30, 74, 157
Washington (La.) Artillery, 81, 237n, 265n
Wauhatchie, Battle of, 142–43, 145–46, 284n
Webb, Alexander, 290n
Weldon Railroad, Battle of, 184, 299n
West, Jason M., 11–12, 38, 224n
West Virginia troops, cavalry, 1st, 277n
Wheat, Chatham Roberdeau, 20–21, 233n
White, James B., 243n
White, Wyman, 272n
White Plains, Va., 53
White's Ford, Crossing at, 61
Whiting, W. H. C., 19, 30, 33, 40, 43–45, 49, 76, 240n
Whitworth, Samuel, 111, 277n
Wilcox, Cadmus M., 54, 160, 172, 254n, 289n, 301n
Wilderness, Battle of the, xiii, 12, 158–66, 214–22, 225n, 230n, 245n, 249n, 251n, 261n, 267n, 279n, 286n, 288n–93n, 300n
Williamsburg, Battle of, 40, 245n
Williamsport, Md., 102, 113–14, 202, 268n
Wilson's Creek, Battle of, 266n
Winchester, Third Battle of, 270n
Winchester, Va., 18–19, 71, 74, 98, 199, 231n
Winston County, Ala., xiv
Wisconsin troops, infantry
—2nd, 256n
—7th, 256n
Wofford, William T., 63, 106, 258n, 279n, 291n

Yellow Tavern, Battle of, 264n, 295n
York, Pa., 102–3
Yorktown, Siege of, 38–40, 73, 251n
Young, James H., 16, 229n
Young, John W., 80, 110, 204, 264n

Zahm, Joseph A., 175, 297n

www.ingramcontent.com/pod-product-compliance
Lightning Source LLC
Chambersburg PA
CBHW030303080526
44584CB00012B/426